25,001
Best Baby Names

Lesley Bolton

SOURCEBOOKS, INC.®
NAPERVILLE, ILLINOIS

Copyright © 2006 by Sourcebooks
Cover illustration © 2006 Shh! Creative
Sourcebooks and the colophon are registered trademarks of
Sourcebooks, Inc.

Published by Sourcebooks, Inc.
P.O. Box 4410, Naperville, Illinois 60567-4410
(630) 961-3900
Fax: (630) 961-2168
www.sourcebooks.com

Library of Congress Cataloging-in-Publication Data

Bolton, Lesley.
   25,001 best baby names / Lesley Bolton.
        p. cm.
   ISBN-13: 978-1-4022-0852-2
   ISBN-10: 1-4022-0852-9
   1. Names, Personal--Dictionaries. 2. Names, Personal--
United States--Dictionaries I. Title.

CS2377.B65 2006
929.4'4--dc22

2006011688

Printed and bound in Canada
TC 10 9 8 7 6 5 4

Contents

Introduction

Let's face it: you have enough to worry about in anticipation of your new arrival. So, why make the baby-naming process any more stressful than it has to be? This is not to undermine the importance of giving your child a name he or she will be proud to say, write, and wear for the rest of his or her life. In fact, a name is one of the greatest gifts you will ever give your child. But the process doesn't have to be one of the horror stories haunting baby showers and parenting circles.

If you are looking for a quick, easy, fun, and—most important—painless approach to baby-naming, *25,001 Best Baby Names* will become your best friend. This book has been designed to set before you the best of the best, from the most popular new names to the treasured classics. And for those of you looking for something a little more exotic, there are plenty of names from countries around the world.

Whether you are looking for a specific meaning or origin or a variation of a popular name, you are given all the information you'll need to make an informed decision. *25,001 Best Baby Names* is chock-full of variety and has the most up-to-date information on baby-naming trends—all in one handy, parent-friendly book. So, if you're ready to call your little one something other than

Baby, you've made that first step in the right direction with this book. Kick back, destress, and enjoy *25,001 Best Baby Names*. Happy baby-naming!

Part One

Fun
Lists

Boys	Girls
Classic Names	
John	Emily
Charles	Ann
George	Elizabeth
Alexander	Mary
Michael	Sarah
Richard	Jane
William	Katherine
Thomas	Margaret
David	Helen
Edward	Christine

Boys	Girls
Biblical Names	
Aaron	Eve
Darius	Sarah
Ezekiel	Deborah
Caleb	Anne
John	Mary
Elijah	Rachel
Zion	Naomi
Samuel	Rebecca
Levi	Dinah
Isaiah	Delilah

Boys	Girls
Nobel Prize–Winners	
Theodor	Wangari
John	Shirin
Roy	Elfriede
Yves	Toni
Richard	Nadine
Robert	Linda
Harold	Christiane
Mohamed	Jody
Barry	Rigoberta
Finn	Aung

Boys	Girls
Exotic Names	
Raines	Amelie
Armel	Angelique
Markum	Giovanna
Aurelio	Deadrana
Dominique	Esme
Lorenzo	Danica
Cloudy	Adriana
Diego	Xanthia
Orlando	Zoe
Adonis	Zenobia

Boys	Girls	Boys	Girls

Influential Names   Powerful Names

Boys	Girls	Boys	Girls
Kyle	Mariam	Corbin	Corianna
Max	Sophie	Dimitri	Gail
Logan	Elizabeth	Raines	Delores
Blake	Celeste	Gregor	Nadia
Nathanial	Anna	Keith	Melinda
Mason	Ashley	Hunter	Marissa
Samuel	Cassandra	Emerson	Natasha
Douglas	Claire	Roderick	Elena
Joshua	Honor	Harvey	Alexandra
Marcus	Hope	Hamilton	Leah

Presidential Names   Olympian Names

Boys	Girls	Boys	Girls
Earnest	Elizabeth	Muhammad	Dorothy
George	Isabel	Jesse	Mary Lou
James	Taylor	Carl	Jackie
Reagan	Miriam	Mark	Wilma
Calvin	Hilary	John	Kristi
Benjamin	Katherine	Eric	Shannon
Adam	Carolyn	Dan	Evelyn
Andrew	Andrea	Bob	Peggy
Abraham	Olivia	Larry	Janet
Dwight	Maria	Irving	Bonnie

Boys	Girls		Boys	Girls
Nicknames as Names			**Children's Lit**	
Greg	Betty		Harry	Charlotte
Dick	Liz		Peter	Mary
Harry	Sue		Edmund	Lucy
Larry	Sasha		Colin	Matilda
Bill	Bobbie		Klaus	Sunny
Bob	Carrie		Henry	Violet
Mike	Dee		Ronald	Hermione
Will	Allie		Tom	Heidi
Matt	Abby		Nigel	Rebecca
Jake	Sandy		James	Susan

Boys	Girls		Boys	Girls
Last Names First			**Forensic Scientists**	
Taylor	Addison		Bryant	Brooke
Wesley	Kelly		Dale	Chelsea
Tanner	Mackenzie		Joshua	April
Murray	Alison		Max	Ava
Grant	Ainsley		Casper	Bree
Ryan	Blair		Craig	Drew
Dillon	Shannon		Keith	Sara
Rhys	Bailey		Bram	Rebecca
Jackson	Hadley		Kyle	Claudia
Douglas	Ashley			

Boys	Girls
Names That Are Candidates for Nicknames	
Christopher	Gabrielle
Alexander	Abigail
Timothy	Kimberly
Benjamin	Gwendolyn
Gregory	Elizabeth
Robert	Deborah
Nicholas	Alexandra
William	Susannah
Franklin	Rebecca
Bradley	Jacqueline

Celebrity Baby Names

Joaquin	Assissi
Roman	Dakota
Marco	Atlanta
Sindri	Ireland
Rio	Remington
Gulliver	Alaia
Hugo	Greta
Lincoln	Keegan
Truman	Satchel
Nikolai	Tenzin

Boys	Girls
Names with Great Expectations	
Romeo	Chastity
Justice	Honor
Alexander	Sunny
Truth	Felicity
Junior	Prudence
Victor	Belle
King	Queen
Arthur	Regina
Jesus	Joy
Beau	Charity

Patriotic Names

Lincoln	Free
Washington	Liberty
Norman	Justice
Columbus	Librada
Knox	Spirit
Crane	Starr
William	Americus
Alamo	Peace
Bragg	Independence
Leavenworth	Eagle

Boys	Girls
The "In Crowd" Names	
Dylan	Piper
Jake	Skye
Max	Taylor
Reese	Lexi
Hunter	Mackenzie
Isaac	Madison
Trey	Dakota
Ethan	Josi
Waylon	Ashland
Cody	Kaylee

Boys	Girls
Urban Names	
Jabari	Juanita
Juwon	Dashawn
Keshoh	Quanisha
Shaquille	Shaldona
Jarvis	Dasmine
Shawnell	Dawntelle
Tyree	Latasha
Tre	Tamika
Damarcus	Tearah
Devonte	Shawanna

Strong Names	
Lars	Christina
Alfonso	Bene
Stephon	Camellia
Evander	Ammalee
Hadar	Elyssa
Ulrich	Hilary
Laskey	Faris
Mungo	Jazzell
Thurmond	Kacy
Maddox	Macaria

Country Names	
Cletus	Randy
Ichabod	Maryann
Ira	Esther
Rusty	Harlee
Wendell	Ruby
Emmett	Daisy
Dustin	Dakota
Wyatt	Bella
Maverick	Dixie
Amos	Abilene

Boys	Girls
Poker Players	
Phil	Cyndy
T.J.	Patti
Johnny	Shana
Miami	Annie
Thuan	Jennifer
Doyle	Evelyn
Stu	Kathy
Eric	Clonie
Preston	Isabelle
Amarillo	Barbara

Boys	Girls
Disney Names	
Aladdin	Ariel
Eric	Lilo
Peter	Wendy
Nemo	Esmeralda
Robin	Belle
Timon	Ursula
Sebastian	Anastasia
Gaston	Dory
Oliver	Aurora
Tod	Marian

Boys	Girls
Most Popular Names of the 1950s	
James	Mary
Michael	Linda
Robert	Patricia
John	Susan
David	Deborah
William	Barbara
Richard	Debra
Thomas	Karen
Mark	Nancy
Charles	Donna

Boys	Girls
Most Popular Names of the 1960s	
Michael	Lisa
David	Mary
John	Susan
James	Karen
Robert	Kimberly
Mark	Patricia
William	Linda
Richard	Donna
Thomas	Michelle
Jeffrey	Cynthia

Boys	Girls
Most Popular Names of the 1970s	
Michael	Jennifer
Christopher	Amy
Jason	Melissa
David	Michelle
James	Kimberly
John	Lisa
Robert	Angela
Brian	Heather
William	Stephanie
Matthew	Nicole

Boys	Girls
Most Popular Names of the 1990s	
Michael	Jessica
Christopher	Ashley
Matthew	Emily
Joshua	Samantha
Jacob	Sarah
Nicholas	Amanda
Andrew	Brittany
Daniel	Elizabeth
Tyler	Taylor
Joseph	Megan

Boys	Girls
Most Popular Names of the 1980s	
Michael	Jessica
Christopher	Jennifer
Matthew	Amanda
Joshua	Ashley
David	Sarah
James	Stephanie
Daniel	Melissa
Robert	Nicole
John	Elizabeth
Joseph	Heather

Boys	Girls
Most Popular Names of the 2000s	
Jacob	Emily
Michael	Madison
Joshua	Emma
Matthew	Hannah
Andrew	Olivia
Christopher	Abigail
Daniel	Ashley
Joseph	Samantha
Ethan	Alexis
William	Elizabeth

★ Most Popular Names of 2007
★ — All names with a ★ in the text denote
Top 100 Names of 2007.

Most Popular Boys Names

1. Jacob	23. Jonathan	45. Jordan
2. Michael	24. Nathan	46. Luke
3. Ethan	25. Samuel	47. Robert
4. Joshua	26. Benjamin	48. Austin
5. Daniel	27. Aiden	49. Landon
6. Christopher	28. Gabriel	50. Cameron
7. Anthony	29. Dylan	51. Thomas
8. William	30. Elijah	52. Aaron
9. Matthew	31. Brandon	53. Lucas
10. Andrew	32. Gavin	54. Aidan
11. Alexander	33. Jackson	55. Connor
12. David	34. Angel	56. Owen
13. Joseph	35. José	57. Hunter
14. Noah	36. Caleb	58. Diego
15. James	37. Mason	59. Jason
16. Ryan	38. Jack	60. Luis
17. Logan	39. Kevin	61. Adrian
18. Jayden	40. Evan	62. Charles
19. John	41. Isaac	63. Juan
20. Nicholas	42. Zachary	64. Brayden
21. Tyler	43. Isaiah	65. Adam
22. Christian	44. Justin	66. Julian

67. Jeremiah
68. Xavier
69. Wyatt
70. Carlos
71. Hayden
72. Sebastian
73. Alex
74. Ian
75. Sean
76. Jaden
77. Jesús
78. Bryan
79. Chase
80. Carter
81. Brian
82. Nathaniel
83. Eric
84. Cole
85. Dominic
86. Kyle
87. Tristan
88. Blake
89. Liam
90. Carson
91. Henry
92. Caden
93. Brady
94. Miguel
95. Cooper
96. Antonio
97. Steven
98. Kaden
99. Richard
100. Timothy

★ Most Popular Names of 2007

Most Popular Girls Names

1. Emily
2. Isabella
3. Emma
4. Ava
5. Madison
6. Sophia
7. Olivia
8. Abigail
9. Hannah
10. Elizabeth
11. Addison
12. Samantha
13. Ashley
14. Alyssa
15. Mia
16. Chloe
17. Natalie
18. Sarah
19. Alexis
20. Grace
21. Ella
22. Brianna
23. Hailey
24. Taylor
25. Anna
26. Kayla
27. Lily

28. Lauren
29. Victoria
30. Savannah
31. Neveah
32. Jasmine
33. Lillian
34. Julia
35. Sofia
36. Kaylee
37. Sydney
38. Gabriella
39. Katherine
40. Alexa
41. Destiny
42. Jessica
43. Morgan
44. Kaitlyn
45. Brooke
46. Allison
47. Makayla
48. Avery
49. Alexandra
50. Jocelyn
51. Audrey
52. Riley

53. Kimberly
54. Maria
55. Evelyn
56. Zoe
57. Brooklyn
58. Angelina
59. Andrea
60. Rachel
61. Madeline
62. Maya
63. Kylie
64. Jennifer
65. Mackenzie
66. Claire
67. Gabrielle
68. Leah
69. Aubrey
70. Arianna
71. Vanessa
72. Trinity
73. Ariana
74. Faith
75. Katelyn
76. Haley
77. Amelia

78. Megan
79. Isabelle
80. Melanie
81. Sara
82. Sophie
83. Bailey
84. Aaliyah
85. Layla
86. Isabel
87. Nicole
88. Stephanie
89. Paige
90. Gianna
91. Autumn
92. Mariah
93. Mary
94. Michelle
95. Jada
96. Gracie
97. Molly
98. Valeria
99. Caroline
100. Jordan

т Most Popular Twin Names of 2007
T — All names with a **T** in the text denote
Top Twin Names of 2007.

1. Jacob, Joshua
2. Matthew, Michael
3. Daniel, David
4. Isaac, Isaiah
5. Ella, Emma
6. Madison, Morgan
7. Taylor, Tyler
8. Landon, Logan
9. Brandon, Bryan
10. Christian, Christopher
11. Gabriella, Isabella
12. Andrew, Matthew
13. Faith, Hope
14. Joseph, Joshua
15. Ethan, Evan
16. Jacob, Joseph
17. Mackenzie, Madison
18. Alexander, Benjamin
19. Caleb, Joshua
20. Hailey, Hannah
21. Isabella, Sophia
22. Madison, Matthew
23. Emily, Ethan
24. Joshua, Matthew
25. Nathaniel, Nicholas
26. Andrew, Anthony
27. Jayden, Jordan
28. Madison, Mason
29. Elijah, Isaiah
30. Alexander, Nicholas
31. Jeremiah, Joshua
32. Emma, Ethan
33. Olivia, Sophia
34. Ava, Emma
35. Haley, Hannah
36. Hayden, Hunter
37. Jacob, Zachary
38. Logan, Luke
39. Natalie, Nathan
40. Benjamin, Samuel
41. Christopher, Nicholas
42. Nathan, Noah
43. Alexander, Christopher
44. James, John

45. John, William
46. Jordan, Justin
47. Megan, Morgan
48. Alexander, Anthony
49. Andrew, William
50. Christopher, Matthew
51. Isabella, Olivia
52. Jacob, Jordan
53. Joseph, Michael
54. Alexander, Andrew
55. Andrew, Jacob
56. Elijah, Ethan
57. Jacob, Matthew
58. Jacob, Samuel
59. James, Joseph
60. Jordan, Joshua
61. Matthew, Ryan
62. Nicholas, Noah
63. Ava, Olivia
64. Emma, Grace
65. Emma, Hannah
66. Jason, Justin
67. Jennifer, Jessica
68. Makayla, Makenzie
69. Natalie, Nicole
70. Zachary, Zoe
71. Ava, Sophia
72. Benjamin, Jacob
73. Emma, Olivia
74. Ethan, Nathan
75. Gabriel, Michael
76. Grace, Olivia
77. Jacob, Justin
78. Jacob, Tyler
79. Jaden, Jordan
80. Jonathan, Joshua
81. José, Juan
82. Logan, Lucas
83. Mark, Matthew
84. Robert, William
85. Samuel, Sophia
86. Abigail, Emily
87. Abigail, Emma
88. Alexander, William
89. Anna, Emma
90. Ashley, Emily
91. Ava, Ella
92. Cameron, Christian

93. Emily, Sarah
94. Emma, Jacob
95. Emma, William
96. Grace, Hannah
97. Hannah, Sarah
98. Jayden, Jaylen
99. Joseph, Nicholas
100. Joshua, Zachary
101. Madison, Megan
102. Parker, Preston

Boys

Aabha (Indian) One who shines
Abha, Abbha

Aabharan (Hindu) One who is treasured; jewel
Abharan, Abharen, Aabharen, Aabharon, Abharon

Aadesh (Indian) A message or command; to make a statement
Adesh, Adhesh, Addesh

Aage (Norse) Representative of ancestors
Age, Ake, Aake

Aarif (Arabic) A learned man
Arif, Aareef, Areef, Aareaf, Areaf, Aareif, Areif, Aarief

*Aaron (Hebrew) One who is exalted; from the mountain of strength
Aaran, Aaren, Aarin, Aaro, Aaronas, Aaronn, Aarron, Aaryn, Eron

Abdi (Hebrew) My servant
Abdie, Abdy, Abdey, Abdee, Abdea

Abdul (Arabic) A servant of God
Abdal, Abdall, Abdalla, Abdallah, Abdel, Abdell, Abdella, Abdellah

Abedi (African) One who worships God
Abedie, Abedy, Abedey, Abedee, Abedea

Abednago (Aramaic) Servant of the god of wisdom, Nabu
Abednego

Abejundio (Spanish) Resembling a bee
Abejundo, Abejundeo, Abedjundiyo, Abedjundeyo

Abiel (Hebrew) God is the father
Abiell, Ahbiell, Ahbiel, Abyel, Aybell, Abyell, Aybel

Abraham (Hebrew) Father of a multitude; father of nations
Abarran, Avraham, Aberham, Abrahamo, Abrahan, Abrahim, Abram, Abrami, Ibrahim

Absalom (Hebrew) The father of peace
Absalon, Abshalom, Absolem, Absolom, Absolon, Avshalom, Avsholom

Abu (African) A father
Abue, Aboo, Abou

Abundio (Spanish) A man of plenty
Abbondio, Abondio, Aboundio, Abundo, Abundeo, Aboundeo, Abondeo

Adael (Hebrew) God witnesses
Adaele, Adayel, Adayele

★Adam (Hebrew) Of the earth
Ad, Adamo, Adams, Adan, Adao, Addam, Addams, Addem

Adamson (English) The son of Adam
Adamsson, Addamson, Adamsun, Adamssun, Addamsun

Addy (Teutonic) One who is awe-inspiring
Addey, Addi, Addie, Addee, Addea, Adi, Ady, Adie

Adelpho (Greek) A brotherly man
Aldelfo, Adelfus, Adelfio, Adelphe

Adil (Arabic) A righteous man; one who is fair and just
Adyl, Adiel, Adeil, Adeel, Adeal, Adyeel

Aditya (Hindi) Of the sun
Adithya, Adithyan, Adityah, Aditeya, Aditeyah

Adonis (Greek) In mythology, a handsome young man loved by Aphrodite
Addonia, Adohnes, Adonys, Adones

★Adrian (Latin) A man from Hadria
Ade, Adiran, Adrain, Adrean, Adreean, Adreyan, Adreeyan, Adriaan

Aekley (English) From the oak tree meadow
Aekly, Aekleigh, Aeklee, Aeklea, Aekleah, Aekli, Aeklie

Afif (Arabic) One who is chaste; pure
Afeef, Afief, Afeif, Affeef, Affif, Afyf, Afeaf

Agamemnon (Greek) One who works slowly; in mythology, the leader of the Greeks at Troy
Agamemno, Agamenon

Aghy (Irish) A friend of the horse
Aghey, Aghi, Aghie, Aghee, Aghea, Aghe

★Aidan (Irish) A fiery young man
Aiden, Aedan, Aeden, Aidano, Aidyn, Ayden, Aydin, Aydan

Aiken (English) Constructed of oak; sturdy
Aikin, Aicken, Aickin, Ayken, Aykin, Aycken, Ayckin

Ainsworth (English) From Ann's estate
Answorth, Annsworth, Ainsworthe, Answorthe, Annsworthe

Ajax (Greek) In mythology, a hero of the Trojan war
Aias, Aiastes, Ajaxx, Ajaxe

Ajit (Indian) One who is invincible
Ajeet, Ajeat, Ajeit, Ajiet, Ajyt

Akiko (Japanese) Surrounded by bright light
Akyko

Akin (African) A brave man; a hero
Akeen, Akean, Akein, Akien, Akyn

Akiva (Hebrew) One who protects or provides shelter
Akyva, Akeeva, Akeava, Akieva, Akeiva, Akeyva

Akmal (Arabic) A perfect man
Aqmal, Akmall, Aqmall, Acmal, Acmall, Ackmal, Ackmall

Alaire (French) Filled with joy
Alair, Alaer, Alaere, Alare, Alayr, Alayre

Alamar (Arabic) Covered with gold
Alamarr, Alemar, Alemarr, Alomar, Alomarr

Alard (German) Of noble strength
Aliard, Allard, Alliard

Albert (German) One who is noble and bright
Alberto, Albertus, Alburt, Albirt, Aubert, Albyrt, Albertos, Albertino

Alcander (Greek) Having strength and power
Alcindor, Alcandor, Alcinder, Alkander, Alkender, Alcender, Alkindor, Alkandor

Alden (English) An old friend
Aldan, Aldin, Aldyn, Aldon, Aldun

Aldo (German) Old or wise one; elder
Aldous, Aldis, Aldus, Alldo, Aldys

Aldred (English) An old advisor
Alldred, Aldraed, Alldraed, Aldread, Alldread

Alejandro (Spanish) Form of Alexander, meaning "a helper and defender of mankind"
Alejandrino, Alejo

★Alex (English) Form of Alexander, meaning "a helper and defender of mankind"
Aleks, Alecks, Alecs, Allex, Alleks, Allecks, Allecs

★ᵀAlexander (Greek) A helper and defender of mankind
Alex, Alec, Alejandro, Alaxander, Aleksandar, Aleksander, Aleksandr, Alesandro, Iskander, Zander

Alfio (Italian) A white-skinned man
Alfeo, Alfiyo, Alfeyo

Alfonso (Italian) Prepared for battle; eager and ready
Alphonso, Alphonse, Affonso, Alfons, Alfonse, Alfonsin, Alfonsino, Alfonz, Alfonzo, Fonso

Algis (German) One who wields a spear
Algiss, Algisse, Algys, Algyss, Algysse

Alon (Hebrew) Of the oak tree
Allona, Allon, Alonn

Alonzo (Spanish) Form of Alfonso, meaning "prepared for battle; eager and ready"
Alonso, Alanso, Alanzo, Allonso, Allonzo, Allohnso, Allohnzo, Alohnso

Aloysius (German) A famous warrior
Ahlois, Aloess, Alois, Aloisio, Aloisius, Aloisio, Aloj, Alojzy

Alpha (Greek) The first-born child; the first letter of the Greek alphabet
Alphah, Alfa, Alfah

Alter (Hebrew) One who is old
Allter, Altar, Alltar

Alton (English) From the old town
Aldon, Aldun, Altun, Alten, Allton, Alltun, Allten

Alvern (Latin) Of the spring's growth
Alverne, Alvarn, Alvarne, Alvurn, Alvurne, Alvirn, Alvirne

Alvis (Norse) In mythology, a dwarf who fell in love with Thor's daughter
Alvise, Alvisse, Alviss, Alvys, Alvyss, Alvysse

Amani (African / Arabic) One who is peaceful / one with wishes and dreams
Amanie, Amany, Amaney, Amanee, Amanye, Amanea, Amaneah

Amari (African) Having great strength; a builder
Amarie, Amaree, Amarea, Amary, Amarey

Amiel (Hebrew) The God of my people
Amyel, Amiell, Amyell

Amil (Hindi) One who is invaluable
Ameel, Ameal, Ameil, Amiel, Amyl

Amit (Hindi) Without
limit; endless
*Ameet, Ameat, Ameit,
Amiet, Amyt*

Amor (French) One who
loves and is loved
Amore

Amory (German) Ruler
and lover of one's home
*Aimory, Amery, Amorey,
Amry, Amori, Amorie,
Amoree, Amorea*

Amos (Hebrew) To carry;
hardworking
Amoss, Aymoss, Aymos

Andino (Italian) Form of
Andrew, meaning "one
who is manly; a warrior"
*Andyno, Andeeno,
Andeano, Andieno,
Andeino*

★ᵀAndrew (Greek) One
who is manly; a warrior
*Andy, Aindrea, Aindreas,
Andie, Andonia, Andor,
Andresj, Andrewes*

Andrik (Slavic) Form of
Andrew, meaning "one
who is manly; a warrior"
*Andric, Andrick, Andryk,
Andryck, Andryc*

★Angel (Greek) A messen-
ger of God
*Andjelko, Ange, Angelino,
Angell, Angelmo, Angelo,
Angie, Angy*

Angus (Scottish) One force;
one strength; one choice
Aengus, Anngus, Aonghus

Anicho (German) An
ancestor
*Anico, Anecho, Aneco,
Anycho, Anyco*

Ankur (Indian) One who is
blossoming; a sapling

Annan (Celtic) From the
brook
Anan

Ansley (English) From the
noble's pastureland
*Ansly, Anslie, Ansli, Anslee,
Ansleigh, Anslea, Ansleah,
Anslye*

Antenor (Spanish) One
who antagonizes
*Antener, Antenar, Antenir,
Antenyr, Antenur*

★ᵀAnthony (Latin) A flour-
ishing man; of an ancient
Roman family
*Antal, Anthone, Anthoney,
Anntoin, Antin, Anton,
Antone, Antonello, **Antonio**,
Txanton*

Antoine (French) Form of
Anthony, meaning "a
flourishing man; of an
ancient Roman family"
*Antione, Antjuan, Antuan,
Antuwain, Antuwaine,
Antuwayne, Antuwon,
Antwahn*

Ara (Armenian / Latin) A legendary king / of the altar; the name of a constellation
Araa, Aira, Arah, Arae, Ahraya

Aram (Assyrian) One who is exalted
Arram

Arcadio (Greek) From an ideal country paradise
Alcadio, Alcado, Alcedio, Arcadios, Arcadius, Arkadi, Arkadios, Arkadius

Arcelio (Spanish) From the altar of heaven
Arcelios, Arcelius, Aricelio, Aricelios, Aricelius

Archard (German) A powerful holy man
Archerd, Archird, Archyrd

Archelaus (Greek) The ruler of the people
Archelaios, Arkelaos, Arkelaus, Arkelaios, Archelaos

Ardal (Gaelic) Having the valor of a bear
Ardghal

Ardell (Latin) One who is eager
Ardel, Ardelle, Ardele

Arden (Latin / English) One who is passionate and enthusiastic / from the valley of the eagles
Ardan, Arrden, Arrdan, Ardin, Arrdin, Ard, Ardyn, Arrdyn

Arduino (German) A valued friend
Ardwino, Arrduino, Ardueno

Ari (Hebrew) Resembling a lion or an eagle
Aree, Arie, Aristide, Aristides, Arri, Ary, Arye, Arrie

Ariel (Hebrew) A lion of God
Arielle, Ariele, Ariell, Arriel, Ahriel, Airial, Arieal, Arial

Aries (Latin) Resembling a ram; the first sign of the zodiac; a constellation
Arese, Ariese

Arion (Greek) A poet or musician
Arian, Arien, Aryon

Aristotle (Greek) Of high quality
Aristotelis, Aristotellis

Arius (Greek) Enduring life; everlasting; immortal
Areos, Areus, Arios

Arledge (English) From the hare's lake
Arlidge, Arlledge, Arllidge, Arrledge, Arrlidge

Arley (English) From the
hare's meadow
*Arlea, Arleigh, Arlie, Arly,
Arleah, Arli, Arlee*

Arliss (Hebrew) Of the
pledge
*Arlyss, Aryls, Arlis, Arlisse,
Arlysse*

Arnold (German) The
eagle ruler
*Arnaldo, Arnaud, Arnauld,
Arnault, Arnd, Arndt,
Arnel, Arnell*

Arthur (Celtic) As strong
as a bear; a hero
*Aart, Arrt, Art, Artair, Arte,
Arther, Arthor, Arthuro*

Arvad (Hebrew) A wanderer; voyager
Arpad

Arvin (English) A friend to
everyone
*Arvinn, Arvinne, Arven,
Arvenn, Arvenne, Arvyn,
Arvynn, Arvynne*

Asaph (Hebrew) One who
gathers or collects
*Asaf, Asaphe, Asafe, Asiph,
Asiphe, Asif, Asife*

Asgard (Norse) From the
courtyard of the gods; in
mythology, the dwelling
place of the gods
Asgarde

Ash (English) From the
ash tree
Ashe

Ashley (English) From the
meadow of ash trees
*Ashely, Asheley, Ashelie,
Ashlan, Ashleigh, Ashlen,
Ashli, Ashlie*

*Ashton (English) From
the ash-tree town
*Asheton, Ashtun, Ashetun,
Ashtin, Ashetin, Ashtyn,
Ashetyn, Aston*

Aslan (Turkish)
Resembling a lion
Aslen, Azlan, Azlen

Athens (Greek) From the
capital of Greece
*Athenios, Athenius,
Atheneos, Atheneus*

Atherton (English) From
the town near the spring
Athertun

Attila (Hungarian) One
who is fatherly
*Atila, Atilano, Atilo, Attilia,
Attilio, Attileo*

Atwell (English) One who
lives at the spring
Attwell, Atwel, Attwel

Atworth (English) One
who lives at the farmstead
*Attworth, Atworthe,
Attworthe*

Aubrey (English) One who rules with elf-wisdom
Aubary, Aube, Aubery, Aubry, Aubury, Aubrian, Aubrien, Aubrion

Auburn (Latin) Having a reddish-brown color
Aubirn, Auburne, Aubyrn, Abern, Abirn, Aburn, Abyrn, Aubern

Audley (English) From the old meadow
Audly, Audleigh, Audlee, Audlea, Audleah, Audli, Audlie

August (Irish) One who is venerable; majestic
Austin, Augustine, Agoston, Aguistin, Agustin, Augustin, Augustyn, Avgustin, Augusteen, Agosteen

*Austin (English) Form of August, meaning "one who is venerable; majestic"
Austen, Austyn, Austan, Auston, Austun

Aviram (Hebrew) My Father is mighty
Avyram, Avirem, Avyrem

Axel (German / Latin / Hebrew) Source of life; small oak / axe / peace
Aksel, Ax, Axe, Axell, Axil, Axill, Axl

Aya (Hebrew) Resembling a bird
Ayah

Ayo (African) Filled with happiness
Ayoe, Ayow, Ayowe

Azamat (Arabic) A proud man; one who is majestic

Azi (African) One who is youthful
Azie, Azy, Azey, Azee, Azea

Azikiwe (African) One who is full of life
Azikiwi, Azikiwie, Azikiwy, Azikiwey, Azikiwee, Azikiwea

Azmer (Islamic) Resembling a lion
Azmar, Azmir, Azmyr, Azmor, Azmur

Azmera (African) The harvester

B

Baakir (African) The eldest child
Baakeer, Baakyr, Baakear, Baakier, Baakeir

Babar (Turkish) Resembling a tiger
Baber, Babir, Babyr, Babor, Babur, Babr

Bacchus (Latin) In mythology, the god of wine
Baccus, Baakus, Baackus, Backus, Bach, Bache

Bachir (Hebrew) The oldest son
Bacheer, Bachear, Bachier, Bacheir, Bachyr

Baha (Arabic) A glorious and splendid man
Bahah

Bailintin (Irish) A valiant man
Bailinten, Bailentin, Bailenten, Bailintyn, Bailentyn

Bain (Irish) A fair-haired man
Baine, Bayn, Bayne, Baen, Baene, Bane, Baines, Baynes

Bajnok (Hungarian) A victorious man
Bajnock, Bajnoc

Bakari (Swahili) One who is promised
Bakarie, Bakary, Bakarey, Bakaree, Bakarea

Bakhit (Arabic) A lucky man
Bakheet, Bakheat, Bakheit, Bakhiet, Bakhyt, Bakht

Bala (Hindi) One who is youthful
Balu, Balue, Balou

Balamani (Indian) A young jewel
Balamanie, Balamany, Balamaney, Balamanee, Balamanea

Balark (Hindi) Born with the rising sun

Balasi (Basque) One who is flat-footed
Balasie, Balasy, Balasey, Balasee, Balasea

Balbo (Latin) One who mutters
Balboe, Balbow, Balbowe, Ballbo, Balbino, Balbi, Balbie, Balby

Balder (English / Norse) Of the brave army / in mythology, the god of light
Baldar, Baldur, Baldor, Baldir, Baldyr

Baldwin (German) A brave friend
Baldwine, Baldwinn, Baldwinne, Baldwen, Baldwenn, Baldwenne, Baldwyn, Baldwynn

Balint (Latin) A healthy and strong man
Balent, Balin, Balen, Balynt, Balyn

Balloch (Scottish) From the grazing land

Bancroft (English) From the bean field
Bancrofte, Banfield, Banfeld, Bankroft, Bankrofte

Bandana (Spanish) A brightly colored headwrap
Bandanah, Bandanna, Bandannah

Bandy (American) A fiesty man
Bandey, Bandi, Bandie, Bandee, Bandea

Bansi (Indian) One who plays the flute
Bansie, Bansy, Bansey, Bansee, Bansea

Bao (Vietnamese / Chinese) To order / one who is prized

Baqir (Arabic) A learned man
Baqeer, Baqear, Baqier, Baqeir, Baqyr, Baqer

Barak (Hebrew) Of the lightning flash
Barrak, Barac, Barrac, Barack, Barrack

Baram (Hebrew) The son of the nation
Barem, Barum, Barom, Barim, Barym

Bard (English) A minstrel; a poet
Barde, Bardo

Barden (English) From the barley valley; from the boar's valley
Bardon, Bardun, Bardin, Bardyn, Bardan, Bardene

Bardol (Basque) A farmer
Bardo, Bartol

Bardrick (Teutonic) An axe ruler
Bardric, Bardrik, Bardryck, Bardryk, Bardryc, Bardarick, Bardaric, Bardarik

Barek (Arabic) One who is noble
Barec, Bareck

Barend (German) The hard bear
Barende, Barind, Barinde, Barynd, Barynde

Barnett (English) Of honorable birth
Barnet, Baronet, Baronett

Barnum (English) From the baron's estate
Barnam, Barnem, Barnom, Barnham, Barnhum, Barnhem

Barr (English) A lawyer
Barre, Bar

Barra (Gaelic) A fair-haired man

Barrett (German / English) Having the strength of a bear / one who argues
Baret, Barrat, Barratt, Barret, Barrette

Barry (Gaelic) A fair-haired man
Barrey, Barri, Barrie, Barree, Barrea, Barrington, Barryngton, Barringtun

Bartholomew (Aramaic) The son of the farmer
Bart, Bartel, Barth, Barthelemy, Bartho, Barthold, Bartholoma, Bartholomaus, Bartlett, Bartol

Bartlett (French) Form of Bartholomew, meaning "the son of the farmer"
Bartlet, Bartlitt, Bartlit, Bartlytt, Bartlyt

Bartley (English) From the meadow of birch trees
Bartly, Bartli, Bartlie, Bartlee, Bartlea, Bartleah, Bartleigh

Bartoli (Spanish) Form of Bartholomew, meaning "the son of the farmer"
Bartolie, Bartoly, Bartoley, Bartolee, Bartoleigh, Bartolea, Bartolo, Bartolio

Barton (English) From the barley town
Bartun, Barten, Bartan, Bartin, Bartyn

Barwolf (English) The ax-wolf
Barrwolf, Barwulf, Barrwulf

Basant (Arabic) One who smiles often
Basante

Base (English) A short man

Bassett (English) A little person
Baset, Basset, Basett

Basy (American) A home-body
Basey, Basi, Basie, Basee, Basea, Basye

Baurice (American) Form of Maurice, meaning "a dark-skinned man; Moorish"
Baurell, Baureo, Bauricio, Baurids, Baurie, Baurin, Baurio, Baurise

Bavol (English) Of the wind
Bavoll, Bavole, Bavolle

Bay (Vietnamese / English) The seventh-born child; born during the month of July / from the bay
Baye, Bae, Bai

Beal (French) A handsome man
Beals, Beale, Beall, Bealle

Beamer (English) One who plays the trumpet
Beamor, Beamir, Beamyr, Beamur, Beamar, Beemer, Beemar, Beemir

Bean (Scottish) One who is lively
Beann, Beane

Becher (Hebrew) The first-born son

Bedar (Arabic) One who is attentive
Beder, Bedor, Bedur, Bedyr, Bedir

Bedell (French) A messenger
Bedel, Bedelle, Bedele, Bedall, Bedal, Bedalle, Bedale

Beircheart (Anglo-Saxon) Of the intelligent army

Bela (Slavic) A white-skinned man
Belah, Bella, Bellah

Belden (English) From the beautiful valley
Beldan, Beldon, Beldun, Beldin, Beldyn, Bellden, Belldan, Belldon, Belldun, Belldin, Belldyn

Belen (Greek) Of an arrow
Belin, Belyn, Belan, Belon, Belun

Belindo (English) A handsome and tender man
Belyndo, Belindio, Belyndio, Belindeo, Belyndeo, Belindiyo, Belyndiyo, Belindeyo

Bellarmine (Italian) One who is handsomely armed
Bellarmin, Bellarmeen, Bellarmeene, Bellarmean, Bellarmeane, Bellarmyn, Bellarmyne

Belton (English) From the beautiful town
Bellton, Beltun, Belltun, Belten, Bellten

Belvin (American) Form of Melvin, meaning "a friend who offers counsel"
Belven, Belvyn, Belvon, Belvun, Belvan

Bem (African) A peaceful man

Ben (English) Form of Benjamin, meaning "son of the south; son of the right hand"
Benn, Benni, Bennie, Bennee, Benney, Benny, Bennea, Benno

★ᵀ**Benjamin** (Hebrew) Son of the south; son of the right hand
Ben, Benejamen, Beniamino, Benjaman, Benjamen, Benjamino, Benjamon, Benjiman, Benjimen

Berdy (German) Having a brilliant mind
Berdey, Berdee, Berdea, Berdi, Berdie

Beresford (English) From the barley ford
Beresforde, Beresfurd, Beresfurde, Beresferd, Beresferde, Berford, Berforde, Berfurd

Berg (German) From the mountain
Bergh, Burg, Burgh

Berkeley (English) From the meadow of birch trees
Berkely, Berkeli, Berkelie, Berkelea, Berkeleah, Berkelee, Berkeleigh, Berkley

Bernard (German) As strong and brave as a bear
Barnard, Barnardo, Barnhard, Barnhardo, Bearnard, Bernardo, Bernarr, Bernd

Berry (English) Resembling a berry fruit
Berrey, Berri, Berrie, Berree, Berrea

Bert (English) One who is illustrious
Berte, Berti, Bertie, Bertee, Bertea, Berty, Bertey

Berthold (German) Having bright strength
Berthoud, Bertol, Bertoll, Bertold, Bertolde, Bertell, Bertel, Bertill

Bethel (Hebrew) The house of God
Bethell, Bethele, Bethelle, Betuel, Betuell, Betuele, Betuelle

Bevis (Teutonic) An archer
Beviss, Bevys, Bevyss, Beavis, Beaviss, Beavys, Beavyss

Biagio (Italian) One who has a stutter
Biaggio

Birney (English) From the island with the brook
Birny, Birnee, Birnea, Birni, Birnie

Black (English) A dark-skinned man
Blak, Blac, Blacke

Blackwell (English) From the dark spring
Blackwel, Blackwelle, Blackwele

Blade (English) One who wields a sword or knife
Blayd, Blayde, Blaid, Blaide, Blaed, Blaede

Blagden (English) From the dark valley
Blagdon, Blagdan, Blagdun, Blagdin, Blagdyn

Blaine (Scottish / Irish) A saint's servant / a thin man
Blayne, Blane, Blain, Blayn, Blaen, Blaene, Blainy, Blainey

Blaise (Latin / American) One with a lisp or a stutter / a fiery man
Blaze, Blaize, Blaiz, Blayze, Blayz, Blaez, Blaeze

★Blake (English) A dark, handsome man
Blayk, Blayke, Blaik, Blaike, Blaek, Blaeke

Bliss (English) Filled with happiness
Blis, Blyss, Blys

Blondell (English) A fair-haired boy
Blondel, Blondele, Blondelle

Boaz (Hebrew) One who is swift
Boaze, Boas, Boase

Bob (English) Form of Robert, meaning "one who is bright with fame"
Bobbi, Bobbie, Bobby, Bobbey, Bobbee, Bobbea

Bogart (French) One who is strong with the bow
Bogaard, Bogaart, Bogaerd, Bogey, Bogie, Bogi, Bogy, Bogee

Bolivar (Spanish) A mighty warrior
Bolevar, Bolivarr, Bolevarr, Bollivar, Bollivarr, Bollevar, Bollevarr

Bonaventure (Latin) One who undertakes a blessed venture
Bonaventura, Buenaventure, Buenaventura, Bueaventure, Bueaventura

Boniface (Latin) Having good fortune; one who is benevolent
Bonifacio, Bonifaceo, Bonifacius, Bonifacios, Bonifaco

Booker (English) One who binds books; a scribe
Bookar, Bookir, Bookyr, Bookur, Bookor

Bosley (English) From the meadow near the forest
Bosly, Boslee, Boslea, Bosleah, Bosleigh, Bosli, Boslie, Bozley

Boston (English) From the town near the forest; from the city of Boston
Bostun, Bostin, Bostyn, Bosten, Bostan

Botolf (English) The messenger wolf
Botolff, Botolph, Botulf, Botulff, Botulph

Boyce (French) One who lives near the forest
Boice, Boyse, Boise

Boyd (Celtic) A blond-haired man
Boyde, Boid, Boide, Boyden, Boydan, Boydin, Boydyn, Boydon

Boynton (Irish) From the town near the river Boyne
Boyntun, Boynten, Boyntin, Boyntan, Boyntyn

Bracken (English) Resembling the large fern
Braken, Brackan, Brakan, Brackin, Brakin, Brackyn, Brakyn, Brackon

Braddock (English) From the broadly spread oak
Bradock, Braddoc, Bradoc, Braddok, Bradok

★**Braden** (Gaelic / English) Resembling salmon / from the wide valley
Bradan, Bradon, Bradin, Bradyn, Braddon, Braddan, Braddin, Brayden

Bradford (English) From the wide ford
Bradforde, Bradferd, Bradferde, Bradfurd, Bradfurde

Bradley (English) From the wide meadow
Bradly, Bradlea, Bradleah, Bradlee, Bradleigh, Bradli, Bradlie

★**Brady** (Irish) The son of a large-chested man
Bradey, Bradee, Bradea, Bradi, Bradie, Braidy, Braidey, Braidee

Bramley (English) From the wild gorse meadow; from the raven's meadow
Bramly, Bramlee, Bramlea, Bramleah, Bramleigh, Bramli, Bramlie

Branch (Latin) An extension
Branche

★T**Brandon** (English) From the broom or gorse hill
Brandun, Brandin, Brandyn, Brandan, Branden, Brannon, Brannun, Brannen

Branton (English) From the broom or gorse town
Brantun, Brantin, Branten, Brantyn, Brantan, Branston, Branstun, Bransten

Braulio (Spanish) One who is glowing
Braulo, Brauleo, Brauliyo, Brauleyo, Bravilio, Braviliyo, Bravileo, Bravileyo

Brazil (English) From the country of Brazil
Brasil, Brazyl, Brasyl

Brendan (Irish) Born to royalty; a prince
Brendano, Brenden, Brendin, Brendon, Brendyn, Brendun

Brennan (Gaelic) A sorrowful man; a teardrop
Brenan, Brenn, Brennen, Brennin, Brennon, Brenin, Brennun, Brennyn

Brent (English) From the hill
Brendt, Brennt, Brentan, Brenten, Brentin, Brenton, Brentun, Brentyn

Brett (Latin) A man from Britain or Brittany
Bret, Breton, Brette, Bretton, Brit, Briton, Britt, Brittain

Brewster (English) One who brews
Brewer, Brewstere

★T**Brian** (Gaelic / Celtic) Of noble birth / having great strength
*Briano, Briant, Brien, Brion, **Bryan**, Bryant, Bryen, Bryent*

Briar (English) Resembling a thorny plant
Brier, Bryar, Bryer

Bruce (Scottish) A man from Brieuse; one who is well-born; from an influential family
Brouce, Brooce, Bruci, Brucie, Brucey, Brucy, Brucee, Brucea

Bruno (German) A brown-haired man
Brunoh, Brunoe, Brunow, Brunowe, Bruin, Bruine, Brunon, Brunun

Buck (English) Resembling a male deer
Buk, Buc, Bucki, Buckie, Bucky, Buckey, Buckee, Buckea

Buckminster (English) From the monastery where deer live
Buckmynster

Bud (English) One who is brotherly
Budd, Buddi, Buddie, Buddee, Buddea, Buddey, Buddy

Budha (Hindi) Another name for the planet Mercury
Budhan, Budhwar

Budhil (Indian) A learned man
Budheel, Budheal, Budheil, Budhiel, Budhyl

Bulat (Russian) Having great strength
Bulatt

Burbank (English) From the riverbank of burrs
Burrbank, Burhbank

Burdett (English) Resembling a bird
Burdet, Burdette, Burdete

Burdon (English) One who lives at the castle
Burdun, Burdan, Burden, Burdin, Burdyn, Burhdon, Burhdun, Burhden

Burgess (German) A free citizen of the town
Burges, Burgiss, Burgis, Burgyss, Burgys, Burgeis

Burke (French) From the fortress on the hill
Berk, Berke, Birk, Bourke, Burk, Birke, Bourk, Byrk

Burne (English) Resembling a bear; from the brook; the brown-haired one
Burn, Beirne, Burnis, Byrn, Byrne, Burns, Byrnes

Burnell (French) The small, brown-haired one
Burnel, Burnelle, Burnele, Brunell, Brunel, Brunele, Brunelle

Burnet (French) Having brown hair
Burnett, Burnete, Burnette, Bernet, Bernett, Bernete, Bernette

Burton (English) From the fortified town
Burtun, Burten, Burtin, Burtyn, Burtan

Butler (English) The keeper of the bottles (wine, liquor)
Buttler, Butlar, Buttlar, Butlor, Buttlor, Butlir, Buttlir, Butlyr

Byron (English) One who lives near the cow sheds
Byrom, Beyren, Beyron, Biren, Biron, Buiron, Byram, Byran

Cable (French) One who makes rope
Cabel, Caibel, Caible, Caybel, Cayble, Caebel, Caeble, Cabe

Caddis (English) Resembling a worsted fabric
Caddys, Caddiss, Caddice, Caddyss

★Cade (English / French) One who is round / of the cask
*Caid, Caide, Cayd, Cayde, Caed, Caede, **Caden**, Cayden*

Cadell (Welsh) Having the spirit of battle
Cadel, Caddell, Caddel

Cadmus (Greek) A man from the east; in mythology, the man who founded Thebes
Cadmar, Cadmo, Cadmos, Cadmuss

Cadogan (Welsh) Having glory and honor during battle
Cadogawn, Cadwgan, Cadwgawn, Cadogaun, Cadwgaun

Caduceus (Greek) The symbol of the medical profession; in mythology, Hermes's insignia
Caduseus, Caducius, Cadusius, Caducios, Cadusios

Cahir (Irish) A mighty warrior
Caheer, Cahear, Cahier, Caheir, Cahyr

Cain (Hebrew) One who wields a spear; something acquired; in the Bible, Adam and Eve's first son who killed his brother Abel
Cayn, Caen, Cane, Caine, Cayne, Caene

Caird (Scottish) A traveling metal worker
Cairde, Cayrd, Cayrde, Caerd, Caerde

Cairn (Gaelic) From the mound of rocks
Cairne, Cairns, Caern, Caerne, Caernes

Caith (Irish) Of the battlefield
Caithe, Cayth, Caythe, Cathe, Caeth, Caethe

Cajetan (English) A man from Gaeta
Cajetano, Cajetanio, Cajetaneo

Calbert (English) A cowboy
Calberte, Calburt, Calburte, Calbirt, Calbirte, Calbyrt, Calbyrte

Cale (English) Form of Charles, meaning "one who is manly and strong / a free man"
Cail, Caile, Cayl, Cayle, Cael, Caele

★ᵀCaleb (Hebrew) Resembling a dog
Cayleb, Caileb, Caeleb, Calob, Cailob, Caylob, Caelob, Kaleb

Calian (Native American) A warrior of life
Calien, Calyan, Calyen

Calix (Greek) A handsome man
Calyx, Calex, Calax, Calox, Calux

Camara (African) One who teaches others

Camden (Gaelic) From the winding valley
Camdene, Camdin, Camdyn, Camdan, Camdon, Camdun

Cameo (English) A small, perfect child
Cammeo

★ᵀCameron (Scottish) Having a crooked nose
Cameren, Cameran, Camerin, Cameryn, Camerun, Camron, Camren, Camran, Tameron

Campbell (Scottish) Having a crooked mouth
Campbel, Cambell, Cambel, Camp, Campe, Cambeul, Cambeull, Campbeul

Candan (Turkish) A sincere man
Canden, Candin, Candyn, Candon, Candun

Canute (Scandinavian) A knot
Cnute, Cnut

Canyon (Spanish / English)
From the footpath / from
the deep ravine
Caniyon, Canyun, Caniyun

Capricorn (Latin) The tenth
sign of the zodiac; the goat

Cargan (Gaelic) From the
small rock
*Cargen, Cargon, Cargun,
Cargin, Cargyn*

★**Carl** (German) Form of
Karl, meaning "a free man"
*Carel, Carlan, Carle,
Carlens, Carlitis, Carlin,
Carlo, **Carlos***

Carlsen (Scandinavian)
The son of Carl
*Carlssen, Carlson, Carlsson,
Carlsun, Carllsun, Carlsin,
Carllsin, Carlsyn*

Carlton (English) From the
free man's town
*Carltun, Carltown, Carston,
Carstun, Carstown,
Carleton, Carletun, Carlten*

Carmichael (Scottish) A
follower of Michael

Carmine (Latin / Aramaic)
A beautiful song / the color
crimson
*Carman, Carmen, Carmin,
Carmino, Carmyne,
Carmon, Carmun, Carmyn*

Carnig (Armenian)
Resembling a lamb
Carnigg, Carnyg, Carnygg

★ᵀ**Carson** (Scottish) The
son of a marsh dweller
*Carsen, Carsun, Carsan,
Carsin, Carsyn*

★**Carter** (English) One who
transports goods; one who
drives a cart
*Cartar, Cartir, Cartyr,
Cartor, Cartur, Cartere,
Cartier, Cartrell*

Cartland (English) From
Carter's land
*Carteland, Cartlan,
Cartlend, Cartelend, Cartlen*

Cary (Celtic / Welsh /
Gaelic) From the river /
from the fort on the hill /
having dark features
*Carey, Cari, Carie, Caree,
Carea, Carry, Carrey, Carri*

Casimir (Slavic) One who
demands peace
*Casimeer, Casmire,
Casimiro, Casmir,
Casimear, Casimyr,
Casimeir, Casimier*

Cassander (Spanish) A
brother of heroes
*Casander, Casandro,
Cassandro, Casandero,
Cassandero*

Cassius (Latin) One who
is empty; hollow; vain
*Cassios, Cassio, Cach,
Cache, Cashus, Cashos,
Cassian, Cassien*

Castel (Spanish) From the castle
Castell, Castal, Castall, Castol, Castoll, Castul, Castull, Castil

Castor (Greek) Resembling a beaver; in mythology, one of the Dioscuri
Castur, Caster, Castar, Castir, Castyr, Castorio, Castoreo, Castoro

Cat (American) Resembling the animal
Catt, Chait, Chaite

Cathal (Gaelic) The ruler of the battle
Cathel, Cathol, Cathul, Cathil, Cathyl

Cathmore (Irish) A renowned fighter
Cathmor, Cathemore, Cathemor

Cato (Latin) One who is all-knowing
Cayto, Caito, Caeto

Caton (Spanish) One who is knowledgable
Caten, Catun, Catan, Catin, Catyn

Cavell (Teutonic) One who is bold
Cavel, Cavele, Cavelle

Caxton (English) From the lump settlement
Caxtun, Caxten

Ceallach (Irish) A bright-headed man
Ceallachan

Celesto (Latin) From heaven
Célestine, Celestino, Celindo, Celestyne, Celestyno

Cephas (Hebrew) As solid as a rock

Cermak (Czech) Resembling a robin
Cermac, Cermack

Chad (English) One who is warlike
Chaddie, Chadd, Chadric, Chadrick, Chadrik, Chadryck, Chadryc, Chadryk

Chadwick (English) From Chad's dairy farm
Chadwik, Chadwic, Chadwyck, Chadwyk, Chadwyc

Chai (Hebrew) A giver of life
Chaika, Chaim, Cahyim, Cahyyam

Chalkley (English) From the chalk meadow
Chalkly, Chalkleigh, Chalklee, Chalkleah, Chalkli, Chalklie, Chalklea

Champion (English) A warrior; the victor
Champeon, Champiun, Champeun, Champ

Chan (Spanish / Sanskrit) Form of John, meaning "God is gracious" / a shining man
Chayo, Chano, Chawn, Chaun

Chanan (Hebrew) God is compassionate
Chanen, Chanin, Chanyn, Chanun, Chanon

Chaniel (Hebrew) The grace of God
Chanyel, Chaniell, Chanyell

Channing (French / English) An official of the church / resembling a young wolf
Channyng, Canning, Cannyng

Chantry (French) One who sings
Chantrey, Chantri, Chantrie, Chantree, Chantrea

Chao (Chinese) The great one

Chappel (English) One who works in the chapel
Capel, Capell, Capello, Cappel, Chappell

★Charles (English / German) One who is manly and strong / a free man
Charls, Chas, Charli, Charlie, Charley, Charly, Charlee, Charleigh, Cale, Chuck, Chick

Charleson (English) The son of Charles
Charlesen, Charlesin, Charlesyn, Charlesan, Charlesun

Charlton (English) From the free man's town
Charleton, Charltun, Charletun, Charleston, Charlestun

Charro (Spanish) A cowboy
Charo

★Chase (English) A huntsman
Chace, Chasen, Chayce, Chayse, Chaise, Chaice, Chaece, Chaese

Chatwin (English) A warring friend
Chatwine, Chatwinn, Chatwinne, Chatwen, Chatwenn, Chatwenne, Chatwyn, Chatwynn

Chaviv (Hebrew) One who is dearly loved
Chaveev, Chaveav, Chaviev, Chaveiv, Chavyv, Chavivi, Chavivie, Chavivy

Chay (Gaelic) From the fairy place
Chaye, Chae

Chelsey (English) From the landing place for chalk
Chelsee, Chelseigh, Chelsea, Chelsi, Chelsie, Chelsy, Chelcey, Chelcy

Cheslav (Russian) From the fortified camp
Cheslaw

Chester (Latin) From the camp of the soldiers
Chet, Chess, Cheston, Chestar, Chestor, Chestur, Chestir, Chestyr

Cheveyo (Native American) A spirit warrior

Chick (English) Form of Charles, meaning "one who is manly and strong / a free man"
Chik, Chicki, Chickie, Chicky, Chickey, Chickee, Chickea, Chic

Chico (Spanish) A boy; a lad

Chien (Vietnamese) A combative man

Chiron (Greek) A wise tutor
Chyron, Chirun, Chyrun

Chogan (Native American) Resembling a blackbird
Chogen, Chogon, Chogun, Chogin, Chogyn

Choni (Hebrew) A gracious man
Chonie, Chony, Choney, Chonee, Chonea

★ᵀ**Christian** (Greek) A follower of Christ
Chrestien, Chretien, Chris, Christan, Christer, Christiano, Christie, Christo

★ᵀ**Christopher** (Greek) One who bears Christ inside
Chris, Kit, Christof, Christofer, Christoffer, Christoforo, Christoforus, Christoph, Christophe, Christophoros

Chuchip (Native American) A deer spirit

Chuck (English) Form of Charles, meaning "one who is manly and strong / a free man"
Chucke, Chucki, Chuckie, Chucky, Chuckey, Chuckee, Chuckea

Chul (Korean) One who stands firm

Chun (Chinese) Born during the spring

Cid (Spanish) A lord
Cyd

Cillian (Gaelic) One who suffers strife

Ciqala (Native American) The little one

Cirrus (Latin) A lock of hair; resembling the cloud
Cyrrus

Clair (Latin) One who is bright
Clare, Clayr, Claer, Clairo, Claro, Claero

Clancy (Celtic) Son of the red-haired warrior
Clancey, Clanci, Clancie, Clancee, Clancea, Clansey, Clansy, Clansi

Clark (English) A cleric; a clerk
Clarke, Clerk, Clerke, Clerc

Claude (English) One who is lame
Claud, Claudan, Claudell, Claidianus, Claudicio, Claudien, Claudino, Claudio

Clay (English) Of the earth's clay

Clayton (English) From the town settled on clay
Claytun, Clayten, Claytin, Claytyn, Claytan, Cleyton, Cleytun, Cleytan

Cleon (Greek) A well-known man
Cleone, Clion, Clione, Clyon, Clyone

Clifford (English) From the ford near the cliff
Cliff, Clyfford, Cliford, Clyford

Cliffton (English) From the town near the cliff
Cliff, Cliffe, Clyff, Clyffe, Clifft, Clift, Clyfft, Clyft

Clinton (English) From the town on the hill
Clynton, Clintun, Clyntun, Clint, Clynt, Clinte, Clynte

Clive (English) One who lives near the cliff
Clyve, Cleve

Cluny (Irish) From the meadow
Cluney, Cluni, Clunie, Clunee, Clunea, Cluneah

Cobden (English) From the cottage in the valley
Cobdenn, Cobdale, Cobdail, Cobdaile, Cobdell, Cobdel, Cobdayl, Cobdayle

Cockrell (French) Resembling a young rooster
Cockrel, Cokrell, Cokrel, Cockrill, Cockril, Cockerel, Cockerell

★Cody (Irish / English) One who is helpful; a wealthy man / acting as a cushion
Codi, Codie, Codey, Codee, Codeah, Codea, Codier, Codyr

Colbert (French) A famous and bright man
Colvert, Culbert, Colburt, Colbirt, Colbyrt, Colbart, Culburt, Culbirt

Colby (English) From the coal town
Colbey, Colbi, Colbie, Colbee, Collby, Coalby, Colbea, Colbeah

⋆Cole (English) Having dark features; having coal-black hair
Coley, Coli, Coly, Colie, Colee, Coleigh, Colea, Colson

Coleridge (English) From the dark ridge
Colerige, Colridge, Colrige

Colgate (English) From the dark gate
Colegate, Colgait, Colegait, Colgayt, Colegayt, Colgaet, Colegaet

⋆Colin (Scottish) A young man; a form of Nicholas, meaning "of the victorious people"
Cailean, Colan, Colyn, Colon, Colun, Colen, Collin, Collan

Colt (English) A young horse; from the coal town
Colte, Colten, Colton, Coltun, Coltan, Coltin, Coltyn, Coltrain

Colter (English) A horse herdsman
Coltere, Coltar, Coltor, Coltir, Coltyr, Coulter, Coultar, Coultir

Comanche (Native American) A tribal name
Comanchi, Comanchie, Comanchee, Comanchea, Comanchy, Comanchey

Comhghall (Irish) A fellow hostage
Cowall, Cowal

Comus (Latin) In mythology, the god of mirth and revelry
Comos, Comes, Comas, Comis, Comys

Conan (English / Gaelic) Resembling a wolf / one who is high and mighty
Conant

Condon (Celtic) A dark, wise man
Condun, Condan, Conden, Condin, Condyn

Cong (Chinese) A clever man

Conn (Irish) The chief
Con

Connecticut (Native American) From the place beside the long river / from the state of Connecticut

Connery (Scottish) A daring man
Connary, Connerie, Conneri, Connerey, Connarie, Connari, Connarey, Conary

⋆Connor (Gaelic) A wolf lover
Conor, Conner, Coner, Connar, Conar, Connur, Conur, Connir, Conir

Conroy (Irish) A wise advisor
Conroye, Conroi

Constantine (Latin) One who is steadfast; firm
Dinos

Consuelo (Spanish) One who offers consolation
Consuel, Consuelio, Consueleo, Consueliyo, Consueleyo

Conway (Gaelic) The hound of the plain; from the sacred river
Conwaye, Conwai, Conwae, Conwy

Cook (English) One who prepares meals for others
Cooke

Cooney (Irish) A handsome man
Coony, Cooni, Coonie, Coonee, Coonea

*Cooper (English) One who makes barrels
Coop, Coopar, Coopir, Coopyr, Coopor, Coopur, Coopersmith, Cupere

Corbett (French) Resembling a young raven
Corbet, Corbete, Corbette, Corbit, Corbitt, Corbite, Corbitte

Corcoran (Gaelic) Having a ruddy complexion
Cochran

Cordero (Spanish) Resembling a lamb
Corderio, Corderiyo, Cordereo, Cordereyo

Corey (Irish) From the hollow; of the churning waters
Cory, Cori, Corie, Coree, Corea, Correy, Corry, Corri

Coriander (Greek) A romantic man; resembling the spice
Coryander, Coriender, Coryender

Corlan (Irish) One who wields a spear
Corlen, Corlin, Corlyn, Corlon, Corlun

Corrado (German) A bold counselor
Corrade, Corradeo, Corradio

Corridon (Irish) One who wields a spear
Corridan, Corridun, Corriden, Corridin, Corridyn

Cortez (Spanish) A courteous man
Cortes

Cosmo (Greek) The order of the universe
Cosimo, Cosmé, Cosmos, Cosmas, Cozmo, Cozmos, Cozmas

Cotton (American) Resembling or farmer of the plant
Cottin, Cotten, Cottyn, Cottun, Cottan

Courtney (English) A courteous man; courtly
Cordney, Cordni, Cortenay, Corteney, Cortni, Cortnee, Cortneigh, Cortney

Covert (English) One who provides shelter
Couvert

Covey (English) A brood of birds
Covy, Covi, Covie, Covee, Covea, Covvey, Covvy, Covvi

Covington (English) From the town near the cave
Covyngton, Covingtun, Covyngtun

Cox (English) A coxswain
Coxe, Coxi, Coxie, Coxey, Coxy, Coxee, Coxea

Coyle (Irish) A leader during battle
Coyl, Coil, Coile

Craig (Gaelic) From the rocks; from the crag
Crayg, Craeg, Craige, Crayge, Craege, Crage, Crag

Crandell (English) From the valley of cranes
Crandel, Crandale, Crandail, Crandaile, Crandayl, Crandayle, Crandael, Crandaele

Crawford (English) From the crow's ford
Crawforde, Crawferd, Crawferde, Crawfurd, Crawfurde

Creed (Latin) A guiding principle; a belief
Creede, Cread, Creade, Creedon, Creadon, Creedun, Creadun, Creedin

Creek (English) From the small stream
Creeke, Creak, Creake, Creik, Creike

Creighton (Scottish) From the border town
Creightun, Crayton, Craytun, Craiton, Craitun, Craeton, Craetun, Crichton

Creketun (English) From the town near the creek
Creketon, Creketen, Creekton, Creektun, Creekten

Crescent (French) One who creates; increasing; growing
Creissant, Crescence, Cressant, Cressent, Crescant

Crogher (Irish) One who loves hounds
Crohoore, Crohoor

Cuarto (Spanish) The fourth-born child
Cuartio, Cuartiyo, Cuarteo, Cuarteyo

Cuetzpalli (Nahuatl) Resembling a lizard
Cuetzpallie, Cuetzpally, Cuetzpalley, Cuetzpallee, Cuetzpallea

Cunningham (Gaelic) From the village of milk
Conyngham, Cuningham, Cunnyngham, Cunyngham

Cuong (Vietnamese) One who is healthy and prosperous

Curcio (French) One who is courteous
Curceo

Curley (English) Having great strength
Curly, Curlie, Curli, Curleigh, Curlee, Curlea

Cuthbert (English) One who is bright and famous
Cuthbeorht, Cuthburt, Cuthbirt, Cuthbyrt

Cyneley (English) From the royal meadow
Cynely, Cyneli, Cynelie, Cynelee, Cynelea, Cyneleah, Cyneleigh

Czar (Russian) An emperor

D

Dabi (Hebrew) One who is dearly loved
Dabie, Daby, Dabey, Dabee, Dabea

Dacey (Gaelic / Latin) A man from the south / a man from Dacia
Dacy, Dacee, Dacea, Daci, Dacie, Daicey, Daicy, Daicee

Dack (English) From the French town of Dax
Dacks

Daedalus (Greek) A craftsman
Daldalos, Dedalus

Dag (Scandinavian) Born during the daylight
Dagney, Dagny, Dagnee, Dagnea, Dagni, Dagnie, Daeg, Dagget

Daijon (American) A gift of hope
Dayjon, Daejon, Dajon

Dainan (Australian) A kind-hearted man
Dainen, Dainon, Dainun, Dainyn, Dainin, Daynan, Daynen, Daynon

Daire (Irish) A wealthy man
*Dair, Daere, Daer, Dayr,
Dayre, Dare, Dari, Darie*

Daivat (Hindi) A powerful
man

Dakarai (African) Filled
with happiness

Dakota (Native American)
A friend to all
*Daccota, Dakoda, Dakodah,
Dakotah, Dakoeta, Dekota,
Dekohta, Dekowta*

Daksha (Indian) A brilliant man
Dakshah

Dallan (Irish) One who is
blind
*Dalan, Dallen, Dalen,
Dallon, Dalon, Dallun,
Dalun*

Dallin (English) From the
valley
Dalin, Dallyn, Dalyn

Damario (Greek /
Spanish) Resembling a
calf / one who is gentle
*Damarios, Damarius,
Damaro, Damero,
Damerio, Damereo,
Damareo, Damerios*

Damian (Greek) One who
tames or subdues others
*Daemon, Daimen, Daimon,
Daman, Damen, Dameon,
Damiano, Damianos*

Damis (Arabic) A dark-
skinned man
Damiss, Damys, Damyss

Danely (Scandinavian) A
man from Denmark
*Daneley, Daneli, Danelie,
Danelee, Daneleigh,
Danelea, Daineley, Dainely*

Dang (Vietnamese) One
who is praiseworthy

Daniachew (African) A
mediator

★ᵀ**Daniel** (Hebrew) God is
my judge
*Dan, Danal, Daneal,
Danek, Danell, Danial,
Daniele, Danil, Danilo*

Danso (African) A reliable
man
Dansoe, Dansow, Dansowe

Dante (Latin) An enduring
man; everlasting
*Dantae, Dantay, Dantel,
Daunte, Dontae, Dontay,
Donte, Dontae*

Danuta (Polish) A gift
from God

Daoud (Arabian) Form of
David, meaning "the
beloved one"
*Daoude, Dawud, Doud,
Daud, Da'ud*

Daphnis (Greek) In
mythology, the son of
Hermes
Daphnys

Dar (Hebrew) Resembling a pearl
Darr

Darcel (French) Having dark features
Darcell, Darcele, Darcelle, Darcio, Darceo

Dardanus (Greek) In mythology, the founder of Troy
Dardanio, Dardanios, Dardanos, Dard, Darde

Darek (English) Form of Derek, meaning "the ruler of the tribe"
Darrek, Darec, Darrec, Darreck, Dareck

Darion (Greek) A gift
Darian, Darien, Dariun, Darrion, Darrian, Darrien, Daryon, Daryan

Darius (Greek) A kingly man; one who is wealthy
Darias, Dariess, Dario, Darious, Darrius, Derrius, Derrious, Derrias

Darlen (American) A sweet man; a darling
Darlon, Darlun, Darlan, Darlin, Darlyn

Darnell (English) From the hidden place
Darnall, Darneil, Darnel, Darnele, Darnelle

Darold (English) Form of Harold, meaning "the ruler of an army"
Darrold, Derald, Derrald, Derold, Derrold

Darren (Gaelic / English) A great man / a gift from God
Darran, Darrin, Darryn, Darron, Darrun, Daren, Darin, Daran

Dart (English / American) From the river / one who is fast
Darte, Darrt, Darrte, Darti, Dartie, Dartee, Dartea, Darty

Darvell (French) From the eagle town
Darvel, Darvele, Darvelle

Das (Indian) A slave; a servant
Dasa

Dasras (Indian) A handsome man

Dasya (Indian) A servant

Daudi (African) One who is dearly loved
Daudie, Daudy, Daudey, Daudee, Daudea

★ᵀDavid (Hebrew) The beloved one
Dave, Davey, Davi, Davidde, Davide, Davie, Daviel, Davin, Daoud

Davis (English) The son of David
Davies, Daviss, Davys, Davyss

Davu (African) Of the beginning
Davue, Davoo, Davou, Davugh

Dayanand (Hindi) A compassionate man
Dayanande, Dayan

Deacon (Greek) The dusty one; a servant
Deecon, Deakon, Deekon, Deacun, Deecun, Deakun, Deekun, Deacan

Dean (English) From the valley; a church official
Deane, Deen, Deene, Dene, Deans, Deens, Deani, Deanie

DeAndre (American) A manly man
D'André, DeAndrae, DeAndray, Diandray, Diondrae, Diondray

Dearon (American) One who is much loved
Dearan, Dearen, Dearin, Dearyn, Dearun

Decimus (Latin) The tenth-born child
Decimos, Decimo, Decimu, Decio

Decker (German / Hebrew) One who prays / a piercing man
Deker, Decer, Dekker, Deccer, Deck, Decke

Declan (Irish) The name of a saint

Dedrick (English) Form of Dietrich, meaning "the ruler of the tribe"
Dedryck, Dedrik, Dedryk, Dedric, Dedryc

Deegan (Irish) A black-haired man
Deagan, Degan, Deegen, Deagen, Degen, Deegon, Deagon, Degon

Deinorus (American) A lively man
Denorius, Denorus, Denorios, Deinorius, Deinorios

Dejuan (American) A talkative man
Dejuane, Dewon, Dewonn, Dewan, Dewann, Dwon, Dwonn, Dajuan

Delaney (Irish / French) The dark challenger / from the elder-tree grove
Delany, Delanee, Delanea, Delani, Delanie, Delainey, Delainy, Delaini

Delaware (English) From the state of Delaware
Delawair, Delaweir, Delwayr, Delawayre, Delawaire, Delawaer, Delawaere

Delius (Greek) A man from Delos
Delios, Delos, Delus, Delo

Dell (English) From the small valley
Delle, Del

Delmon (English) A man of the mountain
Delmun, Delmen, Delmin, Delmyn, Delmont, Delmonte, Delmond, Delmonde

Delsi (American) An easygoing guy
Delsie, Delsy, Delsey, Delsee, Delsea, Delci, Delcie, Delcee

Delvin (English) A godly friend
Delvinn, Delvinne, Delvyn, Delvynn, Delvynne, Delven, Delvenn, Delvenne

Demarcus (American) The son of Marcus
DeMarcus, DaMarkiss, DeMarco, Demarkess, DeMarko, Demarkus, DeMarques, DeMarquez

Dembe (African) A peaceful man
Dembi, Dembie, Dembee, Dembea, Dembey, Demby

Demont (French) Man of the mountain
Demonte, Demond, Demonde, Demunt, Demunte, Demund, Demunde

Denali (American) From the national park
Denalie, Denaly, Denaley, Denalee, Denalea, Denaleigh

Denley (English) From the meadow near the valley
Denly, Denlea, Denleah, Denlee, Denleigh, Denli, Denlie

Denman (English) One who lives in the valley
Denmann, Denmin, Denmyn, Denmen, Denmon, Denmun

Dennis (French) A follower of Dionysus
Den, Denies, Denis, Dennes, Dennet, Denney, Dennie, Denys, Dennys

Dennison (English) The son of Dennis
Denison, Dennisun, Denisun, Dennisen, Denisen, Dennisan, Denisan

Deo (Greek) A godly man

Deonte (French) An outgoing man
Deontay, Deontaye, Deontae, Dionte, Diontay, Diontaye, Diontae

Deotis (American) A learned man; a scholar
Deotiss, Deotys, Deotyss, Deotus, Deotuss

Derek (English) The ruler of the tribe
Dereck, Deric, Derick, Derik, Deriq, Derk, Derreck, Derrek, Darek

Dervin (English) A gifted friend
Dervinn, Dervinne, Dervyn, Dervynn, Dervynne, Dervon, Dervan, Dervun

Deshan (Hindi) Of the nation
Deshal, Deshad

Desiderio (Latin) One who is desired; hoped for
Derito, Desi, Desideratus, Desiderios, Desiderius, Desiderus, Dezi, Diderot

Desmond (Gaelic) A man from South Munster
Desmonde, Desmund, Desmunde, Dezmond, Dezmonde, Dezmund, Dezmunde, Desmee

Desperado (Spanish) A renegade

Destin (French) Recognizing one's certain fortune; fate
Destyn, Deston, Destun, Desten, Destan

Destrey (American) A cowboy
Destry, Destree, Destrea, Destri, Destrie

Deutsch (German) A German

Devanshi (Hindi) A divine messenger
Devanshie, Devanshy, Devanshey, Devanshee, Devanshea

Devante (Spanish) One who fights wrongdoing

Deverell (French) From the riverbank
Deverel, Deveral, Deverall, Devereau, Devereaux, Devere, Deverill, Deveril

Devlin (Gaelic) Having fierce bravery; a misfortunate man
Devlyn, Devlon, Devlen, Devlan, Devlun

*Devon (English) From the beautiful farmland; of the divine
*Devan, Deven, Devenn, **Devin**, Devonn, Devone, Deveon, Devonne*

Dewitt (Flemish) A blond-haired man
DeWitt, Dewytt, DeWytt, Dewit, DeWit, Dewyt, DeWyt

Dexter (Latin) A right-handed man; one who is skillful
Dextor, Dextar, Dextur, Dextir, Dextyr, Dexton, Dextun, Dexten

Dhyanesh (Indian) One who meditates
Dhianesh, Dhyaneshe, Dhianeshe

Dice (American) A gambling man
Dyce

Dichali (Native American) One who talks a lot
Dichalie, Dichaly, Dichaley, Dichalee, Dichalea, Dichaleigh

★Diego (Spanish) Form of James, meaning "he who supplants"
Dyego, Dago

Diesel (American) Having great strength
Deisel, Diezel, Deizel, Dezsel

Dietrich (German) The ruler of the tribe
Dedrick

Digby (Norse) From the town near the ditch
Digbey, Digbee, Digbea, Digbi, Digbie

Diji (African) A farmer
Dijie, Dijee, Dijea, Dijy, Dijey

Dillon (Gaelic) Resembling a lion; a faithful man
Dillun, Dillen, Dillan, Dillin, Dillyn, Dilon, Dilan, Dilin

Dino (Italian) One who wields a little sword
Dyno, Dinoh, Dynoh, Deano, Deanoh, Deeno, Deenoh, Deino

Dinos (Greek) Form of Constantine, meaning "one who is steadfast; firm"
Dynos, Deanos, Deenos, Deinos, Dinose, Dinoz, Dinoze

Dins (American) One who climbs to the top
Dinz, Dyns, Dynz

Dionysus (Greek) The god of wine and revelry
Dion, Deion, Deon, Deonn, Deonys, Deyon, Diandre, Diondre, Dionte

Dior (French) The golden one
D'Or, Diorr, Diorre, Dyor, Deor, Dyorre, Deorre

Diron (American) Form of Darren, meaning "a great man / a gift from God"
Dirun, Diren, Diran, Dirin, Diryn, Dyron, Dyren, Dyran

Dixon (English) The son of Dick
Dixen, Dixin, Dixyn, Dixan, Dixun

Doane (English) From the rolling hills
Doan

Dobber (American) An independent man
Dobbar, Dobbor, Dobbur, Dobbir, Dobbyr

Dobbs (English) A fiery man
Dobbes, Dobes, Dobs

Dobromir (Polish) A good man
Dobromeer, Dobromear, Dobromier, Dobromeir, Dobromere, Dobromyr, Dobrey, Dobree

Domevlo (African) One who doesn't judge others
Domivlo, Domyvlo

Domingo (Spanish) Born on a Sunday
Domyngo, Demingo, Demyngo

★Dominic (Latin) A lord
Demenico, Dom, Domenic, Domenico, Domenique, Domini, Dominick, Dominico

Domnall (Gaelic) A world ruler
Domhnall, Domnull, Domhnull

Don (Scottish) From of Donald, meaning "ruler of the world"
Donn, Donny, Donney, Donnie, Donni, Donnee, Donnea, Donne

Donald (Scottish) Ruler of the world
Don, Donold, Donuld, Doneld, Donild, Donyld

Donar (Teutonic) In mythology, the god of thunder
Doner, Donor, Donur, Donir, Donyr

Dong (Vietnamese) Born during the winter

Dor (Hebrew) Of this generation
Doram, Doriel, Dorli, Dorlie, Dorlee, Dorlea, Dorleigh, Dorly

Doran (Irish) A stranger; one who has been exiled
Doren, Dorin, Doryn

Dorek (Polish) A gift from God
Dorec, Doreck

Dorsey (Gaelic) From the fortress near the sea
Dorsy, Dorsee, Dorsea, Dorsi, Dorsie

Dost (Arabic) A beloved friend
Doste, Daust, Dauste, Dawst, Dawste

Dotson (English) The son of Dot
Dotsen, Dotsan, Dotsin, Dotsyn, Dotsun, Dottson, Dottsun, Dottsin

Dove (American) A peaceful man
Dovi, Dovie, Dovy, Dovey, Dovee, Dovea

Drade (American) A serious-minded man
Draid, Draide, Drayd, Drayde, Draed, Draede, Dradell, Dradel

Drake (English) Resembling a dragon
Drayce, Drago, Drakie, Drako

Dreng (Anglo-Saxon) A mighty warrior; one who is brave
Drenge, Dring, Dringe, Dryng, Drynge

Driscoll (Celtic) A mediator; one who is sorrowful; a messenger
Dryscoll, Driscol, Dryscol, Driskoll, Dryskoll, Driskol, Dryskol, Driskell

Druce (Gaelic / English) A wise man; a druid / the son of Drew
Drews, Drewce, Druece, Druse, Druson, Drusen, Drusin, Drusyn

Drummond (Scottish) One who lives on the ridge
Drummon, Drumond, Drumon, Drummund, Drumund, Drummun, Drumun, Drummand

Duane (Gaelic) A dark or swarthy man
Dewain, Dewayne, Duante, Duayne, Duwain, Duwaine, Duwayne, Dwain

Dublin (Irish) From the capital of Ireland
Dublyn, Dublen, Dublan, Dublon, Dublun

Duc (Vietnamese) One who has upstanding morals

Dude (American) A cow-boy

Due (Vietnamese) A virtuous man

Duke (English) A title of nobility; a leader
Dooke, Dook, Duki, Dukie, Dukey, Duky, Dukee, Dukea

Dumi (African) One who inspires others
Dumie, Dumy, Dumey, Dumee, Dumea

Dumont (French) Man of the mountain
Dumonte, Dumount, Dumounte

Duncan (Scottish) A dark warrior
Dunkan, Dunckan, Dunc, Dunk, Dunck

Dundee (Scottish) From the town on the Firth of Tay
Dundea, Dundi, Dundie, Dundy, Dundey

Dung (Vietnamese) A brave man; a heroic man

Dunton (English) From the town on the hill
Duntun, Dunten, Duntan, Duntin, Duntyn

Durin (Norse) In mythology, one of the fathers of the dwarves
Duryn, Duren, Duran, Duron, Durun

Durjaya (Hindi) One who is difficult to defeat

Durrell (English) One who is strong and protective
Durrel, Durell, Durel

Dustin (English / German) From the dusty area / a courageous warrior
Dustyn, Dusten, Dustan, Duston, Dustun, Dusty, Dustey, Dusti

Duvall (French) From the valley
Duval, Duvale

Dwade (English) A dark traveler
Dwaid, Dwaide, Dwayd, Dwayde, Dwaed, Dwaede

Dwight (Flemish) A white- or blond-haired man
Dwite, Dwhite, Dwyght, Dwighte

Dyami (Native American) Resembling an eagle
Dyamie, Dyamy, Dyamey, Dyamee, Dyamea, Dyame

Dyer (English) A creative man
Dier, Dyar, Diar, Dy, Dye, Di, Die

★Dylan (Welsh) Son of the sea
Dyllan, Dylon, Dyllon, Dylen, Dyllen, Dylun, Dyllun, Dylin

Dymas (Greek) In mythology, the father of Hecabe
Dimas

Dzigbode (African) One who is patient

Eagan (Irish) A fiery man
Eegan, Eagen, Eegen, Eagon, Eegon, Eagun, Eegun

Eagle (Native American) Resembling the bird
Eegle, Eagel, Eegel

Eamon (Irish) Form of Edmund, meaning "a wealthy protector"
Eaman, Eamen, Eamin, Eamyn, Eamun, Eamonn, Eames, Eemon

Ean (Gaelic) Form of John, meaning "God is gracious"
Eion, Eyan, Eyon, Eian

Earl (English) A nobleman
Earle, Erle, Erl, Eorl

Easey (American) An easy-going man
Easy, Easi, Easie, Easee, Easea, Eazey, Eazy, Eazi

Eastman (English) A man from the east
Eestman, East, Easte, Eest, Eeste

Eberlein (German) Resembling a small boar
Eberleen, Eberlean, Eberlien, Eberlin, Eberlyn, Eberle, Eberley, Eberly

Eblis (Arabic) A devilish man
Ebliss, Eblisse, Eblys, Eblyss, Eblysse

Eckhard (German) Of the brave sword point
Eckard, Eckardt, Eckhardt, Ekkehard, Ekkehardt, Ekhard, Ekhardt

Ed (English) Form of Edward, meaning "a wealthy protector"
Edd, Eddi, Eddie, Eddy, Eddey, Eddee, Eddea, Edi

Edan (Celtic) One who is full of fire
Edon, Edun

Edbert (English) One who is prosperous and bright
Edberte, Edburt, Edburte, Edbirt, Edbirte, Edbyrt, Edbyrte

Edenson (English) Son of Eden
Eadenson, Edensun, Eadensun, Edinson, Edinsun, Edensen, Eadensen

Edison (English) Son of Edward
Eddison, Edisun, Eddisun, Edisen, Eddisen, Edisyn, Eddisyn, Edyson

Edlin (Anglo-Saxon) A wealthy friend
Edlinn, Edlinne, Edlyn, Edlynn, Edlynne, Eadlyn, Eadlin, Edlen

Edmar (English) Of the wealthy sea
Edmarr, Eddmar, Eddmarr, Eadmar, Eadmarr

Edmund (English) A wealthy protector
Ed, Eddie, Edmond, Eamon

Edom (Hebrew) A red-haired man
Edum, Edam, Edem, Edim, Edym

Edred (Anglo-Saxon) A king
Edread, Edrid, Edryd

Edward (English) A wealthy protector
Ed, Eadward, Edik, Edouard, Eduard, Eduardo, Edvard, Edvardas, Edwardo

Edwardson (English) The son of Edward
Edwardsun, Eadwardsone, Eadwardsun

Edwin (English) A wealthy friend
Edwinn, Edwinne, Edwine, Edwyn, Edwynn, Edwynne, Edwen, Edwenn

Effiom (African) Resembling a crocodile
Efiom, Effyom, Efyom, Effeom, Efeom

Efigenio (Greek) Form of Eugene, meaning "a well-born man"
Ephigenio, Ephigenios, Ephigenius, Efigenios, Efigenius

Efrain (Spanish) Form of Ephraim, meaning "one who is fertile; productive"
Efraine, Efrayn, Efrayne, Efraen, Efraene, Efrane, Efren, Efran

Efrat (Hebrew) One who is honored
Efratt, Ephrat, Ephratt

Egesa (Anglo-Saxon) One who creates terror
Egessa, Egeslic, Egeslick, Egeslik

Eghert (German) An intelligent man
Egherte, Eghurt, Eghurte, Eghirt, Eghirte, Eghyrt, Eghyrte

Egidio (Italian) Resembling a young goat
Egydio, Egideo, Egydeo, Egidiyo, Egydiyo, Egidius, Egydius, Egidios

Eikki (Finnish) A powerful man
Eikkie, Eikky, Eikkey, Eikkee, Eikkea, Eiki, Eikie, Eiky

Eilert (Scandinavian) Of the hard point
Elert, Eilart, Elart, Eilort, Elort, Eilurt, Elurt, Eilirt

Eilon (Hebrew) From the oak tree
Eilan, Eilin, Eilyn, Eilen, Eilun

Einar (Scandinavian) A leading warrior
Einer, Ejnar, Einir, Einyr, Einor, Einur, Ejnir, Ejnyr

Einri (Teutonic) An intelligent man
Einrie, Einry, Einrey, Einree, Einrea

Eisig (Hebrew) One who laughs often
Eisyg

Eladio (Spanish) A man from Greece
Eladeo, Eladiyo, Eladeyo

Elbert (English / German) A well-born man / a bright man
Elberte, Elburt, Elburte, Elbirt, Elbirte, Ethelbert, Ethelburt, Ethelbirt

Eldan (English) From the valley of the elves

Eldon (English) From the sacred hill
Eldun

Eldorado (Spanish) The golden man

Eldred (English) An old, wise advisor
Eldrid, Eldryd, Eldrad, Eldrod, Edlrud, Ethelred, Ethelread, Eldread

Eldrick (English) An old, wise ruler
Eldrik, Eldric, Eldryck, Eldryk, Eldryc, Eldrich, Eldrych

Eleazar (Hebrew) God will help
Elazar, Eleasar, Eleazaro, Eliazar, Eliezer, Elazaro, Eleazaro, Elazer

Eliachim (Hebrew) God will establish
Eliakim, Elyachim, Elyakim, Eliachym, Eliakym

Elian (Spanish) A spirited man
Elyan, Elien, Elyen, Elion, Elyon, Eliun, Elyun

Elihu (Hebrew) My God is He
Elyhu, Elihue, Elyhue, Elihugh, Elyhugh

★ᵀElijah (Hebrew) Jehovah is my God
Elija, Eliyahu, Eljah, Elja, Elyjah, Elyja, Elijuah, Elyjuah

Elimelech (Hebrew) God is kind
Elymelech, Elimelek, Elimeleck, Elymelek, Elymeleck

Elimu (African) Having knowledge of science
Elymu, Elimue, Elymue, Elimoo, Elymoo

Eliphalet (Hebrew) God is my deliverance
Elifalet, Elifelet, Eliphelet, Elyphalet, Elyfalet, Elyfelet, Elyphelet

Elisha (Hebrew) God is my salvation
Elisee, Eliseo, Elisher, Eliso, Elisio, Elysha, Elysee, Elyseo

Ellory (Cornish) Resembling a swan
Ellorey, Elloree, Ellorea, Ellori, Ellorie, Elory, Elorey, Elorea

Ellsworth (English) From the nobleman's estate
Elsworth, Ellswerth, Elswerth, Ellswirth, Elswirth, Elzie

Elman (English) A nobleman
Elmann, Ellman, Ellmann

Elmo (English / Latin) A protector / an amiable man
Elmoe, Elmow, Elmowe

Elmot (American) A lovable man
Elmott, Ellmot, Ellmott

Elof (Swedish) The only heir
Eluf, Eloff, Eluff, Elov, Ellov, Eluv, Elluv

Elois (German) A famous warrior
Eloys, Eloyis, Elouis

Elpidio (Spanish) A fearless man; having heart
Elpydio, Elpideo, Elpydeo, Elpidios, Elpydios, Elpidius, Elpydius

Elroy (Irish / English) A redhaired young man / a king
Elroi, Elroye, Elric, Elryc, Elrik, Elryk, Elrick, Elryck

Elston (English) From the nobleman's town
Ellston, Elstun, Ellstun, Elson, Ellson, Elsun, Ellsun

Elton (English) From the old town
Ellton, Eltun, Elltun, Elten, Ellten, Eltin, Elltin, Eltyn

Eluwilussit (Native American) A holy man

Elvey (English) An elf warrior
Elvy, Elvee, Elvea, Elvi, Elvie

Elvis (Scandinavian) One who is wise
Elviss, Elvys, Elvyss

Elzie (English) Form of Ellsworth, meaning "from the nobleman's estate"
Elzi, Elzy, Elzey, Elzee, Elzea, Ellzi, Ellzie, Ellzee

Emest (German) One who is serious
Emeste, Emesto, Emestio, Emestiyo, Emesteo, Emesteyo, Emo, Emst

Emil (Latin) One who is eager; an industrious man
Emelen, Emelio, Emile, Emilian, Emiliano, Emilianus, Emilio, Emilion

Emmanuel (Hebrew) God is with us
Manuel, Manny, Em, Eman, Emmannuel

Emrys (Welsh) An immortal man

Enapay (Native American) A brave man
Enapaye, Enapai, Enapae

Enar (Swedish) A great warrior
Ener, Enir, Enyr, Enor, Enur

Endicott (English) From the cottage at the end of the lane
Endicot, Endycott, Endycot, Endecott, Endecot

Endymion (Greek) In mythology, a handsome young man whose youth was preserved in eternal sleep
Endymyon, Endimion, Endimyon, Endymeon, Endimeon

Engelbert (German) As bright as an angel
Englebert, Englbert, Engelburt, Engleburt, Englburt, Englebirt, Engelbirt, Englbirt

Enoch (Hebrew) One who is dedicated to God
Enoc, Enok, Enock

Enrique (Spanish) The ruler of the estate
Enrico, Enriko, Enricko, Enriquez, Enrikay, Enreekay, Enrik, Enric

Enyeto (Native American) One who walks like a bear

Enzo (Italian) The ruler of the estate
Enzio, Enzeo, Enziyo, Enzeyo

Eoin Baiste (Irish) Refers to John the Baptist

Ephraim (Hebrew) One who is fertile; productive
Eff, Efraim, Efram, Efrem, Efrain

★Eric (Scandinavian) Ever the ruler
Erek, Erich, Erick, Erik, Eriq, Erix, Errick, Eryk

Ernest (English) One who is sincere and determined; serious
Earnest, Ernesto, Ernestus, Ernst, Erno, Ernie, Erni, Erney

Eron (Spanish) Form of Aaron, meaning "one who is exalted"
Erun, Erin, Eran, Eren, Eryn

Errigal (Gaelic) From the small church
Errigel, Errigol, Errigul, Errigil, Errigyl, Erigal, Erigel, Erigol

Erskine (Gaelic) From the high cliff
Erskin, Erskyne, Erskyn, Erskein, Erskeine, Erskien, Erskiene

Esam (Arabic) A safeguard
Essam

Esben (Scandinavian) Of God
Esbin, Esbyn, Esban, Esbon, Esbun

Esmé (French) One who is esteemed
Esmay, Esmaye, Esmai, Esmae, Esmeling, Esmelyng

Esmun (American) A kind man
Esmon, Esman, Esmen, Esmin, Esmyn

Esperanze (Spanish) Filled with hope
Esperance, Esperence, Esperenze, Esperanzo, Esperenzo

Estcott (English) From the eastern cottage
Estcot

Esteban (Spanish) One who is crowned in victory
Estebon, Estevan, Estevon, Estefan, Estefon, Estebe, Estyban, Estyvan

★T**Ethan** (Hebrew) One who is firm and steadfast
Ethen, Ethin, Ethyn, Ethon, Ethun, Eitan, Etan, Eithan

Ethanael (American) God has given me strength
Ethaniel, Ethaneal, Ethanail, Ethanale

Ethel (Hebrew) One who is noble
Ethal, Etheal

Etlelooaat (Native American) One who shouts

Eudocio (Greek) One who is respected
Eudoceo, Eudociyo, Eudoceyo, Eudoco

★**Eugene** (Greek) A well-born man
*Eugean, Eugenie, Ugene, Efigenio, Gene, **Owen***

Eulogio (Greek) A reasonable man
Eulogiyo, Eulogo, Eulogeo, Eulogeyo

Euodias (Greek) Having good fortune
Euodeas, Euodyas

Euphemios (Greek) One who is well-spoken
Eufemio, Eufemius, Euphemio, Eufemios, Euphemius, Eufemius

Euphrates (Turkish) From the great river
Eufrates, Euphraites, Eufraites, Euphraytes, Eufraytes

Eusebius (Greek) One who is devout
Esabio, Esavio, Esavius, Esebio, Eusabio, Eusaio, Eusebio, Eusebios

Eustace (Greek) Having an abundance of grapes
Eustache, Eustachios, Eustachius, Eustachy, Eustaquio, Eustashe, Eustasius, Eustatius

★**Evan** (Welsh) Form of John, meaning "God is gracious"
Evann, Evans, Even, Evin, Evon, Evyn, Evian, Evien

Evander (Greek) A benevolent man
Evandor, Evandar, Evandir, Evandur, Evandyr

Evers (English) Resembling a wild boar
Ever, Evert, Everte

Evett (American) A bright man
Evet, Evatt, Evat, Evitt, Evit, Evytt, Evyt

Eyal (Hebrew) Having great strength

Eze (African) A king

Ezeji (African) The king of yams
Ezejie, Ezejy, Ezejey, Ezejee, Ezejea

Ezekiel (Hebrew) Strengthened by God
Esequiel, Ezechiel, Eziechiele, Eziequel, Ezequiel, Ezekial, Ezekyel, Esquevelle, Zeke

F

Factor (English) A businessman
Facter, Factur, Factir, Factyr, Factar

Fairbairn (Scottish) A fair-haired boy
Fayrbairn, Faerbairn, Fairbaern, Fayrbaern, Faerbaern, Fairbayrn, Fayrbayrn, Faerbayrn

Fairbanks (English) From the bank along the path
Fayrbanks, Faerbanks, Farebanks

Faisal (Arabic) One who is decisive; resolute
Faysal, Faesal, Fasal, Feisal, Faizal, Fasel, Fayzal, Faezal

Fakhir (Arabic) A proud man
Fakheer, Fakhear, Fakheir, Fakhier, Fakhyr, Faakhir, Faakhyr, Fakhr

Fakih (Arabic) A legal expert
Fakeeh, Fakeah, Fakieh, Fakeih, Fakyh

Falco (Latin) Resembling a falcon; one who works with falcons
Falcon, Falconer, Falconner, Falk, Falke, Falken, Falkner, Faulconer

Fam (American) A family-oriented man

Fang (Scottish) From the sheep pen
Faing, Fayng, Faeng

Faraji (African) One who provides consolation
Farajie, Farajy, Farajey, Farajee, Farajea

Fardoragh (Irish) Having dark features

Fargo (American) One who is jaunty
Fargoh, Fargoe, Fargouh

Farha (Arabic) Filled with happiness
Farhah, Farhad, Farhan, Farhat, Farhani, Farhanie, Farhany, Farhaney

Fariq (Arabic) One who holds rank as lieutenant general
Fareeq, Fareaq, Fareiq, Farieq, Faryq, Farik, Fareek, Fareak

Farnell (English) From the fern hill
Farnel, Farnall, Farnal, Fernauld, Farnauld, Fernald, Farnald

Farold (English) A mighty traveler
Farould, Farald, Farauld, Fareld

Farran (Irish / Arabic / English) Of the land / a baker / one who is adventurous
Fairran, Fayrran, Faerran, Farren, Farrin, Farron, Ferrin, Ferron

Farrar (English) A blacksmith
Farar, Farrer, Farrier, Ferrar, Ferrars, Ferrer, Ferrier, Farer

Farro (Italian) Of the grain
Farroe, Faro, Faroe, Farrow, Farow

Fatik (Indian) Resembling a crystal
Fateek, Fateak, Fatyk, Fatiek, Fateik

Faust (Latin) Having good luck
Fauste, Faustino, Fausto, Faustos, Faustus, Fauston, Faustin, Fausten

Fawcett (American) An audacious man
Fawcet, Fawcette, Fawcete, Fawce, Fawci, Fawcie, Fawcy, Fawcey

Fawwaz (Arabic) A successful man
Fawaz, Fawwad, Fawad

Fay (Irish) Resembling a raven
Faye, Fai, Fae, Feich

Februus (Latin) A pagan god

Fedor (Russian) A gift from God
Faydor, Feodor, Fyodor, Fedyenka, Fyodr, Fydor, Fjodor

Feechi (African) One who worships God
Feechie, Feechy, Feechey, Feechee, Feachi, Feachie, Feachy, Feachey

Feivel (Hebrew) The brilliant one
Feival, Feivol, Feivil, Feivyl, Feivul, Feiwel, Feiwal, Feiwol

Felim (Gaelic) One who is always good
Felym, Feidhlim, Felimy, Felimey, Felimee, Felimea, Felimi, Felimie

Felipe (Spanish) Form of Phillip, meaning "one who loves horses"
Felippe, Filip, Filippo, Fillip, Flip, Fulop, Fullop, Fulip

Felton (English) From the town near the field
Feltun, Felten, Feltan, Feltyn, Feltin

Fenn (English) From the marsh
Fen

Fergall (Gaelic) A strong and brave man
Fergal, Fearghall, Ferghall, Ferghal, Forgael

Fergus (Gaelic) The first and supreme choice
Fearghas, Fearghus, Feargus, Fergie, Ferguson, Fergusson, Furgus, Fergy

Ferrell (Irish) A brave man; a hero
Ferell, Ferel, Ferrel

Fiacre (Celtic) Resembling a raven
Fyacre, Fiacra, Fyacra, Fiachra, Fyachra, Fiachre, Fyachre

Fielding (English) From the field
Fieldyng, Fielder, Field, Fielde, Felding, Feldyng, Fields

Fiero (Spanish) A fiery man
Fyero

Finbar (Irish) A fair-haired man
Finnbar, Finnbarr, Fionn, Fionnbharr, Fionnbar, Fionnbarr, Fynbar, Fynnbar

Finch (English) Resembling the small bird
Fynch, Finche, Fynche, Finchi, Finchie, Finchy, Finchey, Finchee

Fineas (Egyptian) A dark-skinned man
Fyneas, Finius, Fynius

Finian (Irish) A handsome man; fair
Finan, Finnian, Fionan, Finien, Finnien, Finghin, Finneen, Fineen

Finn (Gaelic) A fair-haired man
Fin, Fynn, Fyn, Fingal, Fingall

Finnegan (Irish) A fair-haired man
Finegan, Finnegen, Finegen, Finnigan, Finigan

Fiorello (Italian) Resembling a little flower
Fiorelo, Fiorelio, Fioreleo, Fiorellio, Fiorelleo

Fitch (English) Resembling an ermine
Fytch, Fich, Fych, Fitche, Fytche

Fitzgerald (English) The son of Gerald
Fytzgerald

Fitzgibbon (English) The son of Gibson
Fytzgibbon, Fitzgibon, Fytzgibon

Flann (Irish) One who has a ruddy complexion
Flan, Flainn, Flannan, Flannery, Flanneri, Flannerie, Flannerey, Flanneree

Flavian (Latin) Having yellow hair
Flavel, Flavelle, Flaviano, Flavien, Flavio, Flavius, Flawiusz, Flaviu

Fletcher (English) One who makes arrows
Fletch, Fletche, Flecher

Flynn (Irish) One who has a ruddy complexion
Flyn, Flinn, Flin, Flen, Flenn, Floinn

Fogarty (Irish) One who has been exiled
Fogartey, Fogartee, Fogartea, Fogarti, Fogartie, Fogerty, Fogertey, Fogerti

Foley (English) A creative man
Foly, Folee, Foleigh, Folea, Foli, Folie

Folker (German) A guardian of the people
Folkar, Folkor, Folkur, Folkir, Folkyr, Folke, Folko, Folkus

Fonso (German) Form of Alfonso, meaning "prepared for battle; eager and ready"
Fonzo, Fonsie, Fonzell, Fonzie, Fonsi, Fonsy, Fonsey, Fonsee

Fontaine (French) From the water source
Fontayne, Fontaene, Fontane, Fonteyne, Fontana, Fountain

Ford (English) From the river crossing
Forde, Forden, Fordan, Fordon, Fordun, Fordin, Fordyn, Forday

Fouad (Arabic) One who
has heart
Fuad

Fred (German) Form of
Frederick, meaning "a
peaceful ruler"
*Freddi, Freddie, Freddy,
Freddey, Freddee, Freddea,
Freddis, Fredis*

Frederick (German) A
peaceful ruler
*Fred, Fredrick, Federico,
Federigo, Fredek, Frederic,
Frederich, Frederico, Frederik,
Fredric*

Freeborn (English) One
who was born a free man
*Freeborne, Freebourn,
Freebourne, Freeburn,
Freeburne, Free*

Fremont (French) The pro-
tector of freedom
*Freemont, Fremonte,
Freemonte, Fremond,
Freemond, Fremonde,
Freemonde, Frimunt*

Friedhelm (German) One
who wears the helmet of
peace
Friedelm, Fridhelm, Fridelm

Frigyes (Hungarian) A
mighty and peaceful ruler

Frode (Norse) A wise man
Froad, Froade

Froyim (Hebrew) A kind man
Froiim

Fructuoso (Spanish) One
who is fruitful
Fructo, Fructoso, Fructuso

Fu (Chinese) A wealthy
man

Fudail (Arabic) Of high
moral character
*Fudaile, Fudayl, Fudayle,
Fudale, Fudael, Fudaele*

Fulbright (English) A bril-
liant man
*Fullbright, Fulbrite,
Fullbrite, Fulbryte,
Fullbryte, Fulbert, Fullbert*

Fulki (Indian) A spark
*Fulkie, Fulkey, Fulky,
Fulkee, Fulkea*

Fullerton (English) From
Fuller's town
*Fullertun, Fullertin,
Fullertyn, Fullertan,
Fullerten*

Fursey (Gaelic) The name
of a missionary saint
*Fursy, Fursi, Fursie, Fursee,
Fursea*

Fyfe (Scottish) A man
from Fifeshire
Fife, Fyffe, Fiffe, Fibh

Fyren (Anglo-Saxon) A
wicked man
*Fyrin, Fyryn, Fyran, Fyron,
Fyrun*

Gabai (Hebrew) A delightful man

Gabbana (Italian) A creative man
Gabbanah, Gabana, Gabanah, Gabbanna, Gabanna

Gabbo (English) To joke or scoff
Gabboe, Gabbow, Gabbowe

Gabor (Hebrew) God is my strength
Gabur, Gabar, Gaber, Gabir, Gabyr

Gabra (African) An offering
Gabre

★ᵀGabriel (Hebrew) A hero of God
Gabrian, Gabriele, Gabrielli, Gabriello, Gaby, Gab, Gabbi, Gabbie

Gad (Hebrew / Native American) Having good fortune / from the juniper tree
Gadi, Gadie, Gady, Gadey, Gadee, Gadea

Gadiel (Arabic) God is my fortune
Gadiell, Gadiele, Gadielle, Gaddiel, Gaddiell, Gadil, Gadeel, Gadeal

Gaffney (Irish) Resembling a calf
Gaffny, Gaffni, Gaffnie, Gaffnee, Gaffnea

Gage (French) Of the pledge
Gaige, Gaege, Gayge

Gahuj (African) A hunter

Gair (Gaelic) A man of short stature
Gayr, Gaer, Gaire, Gayre, Gaere, Gare

Gaius (Latin) One who rejoices
Gaeus

Galal (Arabic) A majestic man
Galall, Gallal, Gallall

Galbraith (Irish) A foreigner; a Scot
Galbrait, Galbreath, Gallbraith, Gallbreath, Galbraithe, Gallbraithe, Galbreathe, Gallbreathe

Gale (Irish / English) A foreigner / one who is cheerful
Gail, Gaill, Gaille, Gaile, Gayl, Gayle, Gaylle, Gayll

Galen (Greek) A healer; one who is calm
Gaelan, Gaillen, Galan, Galin, Galyn, Gaylen, Gaylin, Gaylinn

Gali (Hebrew) From the fountain
Galie, Galy, Galey, Galee, Galea, Galeigh

Galip (Turkish) A victorious man
Galyp, Galup, Galep, Galap, Galop

Gallagher (Gaelic) An eager helper
Gallaghor, Gallaghar, Gallaghur, Gallaghir, Gallaghyr, Gallager, Gallagar, Gallagor

Galt (English) From the high, wooded land
Galte, Gallt, Gallte

Galtero (Spanish) Form of Walter, meaning "the commander of the army"
Galterio, Galteriyo, Galtereo, Galtereyo, Galter, Galteros, Galterus, Gualterio

Gamaliel (Hebrew) God's reward
Gamliel, Gamalyel, Gamlyel, Gamli, Gamlie, Gamly, Gamley, Gamlee

Gameel (Arabic) A handsome man
Gameal, Gamil, Gamiel, Gameil, Gamyl

Gamon (American) One who enjoys playing games
Gamun, Gamen, Gaman, Gamin, Gamyn, Gammon, Gammun, Gamman

Gan (Chinese) A wanderer

Gandy (American) An adventurer
Gandey, Gandi, Gandie, Gandee, Gandea

Gann (English) One who defends with a spear
Gan

Gannon (Gaelic) A fair-skinned man
Gannun, Gannen, Gannan, Gannin, Gannyn, Ganon, Ganun, Ganin

Garcia (Spanish) One who is brave in battle
Garce, Garcy, Garcey, Garci, Garcie, Garcee, Garcea

Gared (English) Form of Gerard, meaning "one who is mighty with a spear"
Garad, Garid, Garyd, Garod, Garud

Garman (English) A spear-man
Garmann, Garmen, Garmin, Garmon, Garmun, Garmyn, Gar, Garr

Garrison (French) Prepared
Garris, Garrish, Garry, Gary

Garrett (English) Form of Gerard, meaning "one who is mighty with a spear"
Garett, Garret, Garretson, Garritt, Garrot, Garrott, Gerrit, Gerritt

Garson (English) The son of Gar (Garrett, Garrison, etc.)
Garrson, Garsen, Garrsen, Garsun, Garrsun, Garsone, Garrsone

Garth (Scandinavian) The keeper of the garden
Garthe, Gart, Garte

Garvey (Gaelic) A rough but peaceful man
Garvy, Garvee, Garvea, Garvi, Garvie, Garrvey, Garrvy, Garrvee

Garvin (English) A friend with a spear
Garvyn, Garven, Garvan, Garvon, Garvun

Gary (English) One who wields a spear
Garey, Gari, Garie, Garea, Garee, Garry, Garrey, Garree

Gassur (Arabic) A courageous man
Gassor, Gassir, Gassyr, Gassar, Gasser

Gaston (French) A man from Gascony
Gastun, Gastan, Gasten, Gascon, Gascone, Gasconey, Gasconi, Gasconie

Gate (American) One who is close-minded
Gates, Gait, Gaite, Gaits, Gaites, Gayt, Gayte, Gayts

★Gavin (Welsh) A little white falcon
Gavan, Gaven, Gavino, Gavyn, Gavynn, Gavon, Gavun, Gavyno

Gazali (African) A mystic
Gazalie, Gazaly, Gazaley, Gazalee, Gazalea, Gazaleigh

Geirleif (Norse) A descendant of the spear
Geirleaf, Geerleif, Geerleaf

Geirstein (Norse) One who wields a rock-hard spear
Geerstein, Gerstein

Gellert (Hungarian) A mighty soldier
Gellart, Gellirt, Gellyrt, Gellort, Gellurt

Genaro (Latin) A dedicated man
Genaroh, Genaroe, Genarow, Genarowe

Gene (English) Form of Eugene, meaning "a well-born man"
Genio, Geno, Geneo, Gino, Ginio, Gineo

Genet (African) From Eden
Genat, Genit, Genyt, Genot, Genut

Genoah (Italian) From the city of Genoa
Genoa, Genovise, Genovize

Geoffrey (English) Form of Jeffrey, meaning "a man of peace"
Geffrey, Geoff, Geoffery, Geoffroy, Geoffry, Geofrey, Geofferi, Geofferie

George (Greek) One who works the earth; a farmer
Georas, Geordi, Geordie, Georg, Georges, Georgi, Georgie, Georgio, Yegor, Jurgen, Joren

Gerald (German) One who rules with the spear
Jerald, Garald, Garold, Gearalt, Geralde, Geraldo, Geraud, Gere, Gerek

Gerard (French) One who is mighty with a spear
Gerord, Gerrard, Gared, Garrett

Geremia (Italian) Form of Jeremiah, meaning "one who is exalted by the Lord"
Geremiah, Geremias, Geremija, Geremiya, Geremyah, Geramiah, Geramia

Germain (French / Latin) A man from Germany / one who is brotherly
Germaine, German, Germane, Germanicus, Germano, Germanus, Germayn, Germayne

Gerry (German) Short form of names beginning with Ger-, such as Gerald or Gerard
Gerrey, Gerri, Gerrie, Gerrea, Gerree

Gershom (Hebrew) One who has been exiled
Gersham, Gershon, Gershoom, Gershem, Gershim, Gershym, Gershum, Gersh

Getachew (African) Their master

Ghazi (Arabic) An invader; a conqueror
Ghazie, Ghazy, Ghazey, Ghazee, Ghazea

Ghoukas (Armenian) Form of Lucas, meaning "a man from Lucania"
Ghukas

Giancarlo (Italian) One who is gracious and mighty
Gyancarlo

Gideon (Hebrew) A mighty warrior; one who fells trees
Gideone, Gidi, Gidon, Gidion, Gid, Gidie, Gidy, Gidey

Gilam (Hebrew) The joy of the people
Gylam, Gilem, Gylem, Gilim, Gylim, Gilym, Gylym, Gilom

Gilbert (French / English)
Of the bright promise / one
who is trustworthy
*Gib, Gibb, Gil, Gilberto,
Gilburt, Giselbert,
Giselberto, Giselbertus*

Gildas (Irish / English)
One who serves God / the
golden one
*Gyldas, Gilda, Gylda, Gilde,
Gylde, Gildea, Gyldea, Gildes*

Giles (Greek) Resembling
a young goat
*Gyles, Gile, Gil, Gilles,
Gillis, Gilliss, Gyle, Gyl*

Gill (Gaelic) A servant
*Gyll, Gilly, Gilley, Gillee,
Gillea, Gilli, Gillie, Ghill*

Gillivray (Scottish) A servant of God
Gillivraye, Gillivrae, Gillivrai

Gilmat (Scottish) One who
wields a sword
Gylmat, Gilmet, Gylmet

Gilmer (English) A famous
hostage
*Gilmar, Gilmor, Gilmur,
Gilmir, Gilmyr, Gillmer,
Gillmar, Gillmor*

Gilon (Hebrew) Filled with joy
*Gilun, Gilen, Gilan, Gilin,
Gilyn, Gilo*

Ginton (Arabic) From the
garden
*Gintun, Gintan, Ginten,
Gintin, Gintyn*

Giovanni (Italian) Form of
John, meaning "God is
gracious"
*Geovani, Geovanney,
Geovanni, Geovanny,
Geovany, Giannino,
Giovan, Giovani, Yovanny*

Giri (Indian) From the
mountain
*Girie, Giry, Girey, Giree,
Girea*

Girvan (Gaelic) The small
rough one
*Gyrvan, Girven, Gyrven,
Girvin, Gyrvin, Girvyn,
Gyrvyn, Girvon*

Giulio (Italian) One who is
youthful
Giuliano, Giuleo

Giuseppe (Italian) Form
of Joseph, meaning "God
will add"
*Giuseppi, Giuseppie,
Giuseppy, Giuseppee,
Giuseppea, Giuseppey,
Guiseppe, Guiseppi*

Gizmo (American) One
who is playful
*Gismo, Gyzmo, Gysmo,
Gizmoe, Gismoe, Gyzmoe,
Gysmoe*

Glade (English) From the
clearing in the woods
*Glayd, Glayde, Glaid,
Glaide, Glaed, Glaede*

Glaisne (Irish) One who is calm; serene
Glaisny, Glaisney, Glaisni, Glaisnie, Glaisnee, Glasny, Glasney, Glasni

Glasgow (Scottish) From the city in Scotland
Glasgo

Glen (Gaelic) From the secluded narrow valley
Glenn, Glennard, Glennie, Glennon, Glenny, Glin, Glinn, Glyn

Glover (English) One who makes gloves
Glovar, Glovir, Glovyr, Glovur, Glovor

Gobind (Sanskrit) The cow finder
Gobinde, Gobinda, Govind, Govinda, Govinde

Goby (American) An audacious man
Gobi, Gobie, Gobey, Gobee, Gobea

Godfrey (German) God is peace
Giotto, Godefroi, Godfry, Godofredo, Goffredo, Gottfrid, Gottfried, Godfried

Godfried (German) God is peace
Godfreed, Gjord

Gogo (African) A grandfatherly man

Goldwin (English) A golden friend
Goldwine, Goldwinn, Goldwinne, Goldwen, Goldwenn, Goldwenne, Goldwyn, Goldwynn

Goode (English) An upstanding man
Good, Goodi, Goodie, Goody, Goodey, Goodee, Goodea

Gordon (Gaelic) From the great hill; a hero
Gorden, Gordin, Gordyn, Gordun, Gordan, Gordi, Gordie, Gordee

Gormley (Irish) The blue spearman
Gormly, Gormlee, Gormlea, Gormleah, Gormleigh, Gormli, Gormlie, Gormaly

Goro (Japanese) The fifth-born child

Gotam (Indian) The best ox
Gotem, Gautam, Gautem, Gautom, Gotom

Gotzon (Basque) A heavenly messenger; an angel

Gower (Welsh) One who is pure; chaste
Gwyr, Gowyr, Gowir, Gowar, Gowor, Gowur

Gozal (Hebrew) Resembling a baby bird
Gozall, Gozel, Gozell, Gozale, Gozele

Grady (Gaelic) One who is famous; noble
Gradey, Gradee, Gradea, Gradi, Gradie, Graidy, Graidey, Graidee

Grand (English) A superior man
Grande, Grandy, Grandey, Grandi, Grandie, Grandee, Grandea, Grander

Granger (English) A farmer
Grainger, Graynger, Graenger, Grange, Graynge, Graenge, Grainge, Grangere

Grant (English) A tall man; a great man
Grante, Graent

Granville (French) From the large village
Granvylle, Granvil, Granvyl, Granvill, Granvyll, Granvile, Granvyle, Grenvill

Gray (English) A gray-haired man
Graye, Grai, Grae, Greye, Grey, Graylon, Graylen, Graylin

Grayson (English) The son of a gray-haired man
Graysen, Graysun, Graysin, Graysyn, Graysan, Graison, Graisun, Graisen

Greenwood (English) From the green forest
Greenwode

Gregory (Greek) One who is vigilant; watchful
Greg, Greggory, Greggy, Gregori, Gregorie, Gregry, Grigori

Gremian (Anglo-Saxon) One who enrages others
Gremien, Gremean, Gremyan

Gridley (English) From the flat meadow
Gridly, Gridlee, Gridlea, Gridleah, Gridleigh, Gridli, Gridlie

Grimaldo (German) A mighty protector
Grymaldo, Grimaldi, Grymaldi, Grimaldie, Grymaldie, Grimaldy, Grymaldy, Grimaldey

Grimm (Anglo-Saxon) One who is fierce; dark
Grimme, Grymm, Grymme

Grimsley (English) From the dark meadow
Grimsly, Grimslee, Grimslea, Grimsleah, Grimsleigh, Grimsli, Grimslie

Griswold (German) From the gray forest
Griswald, Gryswold, Gryswald, Greswold, Greswald

Guban (African) One who has been burnt
Guben, Gubin, Gubyn, Gubon, Gubun

Guedado (African) One who is unwanted

Guerdon (English) A warring man
Guerdun, Guerdan, Guerden, Guerdin, Guerdyn

Guido (Italian) One who acts as a guide
Guidoh, Gwedo, Gwido, Gwydo, Gweedo

Guillaume (French) Form of William, meaning "the determined protector"
Gillermo, Guglielmo, Guilherme, Guillermo, Gwillyn, Gwilym, Guglilmo

Gulshan (Hindi) From the gardens

Gunnar (Scandinavian) A bold warrior
Gunner, Gunnor, Gunnur, Gunnir, Gunnyr

Gunnolf (Norse) A warrior wolf
Gunolf, Gunnulf, Gunulf

Gur (Hebrew) Resembling a lion cub
Guryon, Gurion, Guriel, Guriell, Guryel, Guryell, Guri, Gurie

Gurpreet (Indian) A devoted follower
Gurpreat, Gurpriet, Gurpreit, Gurprit, Gurpryt

Guru (Indian) A teacher; a religious head

Gurutz (Basque) Of the holy cross
Guruts

Gus (German) A respected man; one who is exalted
Guss

Gustav (Scandinavian) Of the staff of the gods
Gus, Gustave, Gussie, Gustaf, Gustof, Tavin

Gusty (American) Of the wind; a revered man
Gustey, Gustee, Gustea, Gusti, Gustie, Gusto

Guwayne (American) Form of Wayne, meaning "one who builds wagons"
Guwayn, Guwain, Guwaine, Guwaen, Guwaene, Guwane

Gwalchmai (Welsh) A battle hawk

Gwandoya (African) Suffering a miserable fate

Gwydion (Welsh) In mythology, a magician
Gwydeon, Gwydionne, Gwydeonne

Gylfi (Scandinavian) A king
Gylfie, Gylfee, Gylfea, Gylfi, Gylfie, Gylphi, Gylphie, Gylphey

Gypsy (English) A wanderer; a nomad
Gipsee, Gipsey, Gipsy, Gypsi, Gypsie, Gypsey, Gypsee, Gipsi

Gyula (Hungarian) One who is honored
Gyulah, Gyulla, Gyullah

H

Habimama (African) One who believes in God
Habymama

Hachiro (Japanese) The eighth-born son
Hachyro

Hadden (English) From the heather-covered hill
Haddan, Haddon, Haddin, Haddyn, Haddun

Hades (Greek) In mythology, the god of the underworld
Hadies, Hadees, Hadiez, Hadeez

Hadriel (Hebrew) The splendor of God
Hadryel, Hadriell, Hadryell

Hadwin (English) A friend in war
Hadwinn, Hadwinne, Hadwen, Hadwenn, Hadwenne, Hadwyn, Hadwynn, Hadwynne

Hafiz (Arabic) A protector
Haafiz, Hafeez, Hafeaz, Hafiez, Hafeiz, Hafyz, Haphiz, Haaphiz

Hagar (Hebrew) A wanderer

Hagen (Gaelic) One who is youthful
Haggen, Hagan, Haggan, Hagin, Haggin, Hagyn, Haggyn, Hagon

Hagop (Armenian) Form of James, meaning "he who supplants"
Hagup, Hagap, Hagep, Hagip, Hagyp

Hagos (African) Filled with happiness

Hahnee (Native American) A beggar
Hahnea, Hahni, Hahnie, Hahny, Hahney

Haim (Hebrew) A giver of live
Hayim, Hayyim

Haines (English) From the vined cottage; from the hedged enclosure
Haynes, Haenes, Hanes, Haine, Hayne, Haene, Hane

Hajari (African) One who takes flight
Hajarie, Hajary, Hajarey, Hajaree, Hajarea

Haji (African) Born during the hajj
Hajie, Hajy, Hajey, Hajee, Hajea

Hakan (Norse / Native American) One who is noble / a fiery man

Hakim (Arabic) One who is wise; intelligent
Hakeem, Hakeam, Hakeim, Hakiem, Hakym

Hal (English) A form of Henry, meaning "the ruler of the house"; a form of Harold, meaning "the ruler of an army"

Halford (English) From the hall by the ford
Hallford, Halfurd, Hallfurd, Halferd, Hallferd

Halig (Anglo-Saxon) A holy man
Halyg

Halil (Turkish) A beloved friend
Haleel, Haleal, Haleil, Haliel, Halyl

Halla (African) An unexpected gift
Hallah, Hala, Halah

Hallberg (Norse) From the rocky mountain
Halberg, Hallburg, Halburg

Halle (Norse) As solid as a rock

Halley (English) From the hall near the meadow
Hally, Halli, Hallie, Halleigh, Hallee, Halleah, Hallea

Halliwell (English) From the holy spring
Haligwell

Hallward (English) The guardian of the hall
Halward, Hallwerd, Halwerd, Hallwarden, Halwarden, Hawarden, Haward, Hawerd

Hamid (Arabic / Indian) A praiseworthy man / a beloved friend
Hameed, Hamead, Hameid, Hamied, Hamyd, Haamid

Hamidi (Swahili) One who is commendable
Hamidie, Hamidy, Hamidey, Hamidee, Hamidea, Hamydi, Hamydie, Hamydee

Hamilton (English) From the flat-topped hill
Hamylton, Hamiltun, Hamyltun, Hamilten, Hamylten, Hamelton, Hameltun, Hamelten

Hamlet (German) From
the little home
*Hamlett, Hammet,
Hammett, Hamnet,
Hamnett, Hamlit, Hamlitt,
Hamoelet*

Hammer (German) One
who makes hammers; a
carpenter
*Hammar, Hammor,
Hammur, Hammir,
Hammyr*

Hampden (English) From
the home in the valley
*Hampdon, Hampdan,
Hampdun, Hampdyn,
Hampdin*

Hancock (English) One
who owns a farm
Hancok, Hancoc

Hanford (English) From
the high ford
*Hanferd, Hanfurd,
Hanforde, Hanferde,
Hanfurde*

Hanisi (Swahili) Born on a
Thursday
*Hanisie, Hanisy, Hanisey,
Hanisee, Hanisea, Hanysi,
Hanysie, Hanysy*

Hank (English) Form of
Henry, meaning "the ruler
of the house"
*Hanke, Hanks, Hanki,
Hankie, Hankee, Hankea,
Hanky, Hankey*

Hanley (English) From the
high meadow
*Hanly, Hanleigh, Hanleah,
Hanlea, Hanlie, Hanli,
Handlea, Handleigh*

Hanna (Arabic) Form of
John, meaning "God is
gracious"
Hannah, Hana, Hanah

Hanoch (Hebrew) One
who is dedicated
Hanock, Hanok, Hanoc

Hanraoi (Irish) Form of
Henry, meaning "the ruler
of the house"

Hansraj (Hindi) The swan
king

Hardik (Indian) One who
has heart
*Hardyk, Hardick, Hardyck,
Hardic, Hardyc*

Hare (English) Resembling
a rabbit

Harence (English) One
who is swift
*Harince, Harense, Harinse,
Harynce, Harynse*

Hari (Indian) Resembling
a lion
*Harie, Hary, Harey, Haree,
Harea*

Harim (Arabic) A superior
man
*Hareem, Haream, Hariem,
Hareim, Harym*

Harkin (Irish) Having dark red hair
Harkyn, Harken, Harkan, Harkon, Harkun

Harlemm (American) A soulful man
Harlam, Harlom, Harlim, Harlym, Harlem

Harlow (English) From the army on the hill
Harlowe, Harlo, Harloe

Harold (Scandinavian) The ruler of an army
Hal, Harald, Hareld, Harry, Darold

Harper (English) One who plays or makes harps
Harpur, Harpar, Harpir, Harpyr, Harpor, Hearpere

Harrington (English) From of Harry's town; from the herring town
Harringtun, Harryngton, Harryngtun, Harington, Haringtun, Haryngton, Haryntun

Harshad (Indian) A bringer of joy
Harsh, Harshe, Harsho, Harshil, Harshyl, Harshit, Harshyt

Hartford (English) From the stag's ford
Harteford, Hartferd, Harteferd, Hartfurd, Hartefurd, Hartforde, Harteforde, Hartferde

Haru (Japanese) Born during the spring

Harvey (English / French) One who is ready for battle / a strong man
Harvy, Harvi, Harvie, Harvee, Harvea, Harv, Harve, Hervey

Hasim (Arabic) One who is decisive
Haseem, Haseam, Hasiem, Haseim, Hasym

Haskel (Hebrew) An intelligent man
Haskle, Haskell, Haskil, Haskill, Haske, Hask

Hasso (German) Of the sun
Hassoe, Hassow, Hassowe

Hassun (Native American) As solid as a stone

Hastiin (Native American) A man

Hastin (Hindi) Resembling an elephant
Hasteen, Hastean, Hastien, Hastein, Hastyn

Hawes (English) From the hedged place
Haws, Hayes, Hays, Hazin, Hazen, Hazyn, Hazon, Hazan

Hawiovi (Native American) One who descends on a ladder
Hawiovie, Hawiovy, Hawiovey, Hawiovee, Hawiovea

Hawkins (English) Resembling a small hawk
Haukins, Hawkyns, Haukyn

Hawthorne (English) From the hawthorn tree
Hawthorn

*ᵀHayden (English) From the hedged valley
Haydan, Haydon, Haydun, Haydin, Haydyn, Haden, Hadan, Hadon

Haye (Scottish) From the stockade
Hay, Hae, Hai

Hazaiah (Hebrew) God will decide
Hazaia, Haziah, Hazia

Hazleton (English) From the hazel tree town
Hazelton, Hazletun, Hazelton, Hazleten, Hazelten

Heath (English) From the untended land of flowering shrubs
Heathe, Heeth, Heethe

Heaton (English) From the town on high ground
Heatun, Heeton, Heetun, Heaten, Heeten

Heber (Hebrew) A partner or companion
Heeber, Hebar, Heebar, Hebor, Heebor, Hebur, Heebur, Hebir

Heimdall (Norse) The white god; in mythology, one of the founders of the human race
Heimdal, Heiman, Heimann

Helio (Greek) Son of the sun
Heleo, Helios, Heleos

Hem (Indian) The golden son

Hemendu (Indian) Born beneath the golden moon
Hemendue, Hemendoo, Hemendou

Hemi (Maori) Form of James, meaning "he who supplants"
Hemie, Hemy, Hemee, Hemea, Hemey

Henderson (Scottish) The son of Henry
Hendrie, Hendries, Hendron, Hendri, Hendry, Hendrey, Hendree, Hendrea

Hendrick (English) Form of Henry, meaning "the ruler of the house"
Hendryck, Hendrik, Hendryk, Hendric, Hendryc

Henley (English) From the high meadow
Henly, Henleigh, Henlea, Henleah, Henlee, Henli, Henlie

★Henry (German) The ruler of the house
Hal, Hank, Harry, Henny, Henree, Henri, Hanraoi, Hendrick

Heraldo (Spanish) Of the divine

Hercules (Greek) In mythology, a son of Zeus who possessed superhuman strength
Herakles, Hercule, Herculi, Herculie, Herculy, Herculey, Herculee, Herculea

Herman (German) A soldier
Hermon, Hermen, Hermun, Hermin, Hermyn, Hermann, Hermie, Herminio

Herne (English) Resembling a heron
Hern, Hearn, Hearne

Hero (Greek) The brave defender
Heroe, Herow, Herowe

Hershel (Hebrew) Resembling a deer
Hersch, Herschel, Herschell, Hersh, Hertzel, Herzel, Herzl, Heschel

Herwin (Teutonic) A friend of war
Herwinn, Herwinne, Herwen, Herwenn, Herwenne, Herwyn, Herwynn, Herwynne

Hesed (Hebrew) A kind man

Hesutu (Native American) A rising yellow-jacket nest
Hesutou, Hesoutou

Hewson (English) The son of Hugh
Hewsun

Hiawatha (Native American) He who makes rivers
Hiawathah, Hyawatha, Hiwatha, Hywatha

Hickok (American) A famous frontier marshal
Hickock, Hickoc, Hikock, Hikoc, Hikok, Hyckok, Hyckock, Hyckoc

Hidalgo (Spanish) The noble one
Hydalgo

Hideaki (Japanese) A clever man; having wisdom
Hideakie, Hideaky, Hideakey, Hideakee, Hideakea

Hieronim (Polish) Form of Jerome, meaning "of the sacred name"
Hieronym, Hieronymos, Hieronimos, Heronim, Heronym, Heronymos, Heronimos

Hietamaki (Finnish) From the sand hill
Hietamakie, Hietamaky, Hietamakey, Hietamakee, Hietamakea

Hieu (Vietnamese) A pious man

Hikmat (Islamic) Filled with wisdom
Hykmat

Hildefuns (German) One who is ready for battle
Hildfuns, Hyldefuns, Hyldfuns

Hillel (Hebrew) One who is praised
Hyllel, Hillell, Hyllell, Hilel, Hylel, Hilell, Hylell

Hiranmay (Indian) The golden one
Hiranmaye, Hiranmai, Hiranmae, Hyranmay, Hyranmaye, Hyranmai, Hyranmae

Hiroshi (Japanese) A generous man
Hiroshie, Hiroshy, Hiroshey, Hiroshee, Hiroshea, Hyroshi, Hyroshie, Hyroshey

Hirsi (African) An amulet
Hirsie, Hirsy, Hirsey, Hirsee, Hirsea

Hisoka (Japanese) One who is secretive
Hysoka, Hisokie, Hysokie, Hisoki, Hysoki, Hisokey, Hysokey, Hisoky

Hitakar (Indian) One who wishes others well
Hitakarin, Hitakrit

Hobart (American) Form of Hubert, meaning "having a shining intellect"
Hobarte, Hoebart, Hoebarte, Hobert, Hoberte, Hoburt, Hoburte, Hobirt

Hoc (Vietnamese) A studious man

Hohberht (German) One who is high and bright
Hohbert, Hohburt, Hohbirt, Hohbyrt, Hoh

Holcomb (English) From the deep valley
Holcom, Holcombe

Holland (American) From the Netherlands
Hollend, Hollind, Hollynd, Hollande, Hollende, Hollinde, Hollynde

Hollis (English) From the holly tree
Hollys, Holliss, Hollyss, Hollace, Hollice, Holli, Hollie, Holly

Holman (English) A man
from the valley
*Holmann, Holmen, Holmin,
Holmyn, Holmon, Holmun*

Holt (English) From the
forest
*Holte, Holyt, Holyte, Holter,
Holtar, Holtor, Holtur, Holtir*

Honaw (Native American)
Resembling a bear
Honawe, Honau

Hondo (African) A warring man
Hondoh, Honda, Hondah

Honesto (Spanish) One
who is honest
*Honestio, Honestiyo,
Honesteo, Honesteyo,
Honestoh*

Honon (Native American)
Resembling a bear
*Honun, Honen, Honan,
Honin, Honyn*

Honovi (Native American)
Having great strength
*Honovie, Honovy, Honovey,
Honovee, Honovea*

Honza (Czech) A gift from
God

Horsley (English) From
the horse meadow
*Horsly, Horslea, Horsleah,
Horslee, Horsleigh, Horsli,
Horslie*

Horst (German) From the
thicket
*Horste, Horsten, Horstan,
Horstin, Horstyn, Horston,
Horstun, Horstman*

Hoshi (Japanese)
Resembling a star
*Hoshiko, Hoshyko, Hoshie,
Hoshee, Hoshea, Hoshy,
Hoshey*

Hototo (Native American)
One who whistles; a war-
rior spirit that sings

Hovannes (Armenian)
Form of John, meaning
"God is gracious"
*Hovennes, Hovann,
Hovenn, Hovane, Hovene,
Hovan, Hoven*

Howard (English) The
guardian of the home
*Howerd, Howord, Howurd,
Howird, Howyrd, Howi,
Howie, Howy*

Howi (Native American)
Resembling a turtle dove

Hrothgar (Anglo-Saxon) A
king
*Hrothgarr, Hrothegar,
Hrothegarr, Hrothgare,
Hrothegare*

Hubert (German) Having
a shining intellect
*Hobart, Huberte, Huburt,
Huburte, Hubirt, Hubirte,
Hubyrt, Hubyrte, Hubie,
Uberto*

Hudson (English) The son of Hugh; from the river
Hudsun, Hudsen, Hudsan, Hudsin, Hudsyn

Hugin (Norse) A thoughtful man
Hugyn, Hugen, Hugan, Hugon, Hugun

Humam (Arabic) A generous and brave man

Hungan (Haitian) A spirit master or priest
Hungen, Hungon, Hungun, Hungin, Hungyn

Hungas (Irish) A vigorous man

★ᵀHunter (English) A great huntsman and provider
Huntar, Huntor, Huntur, Huntir, Huntyr, Hunte, Hunt, Hunting

Husky (American) A big man; a manly man
Huski, Huskie, Huskey, Huskee, Huskea, Husk, Huske

Huslu (Native American) Resembling a hairy bear
Huslue, Huslou

Husto (Spanish) A righteous man
Hustio, Husteo, Hustiyo, Husteyo

Huynh (Vietnamese) An older brother

Hwang (Chinese) Refers to the color yellow
Hwange

Hwitford (English) From the white ford
Hwitforde, Hwitferd, Hwitferde, Hwitfurd, Hwitfurde

I

Iakovos (Hebrew) Form of Jacob, meaning "he who supplants"
Iakovus, Iakoves, Iakovas, Iakovis, Iakovys

★Ian (Gaelic) Form of John, meaning "God is gracious"
Iain, Iaine, Iayn, Iayne, Iaen, Iaene, Iahn

Iavor (Bulgarian) From the sycamore tree
Iaver, Iavur, Iavar, Iavir, Iavyr

Ibrahim (Arabic) Form of Abraham, meaning "father of a multitude; father of nations"
Ibraheem, Ibraheim, Ibrahiem, Ibraheam, Ibrahym

Ichabod (Hebrew) The glory has gone
Ikabod, Ickabod, Icabod, Ichavod, Ikavod, Icavod, Ickavod, Icha

Ichtaca (Nahuatl) A secretive man
Ichtaka, Ichtacka

Ida (Anglo-Saxon) A king
Idah

Idi (African) Born during the holiday of Idd
Idie, Idy, Idey, Idee, Idea

Ido (Arabic / Hebrew) A mighty man / to evaporate
Iddo, Idoh, Iddoh

Idris (Welsh) An eager lord
Idrys, Idriss, Idrisse, Idryss, Idrysse

Iefan (Welsh) Form of John, meaning "God is gracious"
Iefon, Iefen, Iefin, Iefyn, Iefun, Ifan, Ifon, Ifen

Ifor (Welsh) An archer
Ifore, Ifour, Ifoure

Igasho (Native American) A wanderer
Igashoe, Igashow, Igashowe

Ignatius (Latin) A fiery man; one who is ardent
Ignac, Ignace, Ignacio, Ignacius, Ignatious, Ignatz, Ignaz, Ignazio

Igor (Scandinavian / Russian) A hero / Ing's soldier
Igoryok

Ihit (Indian) One who is honored
Ihyt, Ihitt, Ihytt

Ihsan (Arabic) A charitable man
Ihsann, Ihsen, Ihsin, Ihsyn, Ihson, Ihsun

Ike (Hebrew) Form of Isaac, meaning "full of laughter"
Iki, Ikie, Iky, Ikey, Ikee, Ikea

Iker (Basque) A visitor
Ikar, Ikir, Ikyr, Ikor, Ikur

Ilario (Italian) A cheerful man
Ilareo, Ilariyo, Ilareyo, Ilar, Ilarr, Ilari, Ilarie, Ilary

Ilhuitl (Nahuatl) Born during the daytime

Illanipi (Native American) An amazing man
Illanipie, Illanipy, Illanipey, Illanipee, Illanipea

Iluminado (Spanish) One who shines brightly
Illuminado, Iluminato, Illuminato, Iluminados, Iluminatos, Illuminados, Illuminatos

Imaran (Indian) Having great strength
Imaren, Imaron, Imarun, Imarin, Imaryn

Inaki (Basque) An ardent man
Inakie, Inaky, Inakey, Inakee, Inakea, Inacki, Inackie, Inackee

Ince (Hungarian) One who is innocent
Inse

Indiana (English) From the land of the Indians; from the state of Indiana
Indianna, Indyana, Indyanna

Ingemar (Scandinavian) The son of Ing
Ingamar, Ingemur, Ingmar, Ingmur, Ingar, Ingemer, Ingmer

Inger (Scandinavian) One who is fertile
Inghar, Ingher

Ingo (Scandinavian / Danish) A lord / from the meadow
Ingoe, Ingow, Ingowe

Ingram (Scandinavian) A raven of peace
Ingra, Ingrem, Ingrim, Ingrym, Ingrum, Ingrom, Ingraham, Ingrahame, Ingrams

Iniko (African) Born during troubled times
Inicko, Inico, Inyko, Inycko, Inyco

Iorwerth (Welsh) A handsome lord
Ioworth, Iowerthe, Ioworthe, Iowirth, Iowirthe, Iowyrth, Iowyrthe

Iranga (Sri Lankan) One who is special

Irenbend (Anglo-Saxon) From the iron bend
Ironbend

Irwin (English) A friend of the wild boar
Irwinn, Irwinne, Irwyn, Irwynne, Irwine, Irwen, Irwenn, Irwenne

★ᵀ**Isaac** (Hebrew) Full of laughter
Ike, Isaack, Isaak, Isac, Isacco, Isak, Issac, Itzak, Itzhak

★ᵀ**Isaiah** (Hebrew) God is my salvation
Isa, Isaia, Isais, Isia, Isiah, Issiah, Izaiah, Iziah

Iseabail (Hebrew) One who is devoted to God
Iseabaile, Iseabayl, Iseabyle, Iseabael, Iseabaele

Isham (English) From the iron one's estate
Ishem, Ishom, Ishum, Ishim, Ishym, Isenham, Isenhem, Isenhim

Isidore (Greek) A gift of Isis
*Isador, Isadore, Isidor,
Isidoro, Isidorus, Isidro,
Issy, Izidor*

Iskander (Arabic) Form of
Alexander, meaning "a
helper and defender of
mankind"
*Iskinder, Iskandar, Iskindar,
Iskynder, Iskyndar, Iskender,
Iskendar*

Isser (Slavic) One who is
creative
Issar, Issir, Issyr, Issor, Issur

Istu (Native American) As
sweet as sugar
Istue, Istoo, Istou

Istvan (Hungarian) One
who is crowned
*Istven, Istvin, Istvyn, Istvon,
Istvun*

Iulian (Romanian) A
youthful man
Iulien, Iulio, Iuleo

Ivan (Slavic) Form of John,
meaning "God is gra-
cious"
*Ivann, Ivanhoe, Ivano,
Iwan, Iban, Ibano, Ivanti,
Ivantie*

Ives (Scandinavian) The
archer's bow; of the yew
wood
*Ivair, Ivar, Iven, Iver, Ivo,
Ivon, Ivor, Ivaire*

Ivy (English) Resembling
the evergreen vining plant
*Ivee, Ivey, Ivie, Ivi, Ivea,
Iveah*

Iyar (Hebrew) Surrounded
by light
Iyyar, Iyer, Iyyer

J

Ja (Korean / African) A
handsome man / one who
is magnetic

Jabari (African) A valiant
man
*Jabarie, Jabary, Jabarey,
Jabaree, Jabarea*

Jabbar (Indian) One who
consoles others
Jabar

Jabin (Hebrew) God has
built; one who is percep-
tive

Jabon (American) A fiesty
man
*Jabun, Jabin, Jabyn, Jaben,
Jaban*

Jace (Hebrew) God is my
salvation
*Jacen, Jacey, Jacian, Jacy,
Jaice, Jayce, Jaece, Jaycen*

Jacinto (Spanish)
Resembling a hyacinth
Jacynto, Jacindo, Jacyndo, Jacento, Jacendo, Jacenty, Jacentey, Jacentee

★**Jack** (English) Form of John, meaning "God is gracious"
Jackie, Jackman, Jacko, Jacky, Jacq, Jacqin, Jak, Jaq

★**Jackson** (English) The son of Jack or John
Jacksen, Jacksun, Jacson, Jakson, Jaxen, Jaxon, Jaxun, Jaxson

★ᵀ**Jacob** (Hebrew) He who supplants
Jake, James, Kuba, Iakovos, Yakiv, Yankel, Yaqub, Jaco, Jacobo, Jacobi, Jacoby, Jacobie, Jacobey, Jacobo, Jacobus

Jadal (American) One who is punctual
Jadall, Jadel, Jadell

Jade (Spanish) Resembling the green gemstone
Jadee, Jadie, Jayde, Jaden

★ᵀ**Jaden** (Hebrew / English) One who is thankful to God; God has heard / form of Jade, meaning "resembling the green gemstone"
*Jadine, Jadyn, Jadon, **Jayden**, Jadyne, Jaydyn, Jaydon, Jaydine*

Jagan (English) One who is self-confident
Jagen, Jagin, Jagyn, Jagon, Jagun, Jago

Jahan (Indian) Man of the world
Jehan, Jihan, Jag, Jagat, Jagath

Jaidayal (Indian) The victory of kindness
Jadayal, Jaydayal, Jaedayal

Jaime (Spanish) Form of James, meaning "he who supplants"
Jamie, Jaime, Jaimee, Jaimey, Jaimi, Jaimie, Jaimy, Jamee

Jaimin (French) One who is loved
Jaimyn, Jamin, Jamyn, Jaymin, Jaymyn, Jaemin, Jaemyn

Jairdan (American) One who enlightens others
Jardan, Jayrdan, Jaerdan, Jairden, Jarden, Jayrden, Jaerden

Jaja (African) A gift from God

Jajuan (American) One who loves God

★**Jake** (English) Form of Jacob, meaning "he who supplants"
Jaik, Jaike, Jayk, Jayke, Jakey, Jaky

Jakome (Basque) Form of James, meaning "he who supplants"
Jackome, Jakom, Jackom, Jacome

Jaladhi (Hindi) Of the ocean
*Jaladhie, Jaladhy, Jaladhey,
Jaladhee, Jaladi, Jaladie,
Jalady, Jaladey*

Jamal (Arabic) A handsome man
*Jamail, Jahmil, Jam,
Jamaal, Jamy, Jamar*

Jamar (American) Form of
Jamal, meaning "a handsome man"
*Jamarr, Jemar, Jemarr,
Jimar, Jimarr, Jamaar,
Jamari, Jamarie*

★T**James** (Hebrew) Form of
Jacob, meaning "he who
supplants"
*Jaimes, Jaymes, Jame,
Jaym, Jaim, Jaem, Jaemes,
Jamese, Jim, Jaime, Diego,
Hagop, Hemi, Jakome*

Jameson (English) The
son of James
*Jaimison, Jamieson,
Jaymeson, Jamison, Jaimeson,
Jaymison, Jaemeson, Jaemison*

Jamin (Hebrew) The right
hand of favor
*Jamian, Jamiel, Jamon,
Jaymin, Jaemin, Jaymon,
Jaemon, Jaimin*

Janesh (Hindi) A leader of
the people
Janeshe

Japa (Indian) One who chants
Japeth, Japesh, Japendra

Japheth (Hebrew) May he
expand; in the Bible, one
of Noah's sons
*Jaypheth, Jaepheth,
Jaipheth, Jafeth, Jayfeth,
Jaefeth, Jaifeth, Japhet*

Jarah (Hebrew) One who
is as sweet as honey
Jarrah, Jara, Jarra

Jarlath (Irish) A tributary
lord
*Jarleath, Jarlaith, Jarlaeth,
Jarlayth, Jarleeth, Jariath,
Jaryath*

Jarman (German) A man
from Germany
Jarmann, Jerman, Jermann

Jaromir (Slavic) From the
famous spring
*Jaromeer, Jaromear,
Jaromeir, Jaromier, Jaromyr,
Yaromir*

Jaron (Israeli) A song of
rejoicing
*Jaran, Jaren, Jarin, Jarran,
Jarren, Jarrin, Jarron, Jaryn*

Jaroslav (Slavic) Born with
the beauty of spring
Jaroslaw

Jarvis (French) One who
wields a spear
*Jarvee, Jarvell, Jarvey, Jary,
Jervey, Jervis, Jarvys, Jervys*

★T**Jason** (Hebrew / Greek) God is my salvation / a healer; in mythology, the leader of the Argonauts
Jacen, Jaisen, Jaison, Jasen, Jasin, Jasun, Jayson, Jaysen

Jasper (Persian) One who holds the treasure
Jaspar, Jaspir, Jaspyr, Jesper, Jespar, Jespir, Jespyr

Jatan (Indian) One who is nurturing

Javan (Hebrew) Man from Greece; in the Bible, Noah's grandson
Jayvan, Jayven, Jayvern, Jayvon, Javon, Javern, Javen

Jawdat (Arabic) One who is superior
Jaudat

Jay (Latin / Sanskrit) Resembling a jaybird / one who is victorious
Jae, Jai, Jaye, Jayron, Jayronn, Jey

Jean (French) Form of John, meaning "God is gracious"
Jeanne, Jeane, Jene, Jeannot, Jeanot

Jedidiah (Hebrew) One who is loved by God
Jedadiah, Jedediah, Jed, Jedd, Jedidiya, Jedidiyah, Jedadia, Jedadiya

Jeffrey (English) A man of peace
Jeff, Geoffrey, Jeffery, Jeffree

Jehu (Hebrew) He is God
Jayhu, Jahu, Jehue, Jeyhu, Jeyhue, Jayhue, Jahue, Jehew

Jelani (African) One who is mighty; strong
Jelanie, Jelany, Jelaney, Jelanee, Jelanea

Jenci (Hungarian) A well-born man
Jencie, Jency, Jencey, Jencee, Jencea, Jensi, Jensie, Jensy

Jennett (Hindi) One who is heaven-sent
Jenett, Jennet, Jenet, Jennitt, Jenitt, Jennit, Jenit

Jerald (English) Form of Gerald, meaning "one who rules with the spear"
Jeraldo, Jerold, Jerrald, Jerrold

★T**Jeremiah** (Hebrew) One who is exalted by the Lord
Jeremia, Jeremias, Jeremija, Jeremiya, Jeremyah, Jeramiah, Jeramia, Jerram, Geremia

Jermaine (French / Latin) A man from Germany / one who is brotherly
Jermain, Jermane, Jermayne, Jermin, Jermyn, Jermayn, Jermaen, Jermaene

Jerome (Greek) Of the sacred name
Jairome, Jeroen, Jeromo, Jeronimo, Jerrome, Jerom, Jerolyn, Jerolin, Hieronim

Jerram (Hebrew) Form of Jeremiah, meaning "one who is exalted by the Lord"
Jeram, Jerrem, Jerem, Jerrym, Jerym

Jersey (English) From a section of England; one who is calm
Jersy, Jersi, Jersie, Jersee, Jersea

Jesimiel (Hebrew) The Lord establishes
Jessimiel

★ᵀJesse (Hebrew) God exists; a gift from God; God sees all
Jess, Jessey, Jesiah, Jessie, Jessy, Jese, Jessi, Jessee

★Jesus (Hebrew) God is my salvation
*Jesous, Jesues, **Jesús**, Xesus*

Jevon (American) A spirited man
Jeavan, Jeaven, Jeavin, Jevan, Jeven, Jevin, Jevvan, Jevven

Ji (Chinese) One who is organized

Jibben (American) A lively man
Jiben, Jybben, Jyben

Jibril (Arabic) Refers to the archangel Gabriel
Jibryl, Jibri, Jibrie, Jibry, Jibrey, Jibree

Jim (English) Form of James, meaning "he who supplants"
Jimi, Jimmee, Jimmey, Jimmie, Jimmy, Jimmi, Jimbo

Jimoh (African) Born on a Friday
Jymoh, Jimo, Jymo

Jivan (Hindi) A giver of life
Jivin, Jiven, Jivyn, Jivon

Joab (Hebrew) The Lord is my father
Joabb, Yoav

Joachim (Hebrew) One who is established by God; God will judge
Jachim, Jakim, Joacheim, Joaquim, Joaquin, Josquin, Joakim, Joakeen

Joe (English) Form of Joseph, meaning "God will add"
Jo, Joemar, Jomar, Joey, Joie, Joee, Joeye

★ᵀJohn (Hebrew) God is gracious; in the Bible, one of the Apostles
***Sean, Jack, Juan,** Johann, Ian, Ean, **Evan,** Giovanni, Hanna, Hovannes, Iefan, Ivan, Jean, Xoan, Yochanan, Yohan*

Johnavon (American) From God's river
Jonavon, Johnaven, Jonaven

Jokull (Scandinavian) From the glacier
Jokule, Jokulle, Jokul

Jomo (African) One who works the earth; a farmer
Jomoe, Jomow, Jomowe

★T**Jonathan** (Hebrew) A gift of God
Johnathan, Johnathon, Jonathon, Jonatan, Jonaton, Jonathen, Johnathen, Jonaten, Yonatan

★T**Jordan** (Hebrew) Of the down-flowing river; in the Bible, the river where Jesus was baptized
Johrdan, Jordain, Jordaine, Jordane, Jordanke, Jordann, Jorden, Jordaen

Joren (Scandinavian) Form of George, meaning "one who works the earth; a farmer"
Joran, Jorian, Jorien, Joron, Jorun, Joryn, Jorin, Jorn

Jorn (German) A vigilant watchman
Jorne

★T**Joseph** (Hebrew) God will add
Joe, Guiseppe, Yosyp, Jessop, Jessup, Joop, Joos, José, Jose, Josef, Joseito

★T**Joshua** (Hebrew) God is salvation
Josh, Joshuah, Josua, Josue, Joushua, Jozua, Joshwa, Joshuwa

Josiah (Hebrew) God will help
Josia, Josias, Joziah, Jozia, Jozias

Journey (American) One who likes to travel
Journy, Journi, Journie, Journee, Journye, Journea

★T**Juan** (Spanish) Form of John, meaning "God is gracious"
Juanito, Juwan, Jwan

Jubilo (Spanish) One who is rejoicing
Jubylo, Jubilio, Jubylio, Jubileo, Jubyleo

★**Julian** (Greek) The child of Jove; one who is youthful
Juliano, Julianus, Julien, Julyan, Julio, Jolyon, Jullien, Julen

Julius (Greek) One who is youthful
Juleus, Yuliy

Juma (African) Born on a Friday
Jumah

Jumbe (African) Having great strength
Jumbi, Jumbie, Jumby, Jumbey, Jumbee

Jumoke (African) One who is dearly loved
Jumok, Jumoak

Jun (Japanese) One who is obedient

Junaid (Arabic) A warrior
Junaide, Junayd, Junayde, Junade, Junaed, Junaede

Jung (Korean) A righteous man

Jurgen (German) Form of George, meaning "one who works the earth; a farmer"
Jorgen, Jurgin, Jorgin, Jurgyn, Jorgyn

Justice (English) One who upholds moral rightness and fairness
Justyce, Justiss, Justyss, Justis, Justus, Justise

★ᵀJustin (Latin) One who is just and upright
Joost, Justain, Justan, Just, Juste, Justen, Justino, Justo

Justinian (Latin) An upright ruler
Justinien, Justinious, Justinius, Justinios, Justinas, Justinus

Juvenal (Latin) A young boy
Juvinal, Juvenel, Juvinel, Juventino, Juvy, Juvey, Juvee, Juvi

K

Kabir (Indian) A spiritual leader
Kabeer, Kabear, Kabier, Kabeir, Kabyr, Kabar

Kabonesa (African) One who is born during difficult times

Kacancu (African) The firstborn child
Kacancue, Kakancu, Kakancue, Kacanku, Kacankue

Kacey (Irish) A vigilant man; one who is alert
Kacy, Kacee, Kacea, Kaci, Kacie, Kasey, Kasy, Kasi

Kachada (Native American) A white-skinned man

★Kaden (Arabic) A beloved companion
Kadan, Kadin, Kadon, Kaidan, Kaiden, Kaidin, Kaidon, Kaydan

Kadmiel (Hebrew) One who stands before God
Kamiell

Kaemon (Japanese) Full of joy; one who is right-handed
Kamon, Kaymon, Kaimon

Kagen (Irish) A fiery man; a thinker
Kaigen, Kagan, Kaigan, Kaygen, Kaygan, Kaegen, Kaegan

Kahoku (Hawaiian) Resembling a star
Kahokue, Kahokoo, Kahokou

Kaila (Hawaiian) A stylish man
Kayla, Kaela

Kaimi (Hawaiian) The seeker
Kaimie, Kaimy, Kaimey, Kaimee, Kaimea

Kalama (Hawaiian) A source of light
Kalam, Kalame

Kalei (Hawaiian) An attendant of the king

Kali (Polynesian) One who provides comfort
Kalie, Kaly, Kaley, Kalee, Kaleigh, Kalea

Kalidas (Hindi) A poet or musician; a servant of Kali
Kalydas

Kalki (Indian) Resembling a white horse
Kalkie, Kalky, Kalkey, Kalkee, Kalkea

Kalkin (Hindi) The tenth-born child
Kalkyn, Kalken, Kalkan, Kalkon, Kalkun

Kamden (English) From the winding valley
Kamdun, Kamdon, Kamdan, Kamdin, Kamdyn

Kane (Gaelic) The little warrior
Kayn, Kayne, Kaen, Kaene, Kahan, Kahane

Kang (Korean) A healthy man

Kano (Japanese) A powerful man
Kanoe, Kanoh

Kantrava (Indian) Resembling a roaring animal

Kaper (American) One who is capricious
Kahper, Kapar, Kahpar

Kapono (Hawaiian) A righteous man

Karcsi (French) A strong, manly man
Karcsie, Karcsy, Karcsey, Karcsee, Karcsea

Karl (German) A free man
Carl, Karel, Karlan, Karle, Karlens, Karli, Karlin, Karlo, Karlos

Karman (Gaelic) The lord of the manor
Karmen, Karmin, Karmyn, Karmon, Karmun

Karolek (Russian) A small, strong man
Karolec, Karoleck

Kasch (German) Resembling a blackbird
Kasche, Kass, Kas, Kasse

Kasem (Asian) Filled with joy

Kasen (Basque) Protected by a helmet
Kasin, Kasyn, Kason, Kasun, Kasan

Kashka (African) A friendly man
Kashkah

Kashvi (Indian) A shining man
Kashvie, Kashvy, Kashvey, Kashvee, Kashvea

Kasib (Arabic) One who is fertile
Kaseeb, Kaseab, Kasieb, Kaseib, Kasyb

Kasim (Arabic) One who is divided
Kassim, Kaseem, Kasseem, Kaseam, Kasseam, Kasym, Kassym

Kasimir (Slavic) One who demands peace
Kasimeer, Kasimear, Kasimier, Kasimeir, Kasimyr, Kaz, Kazimierz, Kazimir

Katzir (Hebrew) The harvester
Katzyr, Katzeer, Katzear, Katzier, Katzeir

Kaushal (Indian) One who is skilled
Kaushall, Koshal, Koshall

Kazim (Arabic) An even-tempered man
Kazeem, Kazeam, Kaziem, Kazeim, Kazym

Keahi (Hawaiian) Of the flames
Keahie, Keahy, Keahey, Keahee, Keahea

Kealoha (Hawaiian) From the bright path
Keeloha, Kieloha

Kean (Gaelic / English) A warrior / one who is sharp
Keane, Keen, Keene, Kein, Keine, Keyn, Keyne, Kien

Keandre (American) One who is thankful
Kiandre, Keandray, Kiandray, Keandrae, Kiandrae, Keandrai, Kiandrai

Keanu (Hawaiian) Of the mountain breeze
Keanue, Kianu, Kianue, Keanoo, Kianoo, Keanou, Kianou

Keaton (English) From the town of hawks
Keatun, Keeton, Keetun, Keyton, Keytun

Kedar (Arabic) A powerful man
Keder, Kedir, Kedyr, Kadar, Kader, Kadir, Kadyr

Kefir (Hebrew) Resembling a young lion
Kefyr, Kefeer, Kefear, Kefier, Kefeir

Keith (Scottish) Man from the forest
Keithe, Keath, Keathe, Kieth, Kiethe, Keyth, Keythe, Keithen

Kelile (African) My protector
Kelyle

Kellach (Irish) One who suffers strife during battle
Kelach, Kellagh, Kelagh, Keallach

Kelley (Celtic / Gaelic) A warrior / one who defends
Kelly, Kelleigh, Kellee, Kellea, Kelleah, Kelli, Kellie

Kelton (English) From the town of keels
Keldon, Kelltin, Kellton, Kelten, Keltin, Keltun, Kelltun, Keltyn

Kendi (African) One who is much loved
Kendie, Kendy, Kendey, Kendee, Kendea

Kendrick (English / Gaelic) A royal ruler / the champion
Kendric, Kendricks, Kendrik, Kendrix, Kendryck, Kenrick, Kenrik, Kenricks

Kenley (English) From the king's meadow
Kenly, Kenlee, Kenleigh, Kenlea, Kenleah, Kenli, Kenlie

Kenn (Welsh) Of the bright waters

Kennedy (Gaelic) A helmeted chief
Kennedi, Kennedie, Kennedey, Kennedee, Kennedea, Kenadie, Kenadi, Kenady

Kenneth (Irish) Born of the fire; an attractive man
Kennet, Kennett, Kennith, Kennit, Kennitt

Kent (English) From the edge or border
Kentt, Kennt, Kentrell

Kenton (English) From the king's town
Kentun, Kentan, Kentin, Kenten, Kentyn

Kenyon (Gaelic) A blond-haired man
Kenyun, Kenyan, Kenyen, Kenyin

Kepler (German) One who makes hats
Keppler, Kappler, Keppel, Keppeler

Kerbasi (Basque) A warrior
Kerbasie, Kerbasee, Kerbasea, Kerbasy, Kerbasey

Kershet (Hebrew) Of the rainbow

Kesler (American) An energetic man; one who is independent
Keslar, Keslir, Keslyr, Keslor, Keslur

Keung (Chinese) A universal spirit

★Kevin (Gaelic) A beloved and handsome man
Kevyn, Kevan, Keven, Keveon, Kevinn, Kevion, Kevis, Kevon

Khairi (Swahili) A kingly
man
*Khairie, Khairy, Khairey,
Khairee, Khairea*

Khalon (American) A
strong warrior
*Khalun, Khalen, Khalan,
Khalin, Khalyn*

Khayri (Arabic) One who is
charitable
*Khayrie, Khayry, Khayrey,
Khayree, Khayrea*

Khouri (Arabic) A spiritual
man; a priest
*Khourie, Khoury, Khourey,
Khouree, Kouri, Kourie,
Koury, Kourey*

Khushi (Indian) Filled
with happiness
*Khushie, Khushey, Khushy,
Khushee*

Kibbe (Native American) A
nocturnal bird
Kybbe

Kibo (African) From the
highest moutain peak
*Keybo, Keebo, Keabo, Keibo,
Kiebo*

Kidd (English) Resembling
a young goat
Kid, Kydd, Kyd

Kiefer (German) One who
makes barrels
*Keefer, Keifer, Kieffer,
Kiefner, Kieffner, Kiefert,
Kuefer, Kueffner*

Kildaire (Irish) From coun-
ty of Kildare
*Kyldaire, Kildare, Kyldare,
Kildair, Kyldair, Killdaire,
Kylldaire, Kildayr*

Kim (Vietnamese) As precious as gold
Kym

Kimoni (African) A great
man
*Kimonie, Kimony, Kimoney,
Kimonee, Kymoni,
Kymonie, Kymony,
Kymoney*

Kincaid (Celtic) The leader
during battle
*Kincade, Kincayd,
Kincayde, Kincaide,
Kincaed, Kincaede,
Kinkaid, Kinkaide*

Kindin (Basque) The fifth-
born child
*Kinden, Kindan, Kindyn,
Kindon, Kindun*

Kindle (American) To set
aflame
Kindel, Kyndle, Kyndel

King (English) The royal
ruler
Kyng

Kingswell (English) From
the king's spring
*Kinswell, Kyngswell,
Kynswell*

Kinnard (Irish) From the tall hill
Kinard, Kinnaird, Kinaird, Kynnard, Kynard, Kynnaird, Kynaird

Kinsey (English) The victorious prince
Kynsey, Kinsi, Kynsi, Kinsie, Kynsie, Kinsee, Kynsee, Kinsea

Kione (African) One who has come from nowhere

Kioshi (Japanese) One who is quiet
Kioshe, Kioshie, Kioshy, Kioshey, Kioshee, Kyoshi, Kyoshe, Kyoshie

Kipp (English) From the small pointed hill
Kip, Kipling, Kippling, Kypp, Kyp, Kiplyng, Kipplyng, Kippi

Kiri (Vietnamese) Resembling the mountains
Kirie, Kiry, Kirey, Kiree, Kirea

Kirk (Norse) A man of the church
Kyrk, Kerk, Kirklin, Kirklyn

Kirkland (English) From the church's land
Kirklan, Kirklande, Kyrkland, Kyrklan, Kyrklande

Kirkley (English) From the church's meadow
Kirkly, Kirkleigh, Kirklea, Kirkleah, Kirklee, Kirkli, Kirklie

Kirkwood (English) From the church's forest
Kirkwode, Kyrkwood, Kyrkwode

Kisho (Japanese) A self-assured man
Kysho

Kit (English) Form of Christopher, meaning "one who bears Christ inside"
Kitt, Kyt, Kytt

Kitchi (Native American) A brave young man
Kitchie, Kitchy, Kitchey, Kitchee, Kitchea

Kitoko (African) A handsome man
Kytoko

Kivi (Finnish) As solid as stone
Kivie, Kivy, Kivey, Kivee, Kivea

Knight (English) A noble solidier
Knights

Knoton (Native American) Of the wind
Knotun, Knotan, Knoten, Knotin, Knotyn

Knud (Danish) A kind man
Knude

Kody (English) One who is
helpful
*Kodey, Kodee, Kodea, Kodi,
Kodie*

Koen (German) An honest
advisor
Koenz, Kunz, Kuno

Kohana (Native American /
Hawaiian) One who is
swift / the best

Kohler (German) One who
mines coal
Koler

Kojo (African) Born on a
Monday
Kojoe, Koejo, Koejoe

Koka (Hawaiian) A man
from Scotland

Kolbjorn (Swedish)
Resembling a black bear
*Kolbjorne, Kolbjourn,
Kolbjourne*

Konane (Hawaiian) Born
beneath the bright moon
*Konain, Konaine, Konayn,
Konayne, Konaen, Konaene*

Konnor (English) A wolf
lover; one who is strong-
willed
*Konnur, Konner, Konnar,
Konnir, Konnyr*

Koofrey (African)
Remember me
*Koofry, Koofri, Koofrie,
Koofree*

Kordell (English) One who
makes cord
Kordel, Kord, Kordale

Koresh (Hebrew) One who
digs in the earth; a farmer
Koreshe

Kort (Danish) One who
provides counsel
Korte

Kory (Irish) From the hollow; of the churning
waters
*Korey, Kori, Korie, Koree,
Korea, Korry, Korrey, Korree*

Kozma (Greek) One who is
decorated
Kozmah

Kozue (Japanese) Of the
tree branches
Kozu, Kozoo, Kozou

Kraig (Gaelic) From the
rocky place; as solid as a
rock
*Kraige, Krayg, Krayge,
Kraeg, Kraege, Krage*

Kramer (German) A shop-
keeper
*Kramar, Kramor, Kramir,
Kramur, Kramyr, Kraymer,
Kraimer, Kraemer*

Krany (Czech) A man of short stature
Kraney, Kranee, Kranea, Krani, Kranie

Krikor (Armenian) A vigilant watchman
Krykor, Krikur, Krykur

Kristian (Scandinavian) An annointed Christian
Kristan, Kristien, Krist, Kriste, Krister, Kristar, Khristian, Khrist

Kristopher (Scandinavian) A follower of Christ
Khristopher, Kristof, Kristofer, Kristoff, Kristoffer, Kristofor, Kristophor, Krystof

Kuba (Polish) Form of Jacob, meaning "he who supplants"
Kubas

Kuckunniwi (Native American) Resembling a little wolf
Kukuniwi

Kuleen (Indian) A high-born man
Kulin, Kulein, Kulien, Kulean, Kulyn

Kumar (Indian) A prince; a male child

Kuri (Japanese) Resembling a chestnut
Kurie, Kury, Kurey, Kuree, Kurea

Kuron (African) One who gives thanks
Kurun, Kuren, Kuran, Kurin, Kuryn

Kurt (German) A brave counselor
Kurte

Kushal (Indian) A talented man; adroit
Kushall

Kwaku (African) Born on a Wednesday
Kwakue, Kwakou, Kwako, Kwakoe

Kwan (Korean) Of a bold character
Kwon

Kwintyn (Polish) The fifth-born child
Kwentyn, Kwinton, Kwenton, Kwintun, Kwentun, Kwintan, Kwentan, Kwinten

★Kyle (Gaelic) From the narrow channel
Kile, Kiley, Kye, Kylan, Kyrell, Kylen, Kily, Kili

Kylemore (Gaelic) From the great wood
Kylmore, Kylemor, Kylmor

Kyrone (English) Form of Tyrone, meaning "from Owen's land"
Kyron, Keirohn, Keiron, Keirone, Keirown, Kirone

L

Lacey (French) Man from Normandy; as delicate as lace
Lacy, Laci, Lacie, Lacee, Lacea

Lachlan (Gaelic) From the land of lakes
Lachlen, Lachlin, Lachlyn, Locklan, Locklen, Locklin, Locklyn, Loklan

Lachman (Gaelic) A man from the lake
Lachmann, Lockman, Lockmann, Lokman, Lokmann, Lakman, Lakmann

Ladan (Hebrew) One who is alert and aware
Laden, Ladin, Ladyn, Ladon, Ladun

Ladd (English) A servant; a young man
Lad, Laddey, Laddie, Laddy, Laddi, Laddee, Laddea, Ladde

Ladislas (Slavic) A glorious ruler
Lacko, Ladislaus, Laslo, Laszlo, Lazlo, Ladislav, Ladislauv, Ladislao

Lagrand (American) A majestic man
Lagrande

Laibrook (English) One who lives on the road near the brook
Laebrook, Laybrook, Laibroc, Laebroc, Laybroc, Laibrok, Laebrok, Laybrok

Laird (Scottish) The lord of the manor
Layrd, Laerd, Lairde, Layrde, Laerde

Laken (American) Man from the lake
Laike, Laiken, Laikin, Lakin, Lakyn, Lakan, Laikyn, Laeken

Lalam (Indian) The best
Lallam, Lalaam, Lallaam

Lam (Vietnamese) Having a full understanding

Laman (Arabic) A bright and happy man
Lamaan, Lamann, Lamaann

Lamar (German / French) From the renowned land / of the sea
Lamarr, Lamarre, Lemar, Lemarr

Lambert (Scandinavian) The light of the land
Lambart, Lamberto, Lambirt, Landbert, Lambirto, Lambrecht, Lambret, Lambrett

Lambi (Norse) In mythology, the son of Thorbjorn
Lambie, Lamby, Lambey, Lambe, Lambee

Lameh (Arabic) A shining man

Lamorak (English) In Arthurian legend, the brother of Percival
Lamerak, Lamurak, Lamorac, Lamerac, Lamurac, Lamorack, Lamerack, Lamurack

Lander (English) One who owns land
Land, Landers, Landis, Landiss, Landor, Lande, Landry, Landri

★ᵀLandon (English) From the long hill
Landyn, Landan, Landen, Landin, Lando, Langdon, Langden, Langdan

Lane (English) One who takes the narrow path
Laine, Lain, Laen, Laene, Layne, Layn

Langhorn (English) Of the long horn
Langhorne, Lanhorn, Lanhorne

Langilea (Polynesian) Having a booming voice, like thunder
Langileah, Langilia, Langiliah

Langston (English) From the tall man's town
Langsten, Langstun, Langstown, Langstin, Langstyn, Langstan, Langton, Langtun

Langundo (Native American / Polynesian) A peaceful man / one who is graceful

Langworth (English) One who lives near the long paddock
Langworthe, Lanworth, Lanworthe

Lanier (French) One who works with wool

Lantos (Hungarian) One who plays the lute
Lantus

Laochailan (Scottish) One who is waning

Lapidos (Hebrew) One who carries a torch
Lapydos, Lapidot, Lapydot, Lapidoth, Lapydoth, Lapidus, Lapydus

Laquinton (American) Form of Quinton, meaning "from the queen's town or settlement"
Laquinntan, Laquinnten, Laquinntin, Laquinnton, Laquintain, Laquintan, Laquintyn, Laquintynn

Lar (Anglo-Saxon) One who teaches others

Larson (Scandinavian) The son of Lawrence
Larsan, Larsen, Larsun, Larsin, Larsyn

Lasalle (French) From the hall
Lasall, Lasal, Lasale

Lashaun (American) An enthusiastic man
Lashawn, Lasean, Lashon, Lashond

Lassit (American) One who is open-minded
Lassyt, Lasset

Lathan (American) Form of Nathan, meaning "a gift from God"
Lathen, Lathun, Lathon, Lathin, Lathyn, Latan, Laten, Latun

Latimer (English) One who serves as an interpreter
Latymer, Latimor, Latymor, Latimore, Latymore, Lattemore, Lattimore

Latty (English) A generous man
Lattey, Latti, Lattie, Lattee, Lattea

Laurian (English) One who lives near the laurel trees
Laurien, Lauriano, Laurieno, Lawrian, Lawrien, Lawriano, Lawrieno

Lave (Italian) Of the burning rock
Lava

Lawford (English) From the ford near the hill
Lawforde, Lawferd, Lawferde, Lawfurd, Lawfurde

Lawler (Gaelic) A soft-spoken man; one who mutters
Lauler, Lawlor, Loller, Lawlar, Lollar, Loller, Laular, Laulor

Lawley (English) From the meadow near the hill
Lawly, Lawli, Lawlie, Lawleigh, Lawlee, Lawlea, Lawleah

Lawrence (Latin) Man from Laurentum; crowned with laurel
Larance, Laranz, Larenz, Larrance, Larrence, Larrens, Larrey, Larry

Laziz (Arabic) One who is pleasant
Lazeez, Lazeaz, Laziez, Lazeiz, Lazyz

Leaman (American) A powerful man
Leeman, Leamon, Leemon, Leamond, Leamand

Lear (Greek) Of the royalty
Leare, Leer, Leere

Leather (American) As tough as hide
Lether

Leavitt (English) A baker
Leavit, Leavytt, Leavyt, Leavett, Leavet

Leben (English) Filled with hope

Lech (Slavic) In mythology, the founder of the Polish people
Leche

Ledyard (Teutonic) The protector of the nation
Ledyarde, Ledyerd, Ledyerde

Lee (English) From the meadow
Leigh, Lea, Leah, Ley

Leeto (African) One who embarks on a journey
Leato, Leito, Lieto

Legend (American) One who is memorable
Legende, Legund, Legunde

Leighton (English) From the town near the meadow
Leightun, Layton, Laytun, Leyton, Leytun

Lekhak (Hindi) An author
Lekhan

Lema (African) One who is cultivated
Lemah, Lemma, Lemmah

Lemon (American) Resembling the fruit
Lemun, Lemin, Lemyn, Limon, Limun, Limin, Limyn, Limen

Len (Native American) One who plays the flute

Lencho (African) Resembling a lion
Lenchos, Lenchio, Lenchiyo, Lencheo, Lencheyo

Lennart (Scandinavian) One who is brave
Lennert

Lennor (English) A courageous man

Lennox (Scottish) One who owns many elm trees
Lenox, Lenoxe, Lennix, Lenix, Lenixe

Lensar (English) One who stays with his parents
Lenser, Lensor, Lensur

Lenton (American) A pious man
Lentin, Lentyn, Lentun, Lentan, Lenten, Lent, Lente

Leo (Latin) Having the strength of a lion
Lio, Lyo, Leon

Leonard (German) Having the strength of a lion
Len, Lenard, Lenn, Lennard, Lennart, Lennerd, Lennie, Lenny

Leor (Latin) One who listens well
Leore

Lerato (Latin) The song of my soul
Leratio, Lerateo

Leron (French / Arabic) The circle / my song
Lerun, Leran, Leren, Lerin, Leryn

Leroy (French) The king
Leroi, Leeroy, Leeroi, Learoy, Learoi

Levi (Hebrew) We are united as one; in the Bible, one of Jacob's sons
Levie, Levin, Levyn, Levy, Levey, Levee

Li (Chinese) Having great strength

Lian (Chinese) Of the willow

Liang (Chinese) A good man
Lyang

Lidmann (Anglo-Saxon) A man of the sea; a sailor
Lidman, Lydmann, Lydman

Lif (Scandinavian) An energetic man; lively

Lihau (Hawaiian) A spirited man

Like (Asian) A soft-spoken man
Lyke

Lilo (Hawaiian) One who is generous
Lylo, Leelo, Lealo, Leylo, Lielo, Leilo

Lindberg (German) From the linden-tree hill
Lindbergh, Lindburg, Lindburgh, Lindi, Lindie, Lindee, Lindy, Lindey

Lindford (English) From the linden-tree ford
Linford, Lindforde, Linforde, Lyndford, Lynford, Lyndforde, Lynforde

Lindhurst (English) From the village by the linden trees
Lyndhurst, Lindenhurst, Lyndenhurst, Lindhirst, Lindherst, Lyndhirst, Lyndherst, Lindenhirst

Lindley (English) From the meadow of linden trees
Lindly, Lindleigh, Lindlea, Lindleah, Lindlee, Lindli, Lindlie, Lyndley

Lindman (English) One who lives near the linden trees
Lindmann, Lindmon, Lindmonn

Line (English) From the bank

Lion (English) Resembling the animal
Lyon, Lions, Lyons

Lipût (Hungarian) A brave young man

Lisimba (African) One who has been attacked by a lion
Lisymba, Lysimba, Lysymba

Liu (Asian) One who is quiet; peaceful

Llewellyn (Welsh) Resembling a lion
Lewellen, Lewellyn, Llewellen, Llewelyn, Llwewellin, Llew, Llewe, Llyweilun

Lochan (Hindi / Irish) The eyes / one who is lively

★ᵀLogan (Gaelic) From the little hollow
Logann, Logen, Login, Logyn, Logenn, Loginn, Logynn

Lolonyo (African) The beauty of love
Lolonyio, Lolonyeo, Lolonio, Lolonea

Loman (Gaelic) One who is small and bare
Lomann, Loeman, Loemann

Lombard (Latin) One who has a long beard
Lombardi, Lombardo, Lombardie, Lombardy, Lombardey, Lombardee

London (English) From the captial of England
Lundon, Londen, Lunden

Lonzo (Spanish) One who is ready for battle
Lonzio, Lonzeo

Lootah (Native American) Refers to the color red
Loota, Loutah, Louta, Lutah, Luta

Lorcan (Irish) The small fierce one
Lorcen, Lorcin, Lorcyn, Lorcon, Lorcun, Lorkan, Lorken, Lorkin

Lord (English) One who has authority and power
Lorde, Lordly, Lordley, Lordlee, Lordlea, Lordleigh, Lordli, Lordlie

Lore (Basque / English) Resembling a flower / form of Lawrence, meaning "man from Laurentum; crowned with laurel"
Lorea

Lorimer (Latin) One who
makes harnesses
*Lorrimer, Lorimar,
Lorrimar, Lorymar,
Lorrymar, Lorymer,
Lorrymer*

Louis (German) A famous
warrior
*Lew, Lewes, Lewis,
Lodewick, Lodovico, Lou,
Louie, Lucho,* **Luis**

Luba (Yugoslavian) One
who loves and is loved
Lubah

★ᵀLucas (English) A man
from Lucania
*Lukas, Loucas, Loukas,
Luckas, Louckas, Lucus,
Lukus, Ghoukas*

Lucian (Latin) Surrounded
by light
*Luciano, Lucianus, Lucien,
Lucio, Lucjan, Lukianos,
Lukyan, Luce*

Lucky (English) A fortu-
nate man
*Luckey, Luckee, Luckea,
Lucki, Luckie*

Ludlow (English) The
ruler of the hill
Ludlowe

★ᵀLuke (Greek) A man
from Lucania
Luc, Luken

Lunt (Scandinavian) From
the grove
Lunte

Luthando (Latin) One who
is dearly loved

Luther (German) A soldier
of the people
*Louther, Luter, Luthero,
Lutero, Louthero, Luthus,
Luthas, Luthos*

Lux (Latin) A man of the light
*Luxe, Luxi, Luxie, Luxee,
Luxea, Luxy, Luxey*

Ly (Vietnamese) A reasonable man

Lynn (English) A man of
the lake
Linn, Lyn, Lynne, Linne

M

Maahes (Egyptian)
Resembling a lion

Mac (Gaelic) The son of Mac
(Macarthur, Mackinley, etc.)
*Mack, Mak, Macky, Macky,
Macki, Mackie, Mackee,
Mackea*

Macadam (Gaelic) The
son of Adam
*Macadhamh, MacAdam,
McAdam, MacAdhamh*

Macallister (Gaelic) The son of Alistair
MacAlister, McAlister, McAllister, Macalister

Macardle (Gaelic) The son of great courage
MacArdle, McCardle, Macardell, MacArdell, McCardell

Macartan (Gaelic) The son of Artan
MacArtan, McArtan, Macarten, MacArten, McArten

Macarthur (Gaelic) The son of Arthur
MacArthur, McArthur, Macarther, MacArther, McArther

Macauslan (Gaelic) The son of Absalon
MacAuslan, McAuslan, Macauslen, MacAuslen, McAuslen

Maccoll (Gaelic) The son of Coll
McColl, Maccoll, MacColl

Maccrea (Gaelic) The son of grace
McCrea, Macrae, MacCrae, MacCray, MacCrea

Macedonio (Greek) A man from Macedonia
Macedoneo, Macedoniyo, Macedoneyo

Macgowan (Gaelic) The son of a blacksmith
MacGowan, Magowan, McGowan, McGowen, McGown, MacCowan, MacCowen

Machau (Hebrew) A gift from God

Machenry (Gaelic) The son of Henry
MacHenry, McHenry

Machk (Native American) Resembling a bear

Macintosh (Gaelic) The son of the thane
MacIntosh, McIntosh, Macintoshe, MacIntoshe, McIntoshe, Mackintosh, MacKintosh

Mackay (Gaelic) The son of fire
MacKay, McKay, Mackaye, MacKaye, McKaye

Mackinley (Gaelic) The son of the white warrior
MacKinley, McKinley, MacKinlay, McKinlay, Mackinlay, Mackinlie, MacKinlie

Macklin (Gaelic) The son of Flann
Macklinn, Macklyn, Macklynn, Macklen, Macklenn

Maclaine (Gaelic) The son of John's servant
MacLaine, Maclain, MacLain, Maclayn, McLaine, McLain, Maclane, MacLane

Macleod (Gaelic) The son of the ugly one
MacLeod, McLeod, McCloud, MacCloud

Macmurray (Gaelic) The son of Murray
MacMurray, McMurray, Macmurra, MacMurra

Macnab (Gaelic) The son of the abbot
MacNab, McNab

Macon (English / French) To make / from the city in France
Macun, Makon, Makun, Maken, Mackon, Mackun

Macqueen (Gaelic) The son of the good man
MacQueen, McQueen

Macrae (Gaelic) The son of Ray
MacRae, McRae, Macray, MacRay, McRay, Macraye, MacRaye, McRaye

Madden (Pakistani) One who is organized; a planner
Maddon, Maddan, Maddin, Maddyn, Maddun, Maden, Madon, Madun

Maddox (Welsh) The son of the benefactor
Madox, Madocks, Maddocks

Madhur (Indian) A sweet man

Madzimoyo (African) One who is nourished with water
Madzymoyo

Magee (Gaelic) The son of Hugh
MacGee, McGee, MacGhee, Maghee

Maguire (Gaelic) The son of the beige one
Magwire, MacGuire, McGuire, MacGwire, McGwire

Magus (Latin) A sorcerer
Magis, Magys, Magos, Magas, Mages

Mahan (American) A cowboy
Mahahn, Mahen, Mayhan, Maihan, Maehan, Mayhen, Maihen, Maehen

Mahant (Indian) Having a great soul
Mahante

Mahatma (Hindi) Of great spiritual development

Mahfouz (Arabic) One who is protected
Mafouz, Mahfooz, Mafooz, Mahfuz, Mafuz

Mahkah (Native American) Of the earth
Mahka, Makah, Maka

Mahmud (Arabic) One who is praiseworthy
Mahmood, Mahmoud, Mehmood, Mehmud, Mehmoud

Mailhairer (French) An ill-fated man

Maimon (Arabic) One who is dependable; having good fortune
Maymon, Maemon, Maimun, Maymun, Maemun, Mamon, Mamun

Maitland (English) From the meadow land
Maytland, Maetland, Maitlande, Maytlande, Maetlande

Majdy (Arabic) A glorious man
Majdey, Majdi, Majdie, Majdee, Majdea

Makaio (Hawaiian) A gift from God

Makena (Hawaiian) Man of abundance
Makenah

Makin (Arabic) Having great strength
Makeen, Makean, Makein, Makien, Makyn

Makis (Hebrew) A gift from God
Madys, Makiss, Makyss, Makisse, Madysse

Malachi (Hebrew) A messenger of God
Malachie, Malachy, Malaki, Malakia, Malakie, Malaquias, Malechy, Maleki

Malawa (African) A flourishing man

Malcolm (Gaelic) Follower of St. Columbus
Malcom, Malcolum, Malkolm, Malkom, Malkolum

Mali (Indian) A ruler; the firstborn son
Malie, Maly, Maley, Malee, Malea

Mamoru (Japanese) Of the earth
Mamorou, Mamorue, Mamorew, Mamoroo

Manchester (English) From the city in England
Manchestar, Manchestor, Manchestir, Manchestyr, Manchestur

Mandan (Native American) A tribal name
Manden, Mandon, Mandun, Mandin, Mandyn

Mandhatri (Indian) A prince; born to royalty
Mandhatrie, Mandhatry, Mandhatrey, Mandhatree, Mandhatrea

Mani (African) From the mountain
Manie, Many, Maney, Manee, Manea

Manjit (Indian) A conqueror of the mind; having great knowledge
Manjeet, Manjeat, Manjeit, Manjiet, Manjyt

Manley (English) From the man's meadow; from the hero's meadow
Manly, Manli, Manlie, Manlea, Manleah, Manlee, Manleigh

Manmohan (Indian) A handsome and pleasing man
Manmohen, Manmohin, Manmohyn

Mannheim (German) From the hamlet in the swamp
Manheim

Mano (Hawaiian) Resembling a shark
Manoe, Manow, Manowe

Manohar (Indian) A delightful and captivating man
Manoharr, Manohare

Mansel (English) From the clergyman's house
Mansle, Mansell, Mansele, Manselle, Manshel, Manshele, Manshell, Manshelle

Mansfield (English) From the field near the small river
Mansfeld, Maunfield, Maunfeld

Manton (English) From the man's town; from the hero's town
Mantun, Manten, Mannton, Manntun, Mannten

Manu (African) The second-born child
Manue, Manou, Manoo

Manuel (Spanish) Form of Emmanuel, meaning "God is with us"
Manuelo, Manuello, Manolito, Manolo, Manollo, Manny, Manni, Manney

Manya (Indian) A respected man
Manyah

Manzo (Japanese) The third son with ten-thousand-fold strength

Mar (Spanish) Of the sea
Marr, Mare, Marre

Marcel (French) The little warrior
Marceau, Marcelin, Marcellin, Marcellino, Marcell, Marcello, Marcellus, Marcelo

Marden (Old English) From the valley with the pool
Mardin, Mardyn, Mardon, Mardun, Mardan

Mariatu (African) One who is pure; chaste
Mariatue, Mariatou, Mariatoo

Marid (Arabic) A rebellious man
Maryd

Mario (Latin) A manly man
Marius, Marios, Mariano, Marion, Mariun, Mareon

^T**Mark** (Latin) Dedicated to Mars, the god of war
Marc, Markey, Marky, Marki, Markie, Markee, Markea, Markov

Marmion (French) Our little one
Marmyon, Marmeon

Marsh (English) From the marshland
Marshe

Marshall (French / English) A caretaker of horses / a steward
Marchall, Marischal, Marischall, Marschal, Marshal, Marshell, Marshel, Marschall

Marston (English) From the town near the marsh
Marstun, Marsten, Marstin, Marstyn, Marstan

Martin (Latin) Dedicated to Mars, the god of war
Martyn, Mart, Martel, Martell, Marten, Martenn, Marti, Martie

Marvin (Welsh) A friend of the sea
Marvinn, Marvinne, Marven, Marvenn, Marvenne, Marvyn, Marvynn, Marvynne, Mervin

Maryland (English) Honoring Queen Mary; from the state of Maryland
Mariland, Maralynd, Marylind, Marilind, Marylend, Marilend

Masanao (Japanese) A good man

Masao (Japanese) A righteous man

★^T**Mason** (English) One who works with stone
Masun, Masen, Masan, Masin, Masyn, Masson, Massun, Massen

Masselin (French) A young Thomas
Masselyn, Masselen, Masselan, Masselon, Masselun, Maselin, Maselyn, Maselon

Masura (Japanese) A good destiny
Masoura

Matanjah (Hebrew) A gift from God
Matania, Matanya, Matanyahu, Mattania, Mattaniah, Matanyah

Matata (African) One who causes trouble

Matin (Arabic) Having great strength
Maten, Matan, Matyn, Maton, Matun

Matisse (French) One who is gifted
Matiss, Matysse, Matyss, Matise, Matyse

Matlock (American) A rancher
Matlok, Matloc

Matoskah (Native American) Resembling a white bear
Matoska

★ᵀMatthew (Hebrew) A gift from God
Matt, Matvey, Madteo, Madteos, Madtheos, Mat, Mata, Mateo, Mateus, Mateusz

Matunde (African) One who is fruitful
Matundi, Matundie, Matundy, Matundey, Matundee, Matundea

Matvey (Russian) Form of Matthew, meaning "a gift from God"
Matvy, Matvee, Matvea, Matvi, Matvie, Motka, Matviyko

Matwau (Native American) The enemy

Maurice (Latin) A dark-skinned man; Moorish
Maurell, Maureo, Mauricio, Maurids, Maurie, Maurin, Maurio, Maurise, Baurice

Maverick (English) An independent man; a non-conformist
Maveric, Maverik, Mavrick, Mavric, Mavrik

Mawulol (African) One who gives thanks to God

Maximilian (Latin) The greatest
Max, Macks, Maxi, Maxie, Maxy, Maxey, Maxee, Maxea, Maxx

Maxfield (English) From Mack's field
Mackfield, Maxfeld, Macksfeld

Maxwell (English) From Mack's spring
Maxwelle, Mackswell, Maxwel, Mackswel, Mackwelle, Maxwill, Maxwille, Mackswill

Mayer (Latin / German / Hebrew) A large man / a farmer / one who is shining bright
Maier, Mayar, Mayor, Mayir, Mayur, Meyer, Meir, Myer

Mayfield (English) From the strong one's field
Mayfeld, Maifield, Maifeld, Maefield, Maefeld

Mayo (Gaelic) From the yew tree plain
Mayoe, Maiyo, Maeyo, Maiyoe, Maeyoe, Mayoh, Maioh

Mccoy (Gaelic) The son of Coy
McCoy

McKenna (Gaelic) The son of Kenna; to ascend
McKennon, McKennun, McKennen, McKennan

Mckile (Gaelic) The son of Kyle
McKile, Mckyle, McKyle, Mackile, Mackyle, MacKile, MacKyle

Medad (Hebrew) A beloved friend
Meydad

Medgar (German) Having great strength
Medgarr, Medgare, Medgard, Medárd

Medwin (German) A strong friend
Medwine, Medwinn, Medwinne, Medwen, Medwenn, Medwenne, Medwyn, Medwynn

Meged (Hebrew) One who has been blessed with goodness

Mehdi (Arabian) One who is guided
Mehdie, Mehdy, Mehdey, Mehdee, Mehdea

Mehetabel (Hebrew) One who is favored by God
Mehetabell, Mehitabel, Mehitabell, Mehytabel, Mehytabell

Meilyr (Welsh) A regal ruler

Meinrad (German) A strong counselor
Meinred, Meinrod, Meinrud, Meinrid, Meinryd

Meka (Hawaiian) Of the eyes
Mekah

Melancton (Greek) Resembling a black flower
Melankton, Melanctun, Melanktun, Melancten, Melankten, Melanchton, Melanchten, Melanchthon

Mele (Hawaiian) One who is happy

Melesio (Spanish) An attentive man; one who is careful
Melacio, Melasio, Melecio, Melicio, Meliseo, Milesio

Meletius (Greek) A cautious man
Meletios, Meletious, Meletus, Meletos

Meli (Native American) One who is bitter
Melie, Mely, Meley, Melee, Melea, Meleigh

Melker (Swedish) A king
Melkar, Melkor, Melkur, Melkir, Melkyr

Melton (English) From the mill town
Meltun, Meltin, Meltyn, Melten, Meltan

Melville (English) From the mill town
Melvill, Melvil, Melvile, Melvylle, Melvyll, Melvyl, Melvyle

Melvin (English) A friend who offers counsel
Melvinn, Melvinne, Melven, Melvenn, Melvenne, Melvyn, Melvynn, Melvynne, Belvin

Memphis (American) From the city in Tennessee
Memfis, Memphys, Memfys, Memphus, Memfus

Menachem (Hebrew) One who provides comfort
Menaheim, Menahem, Menachim, Menachym, Menahim, Menahym, Machum, Machem

Menassah (Hebrew) A forgetful man
Menassa, Menass, Menas, Menasse, Menasseh

Menefer (Egyptian) Of the beautiful city
Menefar, Menefir, Menefyr, Menefor, Menefur

Menelik (African) The son of a wise man
Menelick, Menelic, Menelyk, Menelyck, Menelyc

Merewood (English) From the forest with the lake
Merwood, Merewode, Merwode

Merlin (Welsh) Of the sea fortress; in Arthurian legend, the wizard and mentor of King Arthur
Merlyn, Merlan, Merlon, Merlun, Merlen, Merlinn, Merlynn, Merlonn

Merrill (English) Of the shining sea
Meril, Merill, Merrel, Merrell, Merril, Meryl, Merryll, Meryll

Merton (English) From the town near the lake
Mertun, Mertan, Merten, Mertin, Mertyn, Murton, Murtun, Murten

Mervin (Welsh) Form of Marvin, meaning "a friend of the sea"
Mervinn, Mervinne, Mervyn, Mervynn, Mervynne, Merven, Mervenn, Mervenne

Meshach (Hebrew) An enduring man
Meshack, Meshac, Meshak, Meeshach, Meeshack, Meeshak, Meeshac

Mhina (African) One who is delightful
Mhinah, Mheena, Mheenah, Mheina, Mheinah, Mhienah, Mhienah, Mhyna

★ᵀ**Michael** (Hebrew) Who is like God?
Makai, Micael, Mical, Micha, Michaelangelo, Michail, Michal, Micheal, Miguel, Mick

Michio (Japanese) One who has the strength of three thousand
Mychio

Mick (English) Form of Michael, meaning "who is like God?"
Micke, Mickey, Micky, Micki, Mickie, Mickee, Mickea, Mickel

Mieko (Japanese) A bright man

Milan (Latin) An eager and hardworking man
Mylan

Miles (German / Latin) One who is merciful / a soldier
Myles, Milo, Mylo, Miley, Mily, Mili, Milie, Milee

Milford (English) From the mill's ford
Millford, Milfurd, Millfurd, Milferd, Millferd, Milforde, Millforde, Milfurde

Miller (English) One who works at the mill
Millar, Millor, Millur, Millir, Millyr, Myller, Millen, Millan

Miloslav (Czech) One who is honored; one who loves glory
Myloslav, Miloslaw, Myloslaw

Milson (English) The son of Miles
Milsun, Milsen, Milsin, Milsyn, Milsan

Mimir (Norse) In mythology, a giant who guarded the well of wisdom
Mymir, Mimeer, Mimyr, Mymeer, Mymyr, Meemir, Meemeer, Meemyr

Miner (Latin / English) One who works in the mines / a youth
Minor, Minar, Minur, Minir, Minyr

Mingan (Native American) Resembling a gray wolf
Mingen, Mingin, Mingon, Mingun, Mingyn

Minh (Vietnamese) A clever man

Minster (English) Of the church
Mynster, Minstar, Mynstar, Minstor, Mynstor, Minstur, Mynstur, Minstir

Miracle (American) An act of God's hand
Mirakle, Mirakel, Myracle, Myrakle

Mirage (French) An illusion
Myrage

Mirumbi (African) Born during a period of rain
Mirumbie, Mirumby, Mirumbey, Mirumbee, Mirumbea

Missouri (Native American) From the town of large canoes; from the state of Missouri
Missourie, Mizouri, Mizourie, Missoury, Mizoury, Missuri, Mizuri, Mizury

Mitali (Indian) A beloved friend
Mitalie, Mitaly, Mitaley, Mitalee, Mitaleigh, Mitalea

Mitsu (Japanese) Of the light
Mytsu, Mitsue, Mytsue

Mochni (Native American) Resembling a talking bird
Mochnie, Mochny, Mochney, Mochnee, Mochnea

Modesty (Latin) One who is without conceit
Modesti, Modestie, Modestee, Modestus, Modestey, Modesto, Modestio, Modestine

Mogens (Dutch) A powerful man
Mogen, Mogins, Mogin, Mogyns, Mogyn, Mogan, Mogans

Mohajit (Indian) A charming man
Mohajeet, Mohajeat, Mohajeit, Mohajiet, Mohajyt

Mohammed (Arabic) One who is greatly praised; the name of the prophet and founder of Islam
Mahomet, Mohamad, Mohamed, Mohamet, Mohammad, Muhammad, Muhammed, Mehmet

Mohave (Native American) A tribal name
Mohav, Mojave

Mojag (Native American) One who is never quiet

Molan (Irish) The servant of the storm
Molen

Momo (American) A warring man

Mona (African) A jealous man
Monah

Mongo (African) A well-known man
Mongoe, Mongow, Mongowe

Mongwau (Native American) Resembling an owl

Monroe (Gaelic) From the mouth of the river Roe
Monro, Monrow, Monrowe, Munro, Munroe, Munrow, Munrowe

Montenegro (Spanish) From the black mountain

Montgomery (French) From Gomeric's mountain
Monty, Montgomerey, Montgomeri, Montgomerie, Montgomeree, Montgomerea

Monty (English) Form of Montgomery, meaning "from Gomeric's mountain"
Montey, Monti, Montie, Montee, Montea, Montes, Montez

Moon (American) Born beneath the moon; a dreamer

Mooney (Irish) A wealthy man
Moony, Mooni, Moonie, Maonaigh, Moonee, Moonea, Moone

Moose (American) Resembling the animal; a big, strong man
Moos, Mooze, Mooz

Moran (Irish) A great man
Morane, Morain, Moraine, Morayn, Morayne, Moraen, Moraene

Morathi (African) A wise man
Morathie, Morathy, Morathey, Morathee, Morathea

Moreland (English) From the moors
Moorland, Morland

Morley (English) From the meadow on the moor
Morly, Morleigh, Morlee, Morlea, Morleah, Morli, Morlie, Moorley

Morpheus (Greek) In mythology, the god of dreams
Morfeus, Morphius, Mofius

Mortimer (French) Of the still water; of the dead sea
Mortymer, Morty, Mortey, Morti, Mortie, Mortee, Mortea, Mort, Morte

Moses (Hebrew) A savior; in the Bible, the leader of the Israelites; drawn from the water
Mioshe, Mioshye, Mohsen, Moke, Moise, Moises, Mose, Moshe

Mostyn (Welsh) From the mossy settlement
Mostin, Mosten, Moston, Mostun, Mostan

Moswen (African) A light-skinned man
Moswenn, Moswenne, Moswin, Moswinn, Moswinne, Moswyn, Moswynn, Moswynne

Moubarak (Arabian) One who is blessed
Mubarak, Moobarak

Mounafes (Arabic) A rival

Muhannad (Arabic) One who wields a sword
Muhanned, Muhanad, Muhaned, Muhunnad, Muhunad, Muhanned, Muhaned

Mukhtar (Arabic) The chosen one
Muktar

Mukisa (Ugandan) Having good fortune
Mukysa

Mulcahy (Irish) A war chief
Mulcahey, Mulcahi, Mulcahie, Mulcahee, Mulcahea

Mundhir (Arabic) One who cautions others
Mundheer, Mundhear, Mundheir, Mundhier, Mundhyr

Murdock (Scottish) From the sea
Murdok, Murdoc, Murdo, Murdoch, Murtagh, Murtaugh, Murtogh, Murtough

Murfain (American) Having a warrior spirit
Murfaine, Murfayn, Murfayne, Murfaen, Murfaene, Murfane

Muriel (Gaelic) Of the shining sea
Muryel, Muriell, Muryell, Murial, Muriall, Muryal, Muryall, Murell

Murphy (Gaelic) A warrior of the sea
Murphey, Murphee, Murphea, Murphi, Murphie, Murfey, Murfy, Murfee

Murray (Gaelic) The lord of the sea
Murrey, Murry, Murri, Murrie, Murree, Murrea, Murry

Murron (Celtic) A bitter man
Murrun, Murren, Murran, Murrin, Murryn

Murtadi (Arabic) One who is content
Murtadie, Murtady, Murtadey, Murtadee, Murtadea

Musad (Arabic) One who is lucky
Musaad, Mus'ad

Mushin (Arabic) A charitable man
Musheen, Mushean, Mushein, Mushien, Mushyn

Muskan (Arabic) One who smiles often
Musken, Muskon, Muskun, Muskin, Muskyn

Muslim (Arabic) An adherent of Islam
Muslym, Muslem, Moslem, Moslim, Moslym

Mustapha (Arabic) The chosen one
Mustafa, Mostapha, Mostafa, Moustapha, Moustafa

Muti (Arabic) One who is obedient
Mutie, Muty, Mutey, Mutee, Mutea, Muta

Myron (Greek) Refers to myrrh, a fragrant oil
Myrun, Myran, Myren, Myrin, Myryn, Miron, Mirun, Miran

Mystique (French) A man with an air of mystery
Mystic, Mistique, Mysteek, Misteek, Mystiek, Mistiek, Mysteeque, Misteeque

Nabendu (Indian) Born beneath the new moon
Nabendue, Nabendoo, Nabendou

Nabhi (Indian) The best
Nabhie, Nabhy, Nabhey, Nabhee, Nabhea

Nabhomani (Indian) Of the sun
Nabhomanie, Nabhomany, Nabhomaney, Nabhomanee, Nabhomanea

Nabil (Arabic) A highborn man
Nabeel, Nabeal, Nabeil, Nabiel, Nabyl

Nabu (Babylonian) In mythology, the god of writing and wisdom
Nabue, Naboo, Nabo, Nebo, Nebu, Nebue, Neboo

Nachshon (Hebrew) An adventurous man; one who is daring
Nachson

Nadav (Hebrew) A generous man
Nadaav

Nadif (African) One who is born between seasons
Nadeef, Nadief, Nadeif, Nadyf, Nadeaf

Nadim (Arabic) A beloved friend
Nadeem, Nadeam, Nadiem, Nadeim, Nadym

Naftali (Hebrew) A struggling man; in the Bible, one of Jacob's sons
Naphtali, Naphthali, Neftali, Nefthali, Nephtali, Nephthali, Naftalie, Naphtalie

Nagel (German) One who makes nails
Nagle, Nagler, Naegel, Nageler, Nagelle, Nagele, Nagell

Nahir (Hebrew) A clear-headed and bright man
Naheer, Nahear, Naheir, Nahier, Nahyr, Naher

Nahum (Hebrew) A compassionate man
Nahom, Nahoum, Nahoom, Nahuem

Naji (Arabic) One who is safe
Najea, Naje, Najee, Najie, Najy, Najey, Nanji, Nanjie

Najib (Arabic) Of noble descent; a highborn man
Najeeb, Najeab, Najeib, Najieb, Najyb, Nageeb, Nageab, Nagyb

Nally (Irish) A poor man
Nalley, Nalli, Nallie, Nallee, Nallea, Nalleigh

Namir (Israeli) Resembling a leopard
Nameer, Namear, Namier, Nameir, Namyr

Nandan (Indian) One who is pleasing
Nanden, Nandin, Nandyn, Nandon, Nandun

Naotau (Indian) Our new son
Naotou

Napier (French / English) A mover / one who takes care of the royal linens
Neper

Napoleon (Italian /
German) A man from
Naples / son of the mists
*Napolean, Napolion,
Napoleone, Napoleane,
Napolione*

Narcissus (Greek)
Resembling a daffodil;
self-love; in mythology, a
youth who fell in love with
his reflection
*Narciso, Narcisse,
Narkissos, Narses, Narcisus,
Narcis, Narciss*

Naresh (Indian) A king
Nareshe, Natesh, Nateshe

Nasih (Arabic) One who
advises others
Nasyh

Natal (Spanish) Born at
Christmastime
*Natale, Natalino, Natalio,
Natall, Natalle, Nataleo,
Natica*

★ᵀ**Nathan** (Hebrew) Form
of Nathaniel, meaning "a
gift from God"
*Nat, Natan, Nate, Nathen,
Nathon, Nathin, Nathyn,
Nathun, Lathan*

★**Nathaniel** (Hebrew) A
gift from God
*Nathan, Natanael,
Nataniel, Nathanael,
Nathaneal, Nathanial,
Nathanyal, Nathanyel,
Nethanel*

Nature (American) An
outdoorsy man
Natural

Navarro (Spanish) From
the plains
*Navaro, Navarrio, Navario,
Navarre, Navare, Nabaro,
Nabarro*

Naveed (Persian) Our best
wishes
*Navead, Navid, Navied,
Naveid, Navyd*

Nazim (Arabian) Of a soft
breeze
*Nazeem, Nazeam, Naziem,
Nazeim, Nazym*

Nebraska (Native
American) From the flat
water land; from the state
of Nebraska

Neckarios (Greek) Of the
nectar; one who is immortal
*Nectaire, Nectarios,
Nectarius, Nektario,
Nektarius, Nektarios,
Nektaire*

Neelotpal (Indian)
Resembling the blue lotus
*Nealotpal, Nielotpal,
Neilotpal, Nilothpal,
Neelothpal*

Negm (Arabian)
Resembling a star

Nehal (Indian) Born during a period of rain
Nehall, Nehale, Nehalle

Nehemiah (Hebrew) God provides comfort
Nehemia, Nechemia, Nechemiah, Nehemya, Nehemyah, Nechemya, Nechemyah

Neil (Gaelic) The champion
Neal, Neale, Neall, Nealle, Nealon, Neel, Neilan, Neile

Neirin (Irish) Surrounded by light
Neiryn, Neiren, Neerin, Neeryn, Neeren

Nelek (Polish) Resembling a horn
Nelec, Neleck

Nelson (English) The son of Neil; the son of a champion
Nealson, Neilson, Neillson, Nelsen, Nilson, Nilsson, Nelli, Nellie

Neptune (Latin) In mythology, god of the sea
Neptun, Neptoon, Neptoone, Neptoun, Neptoune

Neroli (Italian) Resembling an orange blossom
Nerolie, Neroly, Neroley, Neroleigh, Nerolea, Nerolee

Nevan (Irish) The little saint
Naomhan

Neville (French) From the new village
Nev, Nevil, Nevile, Nevill, Nevylle, Nevyl, Nevyle, Nevyll

Newcomb (English) From the new valley
Newcom, Newcome, Newcombe, Neucomb, Neucombe, Neucom, Neucome

Newlin (Welsh) From the new pond
Newlinn, Newlyn, Newlynn, Neulin, Neulinn, Neulyn, Neulynn

Newman (English) A newcomer
Newmann, Neuman, Neumann

Nhat (Vietnamese) Having a long life
Nhatt, Nhate, Nhatte

Niaz (Persian) A gift
Nyaz

Nibaw (Native American) One who stands tall
Nybaw, Nibau, Nybau

★ᵀNicholas (Greek) Of the victorious people
Nick, Nicanor, Niccolo, Nichol, Nicholai, Nicholaus, Nichole, Nicholl, Nichols, Colin

Nick (English) Form of Nicholas, meaning "of the victorious people"
Nik, Nicki, Nickie, Nickey, Nicky, Nickee, Nickea, Niki

Nickler (American) One who is swift
Nikler, Nicler, Nyckler, Nykler, Nycler

Nicomedes (Greek) One who thinks of victory
Nikomedes, Nicomedo, Nikomedo

Nihal (Indian) One who is content
Neehal, Neihal, Niehal, Neahal, Neyhal, Nyhal

Nihar (Indian) Covered with the morning's dew
Neehar, Niehar, Neihar, Neahar, Nyhar

Nikan (Persian) One who brings good things
Niken, Nikin, Nikyn, Nikon, Nikun

Nikshep (Indian) One who is treasured
Nykshep

Nikunja (Indian) From the grove of trees

Nino (Italian / Spanish) God is gracious / a young boy
Ninoshka

Nirad (Indian) Of the clouds
Nyrad

Niran (Thai) The eternal one
Nyran, Niren, Nirin, Niryn, Niron, Nirun, Nyren, Nyrin

Nirav (Indian) One who is quiet
Nyrav

Nirbheet (Indian) A fearless man
Nirbhit, Nirbhyt, Nirbhay, Nirbhaye, Nirbhai, Nirbhae

Niremaan (Arabic) One who shines as brightly as fire
Nyremaan, Nireman, Nyreman

Nishan (Armenian) A sign or symbol

Nishok (Indian) Filled with happiness
Nyshok, Nishock, Nyshock

Nissan (Hebrew) A miracle child
Nisan

Nixkamich (Native American) A grandfatherly man

Niyol (Native American) Of the wind

Njord (Scandinavian) A man from the north
Njorde, Njorth, Njorthe

★ᵀNoah (Hebrew) A peaceful wanderer
Noa

Nodin (Native American) Of the wind
Nodyn, Noden, Nodan, Nodon, Nodun

Nolan (Gaelic) A famous and noble man; a champion of the people
Nolen, Nolin, Nolon, Nolun, Nolyn, Noland, Nolande

North (English) A man from the north
Northe

Northcliff (English) From the northern cliff
Northcliffe, Northclyf, Northclyff, Northclyffe

Norval (Scottish) From the northern valley
Norvall, Norvale, Norvail, Norvaile, Norvayl, Norvayle, Norvael, Norvaele

Norward (English) A guardian of the north
Norwarde, Norwerd, Norwerde, Norwurd, Norwurde

Noshi (Native American) A fatherly man
Noshie, Noshy, Noshey, Noshee, Noshea, Nosh, Noshe

Notaku (Native American) Resembling a growling bear
Notakou, Notakue, Notakoo

Nuhad (Arabic) A brave young man
Nuehad, Nouhad, Neuhad

Nukpana (Native American) An evil man
Nukpanah, Nukpanna, Nukpannah, Nuckpana, Nucpana

Nulte (Irish) A man from Ulster
Nulti, Nultie, Nulty, Nultey, Nultee, Nultea

Nuncio (Spanish) A messenger
Nunzio

Nuriel (Hebrew) God's light
Nuriell, Nuriele, Nurielle, Nuryel, Nuryell, Nuryele, Nuryelle, Nooriel

Nuru (African) My light
Nurue, Nuroo, Nurou, Nourou, Nooroo

Nyack (African) One who is persistent
Niack, Nyak, Niak, Nyac, Niac

Nye (English) One who lives on the island
Nyle, Nie, Nile

Obedience (American) A well-behaved man
Obediance, Obedyence, Obedeynce

Oberon (German) A royal bear; having the heart of a bear
Oberron

Obert (German) A wealthy and bright man
Oberte, Oberth, Oberthe, Odbart, Odbarte, Odbarth, Odbarthe, Odhert

Ochi (African) Filled with laughter
Ochie, Ochee, Ochea, Ochy, Ochey

Odam (English) A son-in-law
Odom, Odem, Odum

Ode (Egyptian / Greek) Traveler of the road / a lyric poem

Oded (Hebrew) One who is supportive and encouraging

Oder (English) From the river
Odar, Odir, Odyr, Odur

Odin (Norse) In mythology, the supreme deity
Odyn, Odon, Oden, Odun

Odinan (Hungarian) One who is wealthy and powerful
Odynan, Odinann, Odynann

Odion (African) The first-born of twins
Odiyon, Odiun, Odiyun

Odissan (African) A wanderer; traveler
Odyssan, Odisan, Odysan, Odissann, Odyssann, Odisann, Odysann

Oengus (Irish) A vigorous man
Oenguss

Offa (Anglo-Saxon) A king
Offah

Ofir (Hebrew) The golden son
Ofeer, Ofear, Ofyr, Ofier, Ofeir, Ofer

Ogaleesha (Native American) A man wearing a red shirt
Ogaleasha, Ogaleisha, Ogaleysha, Ogalesha, Ogaliesha, Ogalisha

Oghe (Irish) One who rides horses
Oghi, Oghie, Oghee, Oghea, Oghy, Oghey

Oguz (Hungarian) An arrow
Oguze, Oguzz, Oguzze

Ohanko (Native American) A reckless man
Ohankio, Ohankiyo

Ojaswit (Indian) A powerful and radiant man
Ojaswyt, Ojaswin, Ojaswen, Ojaswyn, Ojas

Okal (African) To cross
Okall

Okan (Turkish) Resembling a horse
Oken, Okin, Okyn

Okapi (African) Resembling an animal with a long neck
Okapie, Okapy, Okapey, Okapee, Okapea, Okape

Okechuku (African) Blessed by God

Oki (Japanese) From the center of the ocean
Okie, Oky, Okey, Okee, Okea

Oklahoma (Native American) Of the red people; from the state of Oklahoma

Oktawian (African) The eighth-born child
Oktawyan, Oktawean, Octawian, Octawyan, Octawean

Olaf (Scandinavian) The remaining of the ancestors
Olay, Ole, Olef, Olev, Oluf, Uolevi

Olafemi (African) A lucky young man
Olafemie, Olafemy, Olafemey, Olafemee, Olafemea

Oleg (Russian) One who is holy
Olezka

Olimpio (Greek) From Mount Olympus
Olimpo, Olympio, Olympios, Olympus

Olney (English) From the loner's field
Olny, Olnee, Olnea, Olni, Olnie, Ollaneg, Olaneg

Olujimi (African) One who is close to God
Olujimie, Olujimy, Olujimey, Olujimee, Olujimea

Olumide (African) God has arrived
Olumidi, Olumidie, Olumidy, Olumidey, Olumidee, Olumidea, Olumyde, Olumydi

Olumoi (African) One who has been blessed by God
Olumoy

Omeet (Hebrew) My light
Omeete, Omeit, Omeite, Omeyt, Omeyte, Omit, Omeat, Omeate

Omega (Greek) The last great one; the last letter of the Greek alphabet
Omegah

Onaona (Hawaiian) Having a pleasant scent

Ond (Hungarian) The tenth-born child
Onde

Ondrej (Czech) A manly man
Ondrejek, Ondrejec, Ondrousek, Ondravsek

Onkar (Indian) The purest one
Onckar, Oncar, Onkarr, Onckarr, Oncarr

Onofrio (Italain) A defender of peace
Onofre, Onofrius, Onophrio, Onophre, Onfrio, Onfroi

Onslow (Arabic) From the hill of the enthusiast
Onslowe, Ounslow, Ounslowe

Onyebuchi (African) God is in everything
Onyebuchie, Onyebuchy, Onyebuchey, Onyebuchee, Onyebuchea

Oqwapi (Native American) Resembling a red cloud
Oqwapie, Oqwapy, Oqwapey, Oqwapee, Oqwapea

Oram (English) From the enclosure near the riverbank
Oramm, Oraham, Orahamm, Orham, Orhamm

Ordell (Latin) Of the beginning
Ordel, Ordele, Ordelle, Orde

Ordway (Anglo-Saxon) A fighter armed with a spear
Ordwaye, Ordwai, Ordwae

Oren (Hebrew / Gaelic) From the pine tree / a pale-skinned man
Orenthiel, Orenthiell, Orenthiele, Orenthielle, Orenthiem, Orenthium, Orin

Orleans (Latin) The golden child
Orlean, Orleane, Orleens, Orleen, Orleene, Orlins, Olryns, Orlin

Orly (Hebrew) Surrounded by light
Orley, Orli, Orlie, Orlee, Orleigh, Orlea

Ormod (Anglo-Saxon) A sorrowful man

Ormond (English) One who defends with a spear / from the mountain of bears
Ormonde, Ormund, Ormunde, Ormemund, Ormemond, Ordmund, Ordmunde, Ordmond

Ornice (Irish / Hebrew) A pale-skinned man / from the cedar tree
Ornyce, Ornise, Orynse, Orneice, Orneise, Orniece, Orniese, Orneece

Orris (Latin) One who is inventive
Orriss, Orrisse, Orrys, Orryss, Orrysse

Orson (Latin) Resembling a bear; raised by a bear
Orsen, Orsin, Orsini, Orsino, Orsis, Orsonio, Orsinie, Orsiny

Orth (English) An honest man
Orthe

Orton (English) From the settlement by the shore
Ortun, Oraton, Oratun

Orville (French) From the gold town
Orvell, Orvelle, Orvil, Orvill, Orvele, Orvyll, Orvylle, Orvyl

Orwel (Welsh) Of the horizon
Orwell, Orwele, Orwelle

Os (English) The divine

Osborn (Norse) A bear of God
Osborne, Osbourn, Osbourne, Osburn, Osburne

Oscar (English / Gaelic) A spear of the gods / a friend of deer
Oskar, Osker, Oscer, Osckar, Oscker, Oszkar, Oszcar

Osher (Hebrew) A man of good fortune

Osias (Greek) Salvation
Osyas

Osileani (Polynesian) One who talks a lot
Osileanie, Osileany, Osileaney, Osileanee, Osileanea

Oswald (English) The power of God
Oswalde, Osvald, Osvaldo, Oswaldo, Oswell, Osvalde, Oswallt, Osweald

Oswin (English) A friend of God
Oswinn, Oswinne, Oswen, Oswenn, Oswenne, Oswyn, Oswynn, Oswynne

Othniel (Hebrew) God's lion
Othniell, Othnielle, Othniele, Othnyel, Othnyell, Othnyele, Othnyelle

Otmar (Teutonic) A famous warrior
Otmarr, Othmar, Othmarr, Otomar, Ottomar, Otomarr, Ottomarr

Otoahhastis (Native American) Resembling a tall bull

Ottokar (German) A spirited warrior
Otokar, Otokarr, Ottokarr, Ottokars, Otokars, Ottocar, Otocar, Ottocars

Ouray (Native American)
The arrow
Ouraye, Ourae, Ourai

Ourson (French)
Resembling a little bear
*Oursun, Oursoun, Oursen,
Oursan, Oursin, Oursyn*

Ovid (Latin) A shepherd;
an egg
*Ovyd, Ovidio, Ovido,
Ovydio, Ovydo, Ovidiu,
Ovydiu, Ofydd*

*Owen (Welsh / Gaelic)
Form of Eugene, meaning
"a well-born man" / a
youthful man
*Owenn, Owenne, Owin,
Owinn, Owinne, Owyn,
Owynn, Owynne*

Oxton (English) From the
oxen town
*Oxtun, Oxtown, Oxnaton,
Oxnatun, Oxnatown*

Oz (Hebrew) Having great
strength
*Ozz, Ozzi, Ozzie, Ozzy,
Ozzey, Ozzee, Ozzea, Ozi*

Ozni (Hebrew) One who
knows God
*Oznie, Ozny, Ozney,
Oznee, Oznea*

Özséb (Hungarian) A
pious man

Ozuru (Japanese)
Resembling a stork
*Ozurou, Ozourou, Ozuroo,
Ozooroo*

Paavo (Finnish) Form of
Paul, meaning "a small or
humble man"
Paaveli

Pace (Hebrew / English)
Refers to Passover / a
peaceful man
*Paice, Payce, Paece, Pacey,
Pacy, Pacee, Paci, Pacie*

Pacho (Spanish) An independent man; one who is
free

Pachu'a (Native American)
Resembling a water snake

Paco (Spanish) A man
from France
Pacorro, Pacoro, Paquito

Padgett (French) One who
strives to better himself
*Padget, Padgette, Padgete,
Padgeta, Padgetta, Padge,
Paget, Pagett*

Padman (Indian)
Resembling the lotus
Padmann

Padruig (Scottish) Of the royal family

Paine (Latin) Man from the country; a peasant
Pain, Payn, Payne, Paen, Paene, Pane, Paien

Palamedes (English) In Arthurian legend, a knight
Palomydes, Palomedes, Palamydes, Palsmedes, Palsmydes, Pslomydes

Palban (Spanish) A blond-haired man
Palben, Palbin, Palbyn, Palbon, Palbun

Paley (English) Form of Paul, meaning "a small or humble man"
Paly, Pali, Palie, Palee, Palea

Palladin (Greek) Filled with wisdom
Palladyn, Palladen, Palladan, Paladin, Paladyn, Paladen, Paladan

Palmer (English) A pilgrim bearing a palm branch
Pallmer, Palmar, Pallmar, Palmerston, Palmiro, Palmeero, Palmeer, Palmire

Pan (Greek) In mythology, god of the shepherds
Pann

Panama (Spanish) From the canal

Pancho (Spanish) A man from France

Pankaj (Indian) Resembling the lotus flower

Panya (African) Resembling a mouse
Panyah

Panyin (African) The first-born of twins
Panyen

Paras (Hindi) A touchstone
Parasmani, Parasmanie, Parasmany, Parasmaney, Parasmanee

Parkins (English) As solid as a rock; son of Peter
Parkens, Parken, Parkin, Parkyns, Parkyn, Parkinson

Parley (Scottish) A reluctant man
Parly, Parli, Parlie, Parlee, Parlea, Parle

Parmenio (Spanish) A studious man; one who is intelligent
Parmenios, Parmenius

Parounag (Armenian) One who is thankful

Parrish (Latin) Man of the church
Parish, Parrishe, Parishe, Parrysh, Parysh, Paryshe, Parryshe, Parisch

Parry (Welsh) The son of Harry
Parrey, Parri, Parrie, Parree, Parrea

Parthenios (Greek) One who is pure; chaste
Parthenius

Parthik (Greek) One who is pure; chaste
Parthyk, Parthick, Parthyck, Parthic, Parthyc

Pascal (Latin) Born during Easter
Pascale, Pascalle, Paschal, Paschalis, Pascoe, Pascual, Pascuale, Pasqual

Pastor (English) Man of the church
Pastur, Paster, Pastar, Pastir, Pastyr

Patamon (Native American) Resembling a tempest
Patamun, Patamen, Pataman, Patamyn, Patamin

Patch (American) Form of Peter, meaning "as solid and strong as a rock"
Pach, Patche, Patchi, Patchie, Patchy, Patchey, Patchee

★Patrick (Latin) A nobleman; patrician
Packey, Padric, Pat, Patrece, Patric, Patrice, Patreece, Patricio

Patton (English) From the town of warriors
Paten, Patin, Paton, Patten, Pattin, Paddon, Padden, Paddin

Patwin (Native American) A manly man
Patwinn, Patwinne, Patwyn, Patwynne, Patwynn, Patwen, Patwenn, Patwenne

Paul (Latin) A small or humble man
Pauley, Paulie, Pauly, Paley, Paavo

Paurush (Indian) A courageous man
Paurushe, Paurushi, Paurushie, Paurushy, Paurushey, Paurushee

Pavanjit (Indian) Resembling the wind
Pavanjyt, Pavanjeet, Pavanjeat, Pavanjete

Paxton (English) From the peaceful town
Packston, Paxon, Paxten, Paxtun, Packstun, Packsten

Pazel (Hebrew) God's gold; treasured by God
Pazell, Pazele, Pazelle

Pearroc (English) Man of the forest
Pearoc, Pearrok, Pearok, Pearrock, Pearock

Pecos (American) From the river; a cowboy
Pekos, Peckos

Pedro (Spanish) Form of Peter, meaning "as solid and strong as a rock"
Pedrio, Pepe, Petrolino, Piero, Pietro

Pelham (English) From the house of furs; from Peola's home
Pellham, Pelam, Pellam

Pell (English) A clerk or one who works with skins
Pelle, Pall, Palle

Pelon (Spanish) Filled with joy
Pellon

Pelton (English) From the town by the lake
Pellton, Peltun, Pelltun, Peltan, Pelltan, Pelten, Pellten, Peltin

Penda (African) One who is dearly loved
Pendah, Penha, Penhah

Penley (English) From the enclosed meadow
Penly, Penleigh, Penli, Penlie, Penlee, Penlea, Penleah, Pennley

Penrod (German) A respected commander

Pentele (Hungarian) A merciful man
Pentelle, Pentel, Pentell

Penuel (Hebrew) The face of God
Penuell, Penuele, Penuelle

Percival (French) One who can pierce the vale"
Purcival, Percy, Percey, Perci, Percie, Percee, Percea, Persy, Persey, Persi

Peregrine (Latin) One who travels; a wanderer
Perry, Perree, Perrea, Perri, Perrie, Perregrino

Perez (Hebrew) To break through
Peretz

Pericles (Greek) One who is in excess of glory
Perricles, Perycles, Perrycles, Periclees, Perriclees, Peryclees, Perryclees, Periclez

Perk (American) One who is cheerful and jaunty
Perke, Perky, Perkey, Perki, Perkie, Perkee, Perkea

Perkinson (English) The son of Perkin; the son of Peter
Perkynson

Perseus (Greek) In mythology, son of Zeus who slew Medusa
Persius, Persyus, Persies, Persyes

Perth (Celtic) From the thorny thicket
Perthe, Pert, Perte

Perye (English) From the pear tree

Peter (Greek) As solid and strong as a rock
Peder, Pekka, Per, Petar, Pete, Peterson, Petr, Petre, Pierce, Patch, Pedro

Petuel (Hindi) The Lord's vision
Petuell, Petuele, Petuelle

Peyton (English) From the village of warriors
Payton, Peytun, Paytun, Peyten, Payten, Paiton, Paitun, Paiten

Pharis (Irish) A heroic man
Pharys, Pharris, Pharrys

Phex (American) A kind man
Phexx

Philemon (Hebrew) A loving man
Phylemon, Philimon, Phylimon, Philomon, Phylomon, Philamon, Phylamon

Philetus (Greek) A collector
Phyletus, Philetos, Phyletos

Phillip (Greek) One who loves horses
Phil, Philip, Felipe, Filipp, Phillie, Philly

Philo (Greek) One who loves and is loved

Phoebus (Greek) A radiant man
Phoibos

Phomello (African) A successful man
Phomelo

Phong (Vietnamese) Of the wind

Phuc (Vietnamese) One who is blessed
Phuoc

Picardus (Hispanic) An adventurous man
Pycardus, Picardos, Pycardos, Picardas, Pycardas, Picardis, Pycardis, Picardys

Pickworth (English) From the woodcutter's estate
Pikworth, Picworth, Pickworthe, Pikworthe, Picworthe

Pierce (English) Form of Peter, meaning "as solid and strong as a rock"
Pearce, Pears, Pearson, Pearsson, Peerce, Peirce, Pierson, Piersson

Pin (Vietnamese) Filled with joy
Pyn

Pio (Latin) A pious man
Pyo, Pios, Pius, Pyos, Pyus

Pirro (Greek) A red-haired
man
Pyrro

Pitney (English) From the
island of the stubborn
man
*Pitny, Pitni, Pitnie, Pitnee,
Pitnea, Pytney, Pytny, Pytni*

Pittman (English) A laborer
Pyttman, Pitman, Pytman

Plantagenet (French)
Resembling the broom
flower

Poetry (American) A
romantic man
*Poetrey, Poetri, Poetrie,
Poetree, Poetrea, Poet, Poete*

Pollux (Greek) One who is
crowned
*Pollock, Pollok, Polloc,
Pollack, Polloch*

Polo (African) Resembling
an alligator
Poloe, Poloh

Ponce (Spanish) The fifth-
born child
Ponse

Pongor (Hungarian) A
mighty man
Pongorr, Pongoro, Pongorro

Poni (African) The second-
born son
*Ponni, Ponie, Ponnie, Pony,
Ponny, Poney, Ponney, Ponee*

Pons (Latin) From the bridge
Pontius, Ponthos, Ponthus

Poornamruth (Indian)
Full of sweetness
Pournamruth

Poornayu (Indian) Full of
life; blessed with a full life
*Pournayu, Poornayou,
Pournayou, Poornayue,
Pournayue*

Porat (Hebrew) A productive man

Porfirio (Greek) Refers to a
purple coloring
*Porphirios, Prophyrios,
Porfiro, Porphyrios*

Powhatan (Native
American) From the
chief's hill

Prabhakar (Hindu) Of the
sun

Prabhat (Indian) Born
during the morning

Pragun (Indian) One who
is straightforward; honest

Pramod (Indian) A
delightful young man

Pranit (Indian) One who is
humble; modest
Pranyt, Praneet, Praneat

Prasad (Indian) A gift
from God

Prashant (Indian) One who is peaceful; calm
Prashante, Prashanth, Prashanthe

Pratap (Hindi) A majestic man

Pravat (Thai) History

Prem (Indian) An affectionate man

Prentice (English) A student; an apprentice
Prentyce, Prentise, Prentyse, Prentiss, Prentis

Prescott (English) From the priest's cottage
Prescot, Prestcot, Prestcott, Preostcot

^T**Preston** (English) From the priest's town
Prestin, Prestyn, Prestan, Prestun, Presten, Pfeostun

Prewitt (French) A brave young one
Prewet, Prewett, Prewit, Pruitt, Pruit, Pruet, Pruett

Prine (English) One who surpasses others
Pryne

Prometheus (Greek) In mythology, he stole fire from the heavens and gave it to man
Promitheus, Promethius, Promithius

Prop (American) A fun-loving man
Propp, Proppe

Prosper (Latin) A fortunate man
Prospero, Prosperus

Pryderi (Celtic) Son of the sea
Pryderie, Prydery, Pryderey, Pryderee, Pryderea

Prydwen (Welsh) A handsome man
Prydwenn, Prydwenne, Prydwin, Prydwinne, Prydwinn, Prydwyn, Prydwynn, Prydwynne

Pullman (English) One who works on a train
Pulman, Pullmann, Pulmann

Pyralis (Greek) Born of fire
Pyraliss, Pyralisse, Pyralys, Pyralyss, Pyralysse, Pyre

Qabil (Arabic) An able-bodied man
Qabyl, Qabeel, Qabeal, Qabeil, Qabiel

Qadim (Arabic) From an ancient family
Qadeem, Qadiem, Qadeim, Qadym, Qadeam

Qaiser (Arabic) A king; a ruler
Qeyser

Qamar (Arabic) Born beneath the moon
Qamarr, Quamar, Quamarr

Qimat (Hindi) A highly valued man
Qymat

Qing (Chinese) Of the deep water
Qyng

Quaashie (American) An ambitious man
Quashie, Quashi, Quashy, Quashey, Quashee, Quashea, Quaashi, Quaashy

Quaddus (American) A bright man
Quadus, Quaddos, Quados

Quade (Latin) The fourth-born child
Quadrees, Quadres, Quadrys, Quadries, Quadreis, Quadreys, Quadreas, Quadrhys

Quaid (Irish) Form of Walter, meaning "the commander of the army"
Quaide, Quayd, Quayde, Quaed, Quaede

Quashawn (American) A tenacious man
Quashaun, Quasean, Quashon, Quashi, Quashie, Quashee, Quashea, Quashy

Qued (Native American) Wearing a decorated robe

Quentin (Latin) The fifth-born child
Quent, Quenten, Quenton, Quentun, Quentan, Quentyn, Quente, Qwentin

Quick (American) One who is fast; a witty man
Quik, Quicke, Quic

Quillan (Gaelic) Resembling a cub
Quilan, Quillen, Quilen, Quillon, Quilon

Quilliam (Gaelic) Form of William, meaning "the determined protector"
Quilhelm, Quilhelmus, Quilliams, Quilliamson, Quilliamon, Quillem, Quillhelmus, Quilmot

Quimby (Norse) From the woman's estate
Quimbey, Quimbee, Quimbea, Quimbi, Quimbie

Quincy (English) The fifth-born child; from the fifth son's estate
Quincey, Quinci, Quincie, Quincee, Quinncy, Quinnci, Quyncy, Quyncey

Quinlan (Gaelic) A strong and healthy man
Quindlan, Quinlen, Quindlen, Quinian, Quinlin, Quindlin, Quinlyn, Quindlyn

Quinn (Gaelic) One who provides counsel; an intelligent man
Quin, Quinne, Qwinn, Quynn, Qwin, Quiyn, Quyn, Qwinne

Quintavius (American) The fifth-born child
Quintavios, Quintavus, Quintavies

Quinto (Spanish) The fifth-born child
Quynto, Quintus, Quintos, Quinty, Quinti, Quintie, Quintey, Quintee

Quinton (Latin) From the queen's town or settlement
Laquinton

Quintrell (English) An elegant and dashing man
Quintrel, Quintrelle, Quyntrell, Quyntrelle, Quyntrel, Quyntrele, Quintrele

Quirinus (Latin) One who wields a spear
Quirinos, Quirynus, Quirynos, Quirinius, Quirynius

Quito (Spanish) A lively man
Quyto, Quitos, Quytos

Quoc (Vietnamese) A patriot
Quok, Quock

Qutub (Indian) One who is tall

Rabbaanee (African) An easygoing man

Rabbi (Hebrew) The master

Rach (African) Resembling a frog

Radames (Egyptian) A hero
Radamays, Radamayes, Radamais, Radamaise, Radamaes, Radamaese

Radford (English) From the red ford
Radforde, Radferd, Radfurd, Radferde, Radfurde, Redford, Redforde, Raedford

Rafe (Irish) A tough man
Raffe, Raff, Raf, Raif, Rayfe, Raife, Raef, Raefe

Rafi (Arabic) One who is exalted
Rafie, Rafy, Rafey, Rafea, Rafee, Raffi, Raffie, Raffy

Rafiki (African) A gentle friend
Rafikie, Rafikea, Rafikee, Rafiky, Rafikey

Rafiya (African) A dignified man
Rafeeya, Rafeaya, Rafeiya, Rafieya

Raghib (Arabic) One who is desired
Ragheb, Ragheeb, Ragheab, Raghyb, Ragheib, Raghieb

Ragnar (Norse) A warrior who places judgment
Ragnor, Ragner, Ragnir, Ragnyr, Ragnur, Regnar, Regner, Regnir

Rahim (Arabic) A compassionate man
Rahym, Raheim, Rahiem, Raheem, Raheam

Rahimat (Arabic) Full of grace
Rahymat

Rai (Japanese) A trustworthy man; of lightning and thunder

Raiden (Japanese) In mythology, the god of thunder and lightning
Raidon, Rayden, Raydon, Raeden, Raedon, Raden, Radon, Raijin

Raimi (African) A compassionate man
Raimie, Raimy, Raimey, Raimee, Raimea

Rajab (African) A glorified man

Rajan (Indian) A king
Raj, Raja, Rajah

Rajarshi (Indian) The king's sage
Rajarshie, Rajarshy, Rajarshey, Rajarshee, Rajarshea

Rajesh (Hindi) The king's rule

Rajit (Indian) One who is decorated
Rajeet, Rajeit, Rajiet, Rajyt, Rajeat

Rajiv (Hindi) To be striped
Rajyv, Rajeev, Rajeav

Ralph (English) Wolf counsel
Ralf, Ralphe, Ralfe, Ralphi, Ralphie, Ralphee, Ralphea, Ralphy, Raoul

Ram (Hebrew / Sanskrit) A superior man / one who is pleasing
Rahm, Rama, Rahma, Ramos, Rahmos, Ram, Ramm

Rambert (German) Having great strength; an intelligent man
Ramberte, Ramberth, Ramberthe, Ramburt, Ramburte, Ramburth, Ramburthe, Ramhart

Rami (Arabic) A loving man
Ramee, Ramea, Ramie, Ramy, Ramey

Ramiro (Portuguese) A famous counselor; a great judge
Ramyro, Rameero, Rameyro, Ramirez, Ramyrez, Rameerez

Ramsey (English) From the raven island; from the island of wild garlic
Ramsay, Ramsie, Ramsi, Ramsee, Ramsy, Ramsea, Ramzy, Ramzey

Rand (German) One who shields others
Rande

Randall (German) The wolf shield
Randy, Randal, Randale, Randel, Randell, Randl, Randle, Randon, Rendall

Randolph (German) The wolf shield
Randy, Randolf, Ranolf, Ranolph, Ranulfo, Randulfo, Randwulf, Ranwulf, Randwolf

Randy (English) Form of Randall or Randolph, meaning "the wolf shield"
Randey, Randi, Randie, Randee, Randea

Rang (English) Resembling a raven
Range

Rangey (English) From raven's island
Rangy, Rangi, Rangie, Rangee, Rangea

Rangle (American) A cowboy
Rangel

Ranjan (Indian) A delightful boy

Raoul (French) Form of Ralph, meaning "wolf counsel"
Raoule, Raul, Roul, Rowl, Raule, Roule, Rowle

Raqib (Arabic) A glorified man
Raqyb, Raqeeb, Raqeab, Rakib, Rakeeb, Rakeab, Rakyb

Rashard (American) A good-hearted man
Rasherd, Rashird, Rashurd, Rashyrd

Rashaun (American) Form of Roshan, meaning "born during the daylight"
Rashae, Rashane, Rashawn, Rayshaun, Rayshawn, Raishaun, Raishawn, Raeshaun

Ratul (Indian) A sweet man
Ratule, Ratoul, Ratoule, Ratool, Ratoole

Raulo (Spanish) One who is wise
Rawlo

Ravi (Hindi) From the sun
Ravie, Ravy, Ravey, Ravee,
Ravea

Ravid (Hebrew) A wanderer; one who searches
Ravyd, Raveed, Ravead,
Raviyd, Ravied, Raveid

Ravindra (Indian) The strength of the sun
Ravyndra

Ravinger (English) One who lives near the ravine
Ravynger

Rawlins (French) From the renowned land
Rawlin, Rawson,
Rawlinson, Rawlings,
Rawling, Rawls, Rawl,
Rawle

Ray (English) Form of Raymond, meaning "a wise protector"
Rae, Rai, Rayce, Rayder,
Rayse, Raye, Rayford,
Raylen

Rayfield (English) From the field of roe deer
Rayfeld

Rayhurn (English) From the roe deer's stream
Rayhurne, Rayhorn,
Rayhorne, Rayhourn,
Rayhourne

Raymond (German) A wise protector
Ray, Raemond, Raemondo,
Raimond, Raimondo,
Raimund, Raimundo,
Rajmund, Ramon

Rebel (American) An outlaw
Rebell, Rebele, Rebelle, Rebe,
Rebbe, Rebbi, Rebbie,
Rebbea

Redwald (English) Strong counsel
Redwalde, Raedwalde,
Raedwald

Reeve (English) A bailiff
Reve, Reave, Reeford,
Reeves, Reaves, Reves,
Reaford

Regal (American) Born into royalty
Regall

Regan (Gaelic) Born into royalty; the little ruler
Raegan, Ragan, Raygan,
Reganne, Regann, Regane,
Reghan, Reagan

Regenfrithu (English) A peaceful raven

Reggie (Latin) Form of Reginald, meaning "the king's advisor"
Reggi, Reggy, Reggey,
Reggea, Reggee, Reg

Reginald (Latin) The king's advisor
Reggie, Reynold, Raghnall, Rainault, Rainhold, Raonull, Raynald, Rayniero, Regin, Reginaldo

Regine (French) One who is artistic
Regeen, Regeene, Regean, Regeane, Regein, Regeine, Regien, Regiene

Reid (English) A redhaired man; one who lives near the reeds
Read, Reade, Reed, Reede, Reide, Raed

Reilly (Gaelic) An outgoing man
Reilley, Reilli, Reillie, Reillee, Reilleigh, Reillea

Remington (English) From the town of the raven's family
Remyngton, Remingtun, Remyngtun

Renweard (Anglo-Saxon) The guardian of the house
Renward, Renwarden, Renwerd

Renzo (Japanese) The third-born son

Reuben (Hebrew) Behold, a son!
Reuban, Reubin, Reuven, Rouvin, Rube, Ruben, Rubin, Rubino

Rev (American) One who is distinct
Revv, Revin, Reven, Revan, Revyn, Revon, Revun

Rex (Latin) A king
Reks, Recks, Rexs

Rexford (English) From the king's ford
Rexforde, Rexferd, Rexferde, Rexfurd, Rexfurde

Reynold (English) Form of Reginald, meaning "the king's advisor"
Reynald, Reynaldo, Reynolds, Reynalde, Reynolde

Reza (Iranian) One who is content
Rezah, Rezza, Rezzah

Rhydderch (Welsh) Having reddish-brown hair

★Richard (English) A powerful ruler
Rick, Rich, Ricard, Ricardo, Riccardo, Richardo, Richart, Richerd, Rickard, Rickert

Richmond (French / German) From the wealthy hill / a powerful protector
Richmonde, Richmund, Richmunde

Rick (English) Form of Richard, meaning "a powerful ruler"
Ric, Ricci, Ricco, Rickie, Ricki, Ricky, Rico, Rik

Rickward (English) A strong protector
Rickwerd, Rickwood, Rikward, Ricward, Rickweard, Rikweard, Ricweard

Riddock (Irish) From the smooth field
Ridock, Riddoc, Ridoc, Ryddock, Rydock, Ryddoc, Rydoc, Ryddok

Ridgeway (English) One who lives on the road near the ridge
Rydgeway, Rigeway, Rygeway

Rigg (English) One who lives near the ridge
Rig, Ridge, Rygg, Ryg, Rydge, Rige, Ryge, Riggs

Rio (Spanish) From the river
Reo, Riyo, Reyo, Riao, Ryo

Riordain (Irish) A bright man
Riordane, Riordayn, Riordaen, Reardain, Reardane, Reardayn, Reardaen

Riordan (Gaelic) A royal poet; a bard or minstrel
Riorden, Rearden, Reardan, Riordon, Reardon

Ripley (English) From the noisy meadow
Riply, Ripleigh, Ripli, Riplie, Riplea, Ripleah, Riplee, Rip

Rishley (English) From the untamed meadow
Rishly, Rishli, Rishlie, Rishlee, Rishlea, Rishleah, Rishleigh

Rishon (Hebrew) The first-born son
Ryshon, Rishi, Rishie, Rishea, Rishee, Rishy, Rishey

Risley (English) From the brushwood meadow
Risly, Risli, Rislie, Risleigh, Rislea, Risleah, Rislee, Rizley

Riston (English) From the brushwood settlement
Ryston, Ristun, Rystun

Ritter (German) A knight
Rytter, Ritt, Rytt

River (American) From the river
Ryver, Rivers, Ryvers

Roald (Norse) A famous ruler
Roal

Roam (American) One who wanders, searches
Roami, Roamie, Roamy, Roamey, Roamea, Roamee

Roark (Gaelic) A champion
Roarke, Rorke, Rourke, Rork, Rourk, Ruark, Ruarke

★ᵀRobert (German) One who is bright with fame
Bob, Rupert, Riobard, Roban, Robers, Roberto, Robertson, Robartach, Rûbert

Rochester (English) From the stone fortress

Rockford (English) From the rocky ford
Rockforde, Rokford, Rokforde, Rockferd, Rokferd, Rockfurd, Rokfurd

Roderick (German) A famous ruler
Rod, Rodd, Roddi, Roddie, Roddy, Roddee, Roddea, Roddey

Rodney (German / English) From the famous one's island / from the island's clearing
Rodny, Rodni, Rodnie, Rodnea, Rodnee

Rogelio (Spanish) A famous soldier
Rogelo, Rogeliyo, Rogeleo, Rogeleyo, Rojelio, Rojeleo

Roland (German) From the renowned land
Roeland, Rolando, Roldan, Roley, Rollan, Rolland, Rollie, Rollin

Ronald (Norse) The king's advisor
Ranald, Renaldo, Ronal, Ronaldo, Rondale, Roneld, Ronell, Ronello

Ronan (Gaelic) Resembling a little seal

Rong (Chinese) Having glory

Rook (English) Resembling a raven
Rooke, Rouk, Rouke, Ruck, Ruk

Rooney (Gaelic) A red-haired man
Roony, Rooni, Roonie, Roonea, Roonee, Roon, Roone

Roosevelt (Danish) From the field of roses
Rosevelt

Roper (English) One who makes rope
Rapere

Rory (Gaelic) A red-haired man
Rori, Rorey, Rorie, Rorea, Roree, Rorry, Rorrey, Rorri

Roshan (Hindi) Born during the daylight
Rashaun

Roslin (Gaelic) A little red-haired boy
Roslyn, Rosselin, Rosslyn, Rozlin, Rozlyn, Rosling, Rozling

Roswald (German) Of the mighty horses
Rosswald, Roswalt, Rosswalt

Roswell (English) A fascinating man
Rosswell, Rozwell, Roswel, Rozwel

Roth (German) A red-haired man
Rothe

Rousseau (French) A little red-haired boy
Roussell, Russo, Rousse, Roussel, Rousset, Rousskin

Rowdy (English) A boisterous man
Rowdey, Rowdi, Rowdie, Rowdee, Rowdea

Roy (Gaelic / French) A red-haired man / a king
Roye, Roi, Royer, Ruy

Royce (German / French) A famous man / son of the king
Roice, Royse, Roise

Ruadhan (Irish) A red-haired man; the name of a saint
Ruadan, Ruadhagan, Ruadagan

Ruarc (Irish) A famous ruler
Ruarck, Ruarcc, Ruark, Ruarkk, Ruaidhri, Ruaidri

Rubio (Spanish) Resembling a ruby

Rudeger (German) A friendly man
Rudegar, Rudger, Rudgar, Rudiger, Rudigar

Rudolph (German) A famous wolf
Rodolfo, Rodolph, Rodolphe, Rodolpho, Rudy, Rudey, Rudi, Rudie

Rudyard (English) From the red paddock

Rufus (Latin) A red-haired man
Ruffus, Rufous, Ruffous, Rufino, Ruffino

Ruiz (Spanish) A good friend

Rujul (Indian) An honest man
Rujool, Rujoole, Rujule, Rujoul, Rujoule

Rumford (English) From the broad ford
Rumforde, Rumferd, Rumferde, Rumfurd, Rumfurde

Rupert (English) Form of Robert, meaning "one who is bright with fame"
Ruprecht

Rushford (English) From the ford with rushes
Rusheford, Rushforde, Rusheforde, Ryscford

Russell (French) A little red-haired boy
Russel, Roussell, Russ, Rusel, Rusell

Russom (African) The chief; the boss
Rusom, Russome, Rusome

Rusty (English) One who has red hair or a ruddy complexion
Rustey, Rusti, Rustie, Rustee, Rustea, Rust, Ruste, Rustice

Rutherford (English) From the cattle's ford
Rutherfurd, Rutherferd, Rutherforde, Rutherfurde, Rutherferde

Rutledge (Norse / English) From the red ledge / from the root ledge
Routledge, Rotledge, Rootledge

★ᵀRyan (Gaelic) The little ruler; little king
Rian, Rien, Rion, Ryen, Ryon, Ryun, Rhyan, Rhyen

Ryley (English) From the rye clearing
Ryly, Ryli, Rylie, Rylee, Ryleigh, Rylea, Ryleah, Riley

Ryuji (Japanese) The dragon man
Ryujie, Ryujy, Ryujey, Ryujea, Ryujee

S

Saarik (Hindi) Resembling a small songbird
Saarick, Saaric, Sarik, Sarick, Saric, Saariq, Sareek, Sareeq

Saber (French) Man of the sword
Sabere, Sabr, Sabre

Sabir (Arabic) One who is patient
Sabyr, Sabeer, Sabear, Sabeir, Sabier, Sabri, Sabrie, Sabree

Saddam (Arabic) A powerful ruler; the crusher
Saddum, Saddim, Saddym

Sadiq (Arabic) A beloved friend
Sadeeq, Sadyq, Sadeaq, Sadeek, Sadeak, Sadyk, Sadik

Saga (American) A storyteller
Sago

Sagar (Indian / English) A king / one who is wise
Saagar, Sagarr, Saagarr

Sagaz (Spanish) One who is clever
Sagazz

Sagiv (Hebrew) Having great strength
Sagev, Segiv, Segev

Sahaj (Indian) One who is natural

Saieshwar (Hindi) A well-known saint
Saishwar

Sailor (American) Man who sails the seas
Sailer, Sailar, Saylor, Sayler, Saylar, Saelor, Saeler, Saelar

Saith (English) One who is well-spoken
Saithe, Sayth, Saythe, Saeth, Saethe, Sath, Sathe

Sajal (Indian) Resembling a cloud
Sajall, Sajjal, Sajjall

Sajan (Indian) One who is dearly loved
Sajann, Sajjan, Sajjann

Saki (Japanese) One who is cloaked
Sakie, Saky, Sakey, Sakee, Sakea

Salaam (African) Resembling a peach

Salehe (African) A good man
Saleh, Salih

Salim (Arabic) One who is peaceful
Saleem, Salem, Selim

Salute (American) A patriotic man
Saloot, Saloote, Salout, Saloute

Salvador (Spanish) A savior
Sal, Sally, Salvadore, Xalvador

Samanjas (Indian) One who is proper

Samarth (Indian) A powerful man; one who is efficient
Samarthe

Sameen (Indian) One who is treasured
Samine, Sameene, Samean, Sameane, Samyn, Samyne

Sami (Arabic) One who has been exalted
Samie, Samy, Samey, Samee, Samea

Sammohan (Indian) An attractive man
Sammohane

Sampath (Indian) A wealthy man
Sampathe, Sampat

Samson (Hebrew) As bright as the sun; in the Bible, a man with extraordinary strength
Sampson, Sansom, Sanson, Sansone

★ᵀSamuel (Hebrew) God has heard
Sam, Sammie, Sammy, Samuele, Samuello, Samwell, Samuelo, Sammey

Samuru (Japanese) The name of God

Sandburg (English) From the sandy village
Sandbergh, Sandberg, Sandburgh

Sandon (English) From the sandy hill
Sanden, Sandan, Sandun, Sandyn, Sandin

Sanford (English) From the sandy crossing
Sandford, Sanforde, Sandforde, Sanfurd, Sanfurde, Sandfurd, Sandfurde

Sang (Vietnamese) A bright man
Sange

Sanjiro (Japanese) An admirable man
Sanjyro

Sanjiv (Indian) One who lives a long life
Sanjeev, Sanjyv, Sanjeiv, Sanjiev, Sanjeav, Sanjivan

Sanorelle (American) An honest man
Sanorell, Sanorel, Sanorele

Santana (Spanish) A saintly man
Santanna, Santanah, Santannah, Santa

Santo (Italian) A holy man
Sante, Santino, Santos, Santee, Santi, Santie, Santea, Santy

Santob (Hebrew) One who has a good name
Shemtob

Sapan (Indian) A dream or vision
Sapann

Sar (Anglo-Saxon) One who inflicts pain
Sarlic, Sarlik

Sarbajit (Indian) The conquerer
Sarbajeet, Sarbajyt, Sarbajeat, Sarbajet, Sarvajit, Sarvajeet, Sarvajyt, Sarvajeat

Sarojin (Hindu) Resembling a lotus
Saroj

Sarosh (Persian) One who prays
Saroshe

Satayu (Hindi) In Hinduism, the brother of Amavasu and Vivasu
Satayoo, Satayou, Satayue

Satoshi (Japanese) Born from the ashes
Satoshie, Satoshy, Satoshey, Satoshee, Satoshea

Satparayan (Indian) A good-natured man

Saturn (Latin) In mythology, the god of agriculture
Saturnin, Saturno, Saturnino

Satyankar (Indian) One who speaks the truth
Satyancar, Satyancker

Saville (French) From the willow town
Savil, Savile, Savill, Savyile, Savylle, Savyle, Sauville, Sauvile

Savir (Indian) A great leader
Savire, Saveer, Saveere, Savear, Saveare, Savyr, Savyre

Saxe (Swedish) Man from Saxony
Sachs, Sachsen

Saxon (English) A swordsman
Saxen, Saxan, Saxton, Saxten, Saxtan

Sayad (Arabic) An accomplished hunter

Scadwielle (English) From the shed near the spring
Scadwyelle, Scadwiell, Scadwyell, Scadwiel, Scadwyel, Scadwiele, Scadwyele

Scand (Anglo-Saxon) One who is disgraced
Scande, Scandi, Scandie, Scandee, Scandea

Sceotend (Anglo-Saxon) An archer

Schaeffer (German) A steward
Schaffer, Shaeffer, Shaffer, Schaeffur, Schaffur, Shaeffur, Shaffur

Schelde (English) From the river
Shelde

Schneider (German) A tailor
Shneider, Sneider, Snider, Snyder

Schubert (German) One who makes shoes
Shubert, Schuberte, Shuberte, Schubirt, Shubirt, Schuburt, Shuburt

Scirocco (Italian) Of the warm wind
Sirocco, Scyrocco, Syrocco

Scott (English) A man from Scotland
Scot, Scottie, Scotto, Scotty, Scotti, Scottey, Scottee, Scottea

Scowyrhta (Anglo-Saxon) One who makes shoes

Seabury (English) From the village by the sea
Seaburry, Sebury, Seburry, Seaberry, Seabery, Seberry, Sebery

Seaman (English) A mariner

★Sean (Irish) Form of John, meaning "God is gracious"
Shaughn, Shawn, Shaun, Shon, Shohn, Shonn, Shaundre, Shawnel

Seanachan (Irish) One who is wise

Seanan (Hebrew / Irish) A gift from God / an old, wise man
Sinon, Senen, Siobhan

*Sebastian (Greek) The revered one
Sabastian, Seb, Sebastiano, Sebastien, Sebestyen, Sebo, Sebastyn, Sebestyen

Sedgwick (English) From the place of sword grass
Sedgewick, Sedgewyck, Sedgwyck, Sedgewic, Sedgewik, Sedgwic, Sedgwik, Sedgewyc

Seerath (Indian) A great man
Seerathe, Searath, Searathe

Sef (Egyptian) Son of yesterday
Sefe

Seferino (Greek) Of the west wind
Seferio, Sepherino, Sepherio, Seferyno, Sepheryno

Seignour (French) Lord of the house

Selas (African) Refers to the Trinity
Selassi, Selassie, Selassy, Selassey, Selassee, Selassea

Selestino (Spanish) One who is heaven-sent
Selestyno, Selesteeno, Selesteano

Sellers (English) One who dwells in the marshland
Sellars, Sellurs, Sellirs, Sellyrs

Seminole (Native American) A tribal name
Semynole

Seppanen (Finnish) A blacksmith
Sepanen, Seppenen, Sepenen, Seppanan, Sepanan

September (American) Born in the month of September
Septimber, Septymber, Septemberia, Septemberea

Septimus (Latin) The seventh-born child
Septymus

Seraphim (Hebrew) The burning ones; heavenly winged angels
Sarafino, Saraph, Serafin, Serafino, Seraph, Seraphimus, Serafim

Sereno (Latin) One who is calm; tranquil

Serfati (Hebrew) A man from France
Sarfati, Serfatie, Sarfatie, Serfaty, Sarfaty, Serfatey, Sarfatey, Serfatee

Sergio (Latin) An attendant; a servant
Seargeoh, Serge, Sergei, Sergeo, Sergey, Sergi, Sergios, Sergiu

★Seth (Hebrew) One who has been appointed
Sethe, Seath, Seathe, Zeth

Seung (Korean) A victorious successor

Seven (American) Refers to the number; the seventh-born child
Sevin, Sevyn

Sewati (Native American) Resembling a bear claw
Sewatie, Sewaty, Sewatey, Sewatee, Sewatea

Sexton (English) The church's custodian
Sextun, Sextan, Sextin, Sextyn

Seymour (French) From the French town of Saint Maur
Seamore, Seamor, Seamour, Seymore

Shaan (Hebrew) A peaceful man

Shade (English) A secretive man
Shaid, Shaide, Shayd, Shayde, Shaed, Shaede

Shadi (Persian / Arabic) One who brings happiness and joy / a singer
Shadie, Shady, Shadey, Shadee, Shadea

Shadrach (Hebrew) Under the command of the moon god Aku
Shadrack, Shadrick, Shad, Shadd

Shah (Persian) The king

Shai (Hebrew) A gift from God

Shail (Indian) A mountain rock
Shaile, Shayl, Shayle, Shael, Shaele, Shale

Shaka (African) A tribal leader
Shakah

Shakir (Arabic) One who is grateful
Shakeer, Shaqueer, Shakier, Shakeir, Shakear, Shakar, Shaker, Shakyr

Shakur (Arabic) One who is thankful
Shakurr, Shaku

Shannon (Gaelic) Having ancient wisdom
Shanan, Shanen, Shannan, Shannen, Shanon

Shardul (Indian)
Resembling a tiger
Shardule, Shardull,
Shardulle

Shashi (Indian) Of the
moonbeam
Shashie, Shashy, Shashey,
Shashee, Shashea, Shashhi

Shavon (American) One
who is open-minded
Shavaughn, Shavonne,
Shavaun, Shovon,
Shovonne, Shovaun,
Shovaughn

Shaw (English) From the
woodland
Shawe

Shaykeen (American) A
successful man
Shaykean, Shaykein,
Shakeyn, Shakine

Shea (Gaelic) An
admirable man / from the
fairy fortress
Shae, Shai, Shay, Shaye,
Shaylon, Shays

Sheen (English) A shining
man
Sheene, Shean, Sheane

Sheffield (English) From
the crooked field
Sheffeld

Sheldon (English) From
the steep valley
Shelden, Sheldan, Sheldun,
Sheldin, Sheldyn, Shel

Shelley (English) From the
meadow's ledge
Shelly, Shelli, Shellie,
Shellee, Shellea, Shelleigh,
Shelleah

Shelton (English) From
the farm on the ledge
Shellton, Sheltown, Sheltun,
Shelten, Shelny, Shelney,
Shelni, Shelnie

Shem (Hebrew) Having a
well-known name

Shepherd (English) One
who herds sheep
Shepperd, Shep, Shepard,
Shephard, Shepp, Sheppard

Sheridan (Gaelic) A seeker
Sheredan, Sheridon,
Sherridan, Seireadan,
Sheriden, Sheridun,
Sherard, Sherrard

Sherlock (English) A fair-
haired man
Sherlocke, Shurlock,
Shurlocke

Sherman (English) One
who cuts wool cloth
Shermon, Scherman,
Schermann, Shearman,
Shermann, Sherm, Sherme

Sherrerd (English) From
the open field
Shererd, Sherrard, Sherard

Shields (Gaelic) A faithful
protector
Sheelds, Shealds

Shikha (Indian) A fiery man
Shykha

Shiloh (Hebrew) He who was sent
Shilo, Shyloh, Shylo

Shing (Chinese) A victorious man
Shyng

Shino (Japanese) A bamboo stem
Shyno

Shipton (English) From the ship town; from the sheep town

Shiro (Japanese) The fourth-born son
Shyro

Shorty (American) A man who is small in stature
Shortey, Shorti, Shortie, Shortee, Shortea

Shreshta (Indian) The best; one who is superior

Shubhang (Indian) A handsome man

Shuraqui (Arabic) A man from the east

Siamak (Persian) A bringer of joy
Syamak, Siamack, Syamack, Siamac, Syamac

Sidor (Russian) One who is talented
Sydor

Sierra (Spanish) From the jagged mountain range
Siera, Syerra, Syera, Seyera, Seeara

Sigehere (English) One who is victorious
Sygehere, Sigihere, Sygihere

Sigenert (Anglo-Saxon) A king
Sygenert, Siginert, Syginert

Sigmund (German) The victorious protector
Siegmund, Sigmond, Zsigmond, Zygmunt

Sihtric (Anglo-Saxon) A king
Sihtrik, Sihtrick, Syhtric, Syhtrik, Syhtrick, Sihtryc, Sihtryk, Sihtryck

Sik'is (Native American) A friendly man

Sikyahonaw (Native American) Resembling a yellow bear
Sikyahonau, Sykyahonaw, Sykyahonau

Silny (Czech) Having great strength
Silney, Silni, Silnie, Silnee, Silnea

Simbarashe (African) The power of God
Simbarashi, Simbarashie, Simbarashy, Simbarashey, Simbarashee

Simcha (Hebrew) Filled with joy
Symcha, Simha, Symha

Simmons (Hebrew) The son of Simon
Semmes, Simms, Syms, Simmonds, Symonds, Simpson, Symms, Simson

Simon (Hebrew) God has heard
Shimon, Si, Sim, Samien , Semyon, Simen, Simeon, Simone

Sinai (Hebrew) From the clay desert

Sinclair (English) Man from Saint Clair
Sinclaire, Sinclare, Synclair, Synclaire, Synclare

Singer (American) A vocalist
Synger

Sion (Armenian) From the fortified hill
Sionne, Syon, Syonne

Sirius (Greek) Resembling the brightest star
Syrius

Siyavash (Persian) One who owns black horses
Siyavashe

Skerry (Norse) From the rocky island
Skereye, Skerrey, Skerri, Skerrie, Skerree, Skerrea

Slade (English) Son of the valley
Slaid, Slaide, Slaed, Slaede, Slayd, Slayde

Sladkey (Slavic) A glorious man
Sladky, Sladki, Sladkie, Sladkee, Sladkea

Slavomir (Czech) Of renowned glory
Slavomeer, Slavomyr, Slavomere, Slawomir, Slawomeer, Slawomyr, Slawomere

Smith (English) A blacksmith
Smyth, Smithe, Smythe, Smedt, Smid, Smitty, Smittee, Smittea

Snell (Anglo-Saxon) One who is bold
Snel, Snelle, Snele

Solange (French) An angel of the sun

Solaris (Greek) Of the sun
Solarise, Solariss, Solarisse, Solarys, Solaryss, Solarysse, Solstice, Soleil

Somer (French) Born during the summer
Somers, Sommer, Sommers, Sommar, Somar

Somerset (English) From the summer settlement
Sommerset, Sumerset, Summerset

Songaa (Native American) Having great strength
Songan

Sophocles (Greek) An ancient playwright
Sofocles

Sorley (Irish) Of the summer vikings
Sorly, Sorlee, Sorlea, Sorli, Sorlie

Soumil (Indian) A beloved friend
Soumyl, Soumille, Soumylle, Soumill, Soumyll

Southern (English) Man from the south
Sothern, Suthern

Sovann (Cambodian) The golden son
Sovan, Sovane

Spark (English / Latin) A gallant man / to scatter
Sparke, Sparki, Sparkie, Sparky, Sparkey, Sparkee, Sparkea

Squire (English) A knight's companion; the shield-bearer
Squier, Squiers, Squires, Squyre, Squyres

Stanford (English) From the stony ford
Standford, Standforde, Standforde, Stamford, Stamforde

Stanhope (English) From the stony hollow
Stanhop

Stanton (English) From the stone town
Stantown, Stanten, Staunton, Stantan, Stantun

Stark (German) Having great strength
Starke, Starck, Starcke

Stavros (Greek) One who is crowned

Steadman (English) One who lives at the farm
Stedman, Steadmann, Stedmann, Stedeman

Steed (English) Resembling a stallion
Steede, Stead, Steade

*Stephen (Greek) Crowned with garland
Staffan, Steba, Steben, Stefan, Stefano, Steffan, Steffen, Steffon, **Steven,** *Steve*

Sterling (English) One who is highly valued
Sterlyng, Stirling, Sterlyn

Stian (Norse) A voyager; one who is swift
Stig, Styg, Stygge, Stieran, Steeran, Steeren, Steeryn, Stieren

Stilwell (Anglo-Saxon) From the quiet spring
Stillwell, Stilwel, Stylwell, Styllwell, Stylwel, Stillwel

Stobart (German) A harsh man
Stobarte, Stobarth, Stobarthe

Stockley (English) From the meadow of tree stumps
Stockly, Stockli, Stocklie, Stocklee, Stockleigh, Stocklea, Stockleah, Stocleah

Storm (American) Of the tempest; stormy weather; having an impetuous nature
Storme, Stormy, Stormi, Stormie, Stormey, Stormee, Stormea

Stowe (English) A secretive man
Stow, Stowey, Stowy, Stowee, Stowea, Stowi, Stowie

Stratford (English) From the street near the river ford
Strafford, Stratforde, Straford, Strafforde, Straforde

Stratton (Scottish) A homebody
Straton, Stratten, Straten, Strattan, Stratan, Strattun, Stratun

Strider (English) A great warrior
Stryder

Striker (American) An aggressive man
Strike, Stryker, Stryke

Struthers (Irish) One who lives near the brook
Struther, Sruthair, Strother, Strothers

Stuart (English) A steward; the keeper of the estate
Steward, Stewart, Stewert, Stuert, Stu, Stew

Suave (American) A smooth and sophisticated man
Swave

Subhi (Arabic) Born during the early morning hours
Subhie, Subhy, Subhey, Subhee, Subhea

Suffield (English) From the southern field
Suffeld, Suthfeld, Suthfield

Sullivan (Gaelic) Having dark eyes
Sullavan, Sullevan, Sullyvan

Sully (English) From the southern meadow
Sulley, Sulli, Sullie, Sulleigh, Sullee, Sullea, Sulleah, Suthley

Sultan (African / American) A ruler / one who is bold
Sultane, Sulten, Sultun, Sulton, Sultin, Sultyn

Suman (Hindi) A wise man

Sundiata (African) Resembling a hungry lion
Sundyata, Soundiata, Soundyata, Sunjata

Sundown (American) Born at dusk
Sundowne

Su'ud (Arabic) One who has good luck
Suoud

Swahili (Arabic) Of the coastal people
Swahily, Swahiley, Swahilee, Swahiley, Swaheeli, Swaheelie, Swaheely, Swaheeley

Sylvester (Latin) Man from the forest
Silvester, Silvestre, Silvestro, Sylvestre, Sylvestro, Sly, Sevester, Seveste

Syon (Indian) One who is followed by good fortune

Szemere (Hungarian) A man of small stature
Szemir, Szemeer, Szemear, Szemyr

Tabari (Arabic) A famous historian
Tabarie, Tabary, Tabarey, Tabaree, Tabarea

Tabbai (Hebrew) A well-behaved boy
Tabbae, Tabbay, Tabbaye

Tabbart (German) A brilliant man
Tabbert, Tabart, Tabert, Tahbert, Tahberte

Tacari (African) As strong as a warrior
Tacarie, Tacary, Tacarey, Tacaree, Tacarea

Tadao (Japanese) One who is satisfied

Tadeusuz (Polish) One who is worthy of praise
Tadesuz

Tadi (Native American) Of the wind
Tadie, Tady, Tadey, Tadee, Tadea

Tadzi (American / Polish) Resembling the loon / one who is praised
Tadzie, Tadzy, Tadzey, Tadzee, Tadzea

Taft (French / English) From the homestead / from the marshes
Tafte

Taggart (Gaelic) Son of a priest
Taggert, Taggort, Taggirt, Taggyrt

Taghee (Native American) A chief
Taghea, Taghy, Taghey, Taghi, Taghie

Taheton (Native American) Resembling a hawk

Tahmelapachme (Native American) Wielding a dull knife

Tahoe (Native American) From the big water
Taho

Tahoma (Native American) From the snowy mountain peak
Tehoma, Tacoma, Takoma, Tohoma, Tocoma, Tokoma, Tekoma, Tecoma

Taishi (Japanese) An ambitious man
Taishie, Taishy, Taishey, Taishee, Taishea

Taj (Indian) One who is crowned
Tahj, Tajdar

Tajo (Spanish) Born during the daytime

Taksony (Hungarian) One who is content; well-fed
Taksoney, Taksoni, Taksonie, Taksonee, Taksonea, Tas

Talasi (Native American) Resembling a cornflower
Talasie, Talasy, Talasey, Talasee, Talasea

Talford (English) From the high ford
Talforde, Tallford, Tallforde

Talfryn (Welsh) From the high hill
Talfrynn, Talfrin, Talfrinn, Talfren, Talfrenn, Tallfryn, Tallfrin, Tallfren

Talmai (Hebrew) From the furrows
Talmae, Talmay, Talmaye

Talmon (Hebrew) One who is oppressed
Talman, Talmin, Talmyn, Talmen

Talo (Finnish) From the homestead

Tam (Vietnamese / Hebrew) Having heart / one who is truthful

Taman (Hindi) One who is needed

Tamarius (American) A stubborn man
Tamarias, Tamarios, Tamerius, Tamerias, Tamerios

Tameron (American) Form of Cameron, meaning "having a crooked nose"
Tameren, Tameryn, Tamryn, Tamerin, Tamren, Tamrin, Bamron

Tammany (Native American) A friendly chief
Tammani, Tammanie, Tammaney, Tammanee, Tammanea

Tanafa (Polynesian) A drumbeat

Taneli (Hebrew) He will be judged by God
Tanelie, Tanely, Taneley, Tanelee, Tanelea

Tanish (Indian) An ambitious man
Tanishe, Taneesh, Taneeshe, Taneash, Taneashe, Tanysh, Tanyshe

Tanjiro (Japanese) The prized second-born son
Tanjyro

Tank (American) A man who is big and strong
Tankie, Tanki, Tanky, Tankey, Tankee, Tankea

Tanner (English) One who makes leather
Tannere, Tannor, Tannar, Tannir, Tannyr, Tannur, Tannis

Tannon (German) From the fir tree
Tannan, Tannen, Tannin, Tansen, Tanson, Tannun, Tannyn

Tano (Ghanese) From the river
Tanu

Tao (Chinese) One who will have a long life

Taos (Spanish) From the city in New Mexico

Tapani (Hebrew) A victorious man
Tapanie, Tapany, Tapaney, Tapanee, Tapanea

Tapko (American) Resembling an antelope

Tappen (Welsh) From the top of the cliff
Tappan, Tappon, Tappin, Tappyn, Tappun

Taran (Gaelic) Of the thunder
Taren, Taron, Tarin, Taryn, Tarun

Taranga (Indian) Of the waves

Taregan (Native American) Resembling a crane
Taregen, Taregon, Taregin, Taregyn

Tarit (Indian) Resembling lightning
Tarite, Tareet, Tareete, Tareat, Tareate, Taryt, Taryte

Tarn (Norse) From the mountain pool

Tarquin (Latin) One who is impulsive
Tarquinn, Tarquinne, Tarquen, Tarquenn, Tarquenne, Tarquyn, Tarquynn, Tarquynne

Tarrant (American) One who upholds the law
Tarrent, Tarrint, Tarrynt, Tarront, Tarrunt

Tarun (Indian) A youthful man
Taroun, Taroon, Tarune, Taroune, Taroone

Tashi (Tibetan) One who is prosperous
Tashie, Tashy, Tashey, Tashee, Tashea

Tate (English) A cheerful man; one who brings happiness to others
Tayt, Tayte, Tait, Taite, Taet, Taete

Tausiq (Indian) One who provides strong backing
Tauseeq, Tauseaq, Tausik, Tauseek, Tauseak

Tavaris (American) Of misfortune; a hermit
Tavarius, Tavaress, Tavarious, Tavariss, Tavarous, Tevarus, Tavorian, Tavarian

Tavas (Hebrew) Resembling a peacock

Tavi (Aramaic) A good man
Tavie, Tavy, Tavey, Tavee, Tavea

Tavin (German) Form of Gustav, meaning "of the staff of the gods"
Tavyn, Taven, Tavan, Tavon, Tavun, Tava, Tave

Tawa (Native American) Born beneath the sun
Tawah

Tay (Scottish) From the river
Taye, Tae, Tai

Teagan (Gaelic) A handsome man
Teegan, Teygan, Tegan, Teigan

Tecumseh (Native American) A traveler; resembling a shooting star
Tekumseh, Tecumse, Tekumse

Ted (English) Form of Theodore, meaning "a gift from God"
Tedd, Teddy, Teddi, Teddie, Teddee, Teddea, Teddey, Tedric

Tedmund (English) A protector of the land
Tedmunde, Tedmond, Tedmonde, Tedman, Theomund, Theomond, Theomunde, Theomonde

Teetonka (Native American) One who talks too much
Teitonka, Tietonka, Teatonka, Teytonka

Tegene (African) My protector
Tegeen, Tegeene, Tegean, Tegeane

Teiji (Japanese) One who is righteous
Teijo

Teilo (Welsh) A saintly man

Teka (African) He has replaced

Tekeshi (Japanese) A formidable and brave man
Tekeshie, Tekeshy, Tekeshey, Tekeshee, Tekeshea

Telly (Greek) The wisest man
Telley, Tellee, Tellea, Telli, Tellie

Temman (Anglo-Saxon) One who has been tamed

Temple (Latin) From the sacred place
Tempel, Templar, Templer, Templo

Teneangopte (Native American) Resembling a high-flying bird

Tennant (English) One who rents
Tennent, Tenant, Tenent

Tennessee (Native American) From the state of Tennessee
Tenese, Tenesee, Tenessee, Tennese, Tennesee, Tennesse

Teon (Anglo-Saxon) One who harms others

Terence (Latin) From an ancient Roman clan
Tarrants, Tarrance, Tarrence, Tarrenz, Terencio, Terrance, Terrence, Terrey, Terry, Terron

Teris (Irish) The son of Terence
Terys, Teriss, Teryss, Terris, Terrys, Terriss, Terryss

Terrian (American) One who is strong and ambitious
Terrien, Terriun, Terriyn

Terron (English) Form of Terence, meaning "from an ancient Roman clan"
Tarran, Tarren, Tarrin, Tarron, Tarryn, Teron, Teran

Teshi (African) One who is full of laughter
Teshie, Teshy, Teshey, Teshee, Teshea

Tessema (African) One to whom people listen

Tet (Vietnamese) Born on New Year's

Teteny (Hungarian) A chieftain

Teva (Hebrew) A natural man
Tevah

Texas (Native American) One of many friends; from the state of Texas
Texus, Texis, Texes, Texos, Texys

Teyrnon (Celtic) A regal man
Teirnon, Tayrnon, Tairnon, Taernon, Tiarchnach, Tiarnach

Thabo (African) Filled with happiness

Thackary (English) Form of Zachary, meaning "the Lord remembers"
Thackery, Thakary, Thakery, Thackari, Thackarie, Thackarey, Thackaree, Thackarea

Thaddeus (Aramaic) Having heart
Tad, Tadd, Taddeo, Taddeusz, Thad, Thadd, Thaddaios, Thaddaos

Thandiwe (African) One who is dearly loved
Thandie, Thandi, Thandy, Thandey, Thandee, Thandea

Thang (Vietnamese) One who is victorious

Thanus (American) One who owns land

Thao (Vietnamese) One who is courteous

Thatcher (English) One who fixes roofs
Thacher, Thatch, Thatche, Thaxter, Thacker, Thaker, Thackere, Thakere

Thayer (Teutonic) Of the nation's army

Themba (African) One who is trustworthy
Thembah

Theodore (Greek) A gift from God
Ted, Teddy, Teddie, Theo, Theodor

Theron (Greek) A great hunter
Therron, Tharon, Theon, Tharron

Theseus (Greek) In mythology, hero who slew the Minotaur
Thesius, Thesyus

Thinh (Vietnamese) A prosperous man

★Thomas (Aramaic) One of twins
Tam, Tamas, Tamhas, Thom, Thoma, Thomason, Thomson, Thompson, Tip

Thor (Norse) In mythology, god of thunder
Thorian, Thorin, Thorsson, Thorvald, Tor, Tore, Turo, Thorrin

Thorburn (Norse) Thor's bear
Thorburne, Thorbern, Thorberne, Thorbjorn, Thorbjorne, Torbjorn, Torborg, Torben

Thormond (Norse) Protected by Thor
Thormonde, Thormund, Thormunde, Thurmond, Thurmonde, Thurmund, Thurmunde, Thormun

Thorne (English) From the thorn bush
Thorn

Thornycroft (English) From the field of thorn bushes
Thornicroft, Thorneycroft, Thorniecroft, Thorneecroft, Thorneacroft

Thuong (Vietnamese) One who loves tenderly

Thurston (English) From Thor's town; Thor's stone
Thorston, Thorstan, Thorstein, Thorsten, Thurstain, Thurstan, Thursten, Torsten

Thuy (Vietnamese) One who is kind

Tiassale (African) It has been forgotten

Tiberio (Italian) From the Tiber river
Tibero, Tyberio, Tybero, Tiberius, Tiberios, Tyberius, Tyberios

Tibor (Slavic) From the sacred place

Tiburon (Spanish) Resembling a shark

Tiernan (Gaelic) Lord of the manor
Tiarnan, Tiarney, Tierney, Tierny, Tiernee, Tiernea, Tierni, Tiernie

Tilian (Anglo-Saxon) One who strives to better himself
Tilien, Tiliun, Tilion

Tilon (Hebrew) A generous man
Tilen, Tilan, Tilun, Tilin, Tilyn

Tilton (English) From the fertile estate
Tillton, Tilten, Tillten, Tiltan, Tilltan, Tiltin, Tilltin, Tiltun

Timir (Indian) Born in the darkness
Timirbaran

*Timothy (Greek) One
who honors God
*Tim, Timmo, Timmy,
Timmothy, Timmy, Timo,
Timofei, Timofeo*

Tin (Vietnamese) A great
thinker

Tino (Italian) A man of
small stature
*Teeno, Tieno, Teino, Teano,
Tyno*

Tip (American) A form of
Thomas, meaning "one of
twins"
*Tipp, Tipper, Tippy, Tippee,
Tippea, Tippey, Tippi,
Tippie*

Tisa (African) The ninth-
born child
Tisah, Tysa, Tysah

Titus (Greek / Latin) Of
the giants / a great
defender
*Tito, Titos, Tytus, Tytos,
Titan, Tytan, Tyto*

Toa (Polynesian) A brave-
hearted woman

Toan (Vietnamese) One
who is safe
Toane

Tobbar (American) An
active man

Todd (English) Resembling
a fox
Tod

Todor (Bulgarian) A gift
from God
Todos, Todros

Tohon (Native American)
One who loves the water

Tokala (Native American)
Resembling a fox
Tokalo

Toks (American) A care-
free man

Tomer (Hebrew) A man of
tall stature
*Tomar, Tomur, Tomir,
Tomor, Tomyr*

Tomi (Japanese / African) A
wealthy man / of the people
*Tomie, Tomee, Tomea,
Tomy, Tomey*

Tonauac (Aztec) One who
possesses the light

Torger (Norse) The power
of Thor's spear
*Thorger, Torgar, Thorgar,
Terje, Therje*

Torht (Anglo-Saxon) A
bright man
Torhte

Torin (Celtic) One who acts
as chief
*Toran, Torean, Toren, Torion,
Torran, Torrian, Toryn*

Tormaigh (Irish) Having
the spirit of Thor
*Tormey, Tormay, Tormaye,
Tormai, Tormae*

Torr (English) From the tower
Torre

Torrence (Gaelic) From the little hills
Torence, Torrance, Torrens, Torrans, Toran, Torran, Torrin, Torn, Torry

Torry (Norse / Gaelic) Refers to Thor / form of Torrence, meaning "from the little hills"
Torrey, Torree, Torrea, Torri, Torrie, Tory, Torey, Tori

Toshiro (Japanese) One who is talented and intelligent
Toshihiro

Tostig (English) A well-known earl
Tostyg

Toviel (Hebrew) The Lord is good
Toviell, Toviele, Tovielle, Tovi, Tovie, Tovee, Tovea, Tovy

Toyo (Japanese) A man of plenty

Tracy (Gaelic) One who is warlike
Tracey, Traci, Tracie, Tracee, Tracea, Treacy, Trace, Tracen

Travis (French) To cross over
Travys, Traver, Travers, Traviss, Trevis, Trevys, Travus, Traves

Treffen (German) One who socializes
Treffan, Treffin, Treffon, Treffyn, Treffun

Tremain (Celtic) From the town built of stone
Tramain, Tramaine, Tramayne, Tremaine, Tremayne, Tremaen, Tremaene, Tramaen

Tremont (French) From the three mountains
Tremonte, Tremount, Tremounte

Treoweman (English) A loyal man
Treowe

Trevin (English) From the fair town
Trevan, Treven, Trevian, Trevion, Trevon, Trevyn, Trevonn

Trevor (Welsh) From the large village
Trefor, Trevar, Trever, Treabhar, Treveur, Trevir, Trevur

Trey (English) The third-born child
Tre, Trai, Trae, Tray, Traye, Trayton, Treyton, Trayson

Trigg (Norse) One who is truthful
Trygg

Tripp (English) A traveler
*Trip, Trypp, Tryp, Tripper,
Trypper*

Tripsy (American) One
who enjoys dancing
*Tripsey, Tripsee, Tripsea,
Tripsi, Tripsie*

★Tristan (Celtic) A sorrow-
ful man; in Arthurian leg-
end, a knight of the
Round Table
*Trystan, Tris, Tristam,
Tristen, Tristian, Tristin,
Triston, Tristram*

Trocky (American) A
manly man
*Trockey, Trocki, Trockie,
Trockee, Trockea*

Trong (Vietnamese) One
who is respected

Troy (Gaelic) Son of a foot-
soldier
Troye, Troi

Trumbald (English) A bold
man
*Trumbold, Trumbalde,
Trumbolde*

Trygve (Norse) One who
wins with bravery

Tse (Native American) As
solid as a rock

Tsidhqiyah (Hebrew) The
Lord is just
*Tsidqiyah, Tsidhqiya,
Tsdqiya*

Tsubasa (Japanese) A
winged being
*Tsubasah, Tsubase,
Tsubaseh*

Tucker (English) One who
makes garments
*Tuker, Tuckerman,
Tukerman, Tuck, Tuckman,
Tukman, Tuckere, Toukere*

Tuketu (Native American)
Resembling a running
bear
*Tuketue, Tuketoo, Tuketou,
Telutci, Telutcie, Telutcy,
Telutcey, Telutcee*

Tulsi (Indian) A holy man
*Tulsie, Tulsy, Tulsey, Tulsee,
Tulsea*

Tumaini (African) An opti-
mist
*Tumainie, Tumainee,
Tumainy, Tumainey,
Tumayni, Tumaynie,
Tumaynee, Tumayney*

Tunde (African) One who
returns
*Tundi, Tundie, Tundee,
Tundea, Tundy, Tundey*

Tunleah (English) From
the town near the meadow
*Tunlea, Tunleigh, Tunly,
Tunley, Tunlee, Tunli,
Tunlie*

Tupac (African) A messenger warrior
Tupack, Tupoc, Tupock

Turfeinar (Norse) In mythology, the son of Rognvald
Turfaynar, Turfaenar, Turfanar, Turfenar, Turfainar

Tushar (Indian) Of the snow
Tusharr, Tushare

Tusita (Chinese) One who is heaven-sent

Twrgadarn (Welsh) From the strong tower

Txanton (Basque) Form of Anthony, meaning "a flourishing man; of an ancient Roman family"
Txantony, Txantoney, Txantonee, Txantoni, Txantonie, Txantonea

Tybalt (Latin) He who sees the truth
Tybault, Tybalte, Tybaulte

Tye (English) From the fenced-in pasture
Tyg, Tyge, Tie, Tigh, Teyen

Tyfiell (English) Follower of the god Tyr
Tyfiel, Tyfielle, Tyfiele

★ᵀTyler (English) A tiler of roofs
Tilar, Tylar, Tylor, Tiler, Tilor, Ty, Tye, Tylere

Typhoon (Chinese) Of the great wind
Tiphoon, Tyfoon, Tifoon, Typhoun, Tiphoun, Tyfoun, Tifoun

Tyrone (French) From Owen's land
Terone, Tiron, Tirone, Tyron, Ty, Kyrone

Tyson (French) One who is high-spirited; fiery
Thyssen, Tiesen, Tyce, Tycen, Tyeson, Tyssen, Tysen, Tysan

U

U (Korean) A kind and gentle man

Uaithne (Gaelic) One who is innocent; green
Uaithn, Uaythne, Uaythn, Uathne, Uathn, Uaethne, Uaethn

Ualan (Scottish) Form of Valentine, meaning "one who is strong and healthy"
Ualane, Ualayn, Ualayne, Ualen, Ualon

Uba (African) One who is wealthy; lord of the house
Ubah, Ubba, Ubbah

Uberto (Italian) Form of Hubert, meaning "having a shining intellect"
Ulberto, Umberto

Udath (Indian) One who is
noble
Udathe

Uddam (Indian) An excep-
tional man

Uddhar (Indian) One who
is free; an independent
man
Uddharr, Udhar, Udharr

Udell (English) From the
valley of yew trees
*Udale, Udel, Udall, Udayle,
Udayl, Udail, Udaile, Udele*

Udi (Hebrew) One who
carries a torch
*Udie, Udy, Udey, Udee,
Udea*

Udup (Indian) Born
beneath the moon's light
Udupp, Uddup, Uddupp

Udyan (Indian) Of the gar-
den
*Uddyan, Udyann,
Uddyann*

Ugo (Italian) A great
thinker

Uland (English) From the
noble country
*Ulande, Ulland, Ullande,
Ulandus, Ullandus*

Ulhas (Indian) Filled with
happiness
Ulhass, Ullhas, Ullhass

Ull (Norse) Having glory;
in mythology, god of jus-
tice and patron of agriculture
Ulle, Ul, Ule

Ulmer (German) Having
the fame of the wolf
*Ullmer, Ullmar, Ulmarr,
Ullmarr, Ulfmer, Ulfmar,
Ulfmaer*

Ultman (Indian) A godly
man
Ultmann, Ultmane

Umrao (Indian) One who
is noble

Unai (Basque) A shepherd
Unay, Unaye, Unae

Unathi (African) God is
with us
*Unathie, Unathy, Unathey,
Unathee, Unathea*

Uncas (Native American)
Resembling a fox
Unkas, Unckas

Ungus (Irish) A vigorous
man
Unguss

Unique (American) Unlike
others; the only one
*Unikue, Unik, Uniqui,
Uniqi, Uniqe, Unikque,
Unike, Unicke*

Uolevi (Finnish) Form of Olaf, meaning "the remaining of the ancestors"
Uolevie, Uolevee, Uolevy, Uolevey, Uolevea

Upchurch (English) From the upper church
Upchurche

Uranus (Greek) In mythology, the father of the Titans
Urainus, Uraynus, Uranas, Uraynas, Urainas, Uranos, Uraynos, Urainos

Uri (Hebrew) Form of Uriah, meaning "the Lord is my light"
Urie, Ury, Urey, Uree, Urea

Uriah (Hebrew) The Lord is my light
Uri, Uria, Urias, Urija, Urijah, Uriyah, Urjasz, Uriya

Urjavaha (Hindu) Of the Nimi dynasty

Urtzi (Basque) From the sky
Urtzie, Urtzy, Urtzey, Urtzee, Urtzea

Usbeorn (English) A divine warrior

Usher (Latin) From the mouth of the river
Ushar, Ushir, Ussher, Usshar, Usshir

Ushi (Chinese) As strong as an ox
Ushie, Ushy, Ushey, Ushee, Ushea

Utah (Native American) People of the mountains; from the state of Utah

Utsav (Indian) Born during a celebration
Utsavi, Utsave, Utsava, Utsavie, Utsavy, Utsavey, Utsavee, Utsavea

Utt (Arabic) One who is kind and wise
Utte

Uzi (Hebrew) Having great power
Uzie, Uzy, Uzey, Uzee, Uzea, Uzzi, Uzzie, Uzzy

Uzima (African) One who is full of life
Uzimah, Uzimma, Uzimmah, Uzyma, Uzymma, Uyziema, Uzeima, Uzeema

Uzziah (Hebrew) The Lord is my strength
Uzzia, Uziah, Uzia, Uzzya, Uzzyah, Uzyah, Uzya, Uzziel

V

Vachel (French) Resembling a small cow
Vachele, Vachell

Vachlan (English) One who lives near water

Vadar (Dutch) A fatherly man
Vader, Vadyr

Vadhir (Spanish) Resembling a rose
Vadhyr, Vadheer

Vadim (Russian) A good-looking man
Vadime, Vadym, Vadyme, Vadeem, Vadeeme

Vai (Teutonic) A mighty ruler
Vae

Vaijnath (Hindi) Refers to Lord Shiva
Vaejnath, Vaijnathe, Vaejnathe

Valdemar (German) A well-known ruler
Valdemarr, Valdemare, Valto, Valdmar, Valdmarr, Valdimar, Valdimarr

Valentine (Latin) One who is strong and healthy
Val, Valentin, Valentino, Valentyne, Ualan

Valerian (Latin) One who is strong and healthy
Valerien, Valerio, Valerius, Valery, Valeryan, Valere, Valeri, Valerii

Valin (Hindi) The monkey king

Valle (French) From the glen
Vallejo

Valri (French) One who is strong
Valrie, Valry, Valrey, Valree

Vance (English) From the marshland
Vanse

Vanderveer (Dutch) From the ferry
Vandervere, Vandervir, Vandervire, Vandervyr, Vandervyre

Vandy (Dutch) One who travels; a wanderer
Vandey, Vandi, Vandie, Vandee

Vandyke (Danish) From the dike
Vandike

Vanir (Norse) Of the ancient gods

Varante (Arabic) From the river

Vardon (French) From the green hill
Varden, Verdon, Verdun, Verden, Vardun, Vardan, Verddun, Varddun

Varg (Norse) Resembling a wolf

Varick (German) A protective ruler
Varrick, Warick, Warrick

Varius (Latin) A versatile man
Varian, Varinius

Variya (Hindi) The excellent one

Vasava (Hindi) Refers to Indra

Vaschel (Hebrew) From the small ash tree

Vashon (American) The Lord is gracious
Vashan, Vashawn, Vashaun, Vashone, Vashane, Vashayn, Vashayne

Vasin (Indian) A great ruler
Vasine, Vaseen, Vaseene, Vasyn, Vasyne

Vasuki (Hindi) In Hinduism, a serpent king
Vasukie, Vasuky, Vasukey, Vasukee, Vasukea

Vasuman (Indian) Son born of fire

Vasyl (Slavic) A king
Vasil, Vassil, Wasyl

Vatsa (Indian) Our beloved son
Vathsa

Vatsal (Indian) One who is affectionate

Velimir (Croatian) One who wishes for great peace
Velimeer, Velimyr, Velimire, Velimeere, Velimyre

Velyo (Bulgarian) A great man
Velcho, Veliko, Velin, Velko

Vere (French) From the alder tree

Verge (Anglo-Saxon) One who owns four acres

Vernon (French) From the alder-tree grove
Vern, Vernal, Vernard, Verne, Vernee, Vernen, Verney, Vernin

Verrill (French) One who is faithful
Verill, Verrall, Verrell, Verroll, Veryl, Veryll, Verol, Verall

Vibol (Cambodian) A man of plenty
Viboll, Vibole, Vybol, Vyboll, Vybole

Vid (Hungarian) Form of Vito, meaning "one who gives life"
Vida, Vidas, Vidal

Vidal (Spanish) A giver of life
Videl, Videlio, Videlo, Vidalo, Vidalio, Vidas

Vidar (Norse) Warrior of the forest; in mythology, a son of Odin
Vidarr

Vien (Vietnamese) One who is complete; satisfied

Viho (Native American) One who ranks as chief

Vincent (Latin) One who prevails; the conquerer
Vicente, Vicenzio, Vicenzo, Vin, Vince, Vincens, Vincente, Vincentius

Vinod (Indian) One who is a pleasure

Viorel (Romanian) Resembling the bluebell
Viorell, Vyorel, Vyorell

Vipin (Indian) From the forest
Vippin, Vypin, Vypyn, Vyppin, Vyppyn, Vipyn, Vippyn

Vipul (Indian) A man of plenty
Vypul, Vipull, Vypull, Vipool, Vypool

Virag (Hungarian) Resembling a flower

Virgil (Latin) The staff-bearer
Verge, Vergil, Vergilio, Virgilio, Vergilo, Virgilo, Virgilijus

Virginius (Latin) One who is pure; chaste
Virginio, Virgino

Virote (Thai) A powerful man

Vitéz (Hungarian) A courageous warrior

Vito (Latin) One who gives life
Vital, Vitale, Vitalis, Vitaly, Vitas, Vitus, Vitali, Vitaliy, Vid

Vitus (Latin) Giver of life
Wit

Vladimir (Slavic) A famous prince
Vladamir, Vladimeer, Vladimyr, Vladimyre, Vladamyr, Vladamyre, Vladameer, Vladimer

Vladislav (Slavic) One who rules with glory

Volodymyr (Slavic) To rule with peace
Wolodymyr

Vulcan (Latin) In mythology, the god of fire
Vulkan, Vulckan

Vyacheslav (Russian) Form of Wenceslas, meaning "one who receives more glory"

W

Wade (English) To cross the river ford
Wayde, Waid, Waide, Waddell, Wadell, Waydell, Waidell, Waed

Wadley (English) From the meadow near the ford
Wadly, Wadlee, Wadli, Wadlie, Wadleigh

Wadsworth (English) From
the estate near the ford
*Waddsworth, Wadsworthe,
Waddsworthe*

Wafi (Arabic) One who is
trustworthy
*Wafie, Wafy, Wafey, Wafee,
Wafiy, Wafiyy*

Wahab (Indian) A big-
hearted man

Wahchinksapa (Native
American) Having great
wisdom
*Wachinksapa,
Wahchinksap, Wachinksap*

Wainwright (English) One
who builds wagons
*Wainright, Wainewright,
Wayneright, Waynewright,
Waynwright*

Wakil (Arabic) A lawyer; a
trustee
*Wakill, Wakyl, Wakyle,
Wakeel, Wakeele*

Wakiza (Native American)
A desperate fighter
*Wakyza, Wakeza, Wakieza,
Wakeiza*

Walbridge (English) From
the Welshman's bridge
*Wallbridge, Walbrydge,
Wallbrydge*

Waljan (Welsh) The cho-
sen one
*Walljan, Waljen, Walljen,
Waljon, Walljon*

Walker (English) One who
trods the cloth
Walkar, Walkir, Walkor

Walter (German) The com-
mander of the army
*Walther, Walt, Walte,
Walder, Wat, Wouter, Wolter,
Woulter, Galtero, Quaid*

Wamblee (Native American)
Resembling an eagle
*Wambli, Wamblie, Wambly,
Wambley, Wambleigh,
Wamblea*

Wanikiy (Native American)
A savior
*Wanikiya, Wanikie,
Wanikey, Waniki, Wanikee*

Wanjala (African) Born
during a famine
Wanjalla, Wanjal, Wanjall

Warford (English) From
the ford near the weir
*Warforde, Weirford,
Weirforde, Weiford, Weiforde*

Warley (English) From the
meadow near the weir
*Warly, Warleigh, Warlee,
Warlea, Warleah, Warli,
Warlie, Weirley*

Warner (German) Of the
defending army
*Werner, Wernher, Warnher,
Worner, Wornher*

Warra (Aboriginal) Man of
the water
Warrah, Wara, Warah

Warrick (English) Form of Varick, meaning "a protective ruler"
Warrik, Warric, Warick, Warik, Waric, Warryck, Warryk, Warryc

Warrigal (Aboriginal) One who is wild
Warrigall, Warigall, Warigal, Warygal, Warygall

Warrun (Aboriginal) Of the sky
Warun

Warwick (English) From the farm near the weir
Warwik, Warwyck, Warwyk

Wasswa (African) The firstborn of twins
Waswa, Wasswah, Waswah

Wasyl (Ukranian) Form of Vasyl, meaning "a king"
Wasyle, Wasil, Wasile

Watson (English) The son of Walter
Watsin, Watsen, Watsan, Watkins, Watckins, Watkin, Watckin, Wattekinson

Wayne (English) One who builds wagons
Wain, Wanye, Wayn, Waynell, Waynne, Guwayne

Webster (English) A weaver
Weeb, Web, Webb, Webber, Weber, Webbestre, Webestre, Webbe

Wei (Chinese) A brilliant man; having great strength

Wenceslas (Polish) One who receives more glory
Wenceslaus, Wenzel, Vyacheslav

Wendell (German) One who travels; a wanderer
Wendel, Wendale, Wendall, Wendele, Wendal, Windell, Windel, Windal

Wesley (English) From the western meadow
Wes, Wesly, Wessley, Westleigh, Westley, Wesli, Weslie, Wesleigh

Westby (English) From the western farm
Westbey, Wesby, Wesbey, Westbi, Wesbi, Westbie, Wesbie, Westbee

Wharton (English) From the settlement near the weir
Warton, Wharten, Warten, Whartun, Wartun

Whit (English) A white-skinned man
White, Whitey, Whitt, Whitte, Whyt, Whytt, Whytte, Whytey

Whitby (English) From the white farm
Whitbey, Whitbi, Whitbie, Whitbee, Whytbey, Whytby, Whytbi, Whytbie

Whitfield (English) From
the white field
*Whitfeld, Whytfield,
Whytfeld, Witfield, Witfeld,
Wytfield, Wytfeld*

Whitley (English) From
the white meadow
*Whitly, Whitli, Whitlie,
Whitlee, Whitleigh,
Whytley, Whytly, Whytli*

Whitman (English) A
white-haired man
*Whitmann, Witman,
Witmann, Whitmane,
Witmane, Whytman,
Whytmane, Wytman*

Wildon (English) From the
wooded hill
Willdon, Wilden, Willden

Wiley (English) One who
is crafty; from the mead-
ow by the water
*Wily, Wileigh, Wili, Wilie,
Wilee, Wylie, Wyly, Wyley*

Wilford (English) From the
willow ford
*Willford, Wilferd, Willferd,
Wilf, Wielford, Weilford,
Wilingford, Wylingford*

★ᵀWilliam (German) The
determined protector
*Wilek, Wileck, Wilhelm,
Wilhelmus, Wilkes, Wilkie,
Wilkinson, Will, Guillaume,
Quilliam*

Willow (English) Of the
willow tree
Willowe, Willo, Willoe

Wilmer (German) A strong-
willed and well-known man
*Wilmar, Wilmore, Willmar,
Willmer, Wylmer, Wylmar,
Wyllmer, Wyllmar*

Winston (English) Of the joy
stone; from the friendly town
*Win, Winn, Winsten,
Winstonn, Wynstan,
Wynsten, Wynston, Winstan*

Winthrop (English) From
the friendly village
*Winthrope, Wynthrop,
Wynthrope, Winthorp,
Wynthorp*

Winton (English) From the
enclosed pastureland
*Wintan, Wintin, Winten,
Wynton, Wyntan, Wyntin,
Wynten*

Wirt (Anglo-Saxon) One
who is worthy
*Wirte, Wyrt, Wyrte, Wurt,
Wurte*

Wissian (Anglo-Saxon)
One who guides others

Wit (Polish) Form of Vitus,
meaning "giver of life"
Witt

Wlodzimierz (Polish) To
rule with peace
Wlodzimir, Wlodzimerz

Wolfric (German) A wolf ruler
*Wolfrick, Wolfrik, Wulfric,
Wulfrick, Wulfrik, Wolfryk,
Wolfryck, Wolfryc*

Wolodymyr (Ukranian)
Form of Volodymyr, mean-
ing "to rule with peace"
*Wolodimyr, Wolodimir,
Wolodymeer, Wolodimeer*

Woorak (Aboriginal) From
the plains
Woorack, Woorac

★Wyatt (English) Having
the strength of a warrior
*Wyat, Wyatte, Wyate, Wiatt,
Wiatte, Wiat, Wiate, Wyeth*

Wyndham (English) From
the windy village
Windham

Xakery (American) Form
of Zachery, meaning "the
Lord remembers"
*Xaccary, Xaccery, Xach,
Xacharie, Xachery, Xack,
Xackarey, Xackary*

Xalvador (Spanish) Form of
Salvador, meaning "a savior"
*Xalvadore, Xalvadoro,
Xalvadorio, Xalbador,
Xalbadore, Xalbadorio,
Xalbadoro, Xabat*

Xannon (American) From
an ancient family
*Xanon, Xannen, Xanen,
Xannun, Xanun*

Xanthus (Greek) A blond-
haired man
Xanthos, Xanthe, Xanth

★Xavier (Basque / Arabic)
Owner of a new house /
one who is bright
*Xaver, Xever, Xabier,
Xaviere, Xabiere, Xaviar,
Xaviare, Xavior*

Xenocrates (Greek) A foreign ruler

Xesus (Galician) Form of
Jesus, meaning "God is
my salvation"

Xoan (Galician) Form of
John, meaning "God is
gracious"
Xoane, Xohn, Xon

Xue (Chinese) A studious
young man

Xun (Chinese) One who is
swift

Yael (Israeli) Strength of
God
Yaele

Yagil (Hebrew) One who
rejoices, celebrates
Yagill, Yagyl, Yagylle

Yahto (Native American)
Having blue eyes; refers to
the color blue
Yahtoe, Yahtow, Yahtowe

Yahweh (Hebrew) Refers
to God
*Yahveh, Yaweh, Yaveh,
Yehowah, Yehweh, Yehoveh*

Yakiv (Ukranian) Form of
Jacob, meaning "he who
supplants"
*Yakive, Yakeev, Yakeeve,
Yackiv, Yackeev, Yakieve,
Yakiev, Yakeive*

Yakout (Arabian) As precious as a ruby

Yale (Welsh) From the fertile upland
Yayle, Yayl, Yail, Yaile

Yanai (Aramaic) God will
answer
Yanae, Yana, Yani

Yankel (Hebrew) Form of
Jacob, meaning "he who
supplants"
*Yankell, Yanckel, Yanckell,
Yankle, Yanckle*

Yaotl (Aztec) A great war-
rior
*Yaotyl, Yaotle, Yaotel,
Yaotyle*

Yaphet (Hebrew) A handsome man
Yaphett, Yapheth, Yaphethe

Yaqub (Arabic) Form of
Jacob, meaning "he who
supplants"
Ya'qub, Yaqob, Yaqoub

Yardley (English) From the
fenced-in meadow
*Yardly, Yardleigh, Yardli,
Yardlie, Yardlee, Yardlea,
Yarley, Yarly*

Yaromir (Russian) Form of
Jaromir, meaning "from
the famous spring"
*Yaromire, Yaromeer,
Yaromeere, Yaromyr,
Yaromyre*

Yas (Native American)
Child of the snow

Yasahiro (Japanese) One
who is peaceful and calm

Yasin (Arabic) A wealthy
man
*Yasine, Yaseen, Yaseene,
Yasyn, Yasyne, Yasien,
Yasiene, Yasein*

Yasir (Arabic) One who is
well-off financially
*Yassir, Yasser, Yaseer, Yasr,
Yasyr, Yassyr, Yasar, Yassar*

Yaw (African) Born on a
Thursday
Yawo, Yao

Yegor (Russian) Form of George, meaning "one who works the earth; a farmer" *Yegore, Yegorr, Yegeor, Yeorges, Yeorge, Yeorgis*

Yehonadov (Hebrew) A gift from God *Yehonadav, Yehonedov, Yehonedav, Yehoash, Yehoashe, Yeeshai, Yeeshae, Yishai*

Yenge (African) A hard-working man *Yengi, Yengie, Yengy, Yengey, Yengee*

Yeoman (English) A man-servant *Youman, Yoman*

Yestin (Welsh) One who is just and fair *Yestine, Yestyn, Yestyne*

Yigil (Hebrew) He shall be redeemed *Yigile, Yigyl, Yigyle, Yigol, Yigole, Yigit, Yigat*

Yishachar (Hebrew) He will be rewarded *Yishacharr, Yishachare, Yissachar, Yissachare, Yisachar, Yisachare*

Yiska (Native American) The night has gone

Yngve (Scandinavian) Refers to the god Ing

Yo (Cambodian) One who is honest

Yoav (Hebrew) Form of Joab, meaning "the Lord is my father" *Yoave, Yoavo, Yoavio*

Yochanan (Hebrew) Form of John, meaning "God is gracious" *Yochan, Yohannan, Yohanan, Yochannan*

Yohan (German) Form of John, meaning "God is gracious" *Yohanan, Yohann, Yohannes, Yohon, Yohonn, Yohonan*

Yonatan (Hebrew) Form of Jonathan, meaning "a gift of God" *Yonaton, Yohnatan, Yohnaton, Yonathan, Yonathon, Yoni, Yonie, Yony*

Yong (Korean) One who is courageous

York (English) From the yew settlement *Yorck, Yorc, Yorke*

Yosyp (Ukranian) Form of Joseph, meaning "God will add" *Yosip, Yosype, Yosipe*

Yovanny (English) Form of Giovanni, meaning "God is gracious"
Yovanni, Yovannie, Yovannee, Yovany, Yovani, Yovanie, Yovanee

Yukon (English) From the settlement of gold
Youkon, Yucon, Youcon, Yuckon, Youckon

Yuliy (Russian) Form of Julius, meaning "one who is youthful"
Yuli, Yulie, Yulee, Yuleigh, Yuly, Yuley, Yulika, Yulian

Yuudai (Japanese) A great hero
Yudai, Yuudae, Yudae, Yuuday, Yuday

Yves (French) A young archer
Yve, Yvo, Yvon, Yvan, Yvet, Yvete

Zabian (Arabic) One who worships celestial bodies
Zabion, Zabien, Zaabian

Zabulon (Hebrew) One who is exalted
Zabulun, Zabulen

Zacchaeus (Hebrew) Form of Zachariah, meaning "The Lord remembers"
Zachaeus, Zachaios, Zaccheus, Zackaeus, Zacheus, Zackaios, Zaccheo

Zachariah (Hebrew) The Lord remembers
Zacaria, Zacarias, Zaccaria, Zaccariah, Zachaios, Zacharia, Zacharias, Zacherish

★ᵀ**Zachary** (Hebrew) Form of Zachariah, meaning "The Lord remembers"
Zaccary, Zaccery, Zach, Zacharie, Zachery, Zack, Zackarey, Zackary, Thackary, Xakery

Zaci (African) In mythology, the god of fatherhood

Zaden (Dutch) A sower of seeds
Zadin, Zadan, Zadon, Zadun, Zede, Zeden, Zedan

Zadok (Hebrew) One who is righteous; just
Zadoc, Zaydok, Zadock, Zaydock, Zaydoc, Zaidok, Zaidock, Zaidoc

Zador (Hungarian) An ill-tempered man
Zador, Zadoro, Zadorio

Zafar (Arabic) The conquerer; a victorious man
Zafarr, Zaffar, Zhafar, Zhaffar, Zafer, Zaffer

Zahid (Arabic) A pious man
Zahide, Zahyd, Zahyde, Zaheed, Zaheede, Zaheide, Zahiede, Zaheid

Zahir (Arabic) A radiant and flourishing man
Zahire, Zahireh, Zahyr, Zahyre, Zaheer, Zaheere, Zaheir, Zahier

Zahur (Arabic) Resembling a flower
Zahure, Zahureh, Zhahur, Zaahur

Zale (Greek) Having the strength of the sea
Zail, Zaile, Zayl, Zayle, Zael, Zaele

Zamir (Hebrew) Resembling a songbird
Zamire, Zameer, Zameere, Zamyr, Zamyre, Zameir, Zameire, Zamier

Zander (Slavic) Form of Alexander, meaning "a helper and defender of mankind"
Zandros, Zandro, Zandar, Zandur, Zandre

Zanebono (Italian) The good son
Zanbono, Zaynebono, Zaynbono, Zainebono, Zainbono, Zaenebono, Zaenbono

Zareb (African) The protector; guardian
Zarebb, Zaareb, Zarebe, Zarreb, Zareh, Zaareh

Zared (Hebrew) One who has been trapped
Zarede, Zarad, Zarade, Zaared, Zaarad

Zasha (Russian) A defender of the people
Zashah, Zosha, Zoshah, Zashiya, Zoshiya

Zebenjo (African) One who strives to avoid sinning
Zebinjo, Zebenjoe, Zebinjoe

Zeke (English) Form of Ezekiel, meaning "strengthened by God"
Zekiel, Zeek, Zeeke, Zeeq

Zene (African) A handsome man
Zeene, Zeen, Zein, Zeine

Zereen (Arabic) The golden one
Zereene, Zeryn, Zeryne, Zerein, Zereine, Zerrin, Zerren, Zerran

Zeroun (Armenian) One who is respected for his wisdom
Zeroune, Zeroon, Zeroone

Zeth (English) Form of Seth, meaning "one who has been appointed"
Zethe

Ziff (Hebrew) Resembling a wolf
Ziffe, Zif, Zife, Zyf, Zyff, Zyfe, Zyffe

Ziv (Hebrew) A radiant man
Zive, Ziiv, Zivi, Zivie, Zivee, Zivy, Zivey

Ziyad (Arabic) One who betters himself; growth
Ziad

Zlatan (Croatian) The golden son
Zlattan, Zlatane, Zlatann, Zlatain, Zlatayn, Zlaten, Zlaton, Zlatin

Zoan (African) One who takes leave
Zoane

Zoltan (Hungarian) A kingly man; a sultan
Zoltann, Zoltane, Zoltanne, Zsolt, Zsoltan

Zorion (Basque) Filled with happiness
Zorian, Zorien

Zoticus (Greek) Full of life
Zoticos, Zoticas

Zsigmond (Hungairan) Form of Sigmund, meaning "the victorious protector"
Zsigmund, Zsigmonde, Zsigmunde, Zsig, Zsiga

Zubair (Arabic) One who is pure
Zubaire, Zubayr, Zubayre, Zubar, Zubarr, Zubare, Zubaer

Zuberi (African) Having great strength
Zuberie, Zubery, Zuberey, Zuberee, Zubari, Zubarie, Zubary, Zubarey

Zubin (English) One with a toothy grin
Zubine, Zuben, Zuban, Zubun, Zubbin

Zuzen (Basque) One who is just and fair
Zuzenn, Zuzan, Zuzin

Zvonimir (Croatian) The sound of peace
Zvonimirr, Zvonimeer, Zvonimire, Zvonmeere, Zvonimer, Zvonko, Zvoncko

Zygmunt (Polish) Form of Sigmund, meaning "the victorious protector" Zygmund, Zygmont, Zygmond, Zygmunte, Zygmonde, Zygmunde, Zygmonte

Girls

Aadi (Hindi) Child of the beginning
Aadie, Aady, Aadey, Aadee, Aadea, Aadeah, Aadye

Aaralyn (American) Woman with song
Aaralynn, Aaralin, Aaralinn, Aaralinne, Aralyn, Aralynn

Aba (African) Born on a Thursday
Abah, Abba, Abbah

Abarrane (Hebrew) Feminine form of Abraham; mother of a multitude; mother of nations
Abarrayne, Abarraine, Abarane, Abarayne, Abaraine, Abame, Abrahana

Abena (African) Born on a Tuesday
Abenah, Abeena, Abyna, Abina, Abeenah, Abynah, Abinah

Abertha (Welsh) One who is sacrificed
Aberthah

Abhilasha (Hindi) One who is desired
Abhilashah, Abhylasha, Abhylashah

Abiba (African) First child born after the grandmother has died
Abibah, Abeeba, Abyba, Abeebah, Abybah, Abeiba, Abeibah, Abieba

Abiela (Hebrew) My father is Lord
Abielah, Abiella, Abiellah, Abyela, Abyelah, Abyella, Abyellah

★ᵀ**Abigail** (Hebrew) The source of a father's joy
Abbigail, Abigael, Abigale, Abbygail, Abygail, Abygayle, Abbygayle, Abbegale, Abby

Abijah (Hebrew) My father is Lord
Abija, Abisha, Abishah, Abiah, Abia, Aviah, Avia

Abila (Spanish) One who is beautiful
Abilah, Abyla, Abylah

Abilene (American / Hebrew) From a town in Texas / resembling grass
Abalene, Abalina, Abilena, Abiline, Abileene, Abileen, Abileena, Abilyn

Abir (Arabic) Having a fragrant scent
Abeer, Abyr, Abire, Abeere, Abbir, Abhir

Abira (Hebrew) A source of strength; one who is strong
Abera, Abyra, Abyrah, Abirah, Abbira, Abeerah, Abhira

Abra (Hebrew / Arabic) Feminine form of Abraham; mother of a multitude; mother of nations / lesson; example
Abri, Abrah, Abree, Abria, Abbra, Abrah, Abbrah

Academia (Latin) From a community of higher learning
Akademia, Academiah, Akademiah

Acantha (Greek) Thorny; in mythology, a nymph who was loved by Apollo
Akantha, Ackantha, Acanthah, Akanthah, Ackanthah

Accalia (Latin) In mythology, the foster mother of Romulus and Remus
Accaliah, Acalia, Accalya, Acalya, Acca, Ackaliah, Ackalia

Adah (Hebrew) Ornament; beautiful addition to the family
Adda, Adaya, Ada

Adanna (African) Her father's daughter; a father's pride
Adana, Adanah, Adannah, Adanya, Adanyah

Adanne (African) Her mother's daughter; a mother's pride
Adane, Adayne, Adaine, Adayn, Adain, Adaen, Adaene

Adaoma (Ibo) A good woman

Adara (Greek / Arabic) Beautiful girl / chaste one; virgin
Adair, Adare, Adaire, Adayre, Adarah, Adarra, Adaora, Adar

Addin (Hebrew) One who is adorned; voluptuous
Addine, Addyn, Addyne

Adeen (Irish) Little fire shining brightly
Adeene, Adean, Adeane, Adein, Adeine, Adeyn, Adeyne

Adela (German) Of the nobility; serene; of good humor
Adele, Adelia, Adella, Adelle, Adalene, Adelie, Adelina, Adali

Adelpha (Greek) Beloved sister
Adelfa, Adelphe, Adelphie

Adeola (African) One who wears a crown of honor
Adeolah, Adeolla, Adeollah

Adhelle (Teutonic) Lovely
and happy woman
*Adhella, Adhell, Adhele,
Adhela*

Adianca (Native American)
One who brings peace
Adianka, Adyanca, Adyanka

Adira (Hebrew / Arabic)
Powerful, noble woman /
having great strength
*Adirah, Adeera, Adyra,
Adeerah, Adyrah, Adeira,
Adeirah, Adiera*

Admina (Hebrew)
Daughter of the red earth
*Adminah, Admeena,
Admyna, Admeenah,
Admynah, Admeina,
Admeinah, Admiena*

Adolpha (German)
Feminine form of Adolph;
noble she-wolf
*Adolfa, Adolphina,
Adolfina, Adolphine,
Adolfine, Adoqhina*

Adoración (Spanish)
Having the adoration of all

Adra (Arabic) One who is
chaste; a virgin
Adrah

Adrasteia (Greek) One
who will not run away; in
mythology, another name
for Nemesis, the goddess
of vengeance

Adrina (Italian) Having
great happiness
*Adrinna, Adreena, Adrinah,
Adryna, Adreenah, Adrynah*

Aegea (Latin / Greek)
From the Aegean Sea / in
mythology, a daughter of
the sun who was known
for her beauty

Aegina (Greek) In mythology, a sea nymph
Aeginae, Aegyna, Aegynah

Aelfwine (English) A
friend of the elves
*Aelfwyne, Aethelwine,
Aethelwyne*

Aelwen (Welsh) Woman
with a fair brow
*Aelwenn, Aelwenne, Aelwin,
Aelwinn, Aelwinne, Aelwyn,
Aelwynn, Aelwynne*

Aerwyna (English) A
friend of the ocean

Afra (Hebrew / Arabic)
Young doe / white; an
earth color
*Affra, Affrah, Afrah, Afrya,
Afryah, Afria, Affery, Affrie*

Afreda (English / Arabic)
Elf counselor / one who is
created
*Afredah, Afreeda, Aafreeda,
Afrida, Afridah, Aelfraed,
Afreedah, Afryda*

Afrodille (French) Daffodil; showy and vivid
Afrodill, Afrodil, Afrodile, Afrodilla, Afrodila

Afton (English) From the Afton river

Agave (Greek) In mythology, a queen of Thebes

Agnes (Greek) One who is pure; chaste
Agneis, Agnese, Agness, Agnies, Agnus, Agna, Agne, Agnesa, Nessa, Oona

Agraciana (Spanish) One who forgives
Agracianna, Agracyanna, Agracyana, Agraciann, Agraciane, Agracyann, Agracyane, Agracianne

Agrona (Celtic) In mythology, the goddess of war and death
Agronna, Agronia, Agrone

Agurtzane (Basque) Refers to the Virgin Mary; chaste; pure
Aitziber

Ahelia (Hebrew) Breath; a source of life
Ahelie, Ahelya, Aheli, Ahelee, Aheleigh, Ahelea, Aheleah, Ahely

Ahellona (Greek) Woman who has masculine qualities
Ahelona, Ahellonna, Ahelonna

Ahinoam (Hebrew) In the Bible, one of David's wives

Ahuva (Hebrew) One who is dearly loved
Ahuvah, Ahuda, Ahudah

Aiandama (Estonian) Woman who gardens

Aida (English / French / Arabic) One who is wealthy; prosperous / one who is helpful / a returning visitor
Ayda, Aydah, Aidah, Aidee, Aidia, Aieeda, Aaida

Aidan (Gaelic) One who is fiery; little fire
Aiden, Adeen, Aden, Aideen, Adan, Aithne, Aithnea, Ajthne

Aiglentine (French) Resembling the sweetbrier rose
Aiglentina

Aiko (Japanese) Little one who is dearly loved

Ailbhe (Irish) Of noble character; one who is bright

Aileen (Irish / Scottish) Light bearer / from the green meadow
Ailean, Ailein, Ailene, Ailin, Aillen, Ailyn, Alean, Aleane

Ailis (Irish) One who is noble and kind
Ailish, Ailyse, Ailesh, Ailisa, Ailise

Ailna (German) One who is sweet and pleasant; of the nobility
Ailne

Ain (Irish / Arabic) In mythology, a woman who wrote laws to protect the rights of women / precious eye

Aina (African) Child born of a complicated delivery

Aine (Celtic) One who brings brightness and joy

Aingeal (Irish) Heaven's messenger; angel
Aingealag

Aionia (Greek) Everlasting life
Aioniah, Aionea, Aioneah, Ayonia, Ayoniah, Ayonea, Ayoneah

Aira (American) Of the wind
Aera

Airic (Celtic) One who is pleasant and agreeable
Airick, Airik, Aeric, Aerick, Aerik

Aisha (Arabic, African) lively; womanly
Aiesha, Ayisha, Myisha

Aisling (Irish) A dream or vision; an inspiration
Aislin, Ayslin, Ayslinn, Ayslyn, Ayslynn, Aislyn, Aisylnn, Aislinn, Isleen

Aitama (Estonian) One who is helpful
Aitamah, Aytama, Aytamah

Aitheria (Greek) Of the wind
Aitheriah, Aitherea, Aithereah, Aytheria, Aytheriah, Aytherea, Aythereah

Ajaya (Hindi) One who is invincible; having the power of a god
Ajay

Aka (Maori / Turkish) Affectionate one / in mythology, a mother goddess
Akah, Akka, Akkah

Akili (Tanzanian) Having great wisdom
Akilea, Akilee, Akilie, Akylee, Akylie, Akyli, Akileah

Akilina (Latin) Resembling an eagle
Akilinah, Akileena, Akilyna, Akilinna, Ackilina, Acilina, Akylina, Akylyna

Aksana (Russian) Form of Oksana, meaning "hospitality"
Aksanna, Aksanah, Aksannah

Akua (African) Born on a Wednesday

Akuti (Indian) A princess; born to royalty
Akutie, Akutea, Akuteah, Akuty, Akutey, Akutee, Akutye

Alair (French) One who has a cheerful disposition
Alaire, Allaire, Allair, Aulaire, Alayr, Alayre, Alaer, Alaere

Alanza (Spanish) Feminine form of Alonzo; noble and ready for battle

Alaqua (Native American) Resembling the sweet gum tree

Alarice (German) Feminine form of Alaric; ruler of all
Alarise, Allaryce, Alarica, Alarisa, Alaricia, Alrica, Alryca, Alryque

Alaula (Hawaiian) The light of dawn

Alcestis (Greek) In mythology, a woman who died in place of her husband and was later rescued from Hades by Hercules

Alcina (Greek) One who is strong-willed and opinionated
Alceena, Alcyna, Alsina, Alsyna, Alzina, Alcine, Alcinia, Alcyne

Alda (German, Spanish) Long-lived, old; wise; an elder
Aldah, Aldine, Aldina, Aldinah, Aldene, Aldona, Aldeana, Allda

Aldis (English) From the ancient house
Aldys, Aldiss, Aldisse, Aldyss, Aldysse

Aldonsa (Spanish) One who is kind and gracious
Aldonza, Aldonsia, Aldonzia

Aleen (Celtic) Form of Helen, meaning "the shining light"
Aleena, Aleenia, Alene, Alyne, Alena, Alenka, Alynah, Aleine

Alegria (Spanish) One who is cheerful and brings happiness to others
Alegra, Aleggra, Allegra, Alleffra, Allecra

Alera (Latin) Resembling an eagle
Alerra, Aleria, Alerya, Alerah, Alerrah

Alethea (Greek) One who is truthful
Altheia, Lathea, Lathey, Olethea

*Alexandra (Greek) Feminine form of Alexander; a helper and defender of mankind
Alexandria, Alexandrea, Alixandra, Alessandra, Alexis, Alondra, Aleksandra, Alejandra, Sandra, Sandrine, Sasha

Alhena (Arabic) A star in the constellation Gemini
Alhenah, Alhenna, Alhennah

★ᵀ**Alice** (German) Woman of the nobility; truthful; having high moral character
*Alison, **Allison**, **Alyssa**, Alyce, Alicia, Alecia, Alesia, Aleece, Aleecia, Aleesha, Alesha, Lecia*

Alika (Hawaiian) One who is honest
Alicka, Alicca, Alyka, Alycka, Alycca

Alina (Arabic / Polish) One who is noble / one who is beautiful and bright
Aline

Alitash (African) May you always be found
Alytash, Alitasha, Alytasha, Alitashe, Alytashe

★**Aliyah** (Arabic) An ascender; one having the highest social standing
Aaliyah, Aliya, Alliyah, Alieya, Aliyiah, Alliyia, Aleeya, Alee, Aleiya

Almas (Arabic) Resembling a diamond
Almaas

Almira (English) A princess; daughter born to royalty
Almeera, Almeira, Almiera, Almyra, Almirah, Almeerah, Almeirah, Almierah

Almodine (Latin) A highly prized stone
Almondyne, Almondeene, Almondeane, Almondeine, Almondiene

Almunda (Spanish) Refers to the Virgin Mary
Almundena, Almundina

Aloma (Spanish) Form of Paloma, meaning "dove-like"
Alomah, Alomma, Alommah

Alpha (Greek) The first-born child; the first letter of the Greek alphabet

Alphonsine (French) Feminine form of Alphonse; one who is ready for battle
Alphonsina, Alphonsyne, Alphonsyna, Alphonseene, Alphonseena, Alphonseane, Alphonseana, Alphonsiene

Alpina (Scottish) Feminine form of Alpin; blonde; white-skinned
Alpinah, Alpena, Alpeena, Alpyna, Alpeenah, Alpynah, Alpeina, Alpeinah

Alsoomse (Native American) One who is independent

Altagracia (Spanish) The high grace of the Virgin Mary
Alta

Aludra (Arabic) A maiden; the name of a star in the constellation Canis Major
Aloodra

Alura (English) A divine counselor
Allura, Alurea, Alhraed

Alva (Latin) One who has a fair complexion
Alvah

Alvar (German) Of the army of elves
Alvara, Alvaria, Alvarie, Alvare, Alvarr

Alvera (Spanish) Feminine of Alvaro; guardian of all; speaker of the truth
Alveria, Alvara, Alverna, Alvernia, Alvira, Alvyra, Alvarita, Alverra

Alverdine (English) Feminine form of Alfred; one who counsels the elves
Alverdina, Alverdeene, Alverdeena, Alverdeane, Alverdeana, Alverdiene, Alverdiena, Alverdeine

Amada (Spanish) One who is loved by all
Amadia, Amadea, Amadita, Amadah

Amadea (Latin) Feminine form of Amedeo; loved by God
Amadya, Amadia, Amadine, Amadina, Amadika, Amadis

Amadi (African) One who rejoices
Amadie, Amady, Amadey, Amadye, Amadee, Amadea, Amadeah

Amalfi (Italian) From an Italian town overlooking the Gulf of Salerno
Amalfey, Amalfy, Amalfie, Amalfee, Amalfea, Amalfeah

★Amalia (German) One who is industrius and hardworking
Amelia, Amalya, Amalie, Amalea, Amylia, Amyleah, Amilia, Neneca

Amalthea (Greek) One who soothes; in mythology, the foster mother of Zeus
Amaltheah, Amalthia, Amalthya

Amalur (Spanish) From the homeland
Amalure, Amalura, Amaluria

★Amanda (Latin) One who is much loved
Amandi, Amandah, Amandea, Amandee, Amandey, Amande, Amandie, Amandy, Mandy

Amandeep (Indian) Emanating the light of peace
Amanpreet, Amanjot

Amapola (Arabic) Resembling a poppy
Amapolah, Amapolla, Amapollah, Amapolia

Amara (Greek) One who will be forever beautiful
Amarah, Amarya, Amaira, Amaria, Amar, Amari, Amaree, Amarie

★Amber (French) Resembling the jewel; a warm honey color
Ambur, Ambar, Amberly, Amberlyn, Amberli, Amberlee, Ambyr, Ambyre

Ambrosia (Greek) Immortal; in mythology, the food of the gods
Ambrosa, Ambrosiah, Ambrosyna, Ambrosina, Ambrosyn, Ambrosine, Ambrozin, Ambrozyn

America (Latin) A powerful ruler
Americus, Amerika, Amerikus

Amira (Arabic) A princess; one who commands
Amirah, Ameera, Amyra, Ameerah, Amyrah, Ameira, Ameirah, Amiera

Amissa (Hebrew) One who is honest; a friend
Amisa, Amise, Amisia, Amiza, Amysa, Amysia, Amysya, Amyza

Amita (Indian) Feminine form of Amit; without limits; unmeasurable
Amitah, Ameeta, Amyta, Amitha, Ameetah, Amytah, Amieta, Amietah

Amlika (Indian) A nurturing woman; a mother
Amlikah, Amlyka, Amlykah

Amrita (Hindi) Having immortality; full of ambrosia
Amritah, Amritta, Amryta, Amrytta, Amrytte, Amritte, Amryte, Amreeta

Amser (Welsh) A period of time

Amy (Latin) Dearly loved
Aimee, Aimie, Aimi, Aimy, Aimya, Aimey, Amice, Amicia

Anaba (Native American) A woman returning from battle
Anabah, Annaba, Annabah

Anabal (Gaelic) One who is joyful
Anaball, Annabal, Annaball

Anafa (Hebrew) Resembling the heron
Anafah, Anapha, Anaphah

Anarosa (Spanish) A graceful rose
Annarosa, Anarose, Annarose

Anastasia (Greek) One who shall rise again
Anastase, Anastascia, Anastasha, Anastasie, Stacia, Stasia, Stacy, Stacey

Anasuya (Indian) One who is charitable
Anasuyah, Annasuya

Ancina (Latin) Form of Ann, meaning "a woman graced with God's favor"
Ancyna, Anncina, Anncyna, Anceina, Annceina, Anciena, Annciena, Anceena

Andes (Latin) Woman from the Andes

★Andrea (Greek / Latin) Courageous and strong / feminine form of Andrew; womanly
Andria, Andrianna, Andreia, Andreina, Andreya, Andriana, Andreana, Andera

Aneira (Welsh) The golden woman
Aneera, Anyra, Aneirah, Aneerah, Anyrah, Aniera, Anierah, Aneara

★Angela (Greek) A heavenly messenger; an angel
*Angelica, **Angelina**, Angelique, Anjela, Anjelika, Angella, Angelita, Angeline*

Anh (Vietnamese) One who offers safety and peace

Ani (Hawaiian) One who is very beautiful
Aneesa, Aney, Anie, Any, Aany, Aanye, Anea, Aneah

Aniceta (French) One who is unconquerable
Anicetta, Anniceta, Annicetta

Anila (Hindi) Child of the wind
Anilla, Anyla, Anylla, Anilah, Anylah, Anyllah

★ᵀAnna (Latin) A woman graced with God's favor
Annah, Ana, Ann, Anne, Anya, Ane, Annze, Anouche, Annchen, Ancina, Nancy

Annabel (Italian) Graceful and beautiful woman
Annabelle, Annabell, Annabella, Annabele, Anabel, Anabell, Anabelle, Anabella

Annabeth (English) Graced with God's bounty
Anabeth, Annabethe, Annebeth, Anebeth, Anabethe

Annalynn (English) From the graceful lake
Analynn, Annalyn, Annaline, Annalin, Annalinn, Analyn, Analine, Analin

Annmarie (English) Filled with bitter grace
Annemarie, Annmaria, Annemaria, Annamarie, Annamaria, Anamarie, Anamaria, Anamari

Annora (Latin) Having great honor
Anora, Annorah, Anorah, Anoria, Annore, Annorya, Anorya, Annoria

Anona (English)
Resembling a pineapple
*Anonah, Annona,
Annoniah, Annonya,
Annonia*

Anouhea (Hawaiian)
Having a soft, cool fragrance

Ansley (English) From the
noble's pastureland
*Ansly, Anslie, Ansli, Anslee,
Ansleigh, Anslea, Ansleah,
Anslye*

Antalya (Russian) Born with
the morning's first light
*Antaliya, Antalyah,
Antaliyah, Antalia, Antaliah*

Antea (Greek) In mythology, a woman who was
scorned and committed
suicide
Anteia, Anteah

Antje (German) A graceful
woman

An-toan (Vietnamese) Safe
and secure
Toan

Antoinette (French)
Praiseworthy
Toinette

Anuradha (Hindi) In
Hinduism, goddess of
good fortune
Anurada

Anwen (Welsh) A famed
beauty
*Anwin, Anwenne,
Anwinne, Anwyn, Anwynn,
Anwynne, Anwenn,
Anwinn*

Anyango (African) One
who is a good friend

Aolani (Hawaiian) Cloud
from heaven
*Aolaney, Aolanee, Aolaniah,
Aolanie, Aolany, Aolanya,
Aolania, Aolanea*

Apala (African) One who
creates religious music
*Apalla, Appalla, Appala,
Apalah, Apallah, Appallah,
Appalah*

Apara (Yoruban) One who
doesn't remain in one place
*Aparra, Apparra, Appara,
Aparah, Aparrah,
Apparrah, Apparah*

Aphrah (Hebrew) From
the house of dust
Aphra

Aphrodite (Greek) Love; in
mythology, the goddess of
love and beauty
*Afrodite, Afrodita,
Aphrodita, Aphrodyte,
Aphhrodyta, Aphrodytah*

Aponi (Native American)
Resembling a butterfly
Aponni, Apponni, Apponi

Apphia (Hebrew) One who is productive
Apphiah

Apple (American) Sweet fruit; one who is cherished
Appel, Aple, Apel

Apsaras (Indian) In mythology, nature spirits or water nymphs

Aquene (Native American) One who is peaceful
Aqueena, Aqueene, Aqueen

Arama (Spanish) Refers to the Virgin Mary
Aramah, Aramma, Arammah

Aranka (Hungarian) The golden child

Aranrhod (Welsh) A large silver wheel; in mythology, the mother of a sea creature and a blob
Arianrhod, Arianrod

Ararinda (German) One who is tenacious
Ararindah, Ararynda, Araryndah

Arava (Hebrew) Resembling a willow; of an arid land
Aravah, Aravva, Aravvah

Arcadia (Greek / Spanish) Feminine form of Arkadios; woman from Arcadia / one who is adventurous
Arcadiah, Arkadia, Arcadya, Arkadya, Arckadia, Arckadya

Ardara (Gaelic) From the stronghold on the hill
Ardarah, Ardarra, Ardaria, Ardarrah, Ardariah

Ardel (Latin) Feminine form of Ardos; industrious and eager
Ardelle, Ardella, Ardele, Ardelia, Ardelis, Ardela, Ardell

Arden (Latin / English) One who is passionate and enthusiastic / from the valley of the eagles
Ardin, Ardeen, Ardena, Ardene, Ardan, Ardean, Ardine, Ardun

Ardith (Hebrew) From the field of flowers
Ardyth, Ardythe, Ardath, Ardice, Ardise, Ardisa, Ardyce, Ardyse

Ardra (Celtic / Hindi) One who is noble / the goddess of bad luck and misfortune
Ardrah

Argea (Greek) In mythology, the wife of Polynices
Argeia

Arglwyddes (Welsh) A distinguished lady

Argoel (Welsh) A prophetic sign
Argoell, Argoele, Argoelle, Argoela, Argoella

Argraff (Welsh) One who makes an impression
Argraffe, Argrafe

Aria (English) A beautiful melody
Ariah

★Ariana (Welsh / Greek) Resembling silver / one who is holy
*Ariane, Arian, **Arianna**, Arianne, Aerian, Aerion, Arianie, Arieon*

Arietta (Italian) A short but beautiful melody
Arieta, Ariete, Ariet, Ariett, Aryet, Aryeta, Aryetta, Aryette

Arin (English) Form of Erin, meaning "woman of Ireland"
Aryn

Arisje (Danish) One who is superior

Arissa (Greek) One who is superior
Arisa, Aris, Aryssa, Arysa, Arys

Arizona (Native American) From the little spring / from the state of Arizona

Arnette (English) A little eagle
Arnett, Arnetta, Arnete, Arneta, Arnet

Aroha (Maori) One who loves and is loved

Arona (Maori) One who is colorful and vivacious
Aronah, Aronnah, Aronna

Arrosa (Basque) Sprinkled with dew from heaven; resembling a rose
Arrose

Arthurine (English) Feminine form of Arthur; as strong as a she-bear
Arthurina, Arthuretta, Arthuryne, Arthes, Arthene

Artis (Irish / English / Icelandic) Lofy hill; noble / rock / follower of Thor
Artisa, Artise, Artys, Artysa, Artyse, Artiss, Arti, Artina

Arusi (African) A girl born during the time of a wedding
Arusie, Arusy, Arusey, Arusee, Arusea, Aruseah, Arusye

Arwa (Arabic) A female mountain goat

Arya (Indian) One who is noble and honored
Aryah, Aryana, Aryanna, Aryia

Ascención (Spanish) Refers to the Ascension

Aselma (Gaelic) One who is fair-skinned
Aselmah

Asgre (Welsh) Having a noble heart

Ashby (English) Home of the ash tree
Ashbea, Ashbie, Ashbeah, Ashbey, Ashbi, Ashbee

Asherat (Syrian) In mythology, goddess of the sea

Ashima (Hebrew) In the Bible, a deity worshipped at Hamath
Ashimah, Ashyma, Asheema, Ashimia, Ashymah, Asheemah, Asheima, Asheimah

Ashira (Hebrew) One who is wealthy; prosperous
Ashyra, Ashyrah, Ashirah, Asheera, Asheerah, Ashiera, Ashierah, Asheira

★ᵀAshley (English) From the meadow of ash trees
Ashlie, Ashlee, Ashleigh, Ashly, Ashleye, Ashlya, Ashala, Ashleay

Asia (Greek / English) Resurrection / the rising sun; in the Koran, the woman who raised Moses; a woman from the east
Aysia, Asya, Asyah, Azia, Asianne

Asima (Arabic) One who offers protection
Asimah, Aseema, Azima, Aseemah, Asyma, Asymah, Asiema, Asiemah

Asis (African) Of the sun
Asiss, Assis, Assiss

Asli (Turkish) One who is genuine and original
Aslie, Asly, Asley, Aslee, Asleigh, Aslea, Asleah, Alsye

Asma (Arabic) One of high status

Asphodel (Greek) Resembling a lily
Asfodel, Asfodelle, Asphodelle, Asphodela, Asphodella, Asfodela, Asfodella

Assana (Irish) From the waterfall
Assane, Assania, Assanna, Asanna, Asana

Assunta (Latin) One who is raised up
Assuntah, Asunta, Asuntah

Astra (Latin) Of the stars; as bright as a star
Astera, Astrea, Asteria, Astrey, Astara, Astraea, Astrah, Astree

Astrid (Scandinavian / German) One with divine strength
Astryd, Estrid

Asunción (Spanish) Refers to the Virgin Mary's assumption into heaven

Asura (African) Daughter born during the month of Ashur

Athena (Greek) One who is wise; in mythology, the goddess of war and wisdom
Athina, Atheena, Athene

Atthis (Greek) In mythology, the daughter of Cranaus who gave her name to Attica; a woman from Attica

Attracta (Irish) A virtuous woman; a saint
Athracht, Athrachta

Audhilda (Norse) A wealthy woman warrior
Audhild, Audhilde

★Audrey (English) Woman with noble strength
Audree, Audry, Audra, Audrea, Adrey, Audre, Audray, Audrin

Augusta (Latin) Feminine form of Augustus; venerable; majestic
Augustina, Agustina, Augustine, Agostina, Agostine, Augusteen, Augustyna, Agusta

Aulis (Greek) In mythology, a princess of Attica
Auliss, Aulisse, Aulys, Aulyss, Aulysse

Aurear (English) One who plays gentle music
Aureare, Auriar, Auriare, Auryare

Aurora (Latin) Morning's first light; in mythology, the goddess of the dawn
Aurore, Aurea, Aurorette

★Autumn (English) Born in the fall
Autum

★ᵀAva (German / Iranian) A birdlike woman / from the water
Avah, Avalee, Avaleigh, Avali, Avalie, Avaley, Avelaine, Avelina

Avasa (Indian) One who is independent
Avasah, Avassa, Avasia, Avassah, Avasiah, Avasea, Avaseah

Avena (English) From the oat field
Avenah, Aviena, Avyna, Avina, Avinah, Avynah, Avienah, Aveinah

Avera (Hebrew) One who transgresses
Averah, Avyra, Avira

⋆Avery (English) One who is a wise ruler; of the nobility
Avrie, Averey, Averie, Averi, Averee, Averea, Avereah

Aviana (Latin) Blessed with a gracious life
Avianah, Avianna, Aviannah, Aviane, Avianne, Avyana, Avyanna, Avyane

Aviva (Hebrew) One who is innocent and joyful; resembling springtime
Avivi, Avivah, Aviv, Avivie, Avivice, Avni, Avri, Avyva

Awel (Welsh) One who is as refreshing as a breeze
Awell, Awele, Awela, Awella

Awen (Welsh) A fluid essence; a muse; a flowing spirit
Awenn, Awenne, Awin, Awinn, Awinne, Awyn, Awynn, Awynne

Axelle (German / Latin / Hebrew) Source of life; small oak / axe / peace
Axella, Axell, Axele, Axl, Axela, Axelia, Axellia

Ayala (Hebrew) Resembling a gazelle
Ayalah, Ayalla, Ayallah

Ayla (Hebrew) From the oak tree
Aylah, Aylana, Aylanna, Aylee, Aylea, Aylene, Ayleena, Aylena

Aza (Arabic / African) One who provides comfort / powerful
Azia, Aiza, Aizia, Aizha

Azana (African) One who is superior
Azanah, Azanna, Azannah

Azar (Persian) One who is fiery; scarlet
Azara, Azaria, Azarah, Azarra, Azarrah, Azarr

Aznii (Chechen) A famed beauty
Azni, Aznie, Azny, Azney, Aznee, Aznea, Azneah

Azriel (Hebrew) God is my helper
Azrael, Azriell, Azrielle, Azriela, Azriella, Azraela

B

Baba (African) Born on a Thursday
Babah, Babba, Babbah, Baaba

Babette (French) Form of Barbara, meaning "a traveler from a foreign land; a stranger"; form of Elizabeth, meaning "my God is bountiful; God's promise"
Babett, Babete, Babet, Babbet, Babbett, Babbette, Babbete, Babita

Badia (Arabic) An elegant lady; one who is unique
Badiah, Badi'a, Badiya, Badea, Badya, Badeah

Badr (Arabic) Resembling the full moon
Badra, Badriyyah, Badriyah, Badriya, Badriyya, Badrya, Badria

Bahija (Arabic) A cheerful woman
Bahijah, Bahiga, Bahigah, Bahyja, Bahyjah, Bahyga, Bahygah

★Bailey (English) From the courtyard within castle walls; a public official
Bailee, Bayley, Baylee, Baylie, Baili, Bailie, Baileigh, Bayleigh

Baka (Indian) Resembling a crane
Bakah, Bakka, Backa, Bacca

Bakura (Hebrew) Resembling ripened fruit
Bakurah

Baldhart (German) A bold woman having great strength
Balhart, Baldhard, Balhard, Ballard, Balard, Balarde

Baligha (Arabic) One who is forever eloquent
Balighah, Baleegha, Balygha, Baliegha, Baleagha, Baleigha

Banba (Irish) In mythology, a patron goddess of Ireland

Bansuri (Indian) One who is musical
Bansurie, Bansari, Banseri, Bansurri, Bansury, Bansurey, Bansuree, Bansurea

Bara (Hebrew) One who is chosen
Barah, Barra, Barrah

Barbara (Latin) A traveler from a foreign land; a stranger
Barbra, Barbarella, Barbarita, Baibin, Babette, Bairbre, Barbary, Barb

Barika (African) A flourishing woman; one who is successful
Barikah, Baryka, Barikka, Barykka, Baricka, Barycka, Baricca, Barycca

Barr (English) A lawyer
Barre, Bar

Barras (English) From among the trees

Bathild (German) Heroine of a bold battle
Bathilde, Bathilda

Battseeyon (Hebrew) A daughter of Zion
Batseyon, Batseyonne, Battzion, Batzion

Beatha (Celtic) One who gives life
Betha, Beathah, Bethah

Beatrice (Latin) One who blesses others
Beatrix, Beatriz, Beatriss, Beatrisse, Bea, Beatrize, Beatricia, Beatrisa

Bebhinn (Irish) An accomplished singer
Bebhin, Bebhynn, Bebhyn, Bevin, Bevinne, Bevinn, Bevyn

Becky (English) Form of Rebecca, meaning "one who is bound to God"
Beckey, Becki, Beckie, Becca, Becka, Bekka, Beckee, Beckea

Bel (Indian) From the sacred wood

Belisama (Celtic) In mythology, a goddess of rivers and lakes
Belisamah, Belisamma, Belysama, Belisma, Belysma, Belesama

Bellona (Latin) In mythology, the goddess of war
Bellonah, Belona, Bellonna, Belonna, Bellonia, Belonia

Bem (African) A peaceful woman
Berne

Bena (Native American) Resembling a pheasant
Benah, Benna, Bennah

Benigna (Spanish) Feminine form of Benigno; one who is kind; friendly

Benjamina (Hebrew) Feminine form of Benjamin; child of my right hand
Benjameena, Benyamina, Benyameena, Benjameana, Benyameana, Benjamyna, Benyamyna

Bennu (Egyptian) Resembling an eagle

Beomia (Anglo-Saxon) Battle maid
Beomiya, Bemia, Beorhthilde, Beorhthild, Beorhthilda, Beomea, Beomeah

Bernice (Greek) One who brings victory
Berenisa, Berenise, Berenice, Bernicia, Bernisha, Berniss, Bernyce, Bernys

Bertha (German) One who is famously bright and beautiful
Berta, Berthe, Berth, Bertina, Bertyna, Bertine, Bertyne, Birte

Bertilda (English) A luminous battle maiden
Bertilde, Bertild

Bertrade (English) An intelligent advisor
Bertraide, Bertrayde, Bertraed, Beortbtraed, Bertraid, Bertrayd, Bertraede

Beryl (English) Resembling the pale-green precious stone
Beryll, Berylle, Beril, Berill, Berille

Bess (English) Form of Elizabeth, meaning "my God is bountiful; God's promise"
Besse, Bessi, Bessie, Bessy, Bessey, Bessee, Bessea

Beth (English) Form of Elizabeth, meaning "my God is bountiful; God's promise"
Bethe

Bethany (Hebrew) From the house of figs
Bethan, Bethani, Bethanie, Bethanee, Bethaney, Bethane, Bethann, Bethanne

Beyonce (American) One who surpasses others
Beyoncay, Beyonsay, Beyonsai, Beyonsae, Beyonci, Beyoncie, Beyoncee, Beyoncea

Bha (Indian) Having a starlike quality

Bibiana (Italian) Form of Vivian, meaning "lively woman"
Bibiane, Bibianna, Bibianne, Bibiann, Bibine

Bijou (French) As precious as a jewel

Bikita (African) Resembling an anteater
Bikitah, Bikyta, Bykita, Bykyta, Bikeyta, Bikeita, Bikieta, Bikeata

Billie (English) Feminine form of William; having a desire to protect
Billi, Billy, Billey, Billee, Billeigh, Billea, Billeah

Binga (German) From the hollow
Bingah, Bynga, Binge, Bynge, Bingeh, Byngeh

Bisgu (Anglo-Saxon) A compassionate woman
Bisgue, Bysgu, Bysgue

Bixenta (Basque) A victorious woman

Blaine (Scottish / Irish) A saint's servant / a thin woman
Blayne, Blane, Blain, Blayn, Blaen, Blaene

Blair (Scottish) From the field of battle
Blaire, Blare, Blayre, Blaer, Blaere, Blayr

Blake (English) A dark beauty
Blayk, Blayke, Blaik, Blaike, Blaek, Blaeke

Blimah (Hebrew) One resembling a blossom
Blima, Blime, Blyma, Blymah

Blondell (French) A fair-haired woman
Blondelle, Blondele, Blondene, Blondel, Blondela, Blondella

Blythe (English) Filled with happiness
Blyth, Blithe, Blith

Bo-bae (Korean) A treasured child

Bodgana (Polish) A gift of God
Bodganah, Bodganna, Bodgane, Bodgann, Bodganne, Bogna, Bohdana, Bohdanna

Bonamy (French) A very good friend
Bonamey, Bonami, Bonamie, Bonamee, Bonamei, Bonamea, Bonameah

Bonnie (English) Pretty face
Boni, Bona, Bonea, Boneah, Bonee

Borgny (Norwegian) One who offers help
Borgney, Borgni, Borgnie, Borgnee, Borgnea, Borgneah

Boudicca (Celtic) A victorious queen
Boudicea, Bodiccea, Bodicea, Bodicia

Bradana (Scottish) Resembling the salmon
Bradanah, Bradanna, Bradan, Bradane, Bradann, Bradanne, Braydan, Braydana

Brady (Irish) A large-chested woman
Bradey, Bradee, Bradi, Bradie, Bradea, Bradeah

Braima (African) Mother of multitudes
Braimah, Brayma, Braema, Braymah, Braemah

Brandy (English) A woman wielding a sword; an alcoholic drink
Brandey, Brandi, Brandie, Brandee, Branda, Brande, Brandelyn, Brandilyn

Brann (Welsh) A ravenlike woman
Branne, Bran

Braulia (Spanish) One who is glowing
Brauliah, Braulea, Brauleah, Brauliya, Brauliyah

Brazil (Spanish) Of the ancient tree
Brasil, Brazile, Brazille, Brasille, Bresil, Brezil, Bresille, Brezille

Brencis (Slavic) Crowned with laurel

Brenda (Irish) Feminine form of Brendan; a princess; wielding a sword
Brynda, Brinda, Breandan, Brendalynn, Brendolyn, Brend, Brienda

Brenna (Welsh) A raven-like woman
Brinna, Brenn, Bren, Brennah, Brina, Brena, Brenah

★**Brianna** (Irish) Feminine form of Brian; from the high hill; one who ascends
Breanna, Breanne, Breana, Breann, Breeana, Breeanna, Breona, Breonna

Brice (Welsh) One who is alert; ambitious
Bryce

Bridget (Irish) A strong and protective woman; in mythology, goddess of fire, wisdom, and poetry
Bridgett, Bridgette, Briget, Brigette, Bridgit, Bridgitte, Birgit, Birgitte

Brilliant (American) A dazzling and sparkling woman

Brimlad (Anglo-Saxon) From the seaway
Brymlad, Brimlod, Brymlod

Briseis (Greek) In mythology, the Trojan widow abducted by Achilles
Brisys, Brisa, Brisia, Brisha, Brissa, Briza, Bryssa, Brysa

Brittany (English) A woman from Great Britain
Britany, Brittanie, Brittaney, Brittani, Brittanee, Britney, Britnee, Britny

★**Brook** (English) From the running stream
Brooke, *Brookie*, **Brooklyn**, *Brooklynn, Brooklynne*

Brunhild (German) A dark and noble battle maiden; in Norse mythology, queen of the Valkyries
Brunhilde, Brunhilda, Brunnehild, Brunnehilde, Brunnehilda, Brynhild, Brynhilde, Brynhilda

Bupe (African) A hospitable woman

Buthaynah (Arabic) From the soft sand; having soft skin
Buthayna, Buthainah, Buthaina, Buthana, Buthanah

Cable (American) Resembling a heavy rope; having great strength
Cabel

Cabrina (American) Form of Sabrina, meaning "a legendary princess"
Cabrinah, Cabrinna, Cabreena, Cabriena, Cabreina, Cabryna, Cabrine, Cabryne

Cabriole (French) An adorable girl
Cabriolle, Cabrioll, Cabriol, Cabryole, Cabryolle, Cabryoll, Cabryol, Cabriola

Cacalia (Latin) Resembling the flowering plant
Cacaliah, Cacalea, Cacaleah

Caden (English) A battle maiden
Cadan, Cadin, Cadon

Cadence (Latin) Rhythmic and melodious; a musical woman
Cadena, Cadenza, Cadian, Cadienne, Cadianne, Cadiene, Caydence, Cadencia

Cadhla (Irish) A beautiful woman
Cadhlah

Caesaria (Greek) Feminine form of Caesar; an empress
Caesariah, Caesarea, Caesareah, Caezaria, Caezariah, Caezarea, Caezareah, Cesaria

Caia (Latin) One who rejoices
Cai, Cais

Cainwen (Welsh) A beautiful treasure
Cainwenn, Cainwenne, Cainwin, Cainwinn, Cainwinne, Cainwyn, Cainwynn, Cainwynne

Cairo (African) From the city in Egypt

Calais (French) From the city in France

Calantha (Greek) Resembling a lovely flower
Calanthe, Calanthia, Calanthiah, Calantheah, Calanthea

Cale (Latin) A respected woman
Cayl, Cayle, Cael, Caele, Cail, Caile

Caledonia (Latin) Woman of Scotland
Caledoniah, Caledoniya, Caledona, Caledonya, Calydona

California (Spanish) From paradise; from the state of California
Califia

Calise (Greek) A gorgeous woman
Calyse, Calice, Calyce

Calista (Greek) Most beautiful; in mythology, a nymph who changed into a bear and then into the Great Bear constellation
Calissa, Calisto, Callista, Calyssa, Calysta, Calixte, Colista, Collista

Calla (Greek) Resembling
a lily; a beautiful woman
Callah

Callie (Greek) A beautiful girl
Caleigh, Callee, Kali, Kallie

Calligenia (Greek) Daughter
born with beauty
*Caligenia, Calligeniah,
Caligeniah, Callygenia,
Calygenia, Calligenea,
Caligenea*

Caltha (Latin) Resembling
a yellow flower
*Calthah, Calthia, Calthiah,
Caltheah, Calthea*

Calybe (Greek) In mythology, a nymph who was the
wife of Laomedon

Calypso (Greek) A woman
with secrets; in mythology,
a nymph who captivated
Odysseus for seven years

Camassia (American) One
who is aloof
*Camassiah, Camasia,
Camasiah, Camassea,
Camasseah, Camasea,
Camaseah*

Cambay (English) From
the town in India
Cambaye, Cambai, Cambae

Camdyn (English) Of the
enclosed valley
*Camden, Camdan,
Camdon, Camdin*

Cameron (Scottish)
Having a crooked nose
*Cameryn, Camryn, Camerin,
Camren, Camrin, Camron*

Camilla (Italian) Feminine
form of Camillus; a ceremo-
nial attendant; a noble virgin
*Camile, Camille, Camila,
Camillia, Caimile, Camillei,
Cam, Camelai*

Campbell (Scottish)
Having a crooked mouth
*Campbel, Campbelle,
Campbele*

Canace (Greek) Born of
the wind

Candace (Ethiopian /
Greek) A queen / one who
is white and glowing
*Candice, Candiss, Candyce,
Candance, Candys,
Candyss, Candy*

Candida (Latin) White-
skinned
Candide, Candy

Candra (Latin) One who is
glowing

Candy (English) A sweet
girl; form of Candida,
meaning "white-skinned";
form of Candace, mean-
ing "a queen / one who is
white and glowing"
*Candey, Candi, Candie,
Candee, Candea, Candeah*

Caneadea (Native American) From the horizon
Caneadeah, Caneadia, Caneadiah

Canika (American) A woman shining with grace
Canikah, Caneeka, Canicka, Canyka, Canycka, Caneekah, Canickah, Canykah

Canisa (Greek) One who is very much loved
Canisah, Canissa, Canysa, Caneesa, Canyssa

Cannes (French) A woman from Cannes

Cantabria (Latin) From the mountains
Cantabriah, Cantebria, Cantabrea, Cantebrea

Capeka (Slavic) Resembling a young stork
Capekah, Capecca, Capeccah

Caprina (Italian) Woman of the island Capri
Caprinah, Caprinna, Capryna, Capreena, Caprena, Capreenah, Caprynah, Capriena

Cara (Italian / Gaelic) One who is dearly loved / a good friend
Carah, Caralee, Caralie, Caralyn, Caralynn, Carrah, Carra, Chara

Carissa (Greek) A woman of grace
Carisa, Carrisa, Carrissa, Carissima

Carla (Latin) Feminine form of Carl; a free woman
Carlah, Carlana, Carlee, Carleen, Carleigh, Carlena, Carlene, Carletta

Carlessa (American) One who is restless
Carlessah, Carlesa, Carlesah

Carmel (Hebrew) Of the fruitful orchid
Carmela, Carmella, Karmel

Carmen (Latin) A beautiful song
Carma, Carmelita, Carmencita, Carmia, Carmie, Carmina, Carmine, Carmita

Carna (Latin) In mythology, a goddess who ruled the heart

Carni (Latin) One who is vocal
Carnie, Carny, Carney, Carnee, Carnea, Carneah, Carnia, Carniah

Carol (English) Form of Caroline, meaning "joyous song"; feminine form of Charles; a small, strong woman
Carola, Carole, Carolle, Carolla, Caroly, Caroli, Carolie, Carolee

*Caroline (Latin) Joyous song; feminine form of Charles; a small, strong woman
Carol, Carolina, Carolan, Carolann, Carolanne, Carolena, Carolene, Carolena, Caroliana

Carrington (English) A beautiful woman; a woman of Carrington
Carington, Carryngton, Caryngton

Carson (Scottish) Son of the marshland
Carsan, Carsen, Carsin

Caryatis (Greek) In mythology, goddess of the walnut tree
Carya, Cariatis, Caryatiss, Cariatiss, Caryatys, Cariatys, Caryatyss, Cariatyss

Carys (Welsh) One who loves and is loved
Caryss, Carysse, Caris, Cariss, Carisse, Cerys, Ceryss, Cerysse

Cascadia (Latin) Woman of the waterfall
Cascadiya, Cascadea, Cascata

Casey (Greek, Irish) A vigilant woman
Casie, Casy, Caysie, Kasey

Cason (Greek) A seer
Cayson, Caison, Caeson

Cassandra (Greek) An unheeded prophetess; in mythology, King Priam's daughter who foretold the fall of Troy
Casandra, Cassandrea, Cassaundra, Cassondra, Cass, Cassy, Cassey, Cassi

Casta (Spanish) One who is pure; chaste
Castah, Castalina, Castaleena, Castaleina, Castaliena, Castaleana, Castalyna, Castara

Catherine (English) One who is pure; virginal
Catharine, Cathrine, Cathryn, Catherin, Catheryn, Catheryna, Cathi, Cathy, Katherine

Cathresha (American) One who is pure
Cathreshah, Cathreshia, Cathreshiah, Cathreshea, Cathresheah, Cathrisha, Cathrishah, Cathrysha

Catrice (Greek) A wholesome woman
Catrise, Catryce, Catryse, Catreece, Catreese, Catriece, Catriese, Catreice

Cavana (Irish) Feminine form of Cavan; from the hollow
Cavanna, Cavanah, Cavania, Cavaniya, Cavanea, Cavannah

Cayenne (French) Resembling the hot and spicy pepper

Cecilia (Latin) Feminine form of Cecil; one who is blind; patron saint of music
Cecelia, Cecile, Cecilee, Cicely, Cecily, Cecille, Cecilie, Cicilia, Sheila, Silka, Sissy

Celand (Latin) One who is meant for heaven
Celanda, Celande, Celandia, Celandea

Celandine (English) Resembling a swallow
Celandyne, Celandina, Celandyna, Celandeena, Celandena, Celandia, Celandea

Celeste (Latin) A heavenly daughter
Celesta, Celestia, Celesse, Celestiel, Celisse, Celestina, Celestyna, Celestine

Celina (Latin) In mythology, one of the daughters of Atlas who was turned into a star of the Pleiades constellation; feminine form of Celino; of the heavens; form of Selena, meaning "of the moon"
Celena, Celinna, Celene, Celenia, Celenne, Celicia, Celinda, Calina

Celka (Latin) A celestial being
Celkah, Celki, Celkie, Celkee, Celkey, Celky, Celkea, Celkeah

Celosia (Greek) A fiery woman; burning; aflame
Celosiah, Celosea, Celoseah

Cera (French) A colorful woman
Cerah, Cerrah, Cerra

Cerina (Latin) Form of Serena, meaning "having a peaceful disposition"
Cerinah, Ceryna, Cerynah, Cerena, Cerenah, Ceriena, Cerienah, Cereina

Cerise (French) Resembling the cherry
Cerisa

Chadee (French) A divine woman; a goddess
Chadea, Chadeah, Chady, Chadey, Chadi, Chadie

Chai (Hebrew) One who gives life
Chae, Chaili, Chailie, Chailee, Chaileigh, Chaily, Chailey, Chailea

Chailyn (American) Resembling a waterfall
Chailynn, Chailynne, Chaelyn, Chaelynn, Chaelynne, Chaylyn, Chaylynn, Chaylynne

Chakra (Arabic) A center of spiritual energy

Chalette (American) Having good taste
Chalett, Chalet, Chalete, Chaletta, Chaleta

Chalina (Spanish) Form of Rosalina, meaning "resembling a gentle horse / resembling the beautiful and meaningful flower"
Chalinah, Chalyna, Chaleena, Chalena, Charo, Chaliena, Chaleina, Chaleana

Chameli (Hindi) Resembling jasmine
Chamelie, Chamely, Chameley, Chamelee, Chamelea, Chameleah, Chameleigh

Chan (Sanskrit) A shining woman

Chana (Hebrew) Form of Hannah, meaning "having favor and grace"
Chanah, Channa, Chaanach, Chaanah, Chanach, Channah

Chance (American) One who takes risks
Chanci, Chancie, Chancee, Chancea, Chanceah, Chancy, Chancey

Chanda (Sanskrit) An enemy of evil
Chandy, Chaand, Chand, Chandey, Chandee, Chandi, Chandie, Chandea

Chandra (Hindi) Of the moon; another name for the goddess Devi
Chandara, Chandria, Chaundra, Chandrea, Chandreah

Chanel (French) From the canal; a channel
Chanell, Chanelle, Channelle, Chenelle, Chenel, Chenell

Channary (Cambodian) Of the full moon
Channarie, Channari, Channarey, Channaree, Chantrea, Chantria

Chantrice (French) A singer
Chantryce, Chantrise, Chantryse

Chapawee (Native American) Resembling a beaver
Chapawi, Chapawie, Chapawy, Chapawey, Chapawea, Chapaweah

Charbonnet (French) A giving and loving woman
Charbonay, Charbonaye, Charbonae, Charbonai, Charbonnay, Charbonnae, Charbonnai

Charisma (Greek) Blessed with charm
Charismah, Charizma, Charizmah, Charysma, Charyzma, Karisma

Charlesia (American) Feminine form of Charles; small, strong woman
Charlesiah, Charlesea, Charleseah, Charlsie, Charlsi, Charlsy, Charlsey, Charlsee

Charlshea (American) Filled with happiness
Charlsheah, Charlshia, Charlshiah

Charnee (American) Filled
with joy
*Charny, Charney, Charnea,
Charneah, Charni, Charnie*

Charnesa (American) One
who gets attention
*Charnesah, Charnessa,
Charnessah*

Charsetta (American) An
emotional woman
*Charsett, Charsette,
Charset, Charsete, Charseta*

Chartra (American) A
classy lady
Chartrah

Charu (Hindi) One who is
gorgeous
Charoo, Charou

Charumat (Hindi) An intelligent and beautiful woman
Charoomat, Charoumat

Chasia (Hebrew) One who
is protected; sheltered
*Chasiah, Chasea, Chaseah,
Chasya, Chasyah*

Chasidah (Hebrew) A reli-
gious woman; pious
*Chasida, Chasyda,
Chasydah*

Chateria (Vietnamese)
Born beneath the moon-
light
*Chateriah, Chaterea,
Chatereah, Chateriya,
Chateriyah*

Chavi (Egyptian) A pre-
cious daughter
*Chavie, Chavy, Chavey,
Chavee, Chavea, Chaveah*

Chavon (Hebrew) A giver
of life
*Chavonne, Chavonn,
Chavona, Chavonna*

Chazona (Hebrew) A
prophetess
*Chazonah, Chazonna,
Chazonnah*

Cheche (African) A small
woman

Chedra (Hebrew) Filled
with happiness
Chedrah

Cheer (American) Filled
with joy
Cheere

Cheifa (Hebrew) From a
safe harbor
Cheifah, Cheiffa, Cheiffah

Chekia (American) A
saucy woman
*Cheekie, Checki, Checkie,
Checky, Checkey, Checkee,
Checkea, Checkeah*

Chelone (English)
Resembling a flowering
plant

Chelsea (English) From
the landing place for chalk
*Chelcie, Chelsa, Chelsee,
Chelseigh, Chelsey, Chelsi,
Chelsie, Chelsy*

Chemarin (French) A dark
beauty
*Chemarine, Chemaryn,
Chemareen, Chemarein,
Chemarien*

Chemda (Hebrew) A
charismatic woman
Chemdah

Chenille (American) A
soft-skinned woman
*Chenill, Chenil, Chenile,
Chenilla, Chenila*

Chephzibah (Hebrew) Her
father's delight

Cherika (French) One who
is dear
*Chericka, Cheryka,
Cherycka, Cherieka,
Cheriecka, Chereika,
Chereicka, Cheryka*

Cherry (English)
Resembling a fruit-bearing
tree
*Cherrie, Cherri, Cherrey,
Cherree, Cherrea, Cherreah*

Chesney (English) One
who promotes peace
*Chesny, Chesni, Chesnie,
Chesnea, Chesneah,
Chesnee*

Cheyenne (Native
American) Unintelligible
speaker
*Chayanne, Cheyane,
Cheyene, Shayan, Shyann*

Chiante (Italian)
Resembling the wine
*Chianti, Chiantie, Chiantee,
Chianty, Chiantey, Chiantea*

Chiara (Italian) Daughter
of the light
Chiarah, Chiarra, Chiarrah

Chiba (Hebrew) One who
loves and is loved
*Chibah, Cheeba, Cheebah,
Cheiba, Cheibah, Chieba,
Chiebah, Cheaba*

Chickoa (Native American)
Born at daybreak
Chickoah, Chikoa, Chikoah

Chidi (Spanish) One who
is cheerful
*Chidie, Chidy, Chidey,
Chidee, Chidea, Chideah*

Chidori (Japanese)
Resembling a shorebird
*Chidorie, Chidory,
Chidorey, Chidorea,
Chidoreah, Chidoree*

Chikira (Spanish) A talent-
ed dancer
*Chikirah, Chikiera,
Chikierah, Chikeira,
Chikeirah, Chikeera,
Chikeerah, Chikyra*

Chiku (African) A talkative
girl

Chinara (African) God
receives
*Chinarah, Chinarra,
Chinarrah*

Chinue (African) God's own blessing
Chinoo, Chynue, Chynoo

Chiriga (African) One who is triumphant
Chyriga, Chyryga, Chiryga

Chislaine (French) A faithful woman
Chislain, Chislayn, Chislayne, Chislaen, Chislaene, Chyslaine, Chyslain, Chyslayn

Chitsa (Native American) One who is fair
Chitsah, Chytsa, Chytsah

Chizoba (African) One who is well-protected
Chizobah, Chyzoba, Chyzobah

★Chloe (Greek) A flourishing woman; blooming
Clo, Cloe, Cloey, Chloë

Cho (Japanese) Resembling a butterfly

Chofa (Polish) An able-bodied woman
Chofah, Choffa, Choffah

Christina (English) Follower of Christ
Christinah, Cairistiona, Christine, Christin, Christian, Christiana, Christiane, Christianna, Kristina

Chuki (African) Born during an unpleasant time
Chukie, Chuky, Chukey, Chukee, Chukea, Chukeah

Chula (Native American) Resembling a colorful flower
Chulah, Chulla, Chullah

Chulda (Hebrew) One who can tell fortunes
Chuldah

Chun (Chinese) Born during the spring

Chyou (Chinese) Born during autumn

Ciara (Irish) A dark beauty
Ceara, Ciaran, Ciarra, Ciera, Cierra, Ciere, Ciar, Ciarda

Cidrah (American) One who is unlike others
Cidra, Cydrah, Cydra

Cinnamon (American) Resembling the reddish-brown spice
Cinnia, Cinnie

Ciona (American) One who is steadfast
Cionah, Cyona, Cyonah

Claennis (Anglo-Saxon) One who is pure
Claenis, Claennys, Claenys, Claynnis, Claynnys, Claynys, Claynyss

Clancey (American) A light-hearted woman
Clancy, Clanci, Clancie, Clancee, Clancea, Clanceah

★Clara (Latin) One who is famously bright
Clarie, Clarinda, Clarine, Clarita, Claritza, Clarrie, Clarry, Clarabelle, **Claire,** *Clarice*

Clarice (French) A famous woman; also a form of Clara, meaning "one who is famously bright"
Claressa, Claris, Clarisa, Clarise, Clarisse, Claryce, Clerissa, Clerisse

Claudia (Latin / German / Italian) One who is lame
Claudelle, Gladys

Clelia (Latin) A glorious woman
Cloelia, Cleliah, Clelea, Cleleah, Cloeliah, Cloelea, Cloeleah

Clementine (French) Feminine form of Clement; one who is merciful
Clem, Clemence, Clemency, Clementia, Clementina, Clementya, Clementyna, Clementyn

Cleodal (Latin) A glorious woman
Cleodall, Cleodale, Cleodel, Cleodell, Cleodelle

Cleopatra (Greek) A father's glory; of the royal family
Clea, Cleo, Cleona, Cleone, Cleonie, Cleora, Cleta, Cleoni

Clever (American) One who is quick-witted and smart

Cloris (Greek) A flourishing woman; in mythology, the goddess of flowers
Clores, Clorys, Cloriss, Clorisse, Cloryss, Clorysse

Cloud (American) A light-hearted woman
Cloude, Cloudy, Cloudey, Cloudee, Cloudea, Cloudeah, Cloudi, Cloudie

Clydette (American) Feminine form of Clyde, meaning "from the river"
Clydett, Clydet, Clydete, Clydetta, Clydeta

Clymene (Greek) In mythology, the mother of Atlas and Prometheus
Clymena, Clymyne, Clymyn, Clymyna, Clymeena, Clymeina, Clymiena, Clymeana

Clytie (Greek) The lovely one; in mythology, a nymph who was changed into a sunflower
Clyti, Clytee, Clyty, Clytey, Clyte, Clytea, Clyteah

Co (American) A jovial
woman
Coe

Coahoma (Native American)
Resembling a panther

Coby (Hebrew) Feminine
form of Jacob; the supplanter
*Cobey, Cobi, Cobie, Cobee,
Cobea, Cobeah*

Cochava (Hebrew) Having
a starlike quality
*Cochavah, Cochavia,
Cochavea, Cochaviah,
Cochaveah*

Coffey (American) A lovely
woman
*Coffy, Coffe, Coffee, Coffea,
Coffeah, Coffi, Coffie*

Coira (Scottish) Of the
churning waters
Coirah, Coyra, Coyrah

Colanda (American) Form of
Yolanda, meaning "resem-
bling the violet flower"
*Colande, Coland, Colana,
Colain, Colaine, Colane,
Colanna, Corlanda*

Cole (English) A swarthy
woman; having coal-black hair
*Col, Coal, Coale, Coli,
Colie, Coly, Coley, Colee*

Colemand (American) An
adventurer
*Colmand, Colemyan,
Colemyand, Colmyan,
Colmyand*

Colette (French) Victory of
the people
Collette, Kolette

Coligny (French) Woman
from Cologne
*Coligney, Colignie, Coligni,
Colignee, Colignea,
Coligneah*

Colisa (English) A delight-
ful young woman
*Colisah, Colissa, Colissah,
Colysa, Colysah, Colyssa,
Colyssah*

Colola (American) A victorious woman
Colo, Cola

Comfort (English) One
who strengthens or
soothes others
*Comforte, Comfortyne,
Comfortyna, Comforteene,
Comforteena, Comfortene,
Comfortena, Comfortiene*

Conary (Gaelic) A wise
woman
*Conarey, Conarie, Conari,
Conaree, Conarea,
Conareah*

Concordia (Latin) Peace
and harmony; in mytholo-
gy, goddess of peace
*Concordiah, Concordea,
Concord, Concorde,
Concordeah*

Coneisha (American) A giving woman
Coneishah, Coniesha, Conieshah, Conysha, Conyshah, Coneesha, Coneeshah, Coneasha

Constanza (American) One who is strong-willed
Constanzia, Constanzea

Consuela (Spanish) One who provides consolation
Consuelia, Consolata, Consolacion, Chela, Conswela, Conswelia, Conswelea, Consuella

Contessa (Italian) A titled woman; a countess
Countess, Contesse, Countessa, Countesa, Contesa

Cooper (English) One who makes barrels
Couper

Copper (American) A redheaded woman
Coper, Coppar, Copar

Coppola (Italian) A theatrical woman
Copola, Copolla, Coppolla, Coppo, Copla

Coral (English) Resembling the semiprecious sea growth; from the reef
Coralee, Coralena, Coralie, Coraline, Corallina, Coralline, Coraly, Coralyn

Corazon (Spanish) Of the heart
Corazana, Corazone, Corazona

Cordelia (Latin) A good-hearted woman; a woman of honesty
Cordella, Cordelea, Cordilia, Cordilea, Cordy, Cordie, Cordi, Cordee

Corey (Irish) From the hollow; of the churning waters
Cory, Cori, Coriann, Corianne, Corie, Corri, Corrianna, Corrie

Corgie (American) A humorous woman
Corgy, Corgey, Corgi, Corgee, Corgea, Corgeah

Coriander (Greek) A romantic woman; resembling the spice
Coryander, Coriender, Coryender

Corinthia (Greek) A woman of Corinth
Corinthiah, Corinthe, Corinthea, Corintheah, Corynthia, Corynthea, Corynthe

Corky (American) An energetic young woman
Corki, Corkey, Corkie, Corkee, Corkea, Corkeah

Cornelia (Latin) Feminine
form of Cornelius; refer-
ring to a horn
*Cornalia, Corneelija,
Cornela, Cornelija,
Cornelya, Cornella,
Cornelle, Cornie*

Cota (Spanish) A lively
woman
Cotah, Cotta, Cottah

Coty (French) From the
riverbank
*Cotey, Coti, Cotie, Cotee,
Cotea, Coteah*

Courtney (English) A cour-
teous woman; courtly
*Cordney, Cordni, Cortenay,
Corteney, Cortland, Cortnee,
Cortneigh, Cortney, Courteney*

Covin (American) An
unpredictable woman
Covan, Coven, Covyn, Covon

Coy (English) From the
woods, the quiet place
Coye, Coi

Cree (Native American) A
tribal name
Crei, Crey, Crea, Creigh

Creirwy (Welsh) One who
is lucky

Creola (American)
Daughter of American
birth but European heritage
*Creole, Creolla, Criole,
Criola, Criolla, Cryola,
Cryolla*

Cressida (Greek) The gold-
en girl; in mythology, a
woman of Troy
*Cressa, Criseyde, Cressyda,
Crissyda*

Criselda (American) Form
of Griselda, meaning "a
gray-haired battle maid; one
who fights the dark battle"
*Cricelda, Cricely, Crisel,
Criseldis, Crisella, Criselle,
Criselly, Crishelda*

Crishona (American) A
beautiful woman
*Crishonah, Cryshona,
Cryshonah, Crishonna,
Crishonnah, Cryshonna,
Cryshonnah*

Crisiant (Welsh) As clear
as a crystal
*Crisiante, Crisianta,
Crysiant, Crysyant,
Crysianta, Crysiante,
Crysyanta, Crysyante*

Cristos (Greek) A dedicated and faithful woman
Crystos, Christos, Chrystos

Cullodina (Scottish) From
the mossy ground
*Cullodena, Culodina,
Culodena, Cullodyna,
Culodyna*

Cushaun (American) An
elegant lady
*Cushawn, Cusean,
Cushauna, Cushawna,
Cuseana, Cooshaun,
Cooshauna, Cooshawn*

Cwen (English) A royal
woman; queenly
*Cwene, Cwenn, Cwenne,
Cwyn, Cwynn, Cwynne,
Cwin, Cwinn*

Cylee (American) A dar-
ling daughter
*Cyleigh, Cyli, Cylie, Cylea,
Cyleah, Cyly, Cyley*

Cyrene (Greek) In mythol-
ogy, a maiden-huntress
loved by Apollo
*Cyrina, Cyrena, Cyrine,
Cyreane, Cyreana, Cyreene,
Cyreena*

Czigany (Hungarian) A
gypsy girl; one who moves
from place to place
*Cziganey, Czigani,
Cziganie, Cziganee,
Cziganea, Cziganeah*

D

Dacey (Irish) Woman
from the south
*Daicey, Dacee, Dacia, Dacie,
Dacy, Daicee, Daicy, Daci*

Daffodil (French)
Resembling the yellow
flower
*Daffodill, Daffodille,
Dafodil, Dafodill, Dafodille,
Daff, Daffodyl, Dafodyl*

Dagmar (Scandinavian)
Born on a glorious day
*Dagmara, Dagmaria,
Dagmarie, Dagomar,
Dagomara, Dagomar,
Dagomaria, Dagmarr*

Dahlia (Swedish) From the
valley; resembling the
flower
*Dahlea, Dahl, Dahiana,
Dayha, Daleia*

Daira (Greek) One who is
well-informed
Daeira, Danira, Dayeera

Daisy (English) Of the day's
eye; resembling a flower
*Daisee, Daisey, Daisi, Daisie,
Dasie, Daizy, Daysi, Deysi*

Dakota (Native American)
A friend to all
*Dakotah, Dakotta, Dakoda,
Dakodah*

Dalmace (Latin) Woman
from Dalmatia, a region of
Italy
*Dalma, Dalmassa, Dalmatia,
Dalmase, Dalmatea*

Dalmar (African) A versa-
tile woman
*Dalmarr, Dalmare,
Dalmarre*

Damali (Arabic) A beauti-
ful vision
*Damalie, Damaly,
Damaley, Damalee,
Damaleigh, Damalea,
Damaleah*

Damani (American) Of a bright tomorrow
Damanie, Damany, Damaney, Damanee, Damanea, Damaneah

Damaris (Latin) A gentle woman
Damara, Damaress, Damariss, Damariz, Dameris, Damerys, Dameryss, Damiris

Damian (Greek) One who tames or subdues others
Damiane, Daimen, Daimon, Daman, Damen, Dameon, Damiana, Damianna

Dana (English) Woman from Denmark
Daena, Daina, Danaca, Danah, Dane, Danet, Daney, Dania

★Danielle (Hebrew) Feminine form of Daniel; God is my judge
Daanelle, Danee, Danele, Danella, Danelle, Danelley, Danette, Daney

Daphne (Greek) Of the laurel tree; in mythology, a virtuous woman transformed into a laurel tree to protect her from Apollo
Daphna, Daphney, Daphni, Daphnie, Daffi, Daffie, Daffy, Dafna

Darby (English) Of the deer park
Darb, Darbee, Darbey, Darbie, Darrbey, Darrbie, Darrby, Derby, Larby

Daria (Greek) Feminine form of Darius; possessing good fortune; wealthy
Dari, Darian, Dariane, Darianna, Dariele, Darielle, Darien, Darienne

Daring (American) One who takes risks; a bold woman
Daryng, Derring, Dering, Deryng

Darlene (English) Our little darling
Dareen, Darla, Darleane, Darleen, Darleena, Darlena, Darlenny, Darlina

Darnell (English) A secretive woman
Darnelle, Darnella, Darnae, Darnetta, Darnisha, Darnel, Darnele, Darnela

Daryn (Greek) Feminine form of Darin; a gift of God
Darynn, Darynne, Darinne, Daren, Darenn, Darene

Daw (Thai) Of the stars
Dawe

Dawn (English) Born at daybreak; of the day's first light
Dawna, Dawne, Dawnelle, Dawnetta, Dawnette, Dawnielle, Dawnika, Dawnita

Day (American) A father's hope for tomorrow
Daye, Dai, Dae

Daya (Hebrew) Resembling a bird of prey
Dayah, Dayana, Dayanara, Dayania, Dayaniah, Dayanea, Dayaneah

Dayton (English) From the sunny town
Dayten, Daytan

Dea (Greek) Resembling a goddess

Debonnaire (French) One who is suave; nonchalant
Debonair, Debonaire, Debonnayre, Debonayre, Debonaere, Debonnaere

Deborah (Hebrew) Resembling a bee; in the Bible, a prophetess
Debbera, Debbey, Debbi, Debbie, Debbra, Debby, Debee, Debera

Deidre (Gaelic) A broken-hearted or raging woman
Deadra, Dede, Dedra, Deedra, Deedre, Deidra, Deirdre, Deidrie

Deiondre (American) From the lush valley
Deiondra, Deiondria, Deiondrea, Deiondriya

Dekla (Latvian) In mythology, a trinity goddess
Decla, Deckla, Deklah, Decklah, Declah

Delaney (Irish / French) The dark challenger / from the elder-tree grove
Delaina, Delaine, Delainey, Delainy, Delane, Delanie, Delany, Delayna

Delaware (English) From the state of Delaware
Delawair, Delaweir, Delwayr, Delawayre, Delawaire, Delawaer, Delawaere

Delling (Scandinavian) One who is sparkling and witty
Dellyng, Delleng

Delta (Greek) From the mouth of the river; the fourth letter of the Greek alphabet
Dellta, Deltah, Delltah

Delu (African) The sole daughter
Delue, Deloo

Delyth (Welsh) A pretty young woman
Delythe, Delith, Delithe

Demeter (Greek) In mythology, the goddess of the harvest
Demetra, Demitra, Demitras, Dimetria, Demetre, Demetria, Dimitra, Dimitre

Denali (Indian) A superior woman
Denalie, Denaly, Denally, Denalli, Denaley, Denalee, Denallee, Denallie

Dendara (Egyptian) From the town on the river
Dendera, Dendaria, Denderia, Dendarra

Denver (English) From the green valley

Derora (Hebrew) As free as a bird
Derorah, Derorra, Derorit, Drora, Drorah, Drorit, Drorlya, Derorice

Derry (Irish) From the oak grove
Derrey, Derri, Derrie, Derree, Derrea, Derreah

Deryn (Welsh) A birdlike woman
Derran, Deren, Derhyn, Deron, Derrin, Derrine, Derron, Derrynne

Desiree (French) One who is desired
Desaree, Desirae, Desarae, Desire, Desyre, Dezirae, Deziree, Desirat

★Destiny (English) Recognizing one's certain fortune; fate
Destanee, Destinee, Destiney, Destini, Destinie, Destine, Destina, Destyni

Deva (Hindi) A divine being
Devi, Daeva

Devera (Latin) In mythology, goddess of brooms
Deverah

Devika (Indian) The little goddess
Devicka, Devica, Devyka, Devycka, Devyca

Devon (English) From the beautiful farmland; of the divine
Devan, Deven, Devenne, Devin, Devona, Devondra, Devonna, Devonne

Dextra (Latin) Feminine form of Dexter; one who is skillful
Dex

Dharma (Hindi) The universal law of order
Darma

Dhisana (Hindi) In Hinduism, goddess of prosperity
Dhisanna, Disana, Disanna, Dhysana, Dhysanna

Dhyana (Hindi) One who meditates

★Diane (Latin) Of the divine; in mythology, goddess of the moon and the hunt
*Danne, Dayann, Dayanna, Dayanne, Deana, Deane, Deandra, Deann, **Diana***

Diata (African) Resembling a lioness
Diatah, Dyata, Diatta, Dyatah, Dyatta, Diattah, Dyattah

Didina (French) One who is desired
Dideena, Dideina, Didiena, Dideana, Didyna

Dido (Latin) In mythology, the queen of Carthage who committed suicide
Dydo

Didrika (German) Feminine form of Dietrich; the ruler of the people
Diedericka, Diedricka, Diedrika, Dydrika, Didricka

Dielle (Latin) One who worships God
Diele, Diell, Diella, Diela, Diel

Dimity (English) Resembling a sheer cotton fabric
Dimitee, Dimitey, Dimitie, Dimitea, Dimiteah, Dimiti

Dimona (Hebrew) Woman from the south
Dimonah, Dymona, Demona, Demonah, Dymonah

Disa (English) Resembling an orchid

Discordia (Latin) In mythology, goddess of strife
Dyscordia, Diskordia, Dyskordia

Diti (Hindi) In Hinduism, an earth goddess
Dyti, Ditie, Dytie, Dity, Dyty, Ditey, Dytey, Ditee

Ditza (Hebrew) One who brings joy
Ditzah, Diza, Dizah, Dytza, Dytzah, Dyza, Dyzah

Dolores (Spanish) Woman of sorrow; refers to the Virgin Mary
Dalores, Delora, Delores, Deloria, Deloris, Dolorcita, Dolorcitas, Dolorita

Domela (Latin) The lady of the house
Domella, Domele, Domelle, Domell, Domhnulla, Domel

Domina (Latin) An elegant lady
Dominah, Domyna, Domynah

Dominique (French) Feminine form of Dominic; born on the Lord's day
Domaneke, Domanique, Domenica, Domeniga, Domenique, Dominee, Domineek, Domineke

Doreen (French / Gaelic) The golden one / a brooding woman
Dorene, Doreyn, Dorine, Dorreen, Doryne, Doreena, Dore, Doirean

Dorma (Latin) One who is sleeping
Dorrma, Dorrmah, Dormah

Dorothy (Greek) A gift of God
*Dasha, Dasya, Dodie, Dody,
Doe, Doll, Dolley, Dolli*

Dove (American)
Resembling a bird of peace
Duv

Drisana (Indian) Daughter
of the sun
*Dhrisana, Drisanna, Drysana,
Drysanna, Dhrysana,
Dhrisanna, Dhrysanna*

Drury (French) One who is
greatly loved
*Drurey, Druri, Drurie,
Druree, Drurea, Drureah*

Duana (Irish) Feminine
form of Dwayne; little,
dark one
*Duane, Duayna, Duna,
Dwana, Dwayna, Dubhain,
Dubheasa*

Duena (Spanish) One who
acts as a chaperone

Dumia (Hebrew) One who
is silent
*Dumiya, Dumiah,
Dumiyah, Dumea, Dumeah*

Duvessa (Irish) A dark
beauty
*Duvessah, Duvesa,
Dubheasa, Duvesah*

Dylan (Welsh) Daughter of
the waves
*Dylana, Dylane, Dyllan,
Dyllana, Dillon, Dillan,
Dillen, Dillian*

Dympna (Irish) Fawn; the
patron saint of the insane
*Dymphna, Dimpna,
Dimphna*

Dyre (Scandinavian) One
who is dear to the heart

Dysis (Greek) Born at sunset
*Dysiss, Dysisse, Dysys,
Dysyss, Dysysse*

Eadlin (Anglo-Saxon) Born
into royalty
*Eadlinn, Eadlinne, Eadline,
Eadlyn, Eadlynn, Eadlynne,
Eadlina, Eadlyna*

Eadrianne (American)
One who stands out
*Eadrian, Eadriann,
Edriane, Edriana, Edrianna*

Eara (Scottish) Woman
from the east
*Earah, Earra, Earrah, Earia,
Earea, Earie, Eari, Earee*

Earla (English) A great
leader
Earlah

Earna (English) Resembling
an eagle
*Earnah, Earnia, Earnea,
Earniah, Earneah*

Easter (American) Born during the religious holiday
Eastere, Eastre, Eastir, Eastar, Eastor, Eastera, Easteria, Easterea

Easton (American) A wholesome woman
Eastan, Easten, Eastun, Eastyn

Eathelin (English) Noble woman of the waterfall
Eathelyn, Eathelinn, Eathelynn, Eathelina, Eathelyna, Ethelin, Ethelyn, Eathelen

Eathellreda (English) A noble young woman
Eathelreda, Eathellredia, Eathelredia, Eathelredia, Eathelredea, Ethelreda, Ethellreda

Eber (Hebrew) One who moves beyond

Ebere (African) One who shows mercy
Eberre, Ebera, Eberia, Eberea, Eberria, Eberrea, Ebiere, Ebierre

Ebony (Egyptian) A dark beauty
Eboni, Ebonee, Ebonie, Ebonique, Eboney, Ebonea, Eboneah

Ebrel (Cornish) Born during the month of April
Ebrell, Ebrele, Ebrelle, Ebriel, Ebriell, Ebriele, Ebrielle

Ebrill (Welsh) Born in April
Ebrille, Ebril, Evril, Evrill, Evrille

Edalene (Gaelic) A queenly woman; one who is noble
Edaleen, Edaleene, Edalena, Edaleena, Edalyne, Edalyna, Edaline, Edalina

Edana (Irish) Feminine form of Aidan; a fiery woman
Edanah, Edanna, Ena, Ethna, Eithna, Etney, Eideann, Eidana

Edna (Hebrew) One who brings pleasure; a delight
Ednah, Edena, Edenah

Edolia (Teutonic) A woman of good humor
Edoliah, Edolea, Edoleah, Edoli, Edolie, Edoly, Edoley, Edolee

Edra (English) A powerful and mighty woman
Edrah, Edrea, Edreah, Edria, Edriah

Eduarda (Portugese) Feminine form of Edward; a wealthy protector
Eduardia, Eduardea, Edwarda, Edwardia, Edwardea, Eduardina, Eduardyna, Edwardina

Edurne (Basque) Feminine form of Edur; woman of the snow
Edurna, Edurnia, Edurnea, Edurniya

Efterpi (Greek) A maiden
with a pretty face
*Efterpie, Efterpy, Efterpey,
Efterpee, Efterpea, Efterpeah*

Egan (American) A wholesome woman
Egann, Egen, Egun, Egon

Egberta (English) Feminine
form of Egbert; wielding
the shining sword
*Egbertha, Egbertina,
Egbertyna, Egberteena,
Egbertyne, Egberteene,
Egbertine*

Egeria (Latin) A wise counselor; in mythology, a
water nymph
*Egeriah, Egerea, Egereah,
Egeriya, Egeriyah*

Eglah (Hebrew)
Resembling a heifer
*Egla, Eglon, Eglona, Eglia,
Egliah, Eglea, Egleah*

Egzanth (American) A
yellow-haired woman
*Egzanthe, Egzantha,
Egzanthia, Egzanthea,
Egzanthiya, Egzanthya*

Eileen (Gaelic) Form of
Evelyn, meaning "a bird-
like woman"
*Eila, Eileene, Eilena, Eilene,
Eilin, Eilleen, Eily, Eilean*

Eiluned (Welsh) An idol
worshipper
Luned

Eilwen (Welsh) One with a
fair brow
*Eilwenne, Eilwin, Eilwinne,
Eilwyn, Eilwynne*

Eirene (Greek) Form of
Irene, meaning "a peace-
ful woman"
*Eireen, Eireene, Eiren, Eir,
Eireine, Eirein, Eirien, Eiriene*

Eires (Greek) A peaceful
woman
Eiress, Eiris, Eiriss, Eirys, Eiryss

Eirian (Welsh) One who is
bright and beautiful
*Eiriann, Eiriane, Eiriana,
Eirianne, Eirianna*

Ekron (Hebrew) One who
is firmly rooted
Eckron, Ecron

Elaine (French) Form of Helen,
meaning "the shining light"
*Ellaine, Ellayne, Elaina,
Elayna, Elayne, Elaene,
Elaena, Ellaina*

Elana (Hebrew) From the
oak tree
*Elanna, Elanah, Elanie, Elani,
Elany, Elaney, Elanee, Elan*

Elata (Latin) A high-spirited
woman
*Elatah, Elatta, Elattah, Elatia,
Elatea, Elatiah, Elateah*

Elath (Hebrew) From the
grove of trees
*Elathe, Elatha, Elathia,
Elathea*

Eldora (Greek) A gift of
the sun
*Eleadora, Eldorah, Eldorra,
Eldoria, Eldorea*

Eldoris (Greek) Woman of
the sea
*Eldorise, Eldoriss, Eldorisse,
Eldorys, Eldoryss, Eldorysse*

Eldreda (English) Feminine
form of Eldred; one who
provides wise counsel
*Eldredah, Eldrida, Eldridah,
Eldryda, Eldrydah, Eldride,
Eldrede, Eldreada*

Eleacie (American) One
who is forthright
*Eleaci, Eleacy, Eleacey,
Eleacee, Eleacea*

Eleanor (Greek) Form of
Helen, meaning "the shin-
ing light"
*Eleanora, Eleni, Eleonora,
Eleonore, Elinor, Elnora,
Eleanore, Elinora, Nora*

Eleftheria (Greek) An
independent woman; one
who is free
*Eleftheriah, Elefthera,
Elefthereah, Elefteria,
Elefteriah, Elefterea,
Eleftereah, Elepheteria*

Elena (Spanish) Form of
Helen, meaning "the shin-
ing light"
*Elenah, Eleena, Eleenah,
Elyna, Elynah, Elina,
Elinah, Eleni*

Elica (German) One who is
noble
*Elicah, Elicka, Elika, Elyca,
Elycka, Elyka, Elsha, Elsje*

Elida (English) Resembling
a winged creature
*Elidah, Elyda, Eleeda,
Eleda, Elieda, Eleida,
Eleada*

Elidad (Hebrew) Loved by
God
*Elidada, Elidade, Elydad,
Elydada, Elydade*

Elika (Hebrew) God will
judge
*Elikah, Elyka, Elicka,
Elycka, Elica, Elyca*

Eliphal (Hebrew) Delivered
by God
*Eliphala, Eliphall,
Eliphalla, Eliphelet,
Elipheleta*

Elita (Latin) The chosen
one
*Elitah, Elyta, Elytah, Eleta,
Eletah, Elitia, Elitea, Electa*

★**Elizabeth** (Hebrew) My
God is bountiful; God's
promise
*Liz, Elisabet, Elisabeth,
Elisabetta, Elissa, Eliza,
Elizabel, Elizabet, Elsa, Beth,
Babette, Libby, Lisa, Tetty*

★ᵀ**Ella** (German) From a
foreign land
*Elle, Ellee, Ellesse, Elli,
Ellia, Ellie, Elly, Ela*

Ellan (American) A coy woman
Ellane, Ellann

Ellen (English) Form of Helen, meaning "the shining light"
Elin, Elleen, Ellena, Ellene, Ellyn, Elynn, Elen, Ellin

Ellenweorc (Anglo-Saxon) A woman known for her courage

Ellery (English) Form of Hilary, meaning "a cheerful woman"
Ellerey, Elleri, Ellerie, Elleree, Ellerea, Ellereah

Ellette (English) Resembling a little elf
Ellett, Ellete, Elette, Elete, Elletta, Elleta, Eleta, Ellet

Ellyanne (American) A shining and gracious woman
Ellianne, Ellyanna, Ellianna, Ellyann, Elliann, Ellyan, Ellian

Elma (German) Having God's protection
Elmah

Elpida (Greek) Feminine form of Elpidius; filled with hope
Elpidah, Elpyda, Elpeeda, Elpieda, Elpeida, Elpeada, Espe, Elpydah

Elrica (German) A great ruler
Elricah, Elrika, Elrikah, Elryca, Elrycah, Elryka, Elrykah, Elrick

Eltekeh (Hebrew) A God-fearing woman
Elteke, Elteckeh, Eltecke

Elton (American) A spontaneous woman
Elten, Eltan, Eltin, Eltyn, Eltun

Elvia (Irish) A friend of the elves
Elva, Elvie, Elvina, Elvinia, Elviah, Elvea, Elveah, Elvyna

Elvira (Latin) A truthful woman; one who can be trusted
Elvera, Elvita, Elvyra, Elvirah, Elvyrah, Elwira

Elyse (English) Blissful
Elice, Elise, Elle, Elissa, Ilyse

Ema (Polynesian / German) One who is greatly loved / a serious woman

Ember (English) A low-burning fire
Embar, Embir, Embyr

Emiko (Japanese) A child blessed with beauty
Emyko

★ᵀ**Emily** (Latin) An industrious and hardworking woman
Emilee, Emilie, Emilia, Emelia, Emileigh, Emeleigh, Emeli, Emelie

*ᵀEmma (German) One who is complete; a universal woman
Emmy, Emmajean, Emmalee, Emmi, Emmie, Emmaline, Emelina, Emeline

Emmylou (American) A universal ruler
Emmilou, Emmielou, Emylou, Emilou, Emielou

Ena (Irish) A fiery and passionate woman
Enah, Enat, Eny, Enya

Encarnacion (Spanish) Refers to the Incarnation festival

Engelbertha (German) A luminous angel
Engelberta, Engelberthe, Engelberte, Engelbertine, Engelbertina, Engelberteena, Engelberteen, Engelbertyna

Engracia (Spanish) A graceful woman
Engraciah, Engracea, Engraceah

Enslie (American) An emotional woman
Ensli, Ensley, Ensly, Enslee, Enslea, Ensleigh

Eolande (Gaelic) Resembling the violet flower
Eoland, Eolanda, Eolandia, Eolandea

Ephah (Hebrew) Woman of sorrow
Epha, Ephia, Ephea, Ephiah, Epheah

Ephesus (Hebrew) From the desired place

Eranthe (Greek) As delicate as a spring flower
Erantha, Eranth, Eranthia, Eranthea

Erasta (African) A peaceful woman

Ercilia (American) One who is frank
Erciliah, Ercilea, Ercileah, Ercilya, Ercilyah, Erciliya, Erciliyah

Erendira (Spanish) Daughter born into royalty
Erendirah, Erendiria, Erendirea, Erendyra, Erendyria, Erendyrea, Erendeera, Erendiera

Erica (Scandinavian / Latin) Feminine form of Eric; ever the ruler / resembling heather
Erika, Ericka, Erikka, Eryka, Erike, Ericca, Erics, Eiric, Rica

Erimentha (Greek) A devoted protector
Erimenthe, Erimenthia, Erimenthea

*Erin (Gaelic) Woman from Ireland
Erienne, Erina, Erinn, Erinna, Erinne, Eryn, Eryna, Erynn, Arin

Eriphyle (Greek) In mythology, the mother of Alcmaeon
Eriphile, Erifyle, Erifile

Ernestina (German) Feminine form of Ernest; one who is determined; serious
Ernesta, Ernestine, Ernesha, Erna, Ernestyne, Ernestyna, Ernesztina, Earnestyna

Esdey (American) A warm and caring woman
Essdey, Esdee, Esdea, Esdy, Esdey, Esdi, Esdie, Esday

Eshah (African) An exuberant woman
Esha

Eshe (African) Giver of life
Eshey, Eshay, Esh, Eshae, Eshai

Esinam (African) God has heard
Esiname, Esynam, Esinama, Esynama, Esinamia, Esinamea

Esme (French) An esteemed woman
Esmai, Esmae, Esmay, Esmaye, Esmee

Esne (English) Filled with happiness
Esnee, Esney, Esnea, Esni, Esnie, Esny

Essence (American) A perfumed woman
Essince, Esense, Esince, Essynce, Esynce

Esthelia (Spanish) A shining woman
Estheliah, Esthelea, Estheleah, Esthelya, Esthelyah, Estheliya, Estheliyah

Esther (Persian) Resembling the myrtle leaf
Ester, Eszter, Eistir, Eszti

Estrid (Norse) Form of Astrid, meaning "one with divine strength"
Estread, Estreed, Estrad, Estri, Estrod, Estrud, Estryd, Estrida

Etana (Hebrew) A strong and dedicated woman
Etanah, Etanna, Etannah, Etania, Etanea, Ethana, Ethanah, Ethania

Etaney (Hebrew) One who is focused
Etany, Etanie, Etani, Etanee, Etanea

Etenia (Native American) One who is wealthy; prosperous
Eteniah, Etenea, Eteneah, Eteniya, Eteniyah

Eternity (American)
Lasting forever
*Eternitie, Eterniti, Eternitey,
Eternitee, Eternyty, Eternyti,
Eternytie, Eternytee*

Ethna (Irish) A graceful
woman
*Ethnah, Eithne, Ethne,
Eithna, Eithnah*

Eudlina (Slavic) A gener-
ous woman
*Eudlinah, Eudleena,
Eudleenah, Eudleana,
Eudleanah, Eudlyna,
Eudlynah*

Eudocia (Greek) One who
is esteemed
*Eudociah, Eudocea,
Eudoceah, Eudokia, Eudokea,
Eudosia, Eudosea, Eudoxia*

Eugenia (Greek) A well-
born woman
Eugenie, Gina, Zenechka

Eulanda (American) A fair
woman
*Eulande, Euland, Eulandia,
Eulandea*

Eunice (Greek) One who
conquers
*Eunise, Eunyce, Eunis,
Euniss, Eunyss, Eunysse*

Euodias (Hebrew) A traveling woman
Euodia, Euodeas, Euodea

Eurayle (Greek) In mythol-
ogy, a Gorgon
*Euryle, Euraile, Eurale,
Eurael, Euraele*

Eurybia (Greek) In mythology, a sea goddess and
mother of Pallas, Perses,
and Astraios
*Eurybiah, Eurybea,
Eurybeah, Euryba, Eurybah*

Eurynome (Greek) In
mythology, the mother of
the Graces
*Eurynomie, Eurynomi,
Eurynomey, Eurynomee,
Eurynomy, Eurynomea,
Eurynomeah*

Euvenia (American) A
hardworking woman
*Eveniah, Evenea, Eveneah,
Eveniya, Eveniyah*

Eva (Hebrew) Giver of life;
a lively woman
*Eve, Evetta, Evette, Evia,
Eviana, Evie, Evita, Eeva*

Evadne (Greek) In mythology, daughter of Poseidon
and mother of Iamus
*Evadine, Evadna, Euadne,
Euadna, Euadine*

★Evelyn (German) A bird-
like woman
*Evaleen, Evalina, Evaline,
Evalyn, Evelin, Evelina,
Eveline, Evelyne, Eileen*

Everilde (American) A great huntress
Everild, Everilda, Everhilde, Everhild, Everhilda

Evline (French) One who loves nature
Evleen, Evleene, Evlean, Evleane, Evlene, Evlyn, Evlyne

F

Fadhiler (Arabic) A virtuous woman
Fadhyler, Fadheler, Fadheeler, Fadilah, Fadila, Fadillah, Fadyla, Fadylla

Faghira (Arabic) Resembling the jasmine flower
Faghirah, Fagira, Fagirah, Faghyra, Fagheera, Faaghira, Fagheara, Fagheira

Faida (Arabic) One who is bountiful
Faide, Fayda, Fayde, Faeda, Faede

Faillace (French) A delicate and beautiful woman
Faillase, Faillaise, Falace, Falase, Fallase, Fallace

Fairly (English) From the far meadow
Fairley, Fairlee, Fairleigh, Fairli, Fairlie, Faerly, Faerli, Faerlie

★ᵀ**Faith** (English) Having a belief and trust in God
Faythe, Faithe, Faithful, Fayana, Fayanna, Fayanne, Fayane, Fayth

Fakhira (Arabic) A magnificent woman
Fakhirah, Fakhyra, Fakhyrah, Fakheera, Fakira, Fakirah, Fakeera, Fakyra

Fala (Native American) Resembling a crow
Falah, Falla, Fallah

Falesyia (Spanish) An exotic woman
Falesyiah, Falesiya, Falesiyah

Fall (American) Born during the autumn season
Falle

Fallon (Irish) A commanding woman
Fallyn, Faline, Falinne, Faleen, Faleene, Falynne, Falyn, Falina

Falsette (American) A fanciful woman
Falsett, Falset, Falsete, Falsetta, Falseta

Fang (Chinese) Pleasantly fragrant

Fantasia (Latin) From the fantasy land
Fantasiah, Fantasea, Fantasiya, Fantazia, Fantazea, Fantaziya

Faqueza (Spanish) A weakness

Farley (English) From the fern clearing
Farly, Farli, Farlie, Farlee, Farleigh, Farlea, Farleah

Farrow (American) A narrow-minded woman
Farow, Farro, Faro

Fate (Greek) One's destiny
Fayte, Faite, Faete, Faet, Fait, Fayt

Fatima (Arabic) The perfect woman
Fatimah, Fahima, Fahimah

Fatinah (Arabic) A captivating woman
Fatina, Fateena, Fateenah, Fatyna, Fatynah, Fatin, Fatine, Faatinah

Fausta (Italian) A lucky lady; one who is fortunate
Fawsta, Faustina, Faustine, Faustyna, Faustyne, Fausteena, Fausteene, Fawstina

Fauve (French) An uninhibited and untamed woman

Favor (English) One who grants her approval
Faver, Favar, Favorre

Fay (English) From the fairy kingdom; a fairy or an elf
Faye, Fai, Faie, Fae, Fayette, Faylinn, Faylyn, Faylynn

Fayina (Russian) An independent woman
Fayinah, Fayena, Fayeena, Fayeana, Fayiena, Fayeina

February (American) Born in the month of February
Februari, Februarie, Februarey, Februaree, Februarea

Feechi (African) A woman who worships God
Feechie, Feechy, Feechey, Feechee, Fychi, Fychie, Fychey, Fychy

Femay (American) A classy lady
Femaye, Femae, Femai

Femi (African) God loves me
Femmi, Femie, Femy, Femey, Femee, Femea, Femeah

Femise (American) One who desires love
Femeese, Femease, Femice, Femeece, Femeace, Femmis, Femmys

Fenia (Scandinavian) A gold worker
Feniah, Fenea, Feneah, Feniya, Feniyah, Fenya, Fenyah, Fenja

Feo (Greek) A gift from God
Feeo

Fern (English) Resembling
a green shade-loving plant
*Ferne, Fyrn, Fyrne, Furn,
Furne*

Fernilia (American) A suc-
cessful woman
*Ferniliah, Fernilea, Fernileah,
Fernilya, Fernilyah*

Feryal (Arabic) Possessing
the beauty of light
Feryall, Feryale, Feryalle

Fia (Portuguese / Italian /
Scottish) A weaver / from
the flickering fire / arising
from the dark of peace
*Fiah, Fea, Feah, Fya, Fiya,
Fyah, Fiyah*

Fianna (Irish) A warrior
huntress
*Fiannah, Fiana, Fianne,
Fiane, Fiann, Fian*

Fielda (English) From the
field
Fieldah, Felda, Feldah

Fife (American) Having
dancing eyes
*Fyfe, Fifer, Fify, Fifey, Fifee,
Fifea, Fifi, Fifie*

Fifia (African) Born on a
Friday
*Fifiah, Fifea, Fifeah, Fifeea,
Fifeeah*

Filberta (English) Feminine
form of Filibert; a very
brilliant woman
*Filiberta, Filbertha,
Filibertha, Felabeorht,
Felberta, Feliberta,
Felbertha, Felibertha*

Filipa (Spanish) Feminine
form of Phillip; a friend of
horses
*Filipah, Filipina, Filipeena,
Filipyna, Filippa, Fillipa,
Fillippa*

Filomena (Italian) Form of
Philomena, meaning "a
friend of strength"
*Filomina, Filomeena,
Filomyna, Filomenia,
Filominia, Filomeenia,
Filomynia, Filomeana*

Fina (English) Feminine
form of Joseph; God will
add
*Finah, Feena, Fyna, Fifine,
Fifna, Fifne, Fini, Feana*

Findabair (Celtic) Having
fair eyebrows; in mytholo-
gy, the daughter of Medb
*Findabaire, Finnabair,
Finnabaire, Findabhair,
Findabhaire, Findabayr,
Findabayre, Findabare*

Finnea (Gaelic) From the
stream of the wood
*Finneah, Finnia, Fynnea,
Finniah, Fynnia*

Fiona (Gaelic) One who is fair; a white-shouldered woman
Fionna, Fione, Fionn, Finna, Fionavar, Fionnghuala, Fionnuala, Fynballa

Firdaus (Arabic) From the garden in paradise
Firdaws, Firdoos

Flair (English) An elegant woman of natural talent
Flaire, Flare, Flayr, Flayre, Flaer, Flaere

Flame (American) A passionate and fiery woman
Flaym, Flayme, Flaime, Flaim, Flaem, Flaeme

Flamina (Latin) A pious woman
Flaminah, Flamyna, Flamynah, Flamiena, Flamienah, Flameina, Flameinah, Flameena

Flannery (Gaelic) From the flatlands
Flanery, Flanneri, Flannerie, Flannerey, Flannaree, Flannerea

Fleming (English) Woman from Belgium
Flemyng, Flemming, Flemmyng

Fleta (English) One who is swift
Fletah, Flete, Fleda, Flita, Flyta

Flicky (American) A vivacious young woman
Flicki, Flickie, Flickea, Flickeah, Flickee, Flycki, Flyckie, Flyckee

Flirt (American) A playfully romantic woman
Flyrt, Flirti, Flirtie, Flirty, Flirtey, Flirtea, Flirteah, Flirtee

Florence (Latin) A flourishing woman; a blooming flower
Florencia, Florentina, Florenza, Florentine, Florentyna, Florenteena, Florenteene, Florentyne

Florizel (English) A young woman in bloom
Florizell, Florizelle, Florizele, Florizel, Florizella, Florizela, Florazel, Florazell

Fluffy (American) A fun-loving young woman
Fluffey, Fluffi, Fluffea, Fluffeah, Fluffee, Fluffie

Fola (African) Woman of honor
Folah, Folla, Follah

Fontenot (French) One who is special

Forest (English) A woodland dweller
Forrest

Forever (American)
Everlasting

Franchelle (Arabic) A captivating woman
Fatina, Fateena, Fateenah, Fatyna, Fatynah, Fatin, Fatine, Faatinah

Frederica (German)
Peaceful ruler
Freda, Freida, Freddie, Rica

Freira (Spanish) A sister
Freirah, Freyira, Freyirah

Freydis (Norse) Woman born into the nobility
Freydiss, Freydisse, Freydys, Fredyss, Fraidis, Fradis, Fraydis, Fraedis

Frodina (Teutonic) A wise and beloved friend
Frodinah, Frodyna, Frodeena, Frodine, Frodyne, Frodeen, Frodeene, Frodeana

Fuchsia (Latin) Resembling the flower
Fusha, Fushia, Fushea, Fewsha, Fewshia, Fewshea

Fury (Greek) An enraged woman; in mythology, a winged goddess who punished wrongdoers
Furey, Furi, Furie, Furee, Furea, Fureah

G

Gabbatha (Hebrew) From the temple mound
Gabbathah, Gabbathe, Gabatha, Gabbathia, Gabbathea, Gabathia, Gabathea

★T**Gabrielle** (Hebrew) Feminine form of Gabriel; heroine of God
*Gabriel, Gabriela, Gabriele, Gabriell, **Gabriella**, Gabriellen, Gabriellia, Gabrila*

Gaira (Scottish) A petite woman
Gayra, Gara, Gairia, Gairea, Gaera

Galena (Greek) Feminine form of Galen; one who is calm and peaceful
Galene, Galenah, Galenia, Galenea

Galiana (Arabic) The name of a Moorish princess
Galianah, Galianna, Galianne, Galiane, Galian, Galyana, Galyanna, Galyann

Galila (Hebrew) From the rolling hills
Galilah, Gelila, Gelilah, Gelilia, Gelilya, Glila, Glilah, Galyla

Galilee (Hebrew) From the sacred sea
Galileigh, Galilea, Galiley, Galily, Galili, Galilie

Galina (Russian) Form of Helen, meaning "the shining light"
Galinah, Galyna, Galynah, Galeena, Galeenah, Galine, Galyne, Galeene

Gamma (Greek) The third letter of the Greek alphabet
Gammah

Garbi (Basque) One who is pure; clean
Garbie, Garby, Garbey, Garbee, Garbea, Garbeah

Gardenia (English) Resembling the sweet-smelling flower
Gardeniah, Gardenea, Gardeneah, Gardeniya, Gardynia, Gardynea, Gardena, Gardyna

Garima (Indian) A woman of importance
Garimah, Garyma, Gareema, Garymah, Gareemah, Gareama, Gareamah, Gariema

Garnet (English) Resembling the dark-red gem
Garnette, Granata, Grenata, Grenatta

Gasha (Russian) One who is well-behaved
Gashah, Gashia, Gashea, Gashiah, Gasheah

Gath-rimmon (Hebrew) Refers to the pomegranate press

Gavina (Latin) Feminine form of Gavin; resembling the white falcom; woman from Gabio
Gavinah, Gaveena, Gaveenah, Gavyna, Gavynah, Gavenia, Gavenea, Gaveana

Gaza (Hebrew) Having great strength
Gazah, Gazza, Gazzah

Gazit (Hebrew) Of the cut stone
Giza, Gizah, Gisa, Gisah

Geila (Hebrew) One who brings joy to others
Geela, Geelah, Geelan, Geilah, Geiliya, Geiliyah, Gelisa, Gellah

Gemma (Latin) As precious as a jewel
Gemmalyn, Gemmalynn, Gem, Gema, Gemmaline, Jemma

Generosa (Spanish) One who is giving, generous
Generosah, Generose, Generosia, Generosea, Genera

Genevieve (French) White wave; fair-skinned
Genavieve, Geneve, Geneveeve, Genevie, Genivee, Genivieve, Gennie, Genny, Jinelle

Genista (Latin) Resembling the broom plant
Genistah, Geneesta, Ginista, Genysta, Ginysta, Gynysta, Geneasta, Geneista

Georgia (Greek) Feminine form of George; one who works the earth; a farmer; from the state of Georgia
Georgeann, Georgeanne, Georgina, Georgena, Georgene, Georgetta, Georgette, Georgiana, Jeorjia

Geranium (Latin) Resembling the flower; a crane
Geranyum, Geranum

Gerardine (English) Feminine form of Gerard; one who is mighty with a spear
Gerarda, Gerardina, Gerardyne, Gererdina, Gerardyna, Gerrardene, Gerhardina, Gerhardine

Gerizim (Hebrew) From the mountains
Gerizima, Gerizime, Gerizimia, Gerizimea, Gerizym, Gerizyme, Gerizyma, Gerizymea

Gertrude (German) Adored warrior
Geertruide, Geltruda, Geltrudis, Gert, Gerta, Gerte, Gertie, Gertina, Trudy

Gethsemane (Hebrew) Worker of the oil press
Gethsemanie, Gethsemana, Gethsemani, Gethsemaney, Gethsemany, Gethsemanee, Gethsemanea

Gezana (Spanish) Refers to the doctrine of incarnation
Gezanah, Gezanna, Gezania, Gezanea, Gezane, Gizana, Gizane, Gizania

Gibeah (Hebrew) From the hill town
Gibea, Gibia, Gibiah, Gibeon, Gibeona, Gibeonea, Gibeonia, Gibeoneah

Gimbya (African) Daughter born to royalty; a princess
Gimbyah, Gimbiya, Gimbeya, Gimbaya, Gimbiyah, Gimbayah, Gimbeyah

Gina (Japanese / English) A silvery woman / form of Eugenia, meaning "a well-born woman"; form of Jean, meaning "God is gracious"
Geana, Geanndra, Geena, Geina, Gena, Genalyn, Geneene, Genelle

Ginger (English) A lively woman; resembling the spice
Gingee, Gingie, Ginjer, Gingea, Gingy, Gingey, Gingi

Ginny (English) Form of Virginia, meaning "one who is chaste; virginal"
Ginnee, Ginnelle, Ginnette, Ginnie, Ginnilee, Ginna, Ginney, Ginni

Giona (Italian) Resembling the bird of peace
Gionah, Gionna, Gyona, Gyonna, Gionnah, Gyonah, Gyonnah

Giovanna (Italian) Feminine form of Giovanni; God is gracious
Geovana, Geovanna, Giavanna, Giovana, Giovani, Giovanni, Giovanie, Giovanee

Giselle (French) One who offers her pledge
Gisel, Gisela, Gisella, Jiselle

Gita (Hindi / Hebrew) A beautiful song / a good woman
Gitah, Geeta, Geetah, Gitika, Gatha, Gayatri, Gitel, Gittel

Gitana (Spanish) A gypsy woman
Gitanah, Gitanna, Gitannah, Gitane

Githa (Anglo-Saxon) A gift from God
Githah

Gizem (Turkish) A mysterious woman
Gizim, Gizam, Gizym, Gizema, Gizima, Gizyma, Gizama

Gjalp (Norse) In mythology, a frost giantess

Gladys (Welsh) Form of Claudia, meaning "one who is lame"
Gladdis, Gladdys, Gladi, Gladis, Gladyss, Gwladys, Gwyladyss, Gleda

Glenna (Gaelic) From the valley between the hills
Gleana, Gleneen, Glenene, Glenine, Glen, Glenn, Glenne, Glennene

Glenys (Welsh) A holy woman
Glenice, Glenis, Glennice, Glennis, Glennys

Godfreya (German) Feminine form of Godfrey; having the peace of God
Godfredya, Gotfreya, Godafrid, Godafryd

Godiva (English) Gift from God
Godivah, Godgifu, Godyva, Godyvah

Golda (English) Resembling the precious metal
Goldarina, Goldarine, Goldee, Goldi, Goldie, Goldina, Goldy, Goldia

Gordana (Serbian / Scottish) A proud woman / one who is heroic
Gordanah, Gordanna, Gordania, Gordaniya, Gordanea, Gordannah, Gordaniah, Gordaniyah

Gormghlaith (Irish) Woman of sorrow
Gormghlaithe, Gormley, Gormly, Gormlie, Gormli, Gormlee, Gormleigh

★ᵀ**Grace** (Latin) Having God's favor; in mythology, the Graces were the personification of beauty, charm, and grace
Gracee, Gracella, Gracelynn, Gracelynne, Gracey, Gracia, Graciana, Gracie

Granada (Spanish) From the Moorish kingdom
Granadda, Grenada, Grenadda

Greer (Scottish) Feminine form of Gregory; one who is alert and watchful
Grear, Grier, Gryer

Gregoria (Latin) Feminine form of Gregory; one who is alert and watchful
Gregoriana, Gregorijana, Gregorina, Gregorine, Gregorya, Gregoryna, Gregorea, Gregoriya

Greip (Norse) In mythology, a frost giantess

Greta (German) Resembling a pearl
Greeta, Gretal, Grete, Gretel, Gretha, Grethe, Grethel, Gretna

Grid (Norse) One who is peaceful; in mythology, a frost giantess
Gryd

Grimhild (Norse) In mythology, a witch
Grimhilde, Grimhilda, Grimild, Grimilda, Grimilde

Griselda (German) A gray-haired battle maid; one who fights the dark battle
Grezelda, Grizelda, Criselda

Griswalda (German) Woman from the gray woodland
Griswalde, Grizwalda, Grizwalde, Griswald, Grizwald

Guadalupe (Spanish) From the valley of wolves
Guadelupe, Lupe, Lupita

Gudny (Swedish) One who is unspoiled
Gudney, Gudni, Gudnie, Gudne, Gudnee, Gudnea, Gudneah

Gudrun (Scandinavian) A battle maiden
Gudren, Gudrid, Gudrin, Gudrinn, Gudruna, Gudrunn, Gudrunne, Guthrun

Guinevere (Welsh) One who is fair; of the white wave; in mythology, King Arthur's queen
Guenever, Guenevere, Gueniver, Guenna, Guennola, Guinever, Guinna, Gwen

Guiseppina (Italian) Feminine form of Guiseppe; the Lord will add
Giuseppyna, Giuseppa, Giuseppia, Giuseppea, Guiseppie, Guiseppia, Guiseppa, Giuseppina

Gula (Babylonian) In mythology, a goddess
Gulah, Gulla, Gullah

Gulielma (German) Feminine form of Wilhelm; determined protector
Guglielma, Guillelmina, Guillielma, Gulielmina, Guillermina

Gulinar (Arabic) Resembling the pomegranate
Gulinare, Gulinear, Gulineir, Gulinara, Gulinaria, Gulinarea

Gullveig (Norse) In mythology, a dark goddess
Gullveiga, Gullveige, Gulveig, Gulveiga, Gulveige

Gwawr (Welsh) Born with the morning light

Gwendolyn (Welsh) One who is fair; of the white ring
Guendolen, Guendolin, Guendolinn, Guendolynn, Guenna, Gwen, Gwenda, Gwendaline, Wendy

Gwyneth (Welsh) One who is blessed with happiness
Gweneth, Gwenith, Gwenyth, Gwineth, Gwinneth, Gwinyth, Gwynith, Gwynna

Gytha (English) One who is treasured
Gythah

H

Habbai (Arabic) One who is much loved
Habbae, Habbay, Habbaye

Habiba (Arabic) Feminine form of Habib; one who is dearly loved; sweetheart
Habibah, Habeeba, Habyba, Habieba, Habeiba, Habika, Habyka, Habicka

Hachi (Native American / Japanese) From the river / having good fortune
Hachie, Hachee, Hachiko, Hachiyo, Hachy, Hachey, Hachikka

Hadara (Hebrew) A spectacular ornament; adorned with beauty
Hadarah, Hadarit, Haduraq, Hadarra, Hadarrah

Hadeel (Arabic) Resembling a dove
Hadil, Hadyl, Hadeil, Hadiel, Hadeal

Hadiya (Arabic) A gift from God; a righteous woman
Hadiyah, Hadiyyah, Haadiyah, Haadiya, Hadeeya, Hadeeyah, Hadieya, Hadieyah

Hadlai (Hebrew) In a resting state; one who hinders
Hadlae, Hadlay, Hadlaye

Hadley (English) From the field of heather
Hadlea, Hadleigh, Hadly, Hedlea, Hedleigh, Hedley, Hedlie, Hadlee

Hadria (Latin) From the town in northern Italy
Hadrea, Hadriana, Hadriane, Hadrianna, Hadrien, Hadrienne, Hadriah, Hadreah

Hafthah (Arabic) One who is protected by God
Haftha

Hagab (Hebrew) Resembling a grasshopper
Hagabah, Hagaba, Hagabe

Hagai (Hebrew) One who has been abandoned
Hagae, Hagay, Hagaye, Haggai, Haggae, Hagie, Haggie, Hagi

Hagen (Irish) A youthful woman
Hagan, Haggen, Haggan

Haggith (Hebrew) One who rejoices; the dancer
Haggithe, Haggyth, Haggythe, Hagith, Hagithe, Hagyth, Hagythe

Haidee (Greek) A modest woman; one who is well-behaved
Hadee, Haydee, Haydy, Haidi, Haidie, Haydi, Haydie, Haidy

Haimati (Indian) A queen of the snow-covered mountains
Haimatie, Haimaty, Haimatey, Haimatee, Haymati, Haymatie, Haymatee, Haimatea

Haimi (Hawaiian) One who searches for the truth
Haimie, Haimy, Haimey, Haimee, Haymi, Haymie, Haymee, Haimea

Hakana (Turkish) Feminine form of Hakan; ruler of the people; an empress
Hakanah, Hakanna, Hakane, Hakann, Hakanne

Hakkoz (Hebrew) One who has the qualities of a thorn
Hakoz, Hakkoze, Hakoze, Hakkoza, Hakoza

Halak (Hebrew) One who is bald; smooth

Haleigha (Hawaiian) Born with the rising sun
Haleea, Haleya, Halya

★ᵀHaley (English) From the field of hay
Hailey, Hayle, Hailee, Haylee, Haylie, Haleigh, Hayley, Haeleigh

Hall (American) One who is distinguished
Haul

Hallie (Scandinavian, Greek, English) From the hall; woman of the sea; from the field of hay
Halley, Hallie, Halle, Hallee, Hally, Halleigh, Hallea, Halleah

Halo (Latin) Having a blessed aura
Haylo, Haelo, Hailo

Halsey (American) A playful woman
Halsy, Halsee, Halsea, Halsi, Halsie, Halcie, Halcy, Halcey

Halyn (American) A unique young woman
Halynn, Halynne, Halin, Halinn, Halinne

Hamida (Arabic) One who gives thanks
Hamidah, Hamyda, Hameeda, Hameida, Hamieda, Hameada, Hamydah, Hameedah

Hammon (Hebrew) Of the warm springs

Hamula (Hebrew) Feminine form of Hamul; spared by God
Hamulah, Hamulla, Hamullah

Hana (Japanese / Arabic) Resembling a flower blossom / a blissful woman
Hanah, Hanako

Hanan (Arabic) One who shows mercy and compassion

Hang (Vietnamese) Of the moon

Hanika (Hebrew) A graceful woman
Hanikah, Haneeka, Haneekah, Hanyka, Hanykah, Haneika, Haneikah, Hanieka

Hanita (Indian) Favored with divine grace
Hanitah, Hanyta, Haneeta, Hanytah, Haneetah, Haneita, Haneitah, Hanieta

Haniyah (Arabic) One who is pleased; happy
Haniya, Haniyyah, Haniyya, Hani, Hanie, Hanee, Hany, Haney

★ᵀHannah (Hebrew) Having favor and grace; in the Bible, mother of Samuel
Hanalee, Hanalise, Hanna, Hanne, Hannele, Hannelore, Hannie, Hanny, Chana

Hanya (Aboriginal) As solid as a stone

Happy (American) A joyful woman
Happey, Happi, Happie, Happee, Happea

Hara (Hebrew) From the mountainous land
Harah, Harra, Harrah

Haradah (Hebrew) One who is filled with fear
Harada

Harika (Turkish) A superior woman
Harikah, Haryka, Hareeka, Harykah, Hareekah, Hareaka, Hareakah

Harimanti (Indian) Born during the spring
Harimantie, Harymanti, Harimanty, Harymanty, Harymantie, Harimantea, Harymantea

Hariti (Indian) In mythology, the goddess for the protection of children
Haritie, Haryti, Harytie, Haritee, Harytee, Haritea, Harytea

Harla (English) From the fields
Harlah

Harley (English) From the meadow of the hares
Harlea, Harlee, Harleen, Harleigh, Harlene, Harlie, Harli, Harly

Harrell (American) A great leader
Harel, Harell, Harrel, Harelle, Harrelle

Harriet (German) Feminine form of Henry; ruler of the house
Harriett, Hanriette, Hanrietta, Harriette, Harrietta, Harrette, Harriot, Harriotte

Haruma (Hebrew) Feminine form of Harum; one who is elevated

Harva (English) A warrior of the army

Hasibah (Arabic) Feminine form of Hasib; one who is noble and respected
Hasiba, Hasyba, Hasybah, Haseeba, Haseebah, Haseiba, Haseibah, Hasieba

Hasina (African) One who is good and beautiful
Hasinah, Hasyna, Hasynah, Haseena, Haseenah, Hasiena, Hasienah, Haseina

Hatsu (Japanese) The first-born daughter

Haukea (Hawaiian) Of the white snow
Haukia, Haukeah, Haukiah, Haukiya, Haukiyah

Haurana (Hebrew) Feminine form of Hauran; woman from the caves
Hauranna, Hauranah, Haurann, Hauranne, Haurane

Havva (Turkish) A giver of the breath of life
Havvah, Havvia, Havviah

Haya (Japanese / Hebrew) One who is quick and light / form of Havva, meaning "a giver of the breath of life"
Hayah

Hayud (Arabic) From the mountain
Hayuda, Hayudah, Hayood, Hayooda

Hazelelponi (Hebrew) A shadowed woman
Hazelelponie, Hazelelpony, Hazelelponey, Hazelelponee, Hazelelponea

Heartha (Teutonic) A gift from Mother Earth

Heather (English) Resembling the evergreen flowering plant
Hether, Heatha, Heath, Heathe

Hecate (Greek) In mythology, a goddess of fertility and witchcraft
Hekate

Heirnine (Greek) Form of Helen, meaning "the shining light"
Heirnyne, Heirneine, Heirniene, Heirneene, Heirneane

Hel (Norse) In mythology, the goddess of the dead
Hela, Helah

Helen (Greek) The shining light; in mythology, Helen was the most beautiful woman in the world
Helene, Halina, Helaine, Helana, Heleena, Helena, Helenna, Hellen, Aleen, Elaine, Eleanor, Elena, Ellen, Galina, Heirnine, Helice, Leanna, Yalena

Helga (German) A holy woman; one who is successful

Helia (Greek) Daughter of the sun
Heliah, Helea, Heleah, Heliya, Heliyah, Heller, Hellar

Helice (Greek) Form of Helen, meaning "the shining light"
Helyce, Heleece, Heliece, Heleace

Helike (Greek) In mythology, a willow nymph who nurtured Zeus
Helica, Helyke, Helika, Helyka, Helyca

Helle (Greek) In mythology, the daughter of Athamas who escaped sacrifice on the back of a golden ram

Helma (German) Form of Wilhelmina, meaning "determined protector"
Helmah, Helmia, Helmea, Helmina, Helmyna, Helmeena, Helmine, Helmyne

Heloise (French) One who is famous in battle
Helois, Heloisa, Helewidis

Hemanti (Indian) Born during the early winter
Hemantie, Hemanty, Hemantey, Hemantee, Hemantea

Hen (English) Resembling the mothering bird

Henrietta (German) Feminine form of Henry; ruler of the house
Henretta, Henrieta, Henriette, Henrika, Henryetta, Hetta, Hette, Hettie

Hephzibah (Hebrew) She is my delight
Hepsiba, Hepzibeth, Hepsey, Hepsie, Hepsy, Hepzibah, Hepsee, Hepsea

Herdis (Scandinavian) A battle maiden
Herdiss, Herdisse, Herdys, Herdyss, Herdysse

Hermelinda (Spanish) Bearing a powerful shield
Hermelynda, Hermalinda, Hermalynda, Hermelenda, Hermalenda

Hermia (Greek) Feminine form of Hermes; a messenger of the gods
Hermiah, Hermea, Hermila, Hermilla, Hermilda, Herminia, Hermenia, Herma

Hermippe (Greek) In mythology, the mother of Orchomenus
Hermipe, Hermip, Hermipp

Hermona (Hebrew) From the mountain peak
Hermonah, Hermonna, Hermonnah

Hernanda (Spanish) One who is daring
Hernandia, Hernandea, Hernandiya

Herra (Greek) Daughter of the earth
Herrah

Hersala (Spanish) A lovely woman
Hersalah, Hersalla, Hersallah, Hersalia, Hersaliah, Hersalea, Hersaleah

Hesiena (African) The firstborn of twins
Hesienna, Hesienah, Heseina, Hasana, Hasanah, Hasanna, Hasane

Hesione (Greek) In mythology, a Trojan princess saved by Hercules from a sea monster

Hester (Greek) A starlike woman
Hestere, Hesther, Hesta, Hestar

Heven (American) A pretty young woman
Hevin, Hevon, Hevun, Hevven, Hevvin, Hevvon, Hevvun

Hezer (Hebrew) A woman of great strength
Hezir, Hezyr, Hezire, Hezyre, Hezere

Hiah (Korean) A bright woman
Heija, Heijah, Hia

Hiawatha (Native American) She who makes rivers
Hiawathah, Hyawatha, Hiwatha, Hywatha

Hibiscus (Latin) Resembling the showy flower
Hibiskus, Hibyscus, Hibyskus, Hybiscus, Hybiskus, Hybyscus, Hybyskus

Hicks (American) A saucy woman
Hiks, Hycks, Hyks, Hicksi, Hicksie, Hicksee, Hicksy, Hicksey

Hide (Japanese) A superior woman
Hideyo

Hikmah (Arabic) Having great wisdom
Hikmat, Hikma

Hilan (Greek) Filled with happines
Hylan, Hilane, Hilann, Hilanne, Hylane, Hylann, Hylanne

Hilary (Latin) A cheerful woman
Hillary, Hillery, Ellery

Hina (Polynesian) In mythology, a dual goddess symbolizing day and night
Hinna, Henna, Hinaa, Hinah, Heena, Hena

Hind (Arabic) Owning a group of camels; a wife of Muhammed
Hynd, Hinde, Hynde

Hinda (Hebrew)
Resembling a doe
*Hindah, Hindy, Hindey,
Hindee, Hindi, Hindie,
Hynda, Hyndy*

Hiriwa (Polynesian) A silvery woman

Hitomi (Japanese) One
who has beautiful eyes
*Hitomie, Hitomee,
Hitomea, Hitomy, Hitomey*

Holda (German) A secretive
woman; one who is hidden
Holde

Hollander (Dutch) A
woman from Holland
*Hollynder, Hollender,
Holander, Holynder,
Holender, Hollande,
Hollanda*

Holly (English) Of the
holly tree
*Holli, Hollie, Hollee, Holley,
Hollye, Hollyanne, Holle,
Hollea*

Holton (American) One
who is whimsical
*Holten, Holtan, Holtin,
Holtyn, Holtun*

Holy (American) One who
is pious or sacred
*Holey, Holee, Holeigh, Holi,
Holie, Holye, Holea, Holeah*

ᵀHope (English) One who
has high expectations
through faith

Horem (Hebrew) One who
is dedicated to God
*Horema, Horemah, Horym,
Horyma*

Horonaim (Hebrew) Of
the two caverns
*Horonaima, Horonama,
Horonayma, Horonayme,
Horonaem, Horonaema*

Hortensia (Latin) Woman
of the garden
*Hartencia, Hartinsia,
Hortencia, Hortense,
Hortenspa, Hortenxia,
Hortinzia, Hortendana*

Hoshi (Japanese) One who
shines as brightly as a star
*Hoshiko, Hoshie, Hoshee,
Hoshy, Hoshey, Hoshiyo,
Hoshea*

Hourig (Slavic) A small,
fiery woman

Hova (African) Born into
the middle class

Hoyden (American) A
spirited woman
*Hoiden, Hoydan, Hoidan,
Hoydyn, Hoidyn, Hoydin,
Hoidin*

Hudel (Scandinavian) One
who is lovable
*Hudell, Hudele, Hudelle,
Hudela, Hudella*

Hudes (Hebrew) Form of
Judith, meaning " woman
from Judea"

Hudson (English) One who is adventurous; an explorer
Hudsen, Hudsan, Hudsun, Hudsyn, Hudsin

Hueline (German) An intelligent woman
Huelene, Huelyne, Hueleine, Hueliene, Hueleene, Huleane

Huhana (Maori) Form of Susannah, meaning "white lily"
Huhanah, Huhanna, Huhanne, Huhann, Huhane

Humita (Native American) One who shells corn
Humitah, Humyta, Humeeta, Humieta, Humeita, Humeata, Humytah, Humeetah

Hutena (Hurrian) In mythology, the goddess of fate
Hutenah, Hutenna, Hutyna, Hutina

Huwaidah (Arabic) One who is gentle
Huwaydah, Huwaida, Huwayda, Huwaeda, Huwaedah

Huyen (Vietnamese) A woman with jet-black hair

Hvergelmir (Norse) In mythology, the wellspring of cold waters
Hvergelmire, Hvergelmira, Hvergelmeer, Hvergelmeera

Hydeira (Greek) Woman of the water
Hydira, Hydyra, Hydeyra, Hydeera, Hydeara, Hydiera

Hygeia (Greek) In mythology, the goddess of health
Hygia, Hygeiah, Hygea

Hypatia (Greek) An intellectually superior woman
Hypasia, Hypacia, Hypate

Hypermnestra (Greek) In mythology, the mother of Amphiareos

I

Ianeke (Hawaiian) God is gracious
Ianeki, Ianekie, Ianeky, Ianekey, Ianekea, Ianekee

Ianthe (Greek) Resembling the violet flower; in mythology, a sea nymph, a daughter of Oceanus
Iantha, Ianthia, Ianthina, Ianthyna, Ianthea, Ianthiya, Ianthya

Ibtesam (Arabic) One who smiles often
Ibtisam, Ibtysam

Ibtihaj (Arabic) A delight; bringer of joy
Ibtehaj, Ibtyhaj

Ida (Greek) One who is diligent; hardworking; in mythology, the nymph who cared for Zeus on Mount Ida
Idania, Idaea, Idalee, Idaia, Idania, Idalia, Idalie, Idana

Idil (Latin) A pleasant woman
Idyl, Idill, Idyll

Idoia (Spanish) Refers to the Virgin Mary
Idoea, Idurre, Iratze, Izazkun

Idona (Scandinavian) A fresh-faced woman
Idonah, Idonna, Idonnah, Idonia, Idoniah, Idonea, Idoneah, Idonya

Idowu (African) Daughter born after twins

Ife (African) One who loves and is loved
Ifeh, Iffe

Ignatia (Latin) A fiery woman; burning brightly
Igantiah, Ignacia, Ignazia, Iniga

Iheoma (Hawaiian) Lifted up by God

Ikeida (American) A spontaneous woman
Ikeidah, Ikeyda, Ikeydah, Ikeda, Ikedah, Ikieda, Ikiedah, Ikeeda

Ilamay (French) From the island
Ilamaye, Ilamai, Ilamae

Ilandere (American) Moon woman
Ilander, Ilanderre, Ilandera, Ilanderra

Ilia (Greek) From the ancient city
Iliah, Ilea, Ileah, Iliya, Iliyah, Ilya, Ilyah

Ilisapesi (Tonga) The blessed child
Ilisapesie, Ilysapesi, Ilysapesy, Ilisapesy, Ilisapesea, Ilysapesie, Ilysapesea

Ilithyia (Greek) In mythology, goddess of childbirth
Ilithya, Ilithiya, Ilithyiah

Ilma (German) Form of Wilhelmina, meaning "determined protector"
Ilmah, Illma, Illmah

Ilori (African) A special child; one who is treasured
Illori, Ilorie, Illorie, Ilory, Illory, Ilorey, Illorey, Iloree

Ilta (Finnish) Born at night
Iltah, Illta

Ilyse (German / Greek) Born into the nobility / form of Elyse, meaning "blissful"
Ilysea, Ilysia, Ilysse, Ilysea

Imala (Native American) One who disciplines others
Imalah, Imalla, Imallah, Immala, Immalla

Imanuela (Spanish) A
faithful woman
*Imanuella, Imanuel,
Imanuele, Imanuell*

Imari (Japanese) Daughter
of today
*Imarie, Imaree, Imarea,
Imary, Imarey*

Imelda (Italian) Warrior in
the universal battle
Imeldah, Imalda, Imaldah

Imperia (Latin) A majestic
woman
*Imperiah, Imperea,
Impereah, Imperial,
Imperiel, Imperielle,
Imperialle*

Ina (Polynesian) In mythology, a moon goddess
Inah, Inna, Innah

Inaki (Asian) Having a
generous nature
*Inakie, Inaky, Inakey,
Inakea, Inakee*

Inanna (Sumerian) A lady
of the sky; in mythology,
goddess of love, fertility,
war, and the earth
*Inannah, Inana, Inanah,
Inann, Inanne, Inane*

Inara (Arabic) A heaven-
sent daughter; one who
shines with light
*Inarah, Innara, Inarra,
Innarra*

Inari (Finnish / Japanese)
Woman from the lake /
one who is successful
*Inarie, Inaree, Inary,
Inarey, Inarea, Inareah*

Inaya (Arabic) One who
cares for the well-being of
others
Inayah, Inayat

Inca (Indian) An adventurer
*Incah, Inka, Inkah, Incka,
Inckah*

India (English) From the
river; woman from India
*Indea, Indiah, Indeah,
Indya, Indiya, Indee, Inda,
Indy*

Indiana (English) From
the land of the Indians;
from the state of Indiana
*Indianna, Indyana,
Indyanna*

Indiece (American) A
capable woman
*Indeice, Indeace, Indeece,
Indiese, Indeise, Indeese,
Indease*

Indigo (English)
Resembling the plant; a
purplish-blue dye
Indygo, Indeego

Indre (Hindi) Woman of
splendor

Ineesha (American) A sparkling woman
Ineeshah, Ineisha, Ineishah, Iniesha, Inieshah, Ineasha, Ineashah, Ineysha

Ingalls (American) A peaceful woman

Ingegard (Scandinavian) Of the god Ing's kingdom
Ingagard, Ingegerd, Ingagerd, Ingigard, Ingigerd

Ingelise (Danish) Having the grace of the god Ing
Ingelisse, Ingeliss, Ingelyse, Ingelisa, Ingelissa, Ingelysa, Ingelyssa

Inghean (Scottish) Her father's daughter
Ingheane, Inghinn, Ingheene, Ingheen, Inghynn

Inis (Irish) Woman from Ennis
Iniss, Inisse, Innis, Inys, Innys, Inyss, Inysse

Intisar (Arabic) One who is victorious; triumphant
Intisara, Intisarah, Intizar, Intizara, Intizarah, Intisarr, Intysarr, Intysar

Iolanthe (Greek) Resembling a violet flower
Iolanda, Iolanta, Iolantha, Iolante, Iolande, Iolanthia, Iolanthea

Iona (Greek) Woman from the island
Ionna, Ioane, Ioann, Ioanne

Ionanna (Hebrew) Filled with grace
Ionannah, Ionana, Ionann, Ionane, Ionanne

Ionia (Greek) Of the sea and islands
Ionya, Ionija, Ioniah, Ionea, Ionessa, Ioneah, Ioniya

Iosepine (Hawaiian) Form of Josephine, meaning "God will add"
Iosephine, Iosefa, Iosefena, Iosefene, Iosefina, Iosefine, Iosepha, Iosephe

Iowa (Native American) Of the Iowa tribe; from the state of Iowa

Iphedeiah (Hebrew) One who is saved by the Lord
Iphedeia, Iphedia, Iphedea, Iphidea, Iphidia, Iphideia

Iphigenia (Greek) One who is born strong; in mythology, daughter of Agamemnon
Iphigeneia, Iphigenie, Iphagenia, Iphegenia, Iphegenie, Iphegeneia, Ifigenia, Ifegenia

Ipsa (Indian) One who is desired
Ipsita, Ipsyta, Ipseeta, Ipseata, Ipsah

Iratze (Basque) Refers to the Virgin Mary
Iratza, Iratzia, Iratzea, Iratzi, Iratzie, Iratzy, Iratzey, Iratzee

Irem (Turkish) From the heavenly gardens
Irema, Ireme, Iremia, Iremea

Irene (Greek) A peaceful woman; in mythology, the goddess of peace
Ira, Irayna, Ireen, Iren, Irena, Irenea, Irenee, Irenka, Eirene

Ireta (Greek) One who is serene
Iretah, Iretta, Irettah, Irete, Iret, Irett, Ireta

Irma (German) A universal woman
Irmina, Irmine, Irmgard, Irmgarde, Irmagard, Irmagarde, Irmeena, Irmyna

Irodell (American) A peaceful woman
Irodelle, Irodel, Irodele, Irodella, Irodela

Irta (Greek) Resembling a pearl
Irtah

Irune (Basque) Refers to the Holy Trinity
Iroon, Iroone, Iroun, Iroune

★ᵀIsabel (Spanish) Form of Elizabeth, meaning "my God is bountiful; God's promise"
*Isabeau, Isabela, Isabele, Isabelita, Isabell, **Isabella**, **Isabelle**, Ishbel, Ysabel*

Isadore (Greek) A gift from the goddess Isis
Isadora, Isador, Isadoria, Isidor, Isidoro, Isidorus, Isidro, Isidora

Isana (German) A strong-willed woman
Isanah, Isanna, Isane, Isann, Isanne, Isan

Isela (American) A giving woman
Iselah, Isella, Isellah

Isha (Indian / Hebrew) The protector / a lively woman
Ishah

Isleen (Gaelic) Form of Aisling, meaning "a dream or vision; an inspiration"
Isleene, Islyne, Islyn, Isline, Isleine, Isliene, Islene, Isleyne

Isolde (Celtic) A woman known for her beauty; in mythology, the lover of Tristan
Iseult, Iseut, Isold, Isolda, Isolt, Isolte, Isota, Isotta

Isra (Arabic) One who travels in the evening
Israh, Isria, Isrea, Israt

Itiah (Hebrew) One who is comforted by God
Itia, Iteah, Itea, Itiyah, Itiya, Ityah, Itya

Itidal (Arabic) One who is cautious
Itidalle, Itidall, Itidale

Itsaso (Basque) Woman of the ocean
Itassaso, Itassaso, Itassasso

Itxaro (Basque) One who has hope
Itxarro

Iudita (Hawaiian) An affectionate woman
Iuditah, Iudyta, Iudytah, Iudeta, Iudetah

Iuginia (Hawaiian) A high-born woman
Iuginiah, Iuginea, Iugineah, Iugynia, Iugyniah, Iugynea, Iugyneah, Iugenia

Ivory (English) Having a creamy-white complexion; as precious as elephant tusks
Ivorie, Ivorine, Ivoreen, Ivorey, Ivoree, Ivori, Ivoryne, Ivorea

Iwa (Japanese) Of strong character
Iwah

Iwilla (American) She shall rise
Iwillah, Iwilah, Iwila, Iwylla, Iwyllah, Iwyla, Iwylah

Ixchel (Mayan) The rainbow lady; in mythology, the goddess of the earth, moon, and healing
Ixchell, Ixchelle, Ixchela, Ixchella, Ixchal, Ixchall, Ixchalle, Ixchala

Iyabo (African) The mother is home

Izanne (American) One who calms others
Izann, Izane, Izana, Izan, Izanna

Izefia (African) A childless woman
Izefiah, Izefya, Izefiya, Izephia, Izefa, Izepha, Izefea, Izephea

Izolde (Greek) One who is philosophical
Izold, Izolda

J

Jaakkina (Finnish) Feminine form of Jukka; God is gracious
Jakkina, Jaakkinah, Jaakina, Jakina, Jakyna, Jakeena, Jadeana

Jacey (American) Form of Jacinda, meaning "resembling the hyacinth"
Jacee, Jacelyn, Jaci, Jacine, Jacy, Jaicee, Jaycee, Jacie

Jacinda (Spanish)
Resembling the hyacinth
*Jacenda, Jacenia, Jacenta,
Jacindia, Jacinna, Jacinta,
Jacinth, Jacintha, Jacey*

Jacqueline (French)
Feminine form of Jacques;
the supplanter
*Jackie, Xaquelina, Jacalin,
Jacalyn, Jacalynn, Jackalin,
Jackalinne, Jackelyn,
Jacketta, Jackette*

Jaddua (Hebrew) One who
is well-known
Jadduah, Jadua, Jaduah

★Jade (Spanish) Resembling
the green gemstone
*Jada, Jadeana, Jadee,
Jadine, Jadira, Jadrian,
Jadrienne, Jady, Jaden*

Jaden (Hebrew / English)
One who is thankful to
God / form of Jade, mean-
ing "resembling the green
gemstone"
*Jadine, Jadyn, Jadon,
Jayden, Jadyne, Jaydyn,
Jaydon, Jaydine*

Jadwige (Polish) One who
is protected in battle
*Jadwyge, Jadwig, Jadwyg,
Jadwiga, Jadwyga, Jadriga,
Jadryga, Jadreega*

Jadzia (Polish) A princess;
born into royalty
*Jadziah, Jadzea, Jadzeah,
Jadziya, Jadziyah, Jadzya,
Jadzyah*

Jae (English) Feminine
form of Jay; resembling a
jaybird
*Jai, Jaelana, Jaeleah,
Jaeleen, Jaelyn, Jaenelle,
Jaenette, Jaya*

Jael (Hebrew) Resembling
a mountain goat
*Jaella, Jaelle, Jayel, Jaela,
Jaele, Jayil*

Jaen (Hebrew) Resembling
an ostrich
*Jaena, Jaenia, Jaenea,
Jaenne*

Jaffa (Hebrew) A beautiful
woman
Jaffah, Jafit, Jafita

Jahath (Hebrew)
Recognizing the impor-
tance of a union
Jahathe, Jahatha

Jalila (Arabic) An impor-
tant woman; one who is
exalted
*Jalilah, Jalyla, Jalylah,
Jaleela, Jaleelah, Jalil,
Jaleala, Jalealah*

Jamaica (American) From
the island of springs
*Jamaeca, Jamaika,
Jemaica, Jamika, Jamieka,
Jameika, Jamyka, Jemayka*

Jamie (Hebrew) Feminine
form of James; she who
supplants
*Jaima, Jaime, Jaimee,
Jaimelynn, Jaimey, Jaimi,
Jaimie, Jaimy*

Janan (Arabic) Of the heart and soul

Jane (Hebrew) Feminine form of John; God is gracious
Jaina, Jaine, Jainee, Janey, Jana, Janae, Janaye, Jandy, Sine

Janis (English) Feminine form of John; God is gracious
Janice, Janeece, Janess, Janessa, Janesse, Janessia, Janicia, Janiece

Jarah (Hebrew) A sweet and kind woman

Jasher (Hebrew) One who is righteous; upright
Jashiere, Jasheria, Jasherea, Jashera, Jashiera

★Jasmine (Persian) Resembling the climbing plant with fragrant flowers
Jaslyn, Jaslynn, Jasmeen, Jasmin, Jasmina, Jasminda, Jasmyn, Jasmyne

Javiera (Spanish) Feminine form of Xavier; one who is bright; the owner of a new home
Javierah, Javyera, Javyerah, Javeira, Javeirah

Jean (Hebrew) Feminine form of John; God is gracious
Jeanae, Jeanay, Jeane, Jeanee, Jeanelle, Jeanetta, Jeanette, Jeanice, Gina

Jecoliah (Hebrew) All things are possible through the Lord
Jecolia, Jecolea, Jecoleah, Jecholia, Jekolia, Jecoliya, Jekoliya, Jekolea

Jehaleleel (Hebrew) One who praises God
Jehalelel, Jahaleleil, Jehaleliel, Jehalelyl, Jehaleleal

Jehonadab (Hebrew) The Lord gives liberally
Jonadab

Jemima (Hebrew) Dovelike
Jamima, Mima

Jemma (English) Form of Gemma, meaning "as precious as a jewel"
Jemmah, Jema, Jemah, Jemmalyn, Jemalyn, Jemmalynn, Jemalynn

Jena (Arabic) Our little bird
Jenah

★ᵀJennifer (Welsh) One who is fair; a beautiful girl
*Jenefer, Jeni, Jenifer, Jeniffer, Jenn, Jennee, Jenni, Jen, **Jenna***

Jeorjia (American) Form of Georgia, meaning "one who works the earth; a farmer"
Jeorgia, Jeorja, Jorja, Jorjette, Jorgette, Jorjeta, Jorjetta, Jorgete

Jereni (Slavic) One who is peaceful
Jerenie, Jereny, Jereney, Jerenee

Jermaine (French) Woman from Germany
Jermainaa, Jermane, Jermayne, Jermina, Jermana, Jermayna, Jermaen, Jermaena

★ᵀ**Jessica** (Hebrew) The Lord sees all
Jess, Jessa, Jessaca, Jessaka, Jessalin, Jessalyn, Jesse, Jesseca, Yessica

Jethetha (Hebrew) Feminine form of Jetheth; a princess
Jethethia, Jethethea, Jethethiya

Jethra (Hebrew) Feminine form of Jethro; the Lord's excellence; one who has plenty; abudance
Jethrah, Jethria, Jethrea, Jethriya, Jeth, Jethe

Jetta (Danish) Resembling the jet-black lustrous gemstone
Jette, Jett, Jeta, Jete, Jettie, Jetty, Jetti, Jettey

Jewel (French) One who is playful; resembling a precious gem
Jewell, Jewelle, Jewelyn, Jewelene, Jewelisa, Jule, Jewella, Juelline

Jezebel (Hebrew) One who is not exalted; in the Bible, the queen of Israel punished by God
Jessabell, Jetzabel, Jezabel, Jezabella, Jezebelle, Jezibel, Jezibelle, Jezybell

Jie (Chinese) One who is pure; chaste

Jiera (Lithuanian) A lively woman
Jierah, Jyera, Jyerah, Jierra, Jyerra

Jifunza (African) A self-learner
Jifunzah, Jifoonza, Jifoonzah, Jifounza, Jifounzah

Jimmi (English) Feminine form of Jimmy; she who supplants
Jimi, Jimmie, Jimie, Jimmy, Jimmey, Jimmee, Jimmea, Jimy

Jin (Japanese / Chinese) A superior woman / a golden child; one who is elegant

Jinelle (Welsh) Form of Genevieve, meaning "white wave; fair-skinned"
Jinell, Jinele, Jinel, Jynelle, Jynell, Jynele, Jynel

Jinx (Latin) One who performs charms or spells
Jynx, Jinxx, Jynxx

Jiselle (American) Form of Giselle, meaning "one who offers her pledge"
Jisell, Jisele, Jisela, Jizelle, Joselle, Jisella, Jizella, Jozelle

Jo (English) Feminine form of Joseph; God will add
Jobelle, Jobeth, Jodean, Jodelle, Joetta, Joette, Jolinda, Jolisa

Joakima (Hebrew) Feminine form of Joachim; God will judge
Joachima, Joaquina, Joaquine, Joaquima

Jocasta (Greek) In mythology, the queen of Thebes who married her son
Jocastah, Jokasta, Jokastah, Jockasta, Joccasta

★Jocelyn (German / Latin) From the tribe of Gauts / one who is cheerful, happy
Jocelin, Jocelina, Jocelinda, Joceline, Jocelyne, Jocelynn, Jocelynne, Josalind

Joda (Hebrew) An ancestor of Christ

Jokim (Hebrew) Blessed by God
Jokima, Jokym, Jokyme, Jokeem, Jokimia, Jokimea, Joka, Jokeam

Jolan (Greek) Resembling a violet flower
Jola, Jolaine, Jolande, Jolanne, Jolanta, Jolantha, Jolandi, Jolanka

Jolene (English) Feminine form of Joseph; God will add
Joeline, Joeleen, Joeline, Jolaine, Jolean, Joleen, Jolena, Jolina

Jonina (Israeli) Resembling a little dove
Joninah, Jonyna, Jonynah, Joneena, Joneenah, Jonine, Jonyne, Joneene

Jorah (Hebrew) Resembling an autumn rose
Jora

Jord (Norse) In mythology, goddess of the earth
Jorde

★ᵀJordan (Hebrew) Of the down-flowing river; in the Bible, the river where Jesus was baptized
Jardena, Johrdan, Jordain, Jordaine, Jordana, Jordane, Jordanka, Jordann

Josephine (French) Feminine form of Joseph; God will add
Josefina, Josephene, Jo, Josie, Iosepine

Jovana (Spanish) Feminine form of Jovian; daughter of the sky
Jeovana, Jeovanna, Jovanna, Jovena, Jovianne, Jovina, Jovita, Joviana

Joy (Latin) A delight; one who brings pleasure to others
Jioia, Jioya, Joi, Joia, Joie, Joya, Joyann, Joyanna

Joyce (English) One who brings joy to others
Joice, Joyceanne, Joycelyn, Joycelynn, Joyse, Joyceta

Jozachar (Hebrew) God has remembered
Jozachare, Jozachara, Jozacharia, Jozacharea

Judith (Hebrew) Woman from Judea
Judithe, Juditha, Judeena, Judeana, Judyth, Judit, Judytha, Judita, Hudes

★Julia (Latin) One who is youthful; daughter of the sky
Jiulia, Joleta, Joletta, Jolette, Julaine, Julayna, Julee, Juleen, July

July (Latin) Form of Julia, meaning "one who is youthful; daughter of the sky"; born during the month of July
Julye

June (Latin) One who is youthful; born during the month of June
Junae, Junel, Junelle, Junette, Junita, Junia

Justice (English) One who upholds moral rightness and fairness
Justyce, Justiss, Justyss, Justis, Justus, Justise

Juturna (Latin) In mythology, goddess of fountains and springs
Jutorna, Jutourna

Jwahir (African) The golden woman
Jwahyr, Jwaheer, Jwahear

Jyotsna (Indian) Woman of the moonlight

K

Kachina (Native American) A spiritual dancer
Kachine, Kachinah, Kachineh, Kachyna, Kacheena, Kachynah, Kacheenah, Kacheana

Kacondra (American) One who is bold
Kacondrah, Kacondria, Kacondriah, Kacondrea, Kacondreah, Kaecondra, Kaycondra, Kakondra

Kadin (Arabic) A beloved companion
Kadyn, Kadan, Kaden, Kadon, Kadun, Kaedin, Kaeden, Kaydin

Kaelyn (English) A beautiful girl from the meadow
Kaelynn, Kaelynne, Kaelin, Kailyn, Kaylyn, Kaelinn, Kaelinne

Kagami (Japanese) Displaying one's true image
Kagamie, Kagamy, Kagamey, Kagamee, Kagamea

★**Kaila** (Hebrew) Crowned with laurel
Kailah, Kayla, Kailan, Kaleigh, Kalen, Kaley, Kalie, Kalin, Kaylee

Kailasa (Indian) From the silver mountain
Kailasah, Kailassa, Kaylasa, Kaelasa, Kailas, Kailase

Kakra (Egyptian) The younger of twins
Kakrah

Kala (Arabic / Hawaiian) A moment in time / form of Sarah, meaning "a princess; lady"
Kalah, Kalla, Kallah

Kalifa (Somali) A chaste and holy woman
Kalifah, Kalyfa, Kalyfah, Kaleefa, Kaleefah, Kalipha, Kalypha, Kaleepha

Kalinda (Indian) Of the sun
Kalindah, Kalynda, Kalinde, Kalindeh, Kalindi, Kalindie, Kalyndi, Kalyndie

Kallie (English) Form of Callie, meaning "a beautiful girl"
Kalli, Kallita, Kally, Kalley, Kallee, Kalleigh, Kallea, Kalleah

Kalma (Finnish) In mythology, goddess of the dead

Kalpana (Indian) Having a great imagination
Kalpanah, Kalpanna, Kalpannah

Kalwa (Finnish) A heroine

Kalyan (Indian) A beautiful and auspicious woman
Kalyane, Kalyanne, Kalyann, Kaylana, Kaylanna, Kalliyan, Kaliyan, Kaliyane

Kama (Indian) One who loves and is loved
Kamah, Kamma, Kammah

Kamala (Arabic) A woman of perfection
Kamalah, Kammala, Kamalla

Kamaria (African) Of the moon
Kamariah, Kamarea, Kamareah, Kamariya, Kamariyah

Kambiri (African) Newest addition to the family
Kambirie, Kambiry, Kambyry, Kambiree, Kambirea, Kambyree, Kambyrea, Kambyri

Kamea (Hawaiian) The one and only; precious one
Kameo

Kamyra (American)
Surrounded by light
*Kamira, Kamera, Kamiera,
Kameira, Kameera, Kameara*

Kanan (Indian) From the
garden

Kanda (Native American)
A magical woman
Kandah

Kanika (African) A dark,
beautiful woman
*Kanikah, Kanyka, Kanicka,
Kanycka, Kaneeka,
Kaneecka, Kaneaka,
Kaneacka*

Kantha (Indian) A delicate
woman
*Kanthah, Kanthe, Kantheh,
Kanthia, Kanthia, Kanthea,
Kantheah, Kanthiya*

Kanya (Thai) A young girl;
a virgin

Kaoru (Japanese) A fragrant girl
Kaori

Kara (Greek / Italian /
Gaelic) One who is pure /
dearly loved / a good
friend
*Karah, Karalee, Karalie,
Karalyn, Karalynn, Karrah,
Karra, Khara*

Karcsi (French) A joyful
singer
*Karcsie, Karcsy, Karcsey,
Karcsee, Karcsea*

Karen (Greek) Form of
Katherine, meaning "one
who is pure; virginal"
*Karan, Karena, Kariana,
Kariann, Karianna,
Karianne, Karin, Karina*

Karisma (English) Form of
Charisma, meaning
"blessed with charm"
*Kharisma, Karizma,
Kharizma*

Karissa (Greek) Filled with
grace and kindess; very
dear
*Karisa, Karyssa, Karysa,
Karessa, Karesa, Karis, Karise*

Karmel (Latin) Form of
Carmel, meaning "of the
fruitful orchard"
*Karmelle, Karmell,
Karmele, Karmela,
Karmella*

Karnesha (American) A
fiesty woman
*Karneshah, Karnisha,
Karnishah, Karnysha,
Karnyshah*

Karoline (English) A small
and strong woman
*Karolina, Karolinah,
Karolyne, Karrie, Karie,
Karri, Kari, Karry*

Karsten (Greek) The
anointed one
*Karstin, Karstine, Karstyn,
Karston, Karstan, Kiersten,
Keirsten*

Kasey (Irish) Form of Casey, meaning "a vigilant woman"
Kacie, Kaci, Kacy, KC, Kacee, Kacey, Kasie, Kasi

Kashawna (American) One who enjoys debate
Kashawn, Kaseana, Kasean, Kashaun, Kashauna, Kashona, Kashonna

Kashonda (American) A dramatic woman
Kashondah, Kashaunda, Kashaundah, Kashawnda, Kashawndah, Kashanda, Kashandah

Kasi (Indian) From the holy city; shining

Kasmira (Slavice) A peace-maker
Kasmirah, Kasmeera, Kasmeerah, Kasmyra, Kasmyrah, Kazmira, Kazmirah, Kazmyrah

★Katherine (Greek) Form of Catherine, meaning "one who is pure; virginal"
Katharine, Katharyn, Kathy, Kathleen, Katheryn, Kathie, Kathrine, Kathryn, Kaitlyn, Katelyn, Karen, Kay

Katrice (American) A graceful woman
Katryce, Katriece, Katreice, Katreace, Katrise, Katryse, Katriese, Katreise

Katriel (Hebrew) Crowned by God
Katriele, Katrielle, Katriell

Kaveri (Indian) From the sacred river
Kaverie, Kauveri, Kauverie, Kavery, Kaverey, Kaveree, Kaverea, Kauvery

Kavinli (American) One who is eager
Kavinlie, Kavinly, Kavinley, Kavinlee, Kavinlea, Kavinleigh

Kawthar (Arabic) From the river in paradise
Kawthare, Kawthara, Kawtharr

Kay (English / Greek) The keeper of the keys / form of Katherine, meaning "one who is pure; virginal"
Kaye, Kae, Kai, Kaie, Kaya, Kayana, Kayane, Kayanna

Kearney (Irish) The winner
Kearny, Kearni, Kearnie, Kearnee, Kearnea

Keaton (English) From a shed town
Keatan, Keatyn, Keatin, Keatun

Keavy (Irish) A lovely and graceful girl
Keavey, Keavi, Keavie, Keavee, Keavea

Keeya (African) Resembling a flower
Keeyah, Kieya, Keiya, Keyya

Kefira (Hebrew)
Resembling a young
lioness
*Kefirah, Kefiera, Kefeira,
Kefeera, Kefyra, Kephira,
Kepheera, Kepheira*

Keiki (Hawaiian) A precious
baby; resembling an orchid
*Kiki, Kyki, Keeki, Keki,
Keyki, Kaki, Kaeki, Kayki*

Keisha (American) The
favorite child; form of
Kezia, meaning "of the
spice tree"
*Keishla, Keishah, Kecia,
Kesha, Keysha, Keesha,
Kiesha, Keshia*

Kelilah (Hebrew) A victori-
ous woman
*Kelila, Kelula, Kelulah,
Kelyla, Kelylah*

Kempley (English) From
the meadow
*Kemply, Kempli, Kemplie,
Kemplee, Kempleigh,
Kemplea, Kempleah*

Kendra (English) Feminine
form of Kendrick; having
royal power; from the
high hill
*Kendrah, Kendria, Kendrea,
Kindra, Kindria*

Kensington (English) A
brash lady
*Kensyngton, Kensingtyn,
Kinsington, Kinsyngton,
Kinsingtyn*

Kenwei (Arabic)
Resembling a water lily

Kenyangi (Ugandan)
Resembling the white
egret
*Kenyangie, Kenyangy,
Kenyangey, Kenyangee,
Kenyangea*

Kerdonna (American) One
who is loquacious
*Kerdonnah, Kerdona,
Kerdonah, Kerdonia,
Kerdoniah, Kerdonea,
Kerdoneah, Kirdonna*

Kerensa (Cornish) One
who loves and is loved
*Kerinsa, Keransa, Kerensia,
Kerensea, Kerensya, Kerenz,
Kerenza, Keranz*

Kerr (Scottish) From the
marshland

Keshon (American) Filled
with happiness
*Keyshon, Keshawn,
Keyshawn, Kesean, Keysean,
Keshaun, Keyshaun,
Keshonna*

Ketura (Hebrew)
Resembling incense
Keturah, Keturra

Kevina (Gaelic) Feminine
form of Kevin; a beautiful
and beloved child
*Kevinah, Keva, Kevia,
Kevinne, Kevyn, Kevynn,
Kevynne, Keveena*

Keyla (English) A wise daughter

Kezia (Hebrew) Of the spice tree
Keziah, Kesia, Kesiah, Kesi, Kessie, Ketzia, Keisha

Khai (American) Unlike the others; unusual
Khae, Khay, Khaye

Khalida (Arabic) Feminine form of Khalid; an immortal woman
Khalidah, Khaleeda, Khalyda, Khaalida, Khulud, Khulood, Khaleada

Khaliqa (Arabic) Feminine form of Khaliq; a creator; one who is well-behaved
Khaliqah, Khalyqa, Khaleeqa, Kaliqua, Kaleequa, Kalyqua, Khaleaqa, Kaleaqua

Khanh (Vietnamese) Resembling a precious stone
Khann, Khan

Khatiba (Arabic) Feminine form of Khatib; one who leads the prayers; an orator
Khateeba, Khatyba, Khateba, Khatibah, Khateaba

Khatun (Arabic) A daughter born to nobility; a lady
Khatune, Khatoon, Khaatoon, Khanom, Kanom, Khanam, Khaanam, Khatoun

Khayriyyah (Arabic) A charitable woman
Khayriyah, Khariyyah, Khariya, Khareeya

Khepri (Egyptian) Born of the morning sun
Kheprie, Kepri, Keprie, Khepry, Kepry, Khepree, Kepree, Kheprea

Khiana (American) One who is different
Khianna, Khiane, Khianne, Khian, Khyana, Khyanna, Kheana, Kheanna

Ki (Korean) One who is reborn

Kianga (African) Of the sunshine
Kyanga, Keanga

Kichi (Japanese) The fortunate one
Kichie, Kichy, Kichey, Kichee, Kichea

Kidre (American) A loyal woman
Kidrea, Kidreah, Kidria, Kidriah, Kidri, Kidrie, Kidry, Kidrey

Kiele (Hawaiian) Resembling the gardenia
Kielle, Kiel, Kiell, Kiela, Kiella

Kikka (German) The mistress of all
Kika, Kykka, Kyka

Kimana (American) Girl from the meadow
Kimanah, Kimanna, Kimannah, Kymana, Kymanah, Kymanna, Kymannah

Kimball (English) Chief of the warriors; possessing royal boldness
Kimbal, Kimbell, Kimbel, Kymball, Kymbal

★Kimberly (English) Of the royal fortress
Kimberley, Kimberli, Kimberlee, Kimberleigh, Kimberlin, Kimberlyn, Kymberlie, Kymberly

Kimeo (American) Filled with happiness
Kimeyo

Kimetha (American) Filled with joy
Kimethah, Kymetha, Kymethah, Kimethia, Kymethia, Kimethea, Kymethea

Kimiko (Japanese) A noble child; without equal

Kimone (American) A darling daughter
Kymone

Kina (Hawaiian) Woman of China

Kineks (Native American) Resembling a rosebud

Kineta (Greek) One who is active; full of energy
Kinetikos

Kinipela (Hawaiian) One who is fair; white wave

Kinsey (English) The king's victory
Kinnsee, Kinnsey, Kinnsie, Kinsee, Kinsie, Kinzee, Kinzie, Kinzey

Kintra (American) A joyous woman
Kintrah, Kentra, Kentrah, Kintria, Kentria, Kintrea, Kentrea, Kintrey

Kioko (Japanese) A daughter born with happiness

Kirabo (African) A gift from God

Kirima (Eskimo) From the hill
Kirimah, Kiryma, Kirymah, Kirema, Kiremah, Kireema, Kireemah, Kireama

Kismet (English) One's destiny; fate
Kizmet

Kiss (American) A caring and compassionate woman
Kyss, Kissi, Kyssi, Kissie, Kyssie, Kissy, Kyssy, Kissey

Kissa (African) Daughter born after twins
Kissah, Kyssa, Kyssah

Kita (Japanese) Woman from the north

Kobi (American) Woman from California
Kobie, Koby, Kobee, Kobey, Kobea

Koko (Japanese) The stork has come

Kolette (English) Form of Colette, meaning "victory of the people"
Kolete, Kolett, Koleta, Koletta, Kolet

Kolinka (Danish) Born to the victors
Kolinka, Koleenka, Kolynka, Kolenka

Komala (Indian) A delicate and tender woman
Komalah, Komalla, Komal, Komali, Komalie, Komalee, Komaleigh, Komalea

Kona (Hawaiian) A girly woman
Konah, Konia, Koniah, Konea, Koneah, Koni, Konie, Koney

Konane (Hawaiian) Daughter of the moonlight

Kreeli (American) A charming and kind girl
Kreelie, Krieli, Krielie, Kryli, Krylie, Kreely, Kriely, Kryly

Krenie (American) A capable woman
Kreni, Kreny, Kreney, Krenee, Krenea

Kristina (English) Form of Christina, meaning "follower of Christ"
Kristena, Kristine, Kristyne, Kristyna, Krystina, Krystine, Kristjana, Krisalyn

Kumi (Japanese) An everlasting beauty
Kumie, Kumy, Kumey, Kumee, Kumea

Kumiko (Japanese) A child who is forever beautiful
Kumeeko, Kumyko

Kunti (Hindi) In Hinduism, the mother of the Pandavas
Kuntie, Kunty, Kuntey, Kuntea, Koonti, Koontie, Koonty, Koontey

Kuonrada (German) One who provides bold counsel

*Kyla (English) Feminine form of Kyle; from the narrow channel
*Kylah, Kylar, Kyle, Kylee, Kyleigh, Kyley, Kyli, **Kylie***

Kynthia (Greek) In mythology, another name for the moon goddess
Kynthiah, Kynthea, Kinthia, Kinthea, Kynthiya, Kinthiya

L

Labana (Hebrew)
Feminine form of Labon;
white; fair-skinned
*Labanah, Labanna,
Labania, Labanea,
Labaniya, Labannah,
Labaniah, Labaneah*

Labiba (Arabic) Having
great wisdom; one who is
intelligent
*Labibah, Labeeba,
Labeebah, Labyba,
Labybah, Labieba,
Labiebah, Labeiba*

Lacey (French) Woman
from Normandy; as deli-
cate as lace
*Lace, Lacee, Lacene, Laci,
Laciann, Lacie, Lacina, Lacy*

Lachesis (Greek) In
mythology, one of the
three Fates
*Lachesiss, Lachesisse,
Lachesys, Lacheses*

Lacole (American) A sly
woman
Lakole, Lucole, Lukole

Lady (English) One who
kneads bread; the head of
the house
*Lady, Ladee, Ladi, Ladie,
Laidy, Laydy, Laydi, Laydie*

Lael (Hebrew) One who
belongs to God
Laele, Laelle

Laima (Latvian) One who
is fortunate; in mythology,
goddess of luck
Layma, Laema

Lainil (American) A soft-
hearted woman
*Lainill, Lainyl, Lainyll,
Laenil, Laenill, Laenyl,
Laenyll, Laynil*

Lais (Greek) A legendary
courtesan
*Laise, Lays, Layse, Laisa,
Laes, Laese*

Lajita (Indian) A truthful
woman
Lajyta, Lajeeta, Lajeata

Lake (American) From the
still waters
*Laken, Laiken, Layken, Layk,
Layke, Laik, Laike, Laeken*

Lala (Slavic) Resembling a
tulip
Lalah, Lalla, Lallah, Laleh

Lalaine (American) A
hardworking woman
*Lalain, Lalaina, Lalayn,
Lalayne, Lalayna, Lalaen,
Lalaene, Lalaena*

Lalia (Greek) One who is
well-spoken
*Lali, Lallia, Lalya, Lalea,
Lalie, Lalee, Laly, Laley*

Lalita (Indian) A playful and charming woman
Lalitah, Laleeta, Laleetah, Lalyta, Lalytah, Laleita, Laleitah, Lalieta

Lamarian (American) One who is conflicted
Lamariane, Lamarean, Lamareane

Lamia (Greek) In mythology, a female vampire
Lamiah, Lamiya, Lamiyah, Lamea, Lameah

Lamya (Arabic) Having lovely dark lips
Lamyah, Lamyia, Lama

Lanassa (Russian) A light-hearted woman; cheerful
Lanasa, Lanassia, Lanasia, Lanassiya, Lanasiya

Lang (Scandinavian) Woman of great height

Lani (Hawaiian) From the sky; one who is heavenly
Lanikai

Lansing (English) Filled with hope
Lanseng, Lansyng

Lanza (Italian) One who is noble and willing
Lanzah, Lanzia, Lanziah, Lanzea, Lanzeah

Lapis (Egyptian) Resembling the dark-blue gemstone
Lapiss, Lapisse, Lapys, Lapyss, Lapysse

Laquinta (American) The fifth-born child

Laramie (French) Shedding tears of love
Larami, Laramy, Laramey, Laramee, Laramea

Larby (American) Form of Darby, meaning "of the deer park"
Larbey, Larbi, Larbie, Larbee, Larbea

Larch (American) One who is full of life
Larche

Lark (English) Resembling the songbird
Larke

Larue (American) Form of Rue, meaning "a medicinal herb"
LaRue, Laroo, Larou

Lashawna (American) Filled with happiness
Lashauna, Laseana, Lashona, Lashawn, Lasean, Lashone, Lashaun

Lata (Indian) Of the lovely vine
Latah

Latanya (American)
Daughter of the fairy queen
*Latanyah, Latonya,
Latania, Latanja, Latonia,
Latanea*

LaTeasa (Spanish) A flirtatious woman
Lateasa, Lateaza

Latona (Latin) In mytholo-
gy, the Roman equivalent
of Leto, the mother of
Artemis and Apollo
*Latonah, Latonia, Latonea,
Lantoniah, Latoneah*

Latrelle (American) One
who laughs a lot
*Latrell, Latrel, Latrele,
Latrella, Latrela*

Laudonia (Italian) Praises
the house
*Laudonea, Laudoniya,
Laudomia, Laudomea,
Laudomiya*

Laura (Latin) Crowned
with laurel; from the lau-
rel tree
*Lauraine, Lauralee, Laralyn,
Laranca, Larea, Lari,
Lauralee, Lauren, Loretta*

★Lauren (French) Form of
Laura, meaning "crowned
with laurel; from the lau-
rel tree"
*Laren, Larentia, Larentina,
Larenzina, Larren, Laryn,
Larryn, Larrynn*

★Leah (Hebrew) One who
is weary; in the Bible,
Jacob's first wife
*Leia, Leigha, Lia, Liah,
Leeya*

Leanna (Gaelic) Form of
Helen, meaning "the shin-
ing light"
*Leana, Leann, Leanne, Lee-
Ann, Leeann, Leeanne,
Leianne, Leyanne*

Lecia (English) Form of
Alice, meaning "woman of
the nobility; truthful; hav-
ing high moral character"
*Licia, Lecea, Licea, Lisha,
Lysha, Lesha*

Ledell (Greek) One who is
queenly
*Ledelle, Ledele, Ledella,
Ledela, Ledel*

Leela (Indian) An accomplished actress

Legarre (Spanish) Refers
to the Virgin Mary
*Legare, Legarra, Legara,
Lera, Leira*

Legend (American) One
who is memorable
Legende, Legund, Legunde

Legia (Spanish) A bright
woman
*Legiah, Legea, Legeah,
Legiya, Legiyah, Legya,
Legyah*

Lenis (Latin) One who has soft and silky skin
Lene, Leneta, Lenice, Lenita, Lennice, Lenos, Lenys, Lenisse

Leona (Latin) Feminine form of Leon; having the strength of a lion
Leeona, Leeowna, Leoine, Leola, Leone, Leonelle, Leonia, Leonie

Lequoia (Native American) Form of Sequoia, meaning "of the giant redwood tree"
Lequoya, Lequoiya, Lekoya, Lekoia

Lerola (Latin) Resembling a blackbird
Lerolla, Lerolah, Lerolia, Lerolea

★Leslie (Gaelic) From the holly garden; of the gray fortress
Leslea, Leslee, Lesleigh, Lesley, Lesli, Lesly, Lezlee, Lezley

Leucippe (Greek) In mythology, a nymph
Lucippe, Leucipe, Lucipe

Leucothea (Greek) In mythology, a sea nymph
Leucothia, Leucothiah, Leucotheah

Levora (American) A homebody
Levorah, Levorra, Levorrah, Levoria, Levoriah, Levorea, Levoreah, Levorya

Lewa (African) A very beautiful woman
Lewah

Lewana (Hebrew) Of the white moon
Lewanah, Lewanna, Lewannah

Liadan (Irish) An older woman; the gray lady
Leadan, Lyadan

Libby (English) Form of Elizabeth, meaning "my God is bountiful; God's promise"
Libba, Libbee, Libbey, Libbie, Libet, Liby, Lilibet, Lilibeth

Liberty (English) An independent woman; having freedom
Libertey, Libertee, Libertea, Liberti, Libertie, Libertas, Libera, Liber

Libra (Latin) One who is balanced; the seventh sign of the zodiac
Leebra, Leibra, Liebra, Leabra, Leighbra, Lybra

Librada (Spanish) One who is free
Libradah, Lybrada, Lybradah

Lieu (Vietnamese) Of the willow tree

Ligia (Greek) One who is musically talented
Ligiah, Ligya, Ligiya, Lygia, Ligea, Lygea, Lygya, Lygiya

Lila (Arabic / Greek) Born at night / resembling a lily
Lilah, Lyla, Lylah

Lilac (Latin) Resembling the bluish-purple flower
Lilack, Lilak, Lylac, Lylack, Lylak, Lilach

Lilette (Latin) Resembling a budding lily
Lilett, Lilete, Lilet, Lileta, Liletta, Lylette, Lylett, Lylete

Liliha (Hawaiian) One who holds rank as chief

Lilith (Babylonian) Woman of the night
Lilyth, Lillith, Lillyth, Lylith, Lyllith, Lylyth, Lyllyth, Lilithe

★Lillian (Latin) Resembling the lily
Lilian, Liliana, Liliane, Lilianne, Lilias, Lilas, Lillas, Lillias

Lilo (Hawaiian) One who is generous
Lylo, Leelo, Lealo, Leylo, Lielo, Leilo

★Lily (English) Resembling the flower; one who is innocent and beautiful
Leelee, Lil, Lili, Lilie, Lilla, Lilley, Lilli, Lillie

Limor (Hebrew) Refers to myrrh
Limora, Limoria, Limorea, Leemor, Leemora, Leemoria, Leemorea

Lin (Chinese) Resembling jade; from the woodland

Linda (Spanish) One who is soft and beautiful
Lindalee, Lindee, Lindey, Lindi, Lindie, Lindira, Lindka, Lindy, Lynn

Linden (English) From the hill of lime trees
Lindenn, Lindon, Lindynn, Lynden, Lyndon, Lyndyn, Lyndin, Lindin

Lindley (English) From the pastureland
Lindly, Lindlee, Lindleigh, Lindli, Lindlie, Leland, Lindlea

Lindsay (English) From the island of linden trees; from Lincoln's wetland
Lind, Lindsea, Lindsee, Lindseigh, Lindsey, Lindsy, Linsay, Linsey

Lisa (English) Form of Elizabeth, meaning "my God is bountiful; God's promise"
Leesa, Liesa, Lisebet, Lise, Liseta, Lisette, Liszka, Lisebeth

Lishan (African) One who is awarded a medal
Lishana, Lishanna, Lyshan, Lyshana, Lyshanna

Lissie (American) Resembling a flower
Lissi, Lissy, Lissey, Lissee, Lissea

Liv (Scandinavian / Latin) One who protects others / from the olive tree
Livia, Livea, Liviya, Livija, Livvy, Livy, Livya, Lyvia

Liya (Hebrew) The Lord's daughter
Liyah, Leeya, Leeyah, Leaya, Leayah

Lo (American) A fiesty woman
Loe, Low, Lowe

Loicy (American) A delightful woman
Loicey, Loicee, Loicea, Loici, Loicie, Loyce, Loice, Loyci

Lokelani (Hawaiian) Resembling a small red rose
Lokelanie, Lokelany, Lokelaney, Lokelanee, Lokelanea

Loki (Norse) In mythology, a trickster god
Lokie, Lokee, Lokey, Loky, Lokea, Lokeah, Lokia, Lokiah

Lomita (Spanish) A good woman
Lomitah, Lomeeta, Lomeetah, Lomieta, Lomietah, Lomeita, Lomeitah, Lomeata

London (English) From the capital of England

Lorelei (German) From the rocky cliff; in mythology, a siren who lured sailors to their deaths
Laurelei, Laurelie, Loralee, Loralei, Loralie, Loralyn, Lorilee, Lorilyn

Loretta (Italian) Form of Laura, meaning "crowned with laurel; from the laurel tree"
Laretta, Larretta, Lauretta, Laurette, Leretta, Loreta, Lorette, Lorretta

Lorraine (French) From the kingdom of Lothair
Laraine, Larayne, Laurraine, Leraine, Lerayne, Lorain, Loraina, Loraine

Lo-ruhamah (Hebrew) One who does not receive mercy

Louvain (English) From the city in Belgium
Leuven, Loovain

Love (English) One who is full of affection
Lovey, Loveday, Lovette, Lovi, Lovie, Lov, Luv, Luvey

Lovella (Native American) Having a soft spirit
Lovell, Lovela, Lovele, Lovelle, Lovel

Lovely (American) An attractive and pleasant woman
Loveli, Loveley, Lovelie, Lovelee, Loveleigh, Lovelea

Luana (Hawaiian) One who is content and enjoys life
Lewanna, Lou-Ann, Louann, Louanna, Louanne, Luanda, Luane, Luann

Lucretia (Latin) A bringer of light; a successful woman; in mythology, a maiden who was raped by the prince of Rome
Lacretia, Loucrecia, Loucresha, Loucretia, Loucrezia, Lucrece, Lucrecia, Lucreecia

Lucy (Latin) Feminine form of Lucius; one who is illuminated
Luce, Lucetta, Lucette, Luci, Lucia, Luciana, Lucianna, Lucida

Lucylynn (American) A light-hearted woman
Lucylyn, Lucylynne, Lucilynn, Lucilyn, Lucilynne

Ludmila (Slavic) Having the favor of the people
Ludmilah, Ludmilla, Ludmillah, Ludmyla, Ludmylla, Lyubochka, Lyudmila, Lyuha

Luenetter (American) A self-centered woman
Luenette, Luenett, Luenete, Luenet, Luenetta, Lueneta

Luned (Welsh) Form of Eiluned, meaning "an idol worshipper"
Luneda, Lunedia, Lunedea

Lunet (English) Of the crescent moon
Lunett, Lunette, Luneta, Lunete, Lunetta

Lupita (Spanish) Form of Guadalupe, meaning "from the valley of wolves"
Lupe, Lupyta, Lupelina, Lupeeta, Lupieta, Lupeita, Lupeata

Lurissa (American) A beguiling woman
Lurisa, Luryssa, Lurysa, Luressa, Luresa

Luvina (English) Little one who is dearly loved
Luvinah, Luvena, Luvyna, Luveena, Luveina, Luviena, Luveana

Luyu (Native American) Resembling the dove

Lycoris (Greek) Born at twilight
Lycoriss, Lycorisse, Lycorys, Lycorysse, Lycoryss

Lydia (Greek) A beautiful woman from Lydia
Lidia, Lidie, Lidija, Lyda, Lydie, Lydea, Liddy, Lidiy

Lynn (English) Woman of the lake; form of Linda, meaning "one who is soft and beautiful"
Linell, Linnell, Lyn, Lynae, Lyndel, Lyndell, Lynell, Lynelle

Lyric (French) Of the lyre;
the words of a song
*Lyrica, Lyricia, Lyrik,
Lyrick, Lyrika, Lyricka*

Lytanisha (American) A
scintillating woman
*Lytanesha, Lytaniesha,
Lytaneisha, Lytanysha,
Lytaneesha, Lytaneasha*

Maachah (Hebrew) One
who has been oppressed;
in the Bible, one of
David's wives
Maacha

Macanta (Gaelic) A kind
and gentle woman
*Macan, Macantia,
Macantea, Macantah*

Machi (Taiwanese) A good
friend
*Machie, Machy, Machey,
Machee, Machea*

Mackenna (Gaelic)
Daughter of the hand-
some man
*Mackendra, Mackennah,
McKenna, McKendra,
Makenna, Makennah*

★ᵀMackenzie (Gaelic)
Daughter of a wise leader; a
fiery woman; one who is fair
*Mackenzey, Makensie,
Makenzie, M'Kenzie,
McKenzie, Meckenzie,
Mackenzee, Mackenzy*

Macy (French) One who
wields a weapon
*Macee, Macey, Maci, Macie,
Maicey, Maicy, Macea, Maicea*

Mada (Arabic) One who has
reached the end of the path
Madah

Madana (Ethiopian) One
who heals others
*Madayna, Madaina, Madania,
Madaynia, Madainia*

Maddox (English) Born
into wealth and prosperity
Madox, Madoxx, Maddoxx

★Madeline (Hebrew)
Woman from Magdala
*Mada, Madalaina,
Madaleine, Madalena,
Madalene, Madalyn,
Madalynn, Maddelena,
Makelina*

Madhavi (Indian) Feminine
form of Madhav; born in
the springtime
*Madhavie, Madhavee,
Madhavey, Madhavy,
Madhavea*

Madhu (Indian) As sweet
as honey
*Madhul, Madhula, Madhulika,
Madhulia, Madhulea*

Madini (Swahili) As precious as a gemstone
Madinie, Madiny, Madiney, Madinee, Madyny, Madyni, Madinea, Madynie

★ᵀ**Madison** (English) Daughter of a mighty warrior
Maddison, Madisen, Madisson, Madisyn, Madyson

Madoline (English) One who is accomplished with the stringed instrument
Mandalin, Mandalyn, Mandalynn, Mandelin, Mandellin, Mandellyn, Mandolin, Mandolyn

Madonna (Italian) My lady; refers to the Virgin Mary
Madonnah, Madona, Madonah

Maeve (Irish) An intoxicating woman
Mave, Meave, Medb, Meabh

Mafuane (Egyptian) Daughter of the earth
Mafuann, Mafuanne, Mafuana, Mafuanna

Magnolia (French) Resembling the flower
Magnoliya, Magnoliah, Magnolea, Magnoleah, Magnoliyah, Magnolya, Magnolyah

Mahal (Native American) A tender and loving woman
Mahall, Mahale, Mahalle

Mahari (African) One who offers forgiveness
Maharie, Mahary, Maharey, Maharee, Maharai, Maharae, Maharea

Maheona (Native American) A medicine woman
Maheo, Maheonia, Maheonea

Mahesa (Indian) A powerful and great lady
Maheshvari

Mahira (Arabic) A clever and adroit woman
Mahirah, Mahir, Mahire, Mahiria, Mahirea, Maheera, Mahyra, Mahiera

★**Maia** (Latin / Maori) The great one; in mythology, the goddess of spring / a brave warrior
*Maiah, Maya, **Mya**, Maja*

Maida (English) A maiden; a virgin
Maidel, Maidie, Mayda, Maydena, Maydey, Mady, Maegth, Magd

Maiki (Japanese) Resembling the dancing flower
Maikie, Maikei, Maikki, Maikee

Maimun (Arabic) One who is lucky; fortunate
Maimoon, Maimoun

Maimuna (Arabic) One who is trustworthy
Maimoona, Maimouna

Maine (French) From the mainland; from the state of Maine

Maiolaine (French) As delicate as a flower
Maiolainie, Maiolani, Maiolaney, Maiolany, Maiolanee, Maiolayne, Maiolanea

Maisara (Arabic) One who lives an effortless life
Maisarah, Maisarra, Maisarrah

Maisha (African) Giver of life
Maysha, Maishah, Mayshah, Maesha, Maeshah

Maisie (Scottish) Form of Margaret, meaning "resembling a pearl"
Maisee, Maisey, Maisy, Maizie, Mazey, Mazie, Maisi, Maizi

Maitreya (Sanskrit) One who offers love to all
Maitreyah, Maetreya, Maitraya, Maetraya

Majaliwa (Swahili) Filled with God's grace
Majaliwah, Majalewa, Majalywa, Majalewah, Majalywah

Majaya (Indian) A victorious woman
Majayah

Majime (Japanese) An earnest woman

Makala (Hawaiian) Resembling myrtle
Makalah, Makalla, Makallah

Makani (Hawaiian) Of the wind
Makanie, Makaney, Makany, Makanee, Makanea

Makareta (Maori) Form of Margaret, meaning "resembling a pearl / the child of light"
Makaretah, Makarita, Makaryta

Makea (Finnish) One who is sweet
Makeah, Makia, Makiah

Makeda (African) A queenly woman; greatness
Makedah

Makelina (Hawaiian) Form of Madeline, meaning "woman from Magdala"
Makelinah, Makeleena, Makelyna, Makeleana, Makeline, Makelyne, Makeleane, Makeleene

Makena (African) One who is filled with happiness
Makenah, Makeena, Makeenah, Makeana, Makeanah, Makyna, Makynah, Mackena

Malak (Arabic) A heavenly messenger; an angel
Malaka, Malaika, Malayka, Malaeka, Malake, Malayk, Malaek, Malakia

Malati (Indian) Resembling a fragrant flower
Malatie, Malaty, Malatey, Malatee, Malatea

Malcomina (Scottish) Feminine form of Malcolm; devotee of St. Columba
Malcomeena, Malcomyna, Malcominia, Malcominea, Malcomena, Malcomeina, Malcomiena, Malcomeana

Malcsi (Hungarian) An industrious woman
Malcsie, Malcsee, Malcsey, Malcsy, Malksi, Malksie, Malksy, Malksee

Maleda (Ethiopian) Born with the rising sun
Maledah

Mali (Thai / Welsh) Resembling a flower / form of Molly, meaning "star of the sea / from the sea of bitterness"
Malie, Malee, Maleigh, Maly, Maley

Malika (Arabic) Destined to be queen
Malikah, Malyka, Maleeka, Maleika, Malieka, Maliika, Maleaka

Malina (Hawaiian) A peaceful woman
Malinah, Maleena, Maleenah, Malyna, Malynah, Maleina, Maliena, Maleana

Malinka (Russian) As sweet as a little berry
Malinkah, Malynka, Maleenka, Malienka, Maleinka, Maleanka

Maluna (Hawaiian) One who rises above
Maloona, Malunia, Malunai, Maloonia, Maloonai, Malouna, Malounia, Malounai

Malva (Greek) One who is soft and slender
Malvah, Malvia, Malvea

Mana (Polynesian) A charismatic and prestigious woman
Manah

Manal (Arabic) An accomplished woman
Manala, Manall, Manalle, Manalla, Manali

Manami (Japanese) Having a love of the ocean
Manamie, Manamy, Manamey, Manamee, Manamea

Mangena (Hebrew) As sweet as a melody
Mangenah, Mangenna, Mangennah

Manyara (African) A humble woman
Manyarah

Maola (Irish) A handmaiden
Maoli, Maole, Maolie, Maolia, Maoly, Maoley, Maolee, Maolea

Mapenzi (African) One who is dearly loved
Mpenzi, Mapenzie, Mapenze, Mapenzy, Mapenzee, Mapenzea

Maram (Arabic) One who is wished for
Marame, Marama, Marami, Maramie, Maramee, Maramy, Maramey, Maramea

Marcella (Latin) Dedicated to Mars, the God of war
Marcela, Marsela, Marsella, Maricela, Maricel

Marcia (Latin) Feminine form of Marcus; dedicated to Mars, the god of war
Marcena, Marcene, Marchita, Marciana, Marciane, Marcianne, Marcilyn, Marcilynn

Marde (Latin) A woman warrior
Mardane, Mardayne

Mardea (African) The last-born child
Mardeah

Marenda (Latin) An admirable woman
Marendah

Margaret (Greek / Persian) Resembling a pearl / the child of light
Maighread, Mairead, Mag, Maggi, Maggie, Maggy, Maiga, Malgorzata, Megan, Marwarid, Marjorie, Marged, Makareta

Marged (Welsh) Form of Margaret, meaning "resembling a pearl / the child of light"
Margred, Margeda, Margreda

★Maria (Spanish) Form of Mary, meaning "star of the sea / from the sea of bitterness"
Mariah, Marialena, Marialinda, Marialisa, Maaria, Mayria, Maeria, Mariabella

Mariamne (Hebrew) A rebellious woman
Mamre, Meria

Mariane (French) Blend of Mary, meaning "star of the sea / from the sea of bitterness," and Ann, meaning "a woman graced with God's favor"
Mariam, Mariana, Marian, Marion, Maryann, Maryanne, Maryanna, Maryane

Marietta (French) Form of Mary, meaning "star of the sea / from the sea of bitterness"
Mariette, Maretta, Mariet, Maryetta, Maryette, Marieta

Marika (Danish) Form of Mary, meaning "star of the sea / from the sea of bitterness"
Marieke, Marijke, Marike, Maryk, Maryka

Mariko (Japanese) Daughter of Mari; a ball or sphere
Maryko, Mareeko, Marieko, Mareiko

Marilyn (English) Form of Mary, meaning "star of the sea / from the sea of bitterness"
Maralin, Maralyn, Maralynn, Marelyn, Marilee, Marilin, Marillyn, Marilynn

★Marissa (Latin) Woman of the sea
Maressa, Maricia, Marisabel, Marisha, Marisse, Maritza, Mariza, Marrissa

Marjam (Slavic) One who is merry
Marjama, Marjamah, Marjami, Marjamie, Marjamy, Marjamey, Marjamee, Marjamea

Marjani (African) Of the coral reef
Marjanie, Marjany, Marjaney, Marjanee, Marjean, Marjeani, Marjeanie, Marijani

Marjorie (English) Form of Margaret, meaning "resembling a pearl / the child of light"
Marcharie, Marge, Margeree, Margery, Margerie, Margery, Margey, Margi

Marlene (German) Blend of Mary, meaning "star of the sea / from the sea of bitterness," and Magdalene, meaning "woman from Magdala"
Marlaina, Marlana, Marlane, Marlayna, Marlayne, Marleen, Marleena, Marleene

Marlis (German) Form of Mary, meaning "star of the sea / from the sea of bitterness"
Marlisa, Marliss, Marlise, Marlisse, Marlissa, Marlys, Marlyss, Marlysa

Marlo (English) One who resembles driftwood
Marloe, Marlow, Marlowe, Marlon

Marmara (Greek) From the sparkling sea
Marmarra, Marmarah, Marmarrah

Marsala (Italian) From the place of sweet wine
Marsalah, Marsalla, Marsallah

Martha (Aramaic) Mistress of the house; in the Bible, the sister of Lazarus and Mary
Maarva, Marfa, Marhta, Mariet, Marit, Mart, Marta, Marte

Marvina (English) Feminine form of Marvin; friend of the sea
Marvinah, Marveena, Marveene, Marvyna, Marvyne, Marvadene, Marvene, Marvena

Marwarid (Arabic) Form of Margaret, meaning "resembling a pearl / the child of light"
Marwaareed, Marwareed, Marwaryd, Marwaryde, Marwaride

*Mary (Latin / Hebrew) Star of the sea / from the sea of bitterness
Mair, Mal, Mallie, Manette, Manon, Manya, Mare, Maren, Maria, Marietta, Marika, Marilyn, Marlis, Maureen, May, Mindel, Miriam, Molly, Mia

Maryweld (English) Mary of the woods
Marywelde, Marywelda, Mariweld, Mariwelde, Mariwelda

Masami (African / Japanese) A commanding woman / one who is truthful
Masamie, Masamee, Masamy, Masamey, Masamea

Mashaka (African) A troublemaker; a mischievous woman
Mashakah, Mashakia, Mashake, Mashaki, Mashakie, Mashaky, Mashakey, Mashakee

Ma'sma (Arabic) One who is innocent
Maa'sma

Massachusetts (Native American) From the big hill; from the state of Massachusetts
Massachusets, Massachusette, Massachusetta, Massa, Massachute, Massachusta

Mastura (Arabic) One who is pure; chaste
Mastoora, Masturah, Masturia, Masturiya, Mastooria, Mastoura, Mastrouria

Matana (Hebrew) A gift from God
Matanah, Matanna, Matannah, Matai

Matangi (Hindi) In
Hinduism, the patron of
inner thought
*Matangy, Matangie, Matangee,
Matangey, Matangea*

Matsuko (Japanese) Child
of the pine tree

Maureen (Irish) Form of
Mary, meaning "star of
the sea / from the sea of
bitterness"
*Maura, Maurene,
Maurianne, Maurine,
Maurya, Mavra, Maure, Mo*

Mauve (French) Of the
mallow plant
Mawve

Maven (English) Having
great knowledge
Mavin, Mavyn

Maverick (American) One
who is wild and free
*Maverik, Maveryck,
Maveryk, Mavarick, Mavarik*

Mavis (French)
Resembling a songbird
*Mavise, Maviss, Mavisse,
Mavys, Mavyss, Mavysse*

Mawunyaga (African)
God is great

May (Latin) Born during the
month of May; form of Mary,
meaning "star of the sea /
from the sea of bitterness"
*Mae, Mai, Maelynn, Maelee,
Maj, Mala, Mayana, Maye*

★Maya (Indian / Hebrew)
An illusion; a dream / form
of Maia, meaning "the
great one / a brave warrior"

Mayumi (Japanese) One
who embodies truth, wis-
dom, and beauty
*Mayumie, Mayumee,
Mayumy, Mayumey,
Mayumea*

Mazarine (French) Having
deep-blue eyes
*Mazareen, Mazareene,
Mazaryn, Mazaryne,
Mazine, Mazyne, Mazeene*

Mazhira (Hebrew) A shin-
ing woman
*Mazhirah, Mazheera,
Mazhyra, Mazheira,
Mazhiera, Mazheara*

McKayla (Gaelic) A fiery
woman
*McKale, McKaylee,
McKaleigh, McKay,
McKaye, McKaela*

Meara (Gaelic) One who is
filled with happiness
Mearah

Medea (Greek) A cunning
ruler; in mythology, a sor-
ceress
*Madora, Medeia, Media,
Medeah, Mediah, Mediya,
Mediyah*

Medini (Indian) Daughter of the earth
Medinie, Mediny, Mediney, Medinee, Medinea

Meditrina (Latin) The healer; in mythology, goddess of health and wine
Meditreena, Meditryna, Meditriena

Medora (Greek) A wise ruler
Medoria, Medorah, Medorra, Medorea

Medusa (Greek) In mythology, a Gorgon with snakes for hair
Medoosa, Medusah, Medoosah, Medousa, Medousah

Meenakshi (Indian) Having beautiful eyes

★ᵀ**Megan** (Welsh) Form of Margaret, meaning "resembling a pearl / the child of light"
Maegan, Meg, Magan, Magen, Megin, Maygan, Meagan, Meaghan

Mehalia (Hebrew) An affectionate woman
Mehaliah, Mehalea, Mehaleah, Mehaliya, Mehaliyah

Meishan (Chinese) One who is virtuous and beautiful
Meishana, Meishawn, Meishaun, Meishon

Meiwei (Chinese) One who is forever enchanting

Melangell (Welsh) A sweet messenger from heaven
Melangelle, Melangela, Melangella, Melangele, Melangel

★**Melanie** (Greek) A dark-skinned beauty
Malaney, Malanie, Mel, Mela, Melaina, Melaine, Melainey, Melana

Meli (Native American) One who is bitter
Melie, Melee, Melea, Meleigh, Mely, Meley

Melia (Hawaiian / Greek) Resembling the plumeria / of the ash tree; in mythology, a nymph
Melidice, Melitine, Meliah, Meelia, Melya

Melika (Turkish) A great beauty
Melikah, Melicka, Melicca, Melyka, Melycka, Meleeka, Meleaka

Melinda (Latin) One who is sweet and gentle
Melynda, Malinda, Malinde, Mallie, Mally, Malynda, Melinde, Mellinda, Mindy

Melisande (French) Having the strength of an animal
Malisande, Malissande, Malyssandre, Melesande, Melisandra, Melisandre, Melissande, Melissandre

*Melissa (Greek)
Resembling a honeybee;
in mythology, a nymph
*Malissa, Mallissa, Mel,
Melesa, Melessa, Melisa,
Melise, Melisse*

Melita (Greek) As sweet as
honey
*Malita, Malitta, Melida,
Melitta, Melyta, Malyta,
Meleeta, Meleata*

Melka (Polish) A dark-
skinned beauty
Melkah

Melody (Greek) A beauti-
ful song
*Melodee, Melodey, Melodi,
Melodia, Melodie, Melodea*

Menula (Lithuanian) Born
beneath the moon
*Menulah, Menoola,
Menoolah, Menoula,
Menoulah*

Mephaath (Hebrew) A
lustrous woman
*Mephath, Mephatha,
Mephaatha*

Merana (American)
Woman of the waters
*Meranah, Meranna,
Merannah*

Mercer (English) A prosperous merchant

Meredith (Welsh) A great
ruler; protector of the sea
*Maredud, Meridel,
Meredithe, Meredyth,
Meridith, Merridie,
Meradith, Meredydd*

Meribah (Hebrew) A quar-
relsome woman
Meriba

Merope (Greek) In mythol-
ogy, one of the Pleiades
*Meropi, Meropie, Meropy,
Meropey, Meropee, Meropea*

Meroz (Hebrew) From the
cursed plains
Meroza, Merozia, Meroze

Merry (English) One who
is lighthearted and joyful
*Merree, Merri, Merrie,
Merrielle, Merrile, Merrilee,
Merrili, Merrily*

Mertice (English) A well-
known lady
*Mertise, Mertyce, Mertyse,
Mertysa, Mertisa, Mertiece,
Merteace*

Merton (English) From the
village near the pond
Mertan, Mertin, Mertun

Mesopotamia (Hebrew)
From the land between
two rivers
Mesopotama, Mesopotamea

Metea (Greek) A gentle
woman
Meteah, Metia, Metiah

Metin (Greek) A wise counselor
Metine, Metyn, Metyne

Metis (Greek) One who is industrious
Metiss, Metisse, Metys, Metyss, Metysse

Mettalise (Danish) As graceful as a pearl
Metalise, Mettalisse, Mettalisa, Mettalissa

Mhina (African) A delightful lady
Mhinah, Mhinna, Mhena, Mhenah

★**Mia** (Israeli / Latin) Who is like God? / form of Mary, meaning "star of the sea / from the sea of bitterness"
Miah, Mea, Meah, Meya

★ᵀ**Michaela** (Celtic, Gaelic, Hebrew, English, Irish) Feminine form of Michael; who is like God?
*Macaela, MacKayla, **Makayla**, Mak, Mechaela, Meeskaela, Mekea, Micaela*

★**Michelle** (French) Feminine form of Michael; who is like God?
Machelle, Mashelle, M'chelle, Mechelle, Meechelle, Me'Shell, Meshella, Mischa

Michewa (Tibetan) Sent from heaven
Michewah

Michima (Japanese) Possessing beautiful wisdom

Michri (Hebrew) Gift from God
Michrie, Michry, Michrey, Michree, Michrea

Mide (Irish) One who is thirsty
Meeda, Mida

Midori (Japanese) Having green eyes
Midorie, Midory, Midorey, Midoree, Midorea

Mignon (French) One who is cute and petite
Mignonette, Mignonne, Mingnon, Minyonne, Minyonette

Mikaili (African) A godly woman
Mikailie, Mikayli, Mikali, Mikaylie, Mikalie

Mila (Slavic) One who is industrious and hardworking
Milaia, Milaka, Milla, Milia

Milan (Latin) From the city in Italy; one who is gracious
Milaana

Milanka (Croatian) A
sweet young woman
*Milankaa, Milankai,
Milanke, Milankia,
Mylanka, Mylanke*

Milena (Slavic) The
favored one
*Mileena, Milana, Miladena,
Milanka, Mlada, Mladena*

Miliana (Latin) Feminine
of Emeliano; one who is
eager and willing
*Milianah, Milianna,
Miliane, Miliann, Milianne*

Milima (Swahili) Woman
from the mountains
Milimah, Mileema, Milyma

Millo (Hebrew) Defender
of the sacred city
Milloh, Millowe, Milloe

Miloslava (Russian)
Feminine form of
Miloslav; having the favor
and glory of the people
*Miloslavah, Miloslavia,
Miloslavea*

Mima (Hebrew) Form of
Jemima, meaning "our lit-
tle dove"
Mimah, Mymah, Myma

Minda (Native American,
Hindi) Having great
knowledge
*Mindah, Mynda, Myndah,
Menda, Mendah*

Mindel (Hebrew) Form of
Mary, meaning "star of
the sea / from the sea of
bitterness"
*Mindell, Mindelle, Mindele,
Mindela, Mindella*

Mindy (English) Form of
Melinda, meaning "one
who is sweet and gentle"
*Minda, Mindee, Mindi,
Mindie, Mindey, Mindea*

Ming Yue (Chinese) Born
beneath the brigh moon

Mingmei (Chinese) A
bright and beautiful girl

Minjonet (French)
Resembling the small
blue flower
*Minjonett, Minjonete,
Minjonette, Minjoneta,
Minjonetta*

Minka (Teutonic) One who
is resolute; having great
strength
*Minkah, Mynka, Mynkah,
Minna, Minne*

Minowa (Native
American) One who has a
moving voice
*Minowah, Mynowa,
Mynowah*

Minuit (French) Born at
midnight
Minueet

Miracle (American) An act of God's hand
Mirakle, Mirakel, Myracle, Myrakle

Miranda (Latin) Worthy of admiration
Maranda, Myranda, Randi

Mirai (Basque / Japanese) A miracle child / future
Miraya, Mirari, Mirarie, Miraree, Mirae

Miremba (Ugandan) A promoter of peace
Mirembe, Mirem, Mirembah, Mirembeh, Mirema

Miriam (Hebrew) Form of Mary, meaning "star of the sea / from the sea of bitterness"
Mariam, Maryam, Meriam, Meryam, Mirham, Mirjam, Mirjana, Mirriam

Mirinesse (English) Filled with joy
Miriness, Mirinese, Mirines, Mirinessa, Mirinesa

Mirit (Hebrew) One who is strong-willed

Miroslava (Slavic) Feminine form of Miroslav; one who basks in peaceful glory
Miroslavia, Miroslavea, Myroslava, Myroslavia, Myroslavea

Mischa (Russian) Form of Michelle, meaning "who is like God?"
Misha

Mistico (Italian) A mystical woman
Mistica, Mystico, Mystica, Mistiko, Mystiko

Misumi (Japanese) A pure, beautiful woman
Misumie, Misumee, Misumy, Misumey, Misumea

Mitali (Indian) A friendly and sweet woman
Mitalie, Mitalee, Mitaleigh, Mitaly, Mitaley, Meeta, Mitalea

Mitexi (Native American) Born beneath the sacred moon
Mitexie, Mitexee, Mitexy, Mitexey, Mitexa, Mitexea

Miya (Japenese) From the sacred temple
Miyah

Miyo (Japanese) A beautiful daughter
Miyoko

Mizar (Hebrew) A little woman; petite
Mizarr, Mizarre, Mizare, Mizara, Mizaria, Mizarra

Mliss (Cambodian) Resembling a flower
Mlissa, Mlisse, Mlyss, Mlysse, Mlyssa

Mocha (Arabic) As sweet as chocolate
Mochah

Modesty (Latin) One who is without conceit
Modesti, Modestie, Modestee, Modestus, Modestey, Modesta, Modestia, Modestina

Moesha (American) Drawn from the water
Moisha, Moysha, Moeesha, Moeasha, Moeysha

Mohini (Indian) The most beautiful
Mohinie, Mohinee, Mohiny, Mohiney, Mohinea

Moladah (Hebrew) A giver of life
Molada

*★***Molly** (Irish) Form of Mary, meaning "star of the sea / from the sea of bitterness"
Moll, Mollee, Molley, Molli, Mollie, Molle, Mollea, Mali

Mona (Gaelic) One who is born into the nobility
Moina, Monah, Monalisa, Monalissa, Monna, Moyna, Monalysa, Monalyssa

Monahana (Gaelic) A religious woman
Monahanah, Monahanna, Monahannah

Moncha (Irish) A solitary woman
Monchah

Monica (Greek / Latin) A solitary woman / one who advises others
Monnica, Monca, Monicka, Monika, Monike

Monique (French) One who provides wise counsel
Moniqua, Moneeque, Moneequa, Moneeke, Moeneek, Moneaque, Moneaqua, Moneake

Monisha (Hindi) Having great intelligence
Monishah, Monesha, Moneisha, Moniesha, Moneysha, Moneasha

Monroe (Gaelic) Woman from the river
Monrow, Monrowe, Monro

Monserrat (Latin) From the jagged mountain
Montserrat

Montana (Latin) Woman of the mountains; from the state of Montana
Montanna, Montina, Monteene, Montese

Morcan (Welsh) Of the bright sea
Morcane, Morcana, Morcania, Morcanea

Moreh (Hebrew) A great archer; a teacher

★ᵀMorgan (Welsh) Circling the bright sea; a sea dweller
Morgaine, Morgana, Morgance, Morgane, Morganica, Morgann, Morganne, Morgayne

Morguase (English) In Arthurian legend, the mother of Gawain
Marguase, Margawse, Morgawse, Morgause, Margause

Morina (Japanese) From the woodland town
Morinah, Moreena, Moryna, Moriena, Moreina, Moreana

Mubarika (Arabic) One who is blessed
Mubaarika, Mubaricka, Mubaryka, Mubaricca, Mubarycca

Mubina (Arabic) One who displays her true image
Mubeena, Mubinah, Mubyna, Mubeana, Mubiena

Mudan (Mandarin) Daughter of a harmonious family
Mudane, Mudana, Mudayne, Mudaine, Mudann, Mudaen, Mudaena

Mufidah (Arabic) One who is helpful to others
Mufeeda, Mufeyda, Mufyda, Mufeida, Mufieda, Mufeada

Mugain (Irish) In mythology, the wife of the king of Ulster
Mugayne, Mugaine, Mugane, Mugayn, Mugaen, Mugaene, Mugaina, Mugayna

Muirne (Irish) One who is dearly loved
Muirna

Mukantagara (Egyptian) Born during a time of war

Mukarramma (Egyptian) One who is honored and respected
Mukarama, Mukaramma, Mukkarama

Munay (African) One who loves and is loved
Manay, Munaye, Munae, Munai

Munazza (Arabic) An independent woman; one who is free
Munazzah, Munaza, Munazah

Murata (African) A beloved friend
Muraty, Muratia, Murati, Muratie, Muratee, Muratea

Muriel (Irish) Of the shining sea
Merial, Meriel, Merrill, Miureall, Murial, Muriella, Murielle, Merill

Murphy (Celtic) Daughter of a great sea warrior
Murphi, Murphie, Murphey, Murphee, Murfi, Murfy, Murfie, Murphea

Musoke (African) Having the beauty of a rainbow

Mutehhara (Arabic) One who is pure; chaste
Mutehara, Mutehharah, Muteharra, Muteharah

Myisha (Arabic) Form of Aisha, meaning "lively; womanly"
Myesha, Myeisha, Myeshia, Myiesha, Myeasha

Myrina (Latin) In mythology, an Amazon
Myrinah, Myreena, Myreina, Myriena, Myreana

Myrrh (Egyptian) Resembling the fragrant oil

Naama (Hebrew) Feminine form of Noam; an attractive woman; good-looking
Naamah

Naava (Hebrew) A lovely and pleasant woman
Naavah, Nava, Navah, Navit

Nabila (Arabic) Daughter born into nobility; a high-born daughter
Nabilah, Nabeela, Nabyla, Nabeelah, Nabylah, Nabeala, Nabealah

Nachine (Spanish) A fiery young woman
Nacheene, Nachyne, Nachina, Nachinah, Nachyna, Nacheena, Nacheane, Nacheana

Nadda (Arabic) A very generous woman
Naddah, Nada, Nadah

Nadia (Slavic) One who is full of hope
Nadja, Nadya, Naadiya, Nadine, Nadie, Nadiyah, Nadea, Nadija

Nadirah (Arabic) One who is precious; rare
Nadira, Nadyra, Nadyrah, Nadeera, Nadeerah, Nadra, Nadrah

Naeemah (Egyptian) A kind and benevolent woman
Nayma, Nayima, Nayema

Naeva (French) Born in the evening
Naevah, Naevia, Naevea, Nayva, Nayvah, Nayvia, Nayvea

Nafuna (African) A child who is delivered feetfirst
Nafunah, Nafunna, Nafoona, Nafoonah, Naphuna, Naphunah, Naphoona, Naphoonah

Nagesa (African) Born during the time of harvest
Nagesah, Nagessa, Nagessah

Nagge (Hebrew) A radiant woman

Nagina (Arabic) As precious as a pearl
Nageena, Naginah, Nageenah, Nagyna, Nagynah, Nageana, Nageanah

Nailah (Arabic) Feminine form of Nail; a successful woman; the acquirer
Na'ila, Na'ilah, Naa'ilah, Naila, Nayla, Naylah, Naela, Naelah

Najia (Arabic) An independent woman; one who is free
Naajia

Najja (African) The second-born child
Najjah

Namid (Native American) A star dancer
Namide, Namyd, Namyde

Namita (Papuan) In mythology, a mother goddess
Namitah, Nameeta, Namyta, Nameetah, Namytah, Nameata, Nameatah

Nana (Hawaiian / English) Born during the spring; a star / a grandmother or one who watches over children

Nancy (English) Form of Anna, meaning "a woman graced with God's favor"
Nainsey, Nainsi, Nance, Nancee, Nancey, Nanci, Nancie, Nancsi

Nandalia (Australian) A fiery woman
Nandaliah, Nandalea, Nandaleah, Nandali, Nandalie, Nandalei, Nandalee, Nandaleigh

Nandita (Indian) A delightful daughter
Nanditah, Nanditia, Nanditea

Nani (Greek / Hawaiian) A charming woman / one who is beautiful
Nanie, Nanee, Naney, Nany, Nania, Nanya, Naniya, Nanea

Narella (Greek) A bright woman; intelligent
Narellah, Narela, Narelah, Narelle, Narell, Narele

Nascio (Latin) In mythology, goddess of childbirth

Nashita (Arabic) A lively woman; one who is energetic
Nashitah, Nashyta, Nasheeta, Nasheata, Nashieta, Nasheita

Nasiha (Arabic) One who
gives good advice
*Naasiha, Nasihah, Naseeha,
Naseehah, Nasyha, Nasyhah,
Naseaha, Naseahah*

★ᵀ**Natalie** (Latin) Refers to
Christ's birthday; born on
Christmas Day
*Natala, Natalee, Natalene,
Natalia, Natalja, Natalina,
Nataline, Nataly, Natasha*

Natane (Native American)
Her father's daughter
Natanne

Natasha (Russian) Form
of Natalie, meaning "born
on Christmas Day"
*Nastaliya, Nastalya,
Natacha, Natascha,
Natashenka, Natashia,
Natasia, Natosha, Tosha*

Natividad (Spanish)
Refers to the Nativity
*Natividade, Natividada,
Natyvydad, Nativydad,
Natyvidad*

Natsuko (Japanese) Child
born during the summer
Natsu, Natsumi

Navida (Iranian) Feminine
form of Navid; bringer of
good news
*Navyda, Navidah, Navyda,
Naveeda, Naveedah,
Naveada, Naveadah*

Navya (Indian) One who
is youthful
Navyah, Naviya, Naviyah

Nawal (Arabic) A gift of God
*Nawall, Nawalle, Nawala,
Nawalla*

Nawar (Arabic) Resembling
a flower
Nawaar

Nazahah (Arabic) One
who is pure and honest
Nazaha, Nazihah, Naziha

Nechama (Hebrew) One
who provides comfort
*Nehama, Nehamah,
Nachmanit, Nachuma,
Nechamah, Nechamit*

Neda (Slavic) Born on a
Sunday
*Nedda, Nedah, Nedi, Nedie,
Neddi, Neddie, Nedaa*

Neeharika (Indian) Of the
morning dew
*Neharika, Neeharyka,
Neharyka*

Neena (Hindi) A woman
who has beautiful eyes
*Neenah, Neanah, Neana,
Neyna, Neynah*

Nefertiti (Egyptian) A
queenly woman
*Nefertari, Nefertyty,
Nefertity, Nefertitie,
Nefertitee, Nefertytie,
Nefertitea*

Neginoth (Hebrew) An accomplished musician
Neginothe, Negynoth, Negynothe, Neginotha, Negynotha

Nehelamite (Hebrew) A dreamer
Nehelamitte, Nehelamit, Nehelamyte, Nehelamytte, Nehelamyt

Neith (Egyptian) In mythology, goddess of war and hunting
Neitha, Neytha, Neyth, Neit, Neita, Neitia, Neitea, Neithe

Nekana (Spanish) Woman of sorrow
Nekane, Nekania, Nekanea

Neneca (Spanish) Form of Amelia, meaning "one who is industrious and hardworking"
Nenecah, Nenica, Nenneca, Nennica

Neo (African) A gift from God

Nephthys (Egyptian) In mythology, one of the nine most important deities; the lady of the house
Nebt-het, Nebet-het

Nerissa (Italian / Greek) A black-haired beauty / sea nymph
Narissa, Naryssa, Nericcia, Neryssa, Narice, Nerice, Neris

Nessa (Hebrew / Greek) A miracle child / form of Agnes, meaning "one who is pure; chaste"
Nesha, Nessah, Nessia, Nessya, Nesta, Neta, Netia, Nessie

Netis (Native American) One who is trustworthy
Netiss, Netisse, Netys, Netyss, Netysse

★Nevaeh (American) Child from heaven

Nevina (Scottish) Feminine form of Nevin; daughter of a saint
Nevinah, Neveena, Nevyna, Nevinne, Nevynne, Neveene, Neveana, Neveane

Newlyn (Gaelic) Born during the spring
Newlynn, Newlynne, Newlin, Newlinn, Newlinne, Newlen, Newlenn, Newlenne

Neziah (Hebrew) One who is pure; a victorious woman
Nezia, Nezea, Nezeah, Neza, Nezah, Neziya, Neziyah

Niabi (Native American) Resembling a fawn
Niabie, Niabee, Niabey, Niaby, Nyabi, Nyabie, Niabea, Nyabea

Niagara (English) From the famous waterfall
Niagarah, Niagarra, Niagarrah, Nyagara, Nyagarra

*★ᵀ**Nicole** (Greek) Feminine
form of Nicholas; of the
victorious people
*Necole, Niccole, Nichol,
Nichole, Nicholle, Nickol,
Nickole, Nicol*

Nicosia (English) Woman
from the capital of Cyprus
*Nicosiah, Nicosea,
Nicoseah, Nicotia, Nicotea*

Nidia (Spanish) One who
is gracious
*Nydia, Nidiah, Nydiah,
Nidea, Nideah, Nibia,
Nibiah, Nibea*

Nighean (Scottish) A
young woman; a maiden
Nighinn, Nigheen

Nike (Greek) One who
brings victory; in mythology, goddess of victory
Nikee, Nikey, Nykee, Nyke

Nilam (Arabic) Resembling
a precious blue stone
*Neelam, Nylam, Nilima,
Nilyma, Nylyma, Nylima,
Nealam, Nealama*

Nilsine (Scandinavian)
Feminine form of Neil; a
champion
*Nilsina, Nilsyne, Nilsyna,
Nylsine, Nylsyna, Nylsina,
Nylsyne, Nilsa*

Nimeesha (African) A
princess; daughter born to
royalty
*Nimeeshah, Nimiesha,
Nimisha, Nimysha,
Nymeesha, Nymisha,
Nymysha, Nimeasha*

Nini (African) As solid as a
stone
*Ninie, Niny, Niney, Ninee,
Ninea*

Nishan (African) One who
wins awards
*Nishann, Nishanne,
Nishana, Nishanna,
Nyshan, Nyshana*

Nitya (Indian) An eternal
beauty
Nithya, Nithyah, Nityah

Nixie (German) A beauti-
ful water sprite
*Nixi, Nixy, Nixey, Nixee,
Nixea*

Nizhoni (Native American)
A beautiful woman
*Nizhonie, Nyzhoni,
Nyzhonie, Nizhony,
Nizhoney, Nizhonea,
Nyzhony, Nyzhoney*

Nokomis (Native
American) A daughter of
the moon
*Nokomiss, Nokomisse,
Nokomys, Nokomyss,
Nokomysse*

Nolcha (Native American)
Of the sun
Nolchia, Nolchea

Nomusa (African) One
who is merciful
*Nomusah, Nomusha,
Nomusia, Nomusea,
Nomushia, Nomushea*

Nora (English) Form of
Eleanor, meaning "the
shining light"
*Norah, Noora, Norella, Norelle,
Norissa, Norri, Norrie, Norry*

Nordica (German) Woman
from the north
*Nordika, Nordicka,
Nordyca, Nordyka,
Nordycka, Norda, Norell,
Norelle*

Noriko (Japanese) One
who upholds the law
Nori

Nosiwe (African) Mother
of the homeland

Noura (Arabic) Having an
inner light
Nureh, Nourah, Nure

Nsia (African) The sixth-
born child

Nsonowa (African) The
seventh-born child

Nuo (Chinese) A graceful
woman

Nyala (African) Resembling
an antelope
Nyalah, Nyalla, Nyallah

Nyneve (English) In
Arthurian legend, another
name for the lady of the
lake
*Nineve, Niniane, Ninyane,
Nyniane, Ninieve, Niniveve*

Nyura (Ukrainian) A
graceful woman
*Nyrurah, Nyrurra, Niura,
Neura*

Oaisara (Arabic) A great
ruler; an empress
*Oaisarah, Oaisarra,
Oaisarrah*

Oamra (Arabic) Daughter
of the moon
*Oamrah, Oamira, Oamyra,
Oameera*

Oba (African) In mythology, the goddess of rivers
Obah, Obba, Obbah

Obioma (African) A kind
and caring woman
*Obiomah, Obeoma,
Obeomah, Obyoma,
Obyomah*

Octavia (Latin) Feminine form of Octavius; the eighth-born child
Octaviana, Octavianne, Octavie, Octiana, Octoviana, Ottavia, Octavi, Octavy

Odahingum (Native American) Of the rippling waters

Oddrun (Scandinavian) Our secret love

Oddveig (Scandinavian) One who wields a spear

Ode (Egyptian / Greek) Traveler of the road / a lyric poem
Odea

Odessa (Greek) Feminine form of Odysseus; one who wanders; an angry woman
Odissa, Odyssa, Odessia, Odissia, Odyssia, Odysseia

Odina (Latin / Scandinavian) From the mountain / feminine form of Odin, the highest of the gods
Odinah, Odeena, Odeene, Odeen, Odyna, Odyne, Odynn, Odeana

Ogenya (Hebrew) God provides assistance
Ogenyah, Ogeniya, Ogeniyah

Ogin (Native American) Resembling the wild rose

Oheo (Native American) A beautiful woman

Oira (Latin) One who prays to God
Oyra, Oirah, Oyrah

Okalani (Hawaiian) From the heavens
Okalanie, Okalany, Okalaney, Okalanee, Okaloni, Okalonie, Okalonee, Okalony

Okei (Japanese) Woman of the ocean

Oksana (Russian) Hospitality
Oksanah, Oksie, Aksana

Ola (Nigerian / Hawaiian / Norse) One who is precious / giver of life; well-being / a relic of one's ancestors
Olah, Olla, Ollah

Olaide (American) A thoughtful woman
Olaid, Olaida, Olayd, Olayde, Olayda, Olaed, Olaede, Olaeda

Olathe (Native American) A lovely young woman

Olaug (Scandinavian) A loyal woman

Olayinka (Yoruban) Surrounded by wealth and honor
Olayenka, Olayanka

Oldriska (Czech) A noble ruler
Oldryska, Oldri, Oldrie, Oldry, Oldrey, Oldree, Oldrea

Oleda (English) Resembling a winged creature
Oldedah, Oleta, Olita, Olida, Oletah, Olitah, Olidah

Olethea (Latin) Form of Alethea, meaning "one who is truthful"
Oletheia, Olethia, Oletha, Oletea, Olthaia, Olithea, Olathea, Oletia

Olina (Hawaiian) One who is joyous
Oline, Oleen, Oleene, Olyne, Oleena, Olyna, Olin

★ᵀ**Olivia** (Latin) Feminine form of Oliver; of the olive tree; one who is peaceful
Oliviah, Oliva, Olive, Oliveea, Olivet, Olivetta, Olivette, Olivija

Olwen (Welsh) One who leaves a white footprint
Olwynn, Olvyen, Olvyin

Olympia (Greek) From Mount Olympus; a goddess
Olympiah, Olimpe, Olimpia, Olimpiada, Olimpiana, Olypme, Olympie, Olympi

Omri (Arabic) A red-haired woman
Omrie, Omree, Omrea, Omry, Omrey

Omusa (African) One who is adored
Omusah, Omousa, Omousah

Ona (Hebrew) Filled with grace
Onit, Onat, Onah

Ondine (Latin) Resembling a small wave
Ondina, Ondyne, Ondinia, Ondyna

Ondrea (Slavic) Form of Andrea, meaning "courageous and strong / womanly"
Ondria, Ondrianna, Ondreia, Ondreina, Ondreya, Ondriana, Ondreana, Ondera

Oneida (Native American) Our long-awaited daughter
Onieda, Oneyda, Onida, Onyda

Onida (Native American) The one who has been expected
Onidah, Onyda, Onydah

Ontibile (African)
Protected by God
*Ontibyle, Ontybile,
Ontybyle*

Ontina (American) An
open-minded woman
*Ontinah, Onteena,
Onteenah, Onteana,
Onteanah, Ontiena,
Ontienah, Onteina*

Oona (Gaelic) Form of
Agnes, meaning "one who
is pure; chaste"
*Oonaugh, Oonagh, Oonah,
Ouna, Ounah, Ounagh,
Ounaugh*

Opal (Sanskrit) A treas-
ured jewel; resembling the
iridescent gemstone
*Opall, Opalle, Opale,
Opalla, Opala, Opalina,
Opaline, Opaleena*

Ophelia (Greek) One who
offers help to others
*Ofelia, Ofilia, OphÈlie,
Ophelya, Ophilia, Ovalia,
Ovelia, Opheliah*

Ophrah (Hebrew)
Resembling a fawn; from
the place of dust
*Ofra, Ofrit, Ophra, Oprah,
Orpa, Orpah, Ofrat, Ofrah*

Oraleyda (Spanish) Born
with the light of dawn
*Oraleydah, Oraleida,
Oraleidah, Oralida,
Oralidah, Oralyda,
Oralydah, Oraleda*

Orange (Latin) Resembling
the sweet fruit
*Orangetta, Orangia,
Orangina, Orangea*

Orbelina (American) One
who brings excitement
*Orbelinah, Orbeleena,
Orbeleenah, Orbeleana,
Orbeleanah, Orbelyna,
Orbelynah, Orbie*

Orea (Greek) From the
mountains
Oreah

Orenda (Iroquois Indian)
A woman with magical
powers

Oriana (Latin) Born at
sunrise
*Oreana, Orianna, Oriane,
Oriann, Orianne*

Oribel (Latin) A beautiful
golden child
*Orabel, Orabelle, Orabell,
Orabela, Orabella, Oribell,
Oribelle, Oribele*

Orin (Irish) A dark-haired
beauty
*Orine, Orina, Oryna, Oryn,
Oryne*

Orinthia (Hebrew /
Gaelic) Of the pine tree /
a fair lady
*Orrinthia, Orenthia, Orna,
Ornina, Orinthea,
Orenthea, Orynthia,
Orynthea*

Oriole (Latin) Resembling the gold-speckled bird
Oreolle, Oriolle, Oreole, Oriola, Oriolla, Oriol, Oreola, Oreolla

Orion (Greek) The huntress; a constellation

Orithna (Greek) One who is natural
Orithne, Orythna, Orythne, Orithnia, Orythnia, Orithnea, Orythnea, Orithniya

Orla (Gaelic) The golden queen
Orlah, Orrla, Orrlah, Orlagh, Orlaith, Orlaithe, Orghlaith, Orghlaithe

Orna (Irish / Hebrew) One who is pale-skinned / of the cedar tree
Ornah, Ornette, Ornetta, Ornete, Orneta, Obharnait, Ornat

Ornella (Italian) Of the flowering ash tree
Ornelle, Ornell, Ornela, Ornele, Ornel

Ornice (Irish) A pale-skinned woman
Ornyce, Ornise, Orynse, Orneice, Orneise, Orniece, Orniese, Orneece

Ortygia (Greek) In mythology, an island where Artemis and Apollo were born
Ortegia, Ortigia

Orva (Anglo-Saxon / French) A courageous friend / as precious as gold
Orvah

Orynko (Ukrainian) A peaceful woman
Orinko, Orynka, Orinka

Osaka (Japanese) From the city of industry
Osaki, Osakie, Osakee, Osaky, Osakey, Osakea

Osma (English) Feminine form of Osmond; protected by God
Osmah, Ozma, Ozmah

Otina (American) A fortunate woman
Otinah, Otyna, Otynah, Oteena, Oteenah, Oteana, Oteanah, Otiena

Ourania (Greek) A heavenly woman
Ouraniah, Ouranea, Ouraneah, Ouraniya, Ouraniyah

Overton (English) From the upper side of town
Overtown

Owena (Welsh) A high-born woman
Owenah, Owenna, Owennah, Owenia, Owenea

Ozora (Hebrew) One who is wealthy
Ozorah, Ozorra, Ozorrah

P

Paavna (Hindi) One who is pure; chaste
Pavna, Paavnah, Pavnah, Paavani, Pavani, Pavany, Pavaney, Pavanie

Pace (American) A charismatic young woman
Paice, Payce, Paece, Pase, Paise, Payse, Paese

Pacifica (Spanish) A peaceful woman
Pacifika, Pacyfyca, Pacyfyka, Pacifyca, Pacifyka, Pacyfica, Pacyfika

★Page (English) A young assistant
Paige, Payge, Paege

Pageant (American) A dramatic woman
Pagent, Padgeant, Padgent

Paiva (Finnish) Born during daylight
Paeva, Payva

Paki (African) A witness of God
Pakki, Packi, Pacci, Pakie, Pakkie, Paky, Pakky, Pakey

Palakika (Hawaiian) One who is dearly loved
Palakyka, Palakeka, Palakeeka, Palakieka, Palakeika, Palakeaka

Palba (Spanish) A fair-haired woman

Palemon (Spanish) A kindhearted woman
Palemond, Palemona, Palemonda

Palesa (African) Resembling a flower
Palessa, Palesah, Palysa, Palisa, Paleesa

Paloma (Spanish) Dove-like
Palloma, Palomita, Palometa, Peloma, Aloma

Pamela (English) A woman who is as sweet as honey
Pamelah, Pamella, Pammeli, Pammelie, Pameli, Pamelie, Pamelia, Pamelea

Panagiota (Greek) Feminine form of Panagiotis; a holy woman

Panchali (Indian) A princess; a high-born woman
Panchalie, Panchaly, Panchalli, Panchaley, Panchalee, Panchalea, Panchaleigh

Panda (English) Resembling the bamboo-eating animal
Pandah

Pandara (Indian) A good wife
Pandarah, Pandarra, Pandaria, Pandarea

Pandora (Greek) A gifted, talented woman; in mythology, the first mortal woman, who unleashed evil upon the world
Pandorah, Pandorra, Pandoria, Pandorea, Pandoriya

Pantxike (Latin) A woman who is free
Pantxikey, Pantxikye, Pantxeke, Pantxyke

Paras (Indian) A woman against whom others are measured

Parcae (Latin) In mythology, a name that refers to the Fates
Parca, Parcia, Parcee, Parsae, Parsee, Parsia, Parcea

Paris (English) Woman of the city in France
Pariss, Parisse, Parys, Paryss, Parysse

Parry (Welsh) Daughter of Harry
Parri, Parrie, Parrey, Parree, Parrea

Parvani (Indian) Born during a full moon
Parvanie, Parvany, Parvaney, Parvanee, Parvanea

Parvati (Hindi) Daughter of the mountain; in Hinduism, a name for the wife of Shiva
Parvatie, Parvaty, Parvatey, Parvatee, Pauravi, Parvatea, Pauravie, Pauravy

Paterekia (Hawaiian) An upper-class woman
Paterekea, Pakelekia, Pakelekea

Patience (English) One who is patient; an enduring woman
Patiencia, Paciencia, Pacencia, Pacyncia, Pacincia, Pacienca

Patricia (English) Feminine form of Patrick; of noble descent
Patrisha, Patrycia, Patrisia, Patsy, Patti, Patty, Patrizia, Pattie, Trisha

Patrina (American) Born into the nobility
Patreena, Patriena, Patreina, Patryna, Patreana

Paula (English) Feminine form of Paul; a petite woman
Paulina, Pauline, Paulette, Paola, Pauleta, Pauletta, Pauli, Paulete

Pausha (Hindi) Resembling the moon
Paushah

Pax (Latin) One who is
peaceful; in mythology,
the goddess of peace
*Paxi, Paxie, Paxton,
Paxten, Paxtan, Paxy,
Paxey, Paxee*

Pearl (Latin) A precious
gem of the sea
*Pearla, Pearle, Pearlie,
Pearly, Pearline, Pearlina,
Pearli, Pearley*

Pelagia (Greek) Feminine
form of Pelagius; woman
of the sea
*Pelagiah, Pelagea, Pelagiya,
Pelageah, Pelagla, Pelaglah,
Pelagie, Pelagy*

Pelopia (Greek) In mythology, the wife of Thyestes
and mother of Aegisthus
*Pelopiah, Pelopea, Pelopeah,
Pelopiya*

Pembroke (English) From
the broken hill
*Pembrook, Pembrok,
Pembrooke*

Pendant (French) A decorated woman
Pendent, Pendante, Pendente

Penelope (Greek)
Resembling a duck; in
mythology, the faithful
wife of Odysseus
*Peneloppe, Penelopy,
Penelopey, Penelopi,
Penelopie, Penelopee,
Penella, Penelia*

Penia (Greek) In mythology, the personification of
poverty
*Peniah, Penea, Peniya,
Peneah, Peniyah*

Penthesilea (Greek) In
mythology, a queen of the
Amazons

Peony (Greek) Resembling
the flower
*Peoney, Peoni, Peonie,
Peonee, Peonea*

Pepin (French) An awe-
inspiring woman
*Peppin, Pepine, Peppine,
Pipin, Pippin, Pepen,
Pepan, Peppen*

Pepita (Spanish) Feminine
form of Joseph; God will
add
*Pepitah, Pepitta, Pepitia,
Pepitina*

Perdita (Latin) A lost
woman
*Perditah, Perditta, Perdy,
Perdie, Perdi, Perdee,
Perdea, Perdeeta*

Perdix (Latin) Resembling
a partridge
Perdixx, Perdyx, Perdyxx

Peri (Persian / English) In
mythology, a fairy / from
the pear tree
*Perry, Perri, Perie, Perrie,
Pery, Perrey, Perey, Peree*

Perpetua (Latin) One who is constant; steadfast

Persephone (Greek) In mythology, the daughter of Demeter and Zeus who was abducted to the underworld
Persephoni, Persephonie, Persephony, Persephoney, Persephonee, Persefone, Persefoni, Persefonie

Persis (Greek) Woman of Persia
Persiss, Persisse, Persys, Persyss, Persysse

Pesha (Hebrew) A flourishing woman
Peshah, Peshia, Peshiah, Peshea, Pesheah, Peshe

Petronela (Latin) Feminine form of Peter, as solid and strong as a rock
Petronella, Petronelle, Petronia, Petronilla, Petronille, Petrona, Petronia, Petronel

Petunia (English) Resembling the flower
Petuniah, Petuniya, Petunea, Petoonia, Petounia

Phaedra (Greek) A bright woman; in mythology, the wife of Theseus
Phadra, Phaidra, Phedra, Phaydra, Phedre, Phaedre

Phailin (Thai) Resembling a sapphire
Phaylin, Phaelin, Phalin

Phashestha (American) One who is decorated
Phashesthea, Phashesthia, Phashesthiya

Pheakkley (Vietnamese) A faithful woman
Pheakkly, Pheakkli, Pheakklie, Pheakklee, Pheakkleigh, Pheakklea

Pheodora (Greek) A supreme gift
Pheodorah, Phedora, Phedorah

Phernita (American) A well-spoken woman
Pherneeta, Phernyta, Phernieta, Pherneita, Pherneata

Phia (Italian) A saintly woman
Phiah, Phea, Pheah

Philippa (English) Feminine form of Phillip; a friend of horses
Phillippa, Philipa, Phillipa, Philipinna, Philippine, Phillipina, Phillipine, Pilis

Philomena (Greek) A friend of strength
Filomena, Philomina, Mena

Philyra (Greek) A woman
who loves music
Philyre, Philyria, Philyrea

Phoebe (Greek) A bright,
shining woman; in mythol-
ogy, another name for the
goddess of the moon
*Phebe, Phoebi, Phebi,
Phoebie, Phebie, Pheobe,
Phoebee, Phoebea*

Phoena (Greek)
Resembling a mystical bird
*Phoenah, Phoenna, Phena,
Phenna*

Phoenix (Greek) A dark-
red color; in mythology,
an immortal bird
Phuong, Phoenyx

Phyllis (Greek) Of the
foliage; in mythology, a
girl who was turned into
an almond tree
*Phylis, Phillis, Philis,
Phylys, Phyllida, Phylida,
Phillida, Philida*

Pili (Egyptian) The second-
born child
*Pilie, Pily, Piley, Pilee, Pilea,
Pileigh*

Pililani (Hawaiian) Having
great strength
*Pililanie, Pililany, Pililaney,
Pililanee, Pililanea*

Piluki (Hawaiian)
Resembling a small leaf
*Pilukie, Piluky, Pilukey,
Pilukee, Pilukea*

Pineki (Hawaiian)
Resembling a peanut
*Pinekie, Pineky, Pinekey,
Pinekee, Pinekea*

Ping (Chinese) One who is
peaceful
Pyng

Pinga (Inuit) In mythology, goddess of the hunt,
fertility, and healing
Pingah, Pyngah, Pyngah

Pinquana (Native
American) Having a pleas-
ant fragrance
*Pinquan, Pinquann,
Pinquanne, Pinquanna,
Pinquane*

Piper (English) One who
plays the flute
*Pipere, Piperel, Piperell,
Piperele, Piperelle, Piperela,
Piperella, Pyper*

Pippi (French / English) A
friend of horses / a blush-
ing young woman
*Pippie, Pippy, Pippey,
Pippee, Pippea*

Pirouette (French) A ballet
dancer
*Piroette, Pirouett, Piroett,
Piroueta, Piroeta, Pirouetta,
Piroetta, Pirouet*

Pisces (Latin) The twelfth
sign of the zodiac; the fishes
*Pysces, Piscees, Pyscees,
Piscez, Pisceez*

Pithasthana (Hindi) In Hinduism, a name for the wife of Shiva

Platinum (English) As precious as the metal
Platynum, Platnum, Platie, Plati, Platee, Platy, Platey, Platea

Platt (French) From the plains
Platte

Pleshette (American) An extravagent woman
Pleshett, Pleshet, Pleshete, Plesheta, Pleshetta

Pleun (American) One who is good with words
Pleune

Po (Italian) A lively woman

Podarge (Greek) In mythology, one of the Harpies

Poetry (American) A romantic woman
Poetrey, Poetri, Poetrie, Poetree, Poetrea

Polete (Hawaiian) A kind young woman
Polet, Polett, Polette, Poleta, Poletta

Polina (Russian) A small woman
Polinah, Poleena, Poleenah, Poleana, Poleanah, Poliena, Polienah, Poleina

Polyxena (Greek) In mythology, a daughter of Priam and loved by Achilles
Polyxenah, Polyxenia, Polyxenna, Polyxene, Polyxenea

Pomona (Latin) In mythology, goddess of fruit trees
Pomonah, Pomonia, Pomonea, Pamona, Pamonia, Pamonea

Poni (African) The second-born daughter
Ponni, Ponie, Ponnie, Pony, Ponny, Poney, Ponney, Ponee

Poodle (American) Resembling the dog; one with curly hair
Poudle, Poodel, Poudel

Poonam (Hindi) A kind and caring woman
Pounam

Porter (Latin) The doorkeeper

Posala (Native American) Born at the end of spring
Posalah, Posalla, Posallah

Posh (American) A fancy young woman
Poshe, Posha

Potina (Latin) In mythology, goddess of children's food and drink
Potinah, Potyna, Potena, Poteena, Potiena, Poteina, Poteana

Powder (American) A light-hearted woman
Powdar, Powdir, Powdur, Powdor, Powdi, Powdie, Powdy, Powdey

Pragyata (Hindi) One who is knowledgeable

Praise (Latin) One who expresses admiration
Prayse, Praize, Prayze, Praze, Praese, Praeze

Pramada (Indian) One who is indifferent

Pramlocha (Hindi) In Hinduism, a celestial nymph

Precious (American) One who is treasured
Preshis, Preshys

Prima (Latin) The firstborn child
Primalia, Primma, Pryma, Primia, Primea, Preema, Preama

Primola (Latin) Resembling a primrose
Primolah, Primolia, Primoliah, Primolea, Primoleah

Princess (English) A high-born daughter; born to royalty
Princessa, Princesa, Princie, Princi, Princy, Princee, Princey, Princea

Prisca (Latin) From an ancient family
Priscilla, Priscella, Precilla, Presilla, Prescilla, Prisilla, Prisella, Prissy, Prissi

Promise (American) A faithful woman
Promice, Promyse, Promyce, Promis, Promiss, Promys, Promyss

Prudence (English) One who is cautious and exercises good judgment
Prudencia, Prudensa, Prudensia, Prudentia, Predencia, Predentia, Prue, Pru

Pryce (American / Welsh) One who is very dear / an enthusiastic child
Price, Prise, Pryse

Puck (English) A mischievous fairy

Pulcheria (Italian) A chubby baby
Pulcheriah, Pulcherea, Pulchereah, Pulcherya, Pulcheryah, Pulcheriya, Pulcheriyah

Pulika (African) An obedient and well-behaved girl
Pulikah, Pulicca, Pulicka, Pulyka, Puleeka, Puleaka

Pyrena (Greek) A fiery
woman
*Pyrenah, Pyrina, Pyrinah,
Pyryna, Pyrynah, Pyreena,
Pyreenah, Pyriena*

Pyria (American) One who
is cherished
*Pyriah, Pyrea, Pyreah,
Pyriya, Pyriyah, Pyra,
Pyrah*

Qadesh (Syrian) In
mythology, goddess of
love and sensuality
*Quedesh, Qadesha,
Quedesha, Qadeshia,
Quedeshia, Quedeshiya*

Qamra (Arabic) Of the
moon
*Qamrah, Qamar, Qamara,
Qamrra, Qamaria,
Qamrea, Qamria*

Qimat (Indian) A valuable
woman
*Qimate, Qimatte, Qimata,
Qimatta*

Qitarah (Arabic) Having a
nice fragrance
*Qitara, Qytarah, Qytara,
Qitaria, Qitarra, Qitarria,
Qytarra, Qytarria*

Qoqa (Chechen)
Resembling a dove

Quana (Native American)
One who is aromatic;
sweet-smelling
*Quanah, Quanna,
Quannah, Quania,
Quaniya, Quanniya,
Quannia, Quanea*

Querida (Spanish) One
who is dearly loved;
beloved
*Queridah, Queryda,
Querydah, Querrida,
Queridda, Querridda,
Quereeda, Quereada*

Queta (Spanish) Head of
the household
Quetah, Quetta, Quettah

Quiana (American) Living
with grace; heavenly
*Quianah, Quianna,
Quiane, Quian, Quianne,
Quianda, Quiani, Quianita*

Quincy (English) The fifth-
born child
*Quincey, Quinci, Quincie,
Quincee, Quincia, Quinncy,
Quinnci, Quyncy*

Quintana (Latin / English)
The fifth girl / queen's
lawn
*Quintanah, Quinella,
Quinta, Quintina,
Quintanna, Quintann,
Quintara, Quintona*

Quintessa (Latin) Of the essence
Quintessah, Quintesa, Quintesha, Quintisha, Quintessia, Quyntessa, Quintosha, Quinticia

Quinyette (American) The fifth-born child
Quinyett, Quinyet, Quinyeta, Quinyette, Quinyete

Quirina (Latin) One who is contentious
Quirinah, Quiryna, Quirynah, Quireena, Quireenah, Quireina, Quireinah, Quiriena

Quiritis (Latin) In mythology, goddess of motherhood
Quiritiss, Quiritisse, Quirytis, Quirytys, Quiritys, Quirityss

Quiterie (French) One who is peaceful; tranquil
Quiteri, Quitery, Quiterey, Quiteree, Quiterye, Quyterie, Quyteri, Quyteree

R

Rabiah (Egyptian / Arabic) Born in the springtime / of the gentle wind
Rabia, Raabia, Rabi'ah, Rabi

Rachana (Hindi) Born of the creation
Rachanna, Rashana, Rashanda, Rachna

★Rachel (Hebrew) The innocent lamb; in the Bible, Jacob's wife
Rachael, Racheal, Rachelanne, Rachelce, Rachele, Racheli, Rachell, Rachelle, Raquel

Radcliffe (English) Of the red cliffs
Radcleff, Radclef, Radclif, Radclife, Radclyffe, Radclyf, Radcliphe, Radclyphe

Radella (English) An elfin counselor
Radell, Radel, Radele, Radella, Radela, Raedself, Radself, Raidself

Radmilla (Slavic) Hardworking for the people
Radilla, Radinka, Radmila, Redmilla, Radilu

Rafi'a (Arabic) An exalted woman
Rafia, Rafi'ah, Rafee'a, Rafeea, Rafeeah, Rafiya, Rafiyah

Ragnara (Swedish) Feminine form of Ragnar; one who provides counsel to the army
Ragnarah, Ragnarra, Ragnaria, Ragnarea, Ragnari, Ragnarie, Ragnary, Ragnarey

Rahi (Arabic) Born during the springtime
Rahii, Rahy, Rahey, Rahee, Rahea, Rahie

Rahimah (Arabic) A compassionate woman; one who is merciful
Rahima, Raheema, Raheemah, Raheima, Rahiema, Rahyma, Rahymah, Raheama

Raina (Polish) Form of Regina, meaning "a queenly woman"
Raenah, Raene, Rainah, Raine, Rainee, Rainey, Rainelle, Rainy

Raja (Arabic) One who is filled with hope
Rajah

Raleigh (English) From the clearing of roe deer
Raileigh, Railey, Raley, Rawleigh, Rawley, Raly, Rali, Ralie

Ramona (Spanish) Feminine form of Ramon; a wise protector
Ramee, Ramie, Ramoena, Ramohna, Ramonda, Ramonde, Ramonita, Ramonna

Randi (English) Feminine form of Randall; shielded by wolves; form of Miranda, meaning "worthy of admiration"
Randa, Randee, Randelle, Randene, Randie, Randy, Randey, Randilyn

Raquel (Spanish) Form of Rachel, meaning "the innocent lamb"
Racquel, Racquell, Raquela, Raquelle, Roquel, Roquela, Rakel, Rakell

Rasha (Arabic) Resembling a young gazelle
Rashah, Raisha, Raysha, Rashia, Raesha

Ratana (Thai) Resembling a crystal
Ratanah, Ratanna, Ratannah, Rathana, Rathanna

Rati (Hindi) In Hinduism, goddess of passion and lust
Ratie, Ratea, Ratee, Raty, Ratey

Ratri (Indian) Born in the evening
Ratrie, Ratry, Ratrey, Ratree, Ratrea

Rawiyah (Arabic) One who recites ancient poetry
Rawiya, Rawiyya, Rawiyyah

Rawnie (English) An elegant lady
Rawni, Rawny, Rawney, Rawnee, Rawnea

Raya (Israeli) A beloved friend
Rayah

Raymonde (German) Feminine form of Raymond; one who offers wise protection
Raymondi, Raymondie, Raymondee, Raymondea, Raymonda, Raymunde, Raymunda

Rayna (Hebrew / Scandinavian) One who is pure / one who provides wise counsel
Raynah, Raynee, Rayni, Rayne, Raynea, Raynie

Reba (Hebrew) Form of Rebecca, meaning "one who is bound to God"
Rebah, Reeba, Rheba, Rebba, Ree, Reyba, Reaba

*Rebecca (Hebrew) One who is bound to God; in the Bible, the wife of Isaac
Rebakah, Rebbeca, Rebbecca, Rebbecka, Rebeca, Rebeccah, Rebeccea, Becky, Reba

Regan (Gaelic) Born into royalty; the little ruler
Raegan, Ragan, Raygan, Reganne, Regann, Regane, Reghan, Reagan

Regina (Latin) A queenly woman
Regeena, Regena, Reggi, Reggie, Régine, Regine, Reginette, Reginia, Raina

Rehan (Armenian) Resembling a flower
Rehane, Rehann, Rehanne, Rehana, Rehanna, Rehanan, Rehannan, Rehania

Rehema (African) A compassionate woman
Rehemah, Rehemma, Rehemia, Rehemiya, Rehemea

Rehoboth (Hebrew) From the city by the river
Rehobothe, Rehobotha, Rehobothia

Rekha (Indian) One who walks a straight line
Rekhah, Reka, Rekah

Remy (French) Woman from the town of Rheims
Remi, Remie, Remmy, Remmi, Remmie, Remy, Remmey, Remey

Ren (Japanese) Resembling a water lily

Renée (French) One who has been reborn
Ranae, Ranay, Ranée, Renae, Renata, Renay, Renaye, René

Rephidim (Hebrew) One who offers support
Rephidima, Rephydim, Rephydima, Rephidem, Rephydem, Rephedem

Reseda (Latin) Resembling the mignonette flower
Resedah, Reselda, Resedia, Reseldia

Resen (Hebrew) From the head of the stream; refers to a bridle

Reshma (Arabic) Having silky skin
Reshmah, Reshman, Reshmane, Reshmann, Reshmanne, Reshmana, Reshmanna, Reshmaan

Reya (Spanish) A queenly woman
Reyah, Reyeh, Reye, Reyia, Reyiah, Reyea, Reyeah

Reza (Hungarian) Form of Theresa, meaning "a harvester"
Rezah, Rezia, Reziah, Rezi, Rezie, Rezy, Rezee, Resi

Rezeph (Hebrew) As solid as a stone
Rezepha, Rezephe, Rezephia, Rezephah, Rezephiah

Rhea (Greek) Of the flowing stream; in mythology, the wife of Cronus and mother of gods and goddesses
Rea, Rhae, Rhaya, Rhia, Rhiah, Rhiya, Rheya

Rheda (Anglo-Saxon) A divine woman; a goddess
Rhedah

Rhiannon (Welsh) The great and sacred queen
Rheanna, Rheanne, Rhiana, Rhiann, Rhianna, Rhiannan, Rhianon, Rhyan

Rhonda (Welsh) Wielding a good spear
Rhondelle, Rhondene, Rhondiesha, Rhonette, Rhonnda, Ronda, Rondel, Rondelle

Rhys (Welsh) Having great enthusiasm for life
Rhyss, Rhysse, Reece, Reese, Reice, Reise, Reace, Rease

Ria (Spanish) From the river's mouth
Riah

Riane (Gaelic) Feminine form of Ryan; little ruler
Riana, Rianna, Rianne, Ryann, Ryanne, Ryana, Ryanna, Riann

Rica (English) Form of Frederica, meaning "peaceful ruler"; form of Erica, meaning "ever the ruler / resembling heather"
Rhica, Ricca, Ricah, Rieca, Riecka, Rieka, Riqua, Ryca

Riddhi (Indian) A prosperous woman
Riddhie, Riddhy, Riddhey, Riddhee, Riddhea

*Riley (Gaelic) From the rye clearing; a courageous woman
Reilley, Reilly, Rilee, Rileigh, Ryley, Rylee, Ryleigh, Rylie

Rin (Japanese) A pleasant companion
Rinako

Rini (Japanese) Resembling a young rabbit
Rinie, Rinee, Rinea, Riny, Riney

Rio (Spanish) Woman of the river
Rhio

Risa (Latin) One who laughs often
Risah, Reesa, Riesa, Rise, Rysa, Rysah, Riseh, Risako

Rita (Greek) Precious pearl
Ritta, Reeta, Reita, Rheeta, Riet, Rieta, Ritah, Reta

Roberta (English) Feminine form of Robert; one who is bright with fame
Robertah, Robbie, Robin

Rochelle (French) From the little rock
Rochel, Rochele, Rochell, Rochella, Rochette, Roschella, Roschelle, Roshelle

Roja (Spanish) A red-haired lady
Rojah

Rolanda (German) Feminine form of Roland; well-known throughout the land
Rolandah, Rolandia, Roldandea, Rolande, Rolando, Rollanda, Rollande

Romhilda (German) A glorious battle maiden
Romhilde, Romhild, Romeld, Romelde, Romelda, Romilda, Romild, Romilde

Ronli (Hebrew) My joy is the Lord
Ronlie, Ronlee, Ronleigh, Ronly, Ronley, Ronlea, Ronia, Roniya

Ronni (English) Form of Veronica, meaning "displaying her true image"
Ronnie, Ronae, Ronay, Ronee, Ronelle, Ronette, Roni, Ronica, Ronika

Rosalind (German / English) Resembling a gentle horse / form of Rose, meaning "resembling the beautiful and meaningful flower
Ros, Rosaleen, Rosalen, Rosalin, Rosalina, Rosalinda, Rosalinde, Rosaline, Chalina

Rose (Latin) Resembling the beautiful and meaningful flower
Rosa, Rosie, Rosalind

Roseanne (English)
Resembling the graceful
rose
*Ranna, Rosana, Rosanagh,
Rosanna, Rosannah,
Rosanne, Roseann, Roseanna*

Rosemary (Latin /
English) The dew of the
sea / resembling a bitter
rose
*Rosemaree, Rosemarey,
Rosemaria, Rosemarie,
Rosmarie, Rozmary,
Rosamaria, Rosamarie*

Rowan (Gaelic) Of the red-
berry tree
*Rowann, Rowane,
Rowanne, Rowana,
Rowanna*

Rowena (Welsh / German)
One who is fair and slen-
der / having much fame
and happiness
*Rhowena, Roweena,
Roweina, Rowenna,
Rowina, Rowinna,
Rhonwen, Rhonwyn*

Ruana (Indian) One who
is musically inclined
*Ruanah, Ruanna,
Ruannah, Ruane, Ruann,
Ruanne*

Rubaina (Indian) A bright
woman
*Rubaine, Rubain, Rubayne,
Rubayn, Rubayna, Rubana,
Rubane, Rubaena*

Rudella (German) A well-
known woman
*Rudela, Rudelah, Rudell,
Rudelle, Rudel, Rudele,
Rudy, Rudie*

Rue (English, German) A
medicinal herb
Ru, Larue

Rufina (Latin) A red-haired
woman
*Rufeena, Rufeine, Ruffina,
Rufine, Ruffine, Rufyna,
Ruffyna, Rufyne*

Ruhi (Arabic) A spiritual
woman
*Roohee, Ruhee, Ruhie,
Ruhy, Ruhey, Roohi,
Roohie, Ruhea*

Rukmini (Hindi) Adorned
with gold; in Hinduism,
the first wife of Krishna
*Rukminie, Rukminy,
Rukminey, Rukminee,
Rukminea, Rukminni,
Rukminii*

Rumah (Hebrew) One
who has been exalted
*Ruma, Rumia, Rumea,
Rumiah, Rumeah, Rumma,
Rummah*

Rumina (Latin) In mythol-
ogy, a protector goddess of
mothers and babies
*Ruminah, Rumeena,
Rumeenah, Rumeina,
Rumiena, Rumyna,
Rumeinah, Rumienah*

Rupali (Indian) A beautiful
woman
*Rupalli, Rupalie, Rupalee,
Rupallee, Rupal, Rupa,
Rupaly, Rupaley*

Ruqayyah (Arabic) A gen-
tle woman; a daughter of
Muhammad
Ruqayya, Ruqayah, Ruqaya

Rusalka (Slavic) A wood-
land sprite
*Rusalke, Rusalk, Rusalkia,
Rusalkea*

Ruth (Hebrew) A beloved
companion
*Ruthe, Ruthelle, Ruthellen,
Ruthetta, Ruthi, Ruthie,
Ruthina, Ruthine*

Ryba (Slavic) Resembling a fish
Rybah, Rybba, Rybbah

Ryder (American) An
accomplished horsewoman
Rider

Ryo (Japanese) An excellent
woman
Ryoko

Saba (Greek / Arabic)
Woman from Sheba /
born in the morning
*Sabah, Sabaa, Sabba,
Sabbah, Sabaah*

Sabana (Spanish) From the
open plain
*Sabanah, Sabanna, Sabann,
Sabanne, Sabane, Saban*

Sabi (Arabic) A lovely
young lady
*Sabie, Saby, Sabey, Sabee,
Sabbi, Sabbee, Sabea*

Sabirah (Arabic) Having
great patience
*Sabira, Saabira, Sabeera,
Sabiera, Sabeira, Sabyra,
Sabirra, Sabyrra*

Sabra (Hebrew) Resembling
the cactus fruit; to rest
*Sabrah, Sebra, Sebrah,
Sabrette, Sabbra, Sabraa,
Sabarah, Sabarra*

Sabrina (English) A leg-
endary princess
*Sabrinah, Sabrinna,
Sabreena, Sabriena, Sabreina,
Sabryna, Sabrine, Sabryne,
Cabrina, Zabrina*

Sachet (Hindi) Having
consciousness
Sachett, Sachette

Sada (Japanese) The pure
one
*Sadda, Sadaa, Sadako,
Saddaa*

Sadella (American) A beau-
tiful fairylike princess
*Sadel, Sadela, Sadelah,
Sadele, Sadell, Sadellah,
Sadelle, Sydel*

Sadhana (Hindi) A devoted woman
*Sadhanah, Sadhanna,
Sadhannah, Sadhane,
Sadhanne, Sadhann,
Sadhan*

Sadhbba (Irish) A wise woman
Sadhbh, Sadhba

Sadie (English) Form of Sarah, meaning "a princess; lady"
*Sadi, Sady, Sadey, Sadee,
Saddi, Saddee, Sadiey, Sadye*

Sadiya (Arabic) One who is fortunate; lucky
*Sadiyah, Sadiyyah, Sadya,
Sadyah*

Sadzi (American) Having a sunny disposition
*Sadzee, Sadzey, Sadzia,
Sadziah, Sadzie, Sadzya,
Sadzyah, Sadzy*

Safa (Arabic) One who is innocent and pure
*Safah, Saffa, Sapha, Saffah,
Saphah*

Saffron (English) Resembling the yellow flower
*Saffrone, Saffronn,
Saffronne, Safron, Safronn,
Safronne, Saffronah, Safrona*

Saheli (Indian) A beloved friend
*Sahelie, Sahely, Saheley,
Sahelee, Saheleigh, Sahyli,
Sahelea*

Sahila (Indian) One who provides guidance
*Sahilah, Saheela, Sahyla,
Sahiela, Saheila, Sahela,
Sahilla, Sahylla*

Sahkyo (Native American) Resembling the mink
Sakyo

Saida (Arabic) Fortunate one; one who is happy
*Saidah, Sa'ida, Sayida,
Saeida, Saedah, Said,
Sayide, Sayidea*

Saihah (Arabic) One who is useful; good
Saiha, Sayiha

Sailor (American) One who sails the seas
*Sailer, Sailar, Saylor, Sayler,
Saylar, Saelor, Saeler, Saelar*

Saima (Arabic) A fasting woman
Saimah, Saimma, Sayima

Sajni (Indian) One who is dearly loved
*Sajnie, Sajny, Sajney,
Sajnee, Sajnea*

Sakae (Japanese) One who is prosperous
*Sakai, Sakaie, Sakay,
Sakaye*

Sakari (Native American) A sweet girl
*Sakarie, Sakary, Sakarri,
Sakarey, Sakaree, Sakarree,
Sakarah, Sakarrie*

Sakina (Indian / Arabic) A beloved friend / having God-inspired peace of mind
Sakinah, Sakeena, Sakiena, Sakeina, Sakyna, Sakeyna, Sakinna, Sakeana

Sakti (Hindi) In Hinduism, the divine energy
Saktie, Sakty, Sakkti, Sackti, Saktee, Saktey, Saktia, Saktiah

Saku (Japanese) Remembrance of the Lord
Sakuko

Sakura (Japanese) Resembling a cherry blossom
Sakurah, Sakurako, Sakurra

Sala (Hindi) From the sacred sala tree
Salah, Salla, Sallah

Salal (English) An evergreen shrub with flowers and berries
Sallal, Salall, Sallall, Salalle, Salale, Sallale

Salamasina (Samoan) A princess; born to royalty
Salamaseena, Salamasyna, Salamaseana, Salamaseina, Salamasiena

Salina (French) One of a solemn, dignified character
Salin, Salinah, Salinda, Salinee, Sallin, Sallina, Sallinah, Salline

Saloma (Hebrew) One who offers peace and tranquility
Salomah, Salome, Salomia, Salomiah, Schlomit, Shulamit, Salomeaexl, Salomma

Salus (Latin) In mythology, goddess of health and prosperity; salvation
Saluus, Salusse, Saluss

Salwa (Arabic) One who provides comfort; solace
Salwah

Samah (Arabic) A generous, forgiving woman
Sama, Samma, Sammah

*Samantha (Aramaic) One who listens well
Samanthah, Samanthia, Samanthea, Samantheya, Samanath, Samanatha, Samana, Samanitha

Sameh (Arabic) One who forgives
Sammeh, Samaya, Samaiya

Samina (Arabic) A healthy woman
Saminah, Samine, Sameena, Samyna, Sameana, Sameina, Samynah

Samone (Hebrew) Form of Simone, meaning "one who listens well"
Samoan, Samoane, Samon, Samona, Samonia

Samuela (Hebrew)
Feminine form of Samuel;
asked of God
*Samuelah, Samuella,
Samuell, Samuelle,
Sammila, Sammile,
Samella, Samielle*

Sana (Persian / Arabic)
One who emanates light /
brilliance; splendor
*Sanah, Sanna, Sanako,
Sanaah, Sane, Saneh*

Sanaa (Swahili) Beautiful
work of art
Sanae, Sannaa

Sandeep (Punjabi) One
who is enlightened
*Sandeepe, Sandip, Sandipp,
Sandippe, Sandeyp, Sandeype*

Sandhya (Hindi) Born at
twilight; name of the daughter of the god Brahma
*Sandhiya, Sandhyah,
Sandya, Sandyah*

Sandra (Greek) Form of
Alexandra, meaning "a
helper and defender of
mankind"
*Sandrah, Sandrine, Sandy,
Sandi, Sandie, Sandey,
Sandee, Sanda, Sandrica*

Sandrica (Greek) Form of
Sandra, meaning "a helper
and defender of mankind"
*Sandricca, Sandricah,
Sandricka, Sandrickah,
Sandrika, Sandrikah,
Sandryca, Sandrycah*

Sandrine (Greek) Form of
Alexandra, meaning "a
helper and defender of
mankind"
*Sandrin, Sandreana,
Sandreanah, Sandreane,
Sandreen, Sandreena,
Sandreenah, Sandreene*

Sangita (Indian) One who
is musical
*Sangitah, Sangeeta,
Sangeita, Sangyta,
Sangieta, Sangeata*

Saniya (Indian) A moment
in time preserved
*Saniyah, Sanya, Sanea,
Sania*

Sanjna (Indian) A con-
scientous woman

Santana (Spanish) A saint-
ly woman
*Santa, Santah, Santania,
Santaniah, Santaniata,
Santena, Santenah,
Santenna*

Saoirse (Gaelic) An independent woman; having
freedom
Saoyrse

Sapna (Hindi) A dream
come true
*Sapnah, Sapnia, Sapniah,
Sapnea, Sapneah, Sapniya,
Sapniyah*

★ᵀSarah (Hebrew) A princess; lady; in the Bible, wife of Abraham
Sara, Sari, Sariah, Sarika, Saaraa, Sarita, Sarina, Sarra, Kala, Sadie

Saraid (Irish) One who is excellent; superior
Saraide, Saraed, Saraede, Sarayd, Sarayde

Sarama (African / Hindi) A kind woman / in Hinduism, Indra's dog
Saramah, Saramma, Sarrama, Sarramma

Saran (African) One who brings joy to others
Sarane, Sarran, Saranne, Saranna, Sarana, Sarann

Sarasvati (Hindi) In Hinduism, goddess of learning and the arts
Sarasvatti, Sarasvatie, Sarasvaty, Sarasvatey, Sarasvatee, Sarasvatea

Saraswati (Hindi) Owning water; in Hinduism, a river goddess
Saraswatti, Saraswatie, Saraswaty, Saraswatey, Saraswatee, Saraswatea

Sardinia (Italian) Woman from a mountainous island
Sardiniah, Sardinea, Sardineah, Sardynia, Sardyniah, Sardynea, Sardyneah

Sasa (Japanese) One who is helpful; gives aid
Sasah

Sasha (Russian) Form of Alexandra, meaning "a helper and defender of mankind"
Sascha, Sashenka, Saskia

Sauda (Swahili) A dark beauty
Saudaa, Sawda, Saudda

★Savannah (English) From the open grassy plain
Savanna, Savana, Savanne, Savann, Savane, Savanneh

Savarna (Hindi) Daughter of the ocean
Savarnia, Savarnea, Savarniya, Savarneia

Savitri (Hindi) In Hinduism, the daughter of the god of the sun
Savitari, Savitrie, Savitry, Savitarri, Savitarie, Savitree, Savitrea, Savitrey

Savvy (American) Smart and perceptive woman
Savy, Savvi, Savvie, Savvey, Savee, Savvee, Savvea, Savea

Sayyida (Arabic) A mistress
Sayyidah, Sayida, Sayyda, Seyyada, Seyyida, Seyada, Seyida

Scelflesh (English) From
the meadow

Schaaph (Hebrew) One
who is thoughtful
Schaph, Schaphe

Scota (Irish) Woman of
Scotland
*Scotta, Scotah, Skota,
Skotta, Skotah*

Sea'iqa (Arabic) Thunder
and lightning
Seaqa, Seaqua

Season (Latin) A fertile
woman; one who
embraces change
*Seazon, Seeson, Seezon,
Seizon, Seasen, Seasan,
Seizen, Seizan*

Sebille (English) In
Arthurian legend, a fairy
*Sebylle, Sebill, Sebile,
Sebyle, Sebyl*

Secunda (Latin) The second-
born child
*Secundah, Secuba,
Secundus, Segunda,
Sekunda*

Seda (Armenian) Voices of
the forest
Sedda, Sedah, Seddah

Sedona (American)
Woman from a city in
Arizona
*Sedonah, Sedonna,
Sedonnah, Sedonia,
Sedonea*

Seema (Greek) A symbol;
a sign
*Seyma, Syma, Seama,
Seima, Siema*

Sefarina (Greek) Of a gen-
tle wind
*Sefarinah, Sefareena,
Sefareenah, Sefaryna,
Sefarynah, Sefareana,
Sefareanah*

Seiko (Japanese) The force
of truth

Selene (Greek) Of the moon
*Sela, Selena, Selina, Celina,
Zalina*

Sema (Arabic) A divine
omen; a known symbol
Semah

Senalda (Spanish) A sign;
a symbol
*Senaldah, Senaldia,
Senaldiya, Senaldea,
Senaldya*

September (American)
Born in the month of
September
*Septimber, Septymber,
Septemberia, Septemberea*

Sequoia (Native American)
Of the giant redwood tree
Sekwoya, Lequoia

Serafina (Latin) A seraph; a heavenly winged angel
Serafinah, Serafine, Seraphina, Serefina, Seraphine, Sera

Serena (Latin) Having a peaceful disposition
Serenah, Serene, Sereena, Seryna, Serenity, Serenitie, Serenitee, Serepta, Cerina, Xerena

Serendipity (American) A fateful meeting; having good fortune
Serendipitey, Serendipitee, Serendipiti, Serendipitie, Serendypyty

Sevati (Indian) Resembling the white rose
Sevatie, Sevatti, Sevate, Sevatee, Sevatea, Sevaty, Sevti

Shabana (Arabic) A maiden belonging to the night
Shabanah, Shabanna, Shabaana, Shabanne, Shabane

Shabnan (Persian) A falling raindrop
Shabnane, Shabnann, Shabnanne

Shadha (Arabic) An aromatic fragrance
Shadhah

Shafiqa (Arabic) A compassionate woman
Shafiqah, Shafiqua, Shafeeqa, Shafeequa

Shai (Gaelic) A gift of God
Shay, Shae, Shayla, Shea, Shaye

Sha'ista (Arabic) One who is polite and well-behaved
Shaistah, Shaista, Shaa'ista, Shayista, Shaysta

Shakila (Arabic) Feminine form of Shakil; beautiful one
Shakilah, Shakela, Shakeela, Shakeyla, Shakyla, Shakeila, Shakiela, Shakina

Shakira (Arabic) Feminine form of Shakir; grateful; thankful
Shakirah, Shakiera, Shaakira, Shakeira, Shakyra, Shakeyra, Shakura, Shakirra

Shakti (Indian) A divine woman; having power
Shaktie, Shakty, Shaktey, Shaktee, Shaktye, Shaktea

Shaliqa (Arabic) One who is sisterly
Shaliqah, Shaliqua, Shaleeqa, Shaleequa, Shalyqa, Shalyqua

Shamima (Arabic) A
woman full of flavor
*Shamimah, Shameema,
Shamiema, Shameima,
Shamyma, Shameama*

Shandy (English) One who
is rambunctious; boisterous
*Shandey, Shandee, Shandi,
Shandie, Shandye, Shandea*

Shani (African) A mar-
velous woman
*Shanie, Shany, Shaney,
Shanee, Shanni, Shanea,
Shannie, Shanny*

Shanley (Gaelic) Small
and ancient woman
*Shanleigh, Shanlee, Shanly,
Shanli, Shanlie, Shanlea*

Shannon (Gaelic) Having
ancient wisdom; river
name
*Shanon, Shannen,
Shannan, Shannin,
Shanna, Shannae,
Shannun, Shannyn*

Shaquana (American)
Truth in life
*Shaqana, Shaquanah,
Shaquanna, Shaqanna,
Shaqania*

Sharifah (Arabic) Feminine
form of Sharif; noble;
respected; virtuous
*Sharifa, Shareefa, Sharufa,
Sharufah, Sharyfa, Sharefa,
Shareafa, Shariefa*

Sharik (African) One who
is a child of God
*Shareek, Shareake,
Sharicke, Sharick, Sharike,
Shareak, Sharique, Sharyk*

Sharikah (Arabic) One
who is a good companion
*Sharika, Shareeka,
Sharyka, Shareka,
Shariqua, Shareaka*

Sharlene (French)
Feminine form of Charles;
petite and womanly
*Sharleene, Sharleen,
Sharla, Sharlyne, Sharline,
Sharlyn, Sharlean,
Sharleane*

Sharon (Hebrew) From
the plains; a flowering
shrub
*Sharron, Sharone,
Sharona, Shari, Sharis,
Sharne, Sherine, Sharun*

Shasta (Native American)
From the triple-peaked
mountain
*Shastah, Shastia, Shastiya,
Shastea, Shasteya*

Shawnee (Native
American) A tribal name
*Shawni, Shawnie,
Shawnea, Shawny,
Shawney, Shawnea*

Shayla (Irish) Of the fairy palace; form of Shai, meaning "a gift of God"
Shaylah, Shaylagh, Shaylain, Shaylan, Shaylea, Shayleah, Shaylla, Sheyla

Shaylee (Gaelic) From the fairy palace; a fairy princess
Shalee, Shayleigh, Shailee, Shaileigh, Shaelee, Shaeleigh, Shayli, Shaylie

Sheehan (Celtic) Little peaceful one; peacemaker
Shehan, Sheyhan, Shihan, Shiehan, Shyhan, Sheahan

Sheela (Indian) One of cool conduct and character
Sheelah, Sheetal

Sheena (Gaelic) God's gracious gift
Sheenah, Shena, Shiena, Sheyna, Shyna, Sheana, Sheina

Sheherezade (Arabic) One who is a city dweller

Sheila (Irish) Form of Cecilia, meaning "one who is blind"
Sheilah, Sheelagh, Shelagh, Shiela, Shyla, Selia, Sighle, Sheiletta

Shelby (English) From the willow farm
Shelbi, Shelbey, Shelbie, Shelbee, Shelbye, Shelbea

Sheridan (Gaelic) One who is wild and untamed; a searcher
Sheridann, Sheridanne, Sherydan, Sherridan, Sheriden, Sheridon, Sherrerd, Sherida

Sheshebens (Native American) Resembling a small duck

Shifra (Hebrew) A beautiful midwife
Shifrah, Shiphrah, Shiphra, Shifria, Shifriya, Shifrea

Shikha (Indian) Flame burning brightly
Shikhah, Shikkha, Shekha, Shykha

Shima (Native American) Little mother
Shimah, Shimma, Shyma, Shymah

Shina (Japanese) A virtuous woman; having goodness
Shinah, Shinna, Shyna, Shynna

Shobha (Indian) An attractive woman
Shobhah, Shobbha, Shoba, Shobhan, Shobhane

Shoshana (Arabic) Form of Susannah, meaning "white lily"
Shosha, Shoshan, Shoshanah, Shoshane, Shoshanha, Shoshann, Shoshanna, Shoshannah

Shradhdha (Indian) One who is faithful; trusting
Shraddha, Shradha, Shradhan, Shradhane

Shruti (Indian) Having good hearing
Shrutie, Shruty, Shrutey, Shrutee, Shrutye, Shrutea

Shunnareh (Arabic) Pleasing in manner and behavior
Shunnaraya, Shunareh, Shunarreh

Shyann (English) Form of Cheyenne, meaning "unintelligible speaker"
Shyanne, Shyane, Sheyann, Sheyanne, Sheyenne, Sheyene

Shysie (Native American) A quiet child
Shysi, Shysy, Shysey, Shysee, Shycie, Shyci, Shysea, Shycy

Sibyl (English) A prophetess; a seer
Sybil, Sibyla, Sybella, Sibil, Sibella, Sibilla, Sibley, Sibylla

Siddhi (Hindi) Having spiritual power
Sidhi, Syddhi, Sydhi

Sidero (Greek) In mythology, stepmother of Pelias and Neleus
Siderro, Sydero, Sideriyo

Sieglinde (German) Winning a gentle victory

★Sierra (Spanish) From the jagged mountain range
Siera, Syerra, Syera, Seyera, Seeara

Sigfreda (German) A woman who is victorious
Sigfreeda, Sigfrida, Sigfryda, Sigfreyda, Sigfrieda, Sigfriede, Sigfrede

Sigismonda (Teutonic) A victorious defender
Sigismunda

Signia (Latin) A distinguishing sign
Signiya, Signea, Signeia, Signeya, Signa

Sigyn (Norse) In mythology, the wife of Loki

Sihu (Native American) As delicate as a flower

Silka (Latin) Form of Cecelia, meaning "one who is blind"
Silke, Silkia, Silkea, Silkie, Silky, Silkee, Sylka, Sylke

Sima (Arabic) One who is treasured; a prize
Simma, Syma, Simah, Simia, Simiya

Simone (French) One who listens well
Sim, Simonie, Symone, Samone

Simran (Indian) One who meditates
Simrana, Simrania, Simrann, Simranne, Simrane, Simranna

Sine (Scottish) Form of Jane, meaning "God is gracious"
Sinead, Sineidin, Sioned, Sionet, Sion, Siubhan, Siwan, Sineh

Sinobia (Greek) Form of Zenobia, meaning "child of Zeus"
Sinobiah, Sinobya, Sinobe, Sinobie, Sinovia, Senobia, Senobya, Senobe

Sinopa (Native American) Resembling a fox

Sinope (Greek) In mythology, one of the daughters of Asopus

Siran (Armenian) An alluring and lovely woman

Siren (Greek) In mythology, a sea nymph whose beautiful singing lured sailors to their deaths; refers to a seductive and beautiful woman
Sirene, Sirena, Siryne, Siryn, Syren, Syrena, Sirine, Sirina

Siria (Spanish / Persian) Bright like the sun / a glowing woman
Siriah, Sirea, Sireah, Siriya, Siriyah, Sirya, Siryah

Siroun (Armenian) A lovely woman
Sirune

Sirpuhi (Armenian) One who is holy; pious
Sirpuhie, Sirpuhy, Sirpuhey, Sirpuhea, Sirpuhee

Sissy (English) Form of Cecilia, meaning "one who is blind"
Sissey, Sissie, Sisley, Sisli, Sislee, Sissel, Sissle, Syssy

Sita (Hindi) In Hinduism, goddess of the harvest and wife of Rama

Sive (Irish) A good and sweet girl
Sivney, Sivny, Sivni, Sivnie, Sivnee, Sivnea

Sloane (Irish) A strong protector; a woman warrior
Sloan, Slone

Smita (Indian) One who smiles a lot

Snana (Native American) Having a sound like bells
Snanah, Snanna, Snannah

Snow (American) Frozen rain
Snowy, Snowie, Snowi, Snowey, Snowee, Snowea, Sno

Snowdrop (English) Resembling a small white flower

Solana (Latin / Spanish) Wind from the east / of the sunshine
Solanah, Solanna, Solann, Solanne

Solange (French) One who is religious and dignified

Solaris (Greek) Of the sun
Solarise, Solariss, Solarisse, Solarys, Solaryss, Solarysse, Sol, Soleil

Solita (Latin) One who is solitary
Solitah, Solida, Soledad, Soledada, Soledade

Somatra (Indian) Of the excellent moon

Sona (Arabic) The golden one
Sonika, Sonna

Sonora (Spanish) A pleasant-sounding woman
Sonorah, Sonoria, Sonorya, Sonoriya

Soo (Korean) Having an excellent long life

★ᵀSophie (Greek) Wisdom
*Sophia, Sofiya, Sofie, **Sofia**, Sofi, Sofiyko, Sofronia, Sophronia, Zofia*

Sorina (Romanian) Feminine form of Sorin; of the sun
Sorinah, Sorinna, Sorinia, Soriniya, Sorinya, Soryna, Sorynia, Sorine

Sorrel (French) From the surele plant
Sorrell, Sorrelle, Sorrele, Sorrela, Sorrella

Sparrow (English) Resembling a small song-bird
Sparro, Sparroe, Sparo, Sparow, Sparowe, Sparoe

Sslama (Egyptian) One who is peaceful

Stacey (English) Form of Anastasia, meaning "one who shall rise again"
Stacy, Staci, Stacie, Stacee, Stacia, Stasia, Stasy, Stasey

Stella (English) Star of the sea
Stela, Stelle, Stele, Stellah, Stelah

★Stephanie (Greek) Feminine form of Stephen; crowned in victory
Stephani, Stephany, Stephaney, Stephanee, Stephene, Stephana, Stefanie, Stefani

Stevonna (Greek) A crowned lady
Stevonnah, Stevona, Stevonah, Stevonia, Stevonea, Stevoniya

Struana (Scottish) From the stream
Struanna, Struanah, Struanne, Struan, Struann, Struane

Styx (Greek) In mythology, the river of the underworld
Stixx, Styxx, Stix

Suave (American) A smooth and courteous woman
Swave

Subhadra (Hindi) In Hinduism, the sister of Krishna

Subhaga (Indian) A fortunate person

Subhuja (Hindi) An auspicious celestial damsel

Subira (African) One who is patient
Subirah, Subirra, Subyra, Subyrra, Subeera, Subeara, Subeira, Subiera

Suhaila (Arabic) Feminine form of Suhail; the second brightest star
Suhayla, Suhaela, Suhala, Suhailah, Suhaylah, Suhaelah, Suhalah

Sulwyn (Welsh) One who shines as bright as the sun
Sulwynne, Sulwynn, Sulwinne, Sulwin, Sulwen, Sulwenn, Sulwenne

Sumana (Indian) A good-natured woman
Sumanah, Sumanna, Sumane, Sumanne, Sumann

Sumi (Japanese) One who is elegant and refined
Sumie

Sumitra (Indian) A beloved friend
Sumitrah, Sumita, Sumytra, Sumyta, Sumeetra, Sumeitra, Sumietra, Sumeatra

Summer (American) Refers to the season; born in summer
Sommer, Sumer, Somer, Somers

Suna (Turkish) A swan-like woman

Sunanda (Indian) Having a sweet character
Sunandah, Sunandia, Sunandiya, Sunandea, Sunandya

Sunila (Indian) Feminine form of Sunil; very blue
Sunilah, Sunilla, Sunilya, Suniliya

Sunniva (English) Gift of the sun
Synnove, Synne, Synnove, Sunn

Surabhi (Indian) Having a lovely fragrance
Surbhii, Surabhie, Surabhy, Surabhey, Surabhee, Surabhea

Susannah (Hebrew) White lily
Susanna, Susanne, Susana, Susane, Susan, Suzanna, Suzannah, Suzanne, Shoshana, Huhana

Sushanti (Indian) A peaceful woman; tranquil
Sushantie, Sushanty, Sushantey, Sushantee, Sushantea

Suzu (Japanese) One who is long-lived
Suzue, Suzuko

Swanhilda (Norse) A woman warrior; in mythology, the daughter of Sigurd
Swanhild, Swanhilde, Svanhilde, Svanhild, Svenhilde, Svenhilda

Swarupa (Indian) One who is devoted to the truth

★Sydney (English) Of the wide meadow
Sydny, Sydni, Sydnie, Sydnea, Sydnee, Sidney, Sidne, Sidnee

T

Taariq (Swahili) Resembling the morning star
Tariq, Taarique, Tarique

Tabia (African / Egyptian) One who makes incantations / a talented woman
Tabiah, Tabya, Tabea, Tabeah, Tabiya

Tabita (African) A graceful woman
Tabitah, Tabyta, Tabytah, Tabeeta, Tabeata, Tabieta, Tabeita

Tabitha (Greek) Resembling a gazelle; known for beauty and grace
Tabithah, Tabbitha, Tabetha, Tabbetha, Tabatha, Tabbatha, Tabotha, Tabbotha

Tabora (Spanish) One who plays a small drum
Taborah, Taborra, Taboria, Taborya

Tacincala (Native American) Resembling a deer
Tacincalah, Tacyncala, Tacyncalah, Tacincalla, Tacyncalla

Tahsin (Arabic) Beautification; one who is praised
Tahseen, Tahsene, Tahsyne, Tasine, Tahseene, Tahsean, Tahseane

Tahzib (Arabic) One who is educated and cultured
Tahzeeb, Tahzebe, Tahzybe, Tazib, Tazyb, Tazeeb, Tahzeab, Tazeab

Taithleach (Gaelic) A quiet and calm young lady

Takako (Japanese) A lofty child

Takoda (Native American) Friend to everyone
Takodah, Takodia, Takodya, Takota

Tala (Native American) A stalking wolf
Talah, Talla

Talia (Hebrew / Greek) Morning dew from heaven / blooming
Taliah, Talea, Taleah, Taleya, Tallia, Talieya, Taleea, Taleia

Talihah (Arabic) One who seeks knowledge
Taliha, Talibah, Taliba, Talyha, Taleeah, Taleahah

Taline (Armenian) Of the monestary
Talene, Taleen, Taleene, Talyne, Talinia, Talinya, Taliniya

Talisa (American) Consecrated to God
Talisah, Talysa, Taleesa, Talissa, Talise, Taleese, Talisia, Talisya

Talisha (American) A damsel; an innocent
Talesha, Taleisha, Talysha, Taleesha, Tylesha, Taleysha, Taleshia, Talishia

Talitha (Arabic) A maiden; young girl
Talithah, Taletha, Taleetha, Talytha, Talithia, Talethia, Tiletha, Talith

Tamanna (Indian) One who is desired
Tamannah, Tamana, Tamanah, Tammana, Tammanna

Tamasha (African) Pageant winner
Tamasha, Tomosha, Tomasha, Tamashia, Tamashya

Tamesis (Celtic) In mythology, the goddess of water; source of the name for the river Thames
Tamesiss, Tamesys, Tamesyss

Tangia (American) The angel
Tangiah, Tangya, Tangiya, Tangeah

Tani (Japanese / Melanesian / Tonkinese) From the valley / a sweetheart / a young woman
Tanie, Tany, Taney, Tanee, Tanni, Tanye, Tannie, Tanny

Tania (Russian) Queen of the fairies
Tanya, Tannie, Tanny, Tanika

Tanner (English) One who tans hides
Taner, Tannar, Tannor, Tannis

Tansy (English / Greek) An aromatic yellow flower / having immortality
Tansey, Tansi, Tansie, Tansee, Tansye, Tansea, Tancy, Tanzy

Tanushri (Indian) One who is beautiful; attractive
Tanushrie, Tanushry, Tanushrey, Tanushree, Tanushrea

Tanvi (Indian) Slender and beautiful woman
Tanvie, Tanvy, Tanvey, Tanvee, Tanvye, Tannvi, Tanvea

Tapati (Indian) In mythology, the daughter of the sun god
Tapatie, Tapaty, Tapatey, Tapatee, Tapatye, Tapatea

Taphath (Hebrew) In the Bible, Solomon's daughter
Tafath, Taphathe, Tafathe

Tara (Gaelic / Indian) Of the tower; rocky hill / star; in mythology, an astral goddess
Tarah, Tarra, Tayra, Taraea, Tarai, Taralee, Tarali, Taraya

Tarachand (Indian) Silver star
Tarachande, Tarachanda, Tarachandia, Tarachandea, Tarachandiya, Tarachandya

Taree (Japanese) A bending branch
Tarea, Tareya

Taregan (Native American) Resembling a crane
Tareganne, Taregann

Tareva-chine(shanay) (Native American) One with beautiful eyes

Tariana (American) From the holy hillside
Tariana, Tarianna, Taryana, Taryanna

Tarika (Indian) A starlet
Tarikah, Taryka, Tarykah, Taricka, Tarickah

Tarisai (African) One to behold; to look at
Tarysai

Tasanee (Thai) A beautiful view
Tasane, Tasani, Tasanie, Tasany, Tasaney, Tasanye, Tasanea

Taskin (Arabic) One who provides peace; satisfaction
Taskine, Taskeen, Taskeene, Taskyne, Takseen, Taksin, Taksyn

Tasnim (Arabic) From the fountain of paradise
Tasnime, Tasneem, Tasneeme, Tasnyme, Tasnym, Tasneam, Tasneame

Tatum (English) Bringer of joy; spirited
Tatom, Tatim, Tatem, Tatam, Tatym

Tavi (Aramaic) One who is well-behaved
Tavie, Tavee, Tavy, Tavey, Tavea

★ᵀ**Taylor** (English) Cutter of cloth; one who alters garments
Tailor, Taylore, Taylar, Tayler, Talour, Taylre, Tailore, Tailar

Teamhair (Irish) In mythology, a place where kings met
Teamhaire, Teamhare, Teamharre

Tehya (Native American) One who is precious
Tehyah, Tehiya, Tehiyah

Teigra (Greek) Resembling a tiger
Teigre

Telephassa (Latin) In mythology, the queen of Tyre
Telephasa, Telefassa, Telefasa

Temperance (English) Having self-restraint
Temperence, Temperince, Temperancia, Temperanse, Temperense, Temperinse

Tendai (African) Thankful to God
Tenday, Tendae, Tendaa, Tendaye

Tender (American) One who is sensitive; young and vulnerable
Tendere, Tendera, Tenderia, Tenderre, Tenderiya

Teranika (Gaelic) Victory of the earth
Teranikah, Teranieka, Teraneika, Teraneeka, Teranica, Teranicka, Teranicca, Teraneaka

Terpsichore (Greek) In mythology, the muse of dancing and singing
Terpsichora, Terpsichoria, Terpsichoriya

Terra (Latin) From the earth; in mythology, an earth goddess
Terrah, Terah, Teralyn, Terran, Terena, Terenah, Terenna, Terrena

Terrian (Greek) One who is innocent
Terriane, Terrianne, Terriana, Terianna, Terian, Terianne

Teryl (English) One who is vivacious and bright
Terryl, Teryll, Terylle, Terryll

Tetsu (Japanese) A strong woman
Tetsue

Tetty (English) Form of Elizabeth, meaning "my God is bountiful; God's promise"
Tettey, Tetti, Tettie, Tettee, Tettea

Tevy (Cambodian) An angel
Tevey, Tevi, Tevie, Tevee, Tevea

Thandiwe (African) The loving one
Thandywe, Thandiewe, Thandeewe, Thandie, Thandi, Thandee, Thandy, Thandey

Thao (Vietnamese) One who is respectful of her parents

Thara (Arabic) One who is wealthy; prosperous
Tharah, Tharra, Tharrah, Tharwat

Thelma (Greek) One who is ambitious and willful
Thelmah, Telma, Thelmai, Thelmia, Thelmalina

Thelred (English) One who is well-advised
Thelrede, Thelread, Thelredia, Thelredina, Thelreid, Thelreed, Thelryd

Thema (African) A queen
Themah, Theema, Thyma, Theyma, Theama

Theora (Greek) A watcher
Theorra, Theoria, Theoriya, Theorya

Theresa (Greek) A harvester
Teresa, Theresah, Theresia, Therese, Thera, Tresa, Tressa, Tressam, Reese, Reza

Theta (Greek) Eighth letter of the Greek alphabet
Thetta

Thistle (English) Resembling the prickly, flowered plant
Thistel, Thissle, Thissel

Thomasina (Hebrew) Feminine form of Thomas; a twin
Thomasine, Thomsina, Thomasin, Tomasina, Tomasine, Thomasa, Thomaseena, Thomaseana

Thoosa (Greek) In mythology, a sea nymph
Thoosah, Thoosia, Thoosiah, Thusa, Thusah, Thusia, Thusiah, Thousa

Thorberta (Norse) Brilliance of Thor
Thorbiartr, Thorbertha

Thordia (Norse) Spirit of Thor
Thordiah, Thordis, Tordis, Thordissa, Tordissa, Thoridyss

Thuy (Vietnamese) One who is gentle and pure
Thuye, Thuyy, Thuyye

Thy (Vietnamese / Greek) A poet / one who is untamed
Thye

Tia (Spanish / Greek) An aunt / daughter born to royalty
Tiah, Tea, Teah, Tiana, Teea, Tya, Teeya, Tiia

Tiberia (Italian) Of the Tiber river
Tiberiah, Tiberiya, Tiberya, Tibeeria, Tibearia, Tibieria, Tibeiria

Tiegan (Aztec) A little princess in a big valley
Tiegann, Tieganne

Tierney (Gaelic) One who is regal; lordly
Tiernie, Tierni, Tiernee, Tierny, Tiernea

Tiffany (Greek) Lasting love
Tiffaney, Tiffani, Tiffanie, Tiffanee, Tifany, Tifaney, Tifanee, Tifani

Timothea (English) Feminine form of Timothy; honoring God
Timotheah, Timothia, Timothya, Timothiya

Tina (English) From the river; also shortened form of names ending in -tina
Tinah, Teena, Tena, Teyna, Tyna, Tinna, Teana

Ting (Chinese) Graceful and slim woman

Tirza (Hebrew) One who is pleasant; a delight
Tirzah

Tisa (African) The ninth-born child
Tisah, Tiza

Tita (Latin) Holding a title of honor
Titah, Teeta, Tyta, Teata

Tivona (Hebrew) Lover of nature
Tivonna, Tivone, Tivonia, Tivoniya

Toan (Vietnamese) Form of An-toan, meaning "safe and secure"
Toane, Toanne

Toinette (French) Form of Antoinette, meaning "praiseworthy"
Toinett, Toinete, Toinet, Toineta, Toinetta, Tola

Toki (Japanese / Korean) One who grasps opportunity; hopeful / resembling a rabbit
Tokie, Toky, Tokey, Tokye, Tokiko, Tokee, Tokea

Tola (Polish / Cambodian)
Form of Toinette, mean-
ing "praiseworthy" / born
during October
Tolah, Tolla, Tollah

Topanga (Native American)
From above or a high place
Topangah

Topaz (Latin) Resembling
a yellow gemstone
*Topazz, Topaza, Topazia,
Topaziya, Topazya, Topazea*

Tordis (Norse) A goddess
*Tordiss, Tordisse, Tordys,
Tordyss, Tordysse*

Torny (Norse) New; just
discovered
*Torney, Tornie, Torni, Torne,
Torn, Tornee, Tornea*

Torunn (Norse) Thor's love
Torun, Torrun, Torrunn

Tory (American) Form of
Victoria, meaning "victorious
woman; winner; conqueror"
*Torry, Torey, Tori, Torie,
Torree, Tauri, Torye, Toya*

Tosca (Latin) From the
Tuscany region
*Toscah, Toscka, Toska,
Tosckah, Toskah*

Tosha (English) Form of
Natasha, meaning "born
on Christmas"
*Toshah, Toshiana, Tasha,
Tashia, Tashi, Tassa*

Tourmaline (Singhalese) A
stone of mixed colors
*Tourmalyne, Tourmalina,
Tourmalinia*

Tova (Hebrew) One who is
well-behaved
*Tovah, Tove, Tovi, Toba,
Toibe, Tovva*

Treasa (Irish) Having great
strength
*Treasah, Treesa, Treisa,
Triesa, Treise, Treese,
Toirease*

★Trinity (Latin) The holy
three
*Trinitey, Triniti, Trinitie,
Trinitee, Trynity, Trynitey,
Tryniti, Trynitie*

Trisha (Latin) Form of
Patricia, meaning "of
noble descent"
*Trishah, Trishia, Tricia,
Trish, Trissa, Trisa*

Trishna (Polish) In mythol-
ogy, the goddess of the
deceased, protector of
graves
*Trishnah, Trishnia,
Trishniah, Trishnea,
Trishneah, Trishniya,
Trishniyah, Trishnya*

Trisna (Indian) The one
desired
*Trisnah, Trisnia, Trisniah,
Trisnea, Trisneah, Trisniya,
Trisniyah, Trisnya*

Trudy (German) Form of Gertrude, meaning "adored warrior"
Trudey, Trudi, Trudie, Trude, Trudye, Trudee, Truda, Trudia

Trupti (Indian) State of being satisfied
Truptie, Trupty, Truptey, Truptee, Trupte, Truptea

Tryamon (English) In Arthurian legend, a fairy princess
Tryamonn, Tryamonne, Tryamona, Tryamonna

Tryna (Greek) The third-born child
Trynah

Tsifira (Hebrew) One who is crowned
Tsifirah, Tsifyra, Tsiphyra, Tsiphira, Tsipheera, Tsifeera

Tuccia (Latin) A vestal virgin

Tula (Hindi) Balance; a sign of the zodiac
Tulah, Tulla, Tullah

Tullia (Irish) One who is peaceful
Tulliah, Tullea, Tulleah, Tullya, Tulia, Tulea, Tuleah, Tulya

Tusti (Hindi) One who brings happiness and peace
Tustie, Tusty, Tustey, Tustee, Tuste, Tustea

Tutilina (Latin) In mythology, the protector goddess of stored grain
Tutilinah, Tutileena, Tutileana, Tutilyna, Tutileina, Tutiliena, Tutilena, Tutylina

Tuuli (Finnish) Of the wind
Tuulie, Tuulee, Tuula, Tuuly, Tuuley, Tuulea

Tuyet (Vietnamese) Snow white woman
Tuyett, Tuyete, Tuyette, Tuyeta, Tuyetta

Tyler (English) Tiler of roofs

Tyme (English) The aromatic herb thyme
Time, Thyme, Thime

Tyne (English) Of the river
Tyna

Tyro (Greek) In mythology, a woman who bore twin sons to Poseidon

Tzidkiya (Hebrew) Righteousness of the Lord
Tzidkiyah, Tzidkiyahu

Tzigane (Hungarian) A gypsy
Tzigan, Tzigain, Tzigaine, Tzigayne

U

U (Korean) One who is gentle and considerate

Uadjit (Egyptian) In mythology, a snake goddess
Ujadet, Uajit, Udjit, Ujadit

Ualani (Hawaiian) Of the heavenly rain
Ualanie, Ualany, Ualaney, Ualanee, Ualanea, Ualania, Ualana

Udavine (American) A thriving woman
Udavyne, Udavina, Udavyna, Udevine, Udevyne, Udevina, Udevyna

Udele (English) One who is wealthy; prosperous
Udelle, Udela, Udella, Udelah, Udellah, Uda, Udah

Uela (American) One who is devoted to God
Uelah, Uella, Uellah

Uganda (African) From the country in Africa
Ugandah, Ugaunda, Ugaundah, Ugawnda, Ugawndah, Ugonda, Ugondah

Ugolina (German) Having a bright spirit; bright mind
Ugolinah, Ugoleena, Ugoliana, Ugolyna, Ugoline, Ugolyn, Ugolyne

Ulalia (Greek) Form of Eulalia, meaning "well-spoken"
Ulaliah, Ulalya, Ulalyah

Ulan (African) Firstborn of twins
Ulann, Ulanne

Ulima (Arabic) One who is wise and astute
Ulimah, Ullima, Ulimma, Uleema, Uleama, Ulyma, Uleima, Uliema

Ulla (German) A willful woman
Ullah, Ullaa, Ullai, Ullae

Uma (Hindi) Mother; in mythology, the goddess of beauty and sunlight
Umah, Umma

Umberla (French) Feminine form of Umber; providing shade; of an earth color
Umberlah, Umberly, Umberley, Umberlee, Umberleigh, Umberli, Umberlea, Umberlie

Ummi (African) Born of my mother
Ummie, Ummy, Ummey, Ummee, Umi

Unity (American) Woman who upholds oneness; togetherness
Unitey, Unitie, Uniti, Unitee, Unitea, Unyty, Unytey, Unytie

Ura (Indian) Loved from the heart
Urah, Urra

Ural (Slavic) From the mountains
Urall, Urale, Uralle

Urbai (American) One who is gentle
Urbae, Urbay, Urbaye

Urbana (Latin) From the city; city dweller
Urbanah, Urbanna, Urbane, Urbania, Urbanya, Urbanne

Uriela (Hebrew) The angel of light
Uriella, Urielle, Uriel, Uriele, Uriell

Urta (Latin) Resembling the spiny plant
Urtah

Utah (Native American) People of the mountains; from the state of Utah

Uzoma (African) One who takes the right path
Uzomah, Uzomma, Uzommah

Uzzi (Hebrew / Arabic) God is my strength / a strong woman
Uzzie, Uzzy, Uzzey, Uzzee, Uzi, Uzie, Uzy, Uzey

V

Vala (German) The chosen one; singled out
Valah, Valla

Valda (Teutonic / German) Spirited in battle / famous ruler
Valdah, Valida, Velda, Vada, Vaida, Vayda, Vaeda

Valdis (Norse) In mythology, the goddess of the dead
Valdiss, Valdys, Valdyss

Valencia (Spanish) One who is powerful; strong; from the city of Valencia
Valenciah, Valyncia, Valencya, Valenzia, Valancia, Valenica, Valanca, Valecia

Valentina (Latin) One who is vigorous and healthy
Valentinah, Valentine, Valenteena, Valenteana, Valentena, Valentyna, Valantina, Valentyne

★**Valerie** (Latin) Feminine form of Valerius; strong and valiant
Valeri, Valeree, Valerey, Valery, Valarie, Valari, **Valeria**, *Vallery*

Vandani (Hindi) One who is honorable and worthy
Vandany, Vandaney, Vandanie, Vandanee, Vandania, Vandanya

★**Vanessa** (Greek) Resembling a butterfly
Vanessah, Vanesa, Vannesa, Vannessa, Vanassa, Vanasa, Vanessia, Vanysa, Yanessa

Vanity (English) Having excessive pride
Vanitey, Vanitee, Vaniti, Vanitie, Vanitty, Vanyti, Vanyty, Vanytie

Vanmra (Russian) A stranger; from a foreign place
Vanmrah

Varda (Hebrew) Resembling a rose
Vardah, Vardia, Vardina, Vardissa, Vardita, Vardysa, Vardyta, Vardit

Varuna (Hindi) Wife of the sea
Varunah, Varuna, Varun, Varunani, Varuni

Vashti (Persian) A lovely woman
Vashtie, Vashty, Vashtey, Vashtee

Vasta (Persian) One who is pretty
Vastah

Vasteen (American) A capable woman
Vasteene, Vastiene, Vastien, Vastein, Vasteine, Vastean, Vasteane

Vasuda (Hindi) Of the earth
Vasudah, Vasudhara, Vasundhara, Vasudhra, Vasundhra

Vayu (Hindi) A vital life force; the air
Vayyu

Vedette (French) From the guard tower
Vedete, Vedett, Vedet, Vedetta, Vedeta

Vedi (Sanskrit) Filled with wisdom
Vedie, Vedy, Vedey, Vedee, Vedea, Vedeah

Vega (Latin) A falling star
Vegah

Vellamo (Finnish) In mythology, the goddess of the sea
Velamo, Vellammo

Ventana (Spanish) As transparent as a window
Ventanah, Ventanna, Ventane, Ventanne

Venus (Greek) In mythology, the goddess of love and beauty
Venis, Venys, Vynys, Venusa, Venusina, Venusia

Veradis (Latin) One who is genuine; truthful
Veradise, Veradys, Veradisa, Verdissa, Veradysa, Veradyssa, Veradisia, Veraditia

Verda (Latin) Springlike; one who is young and fresh
Verdah, Verdea, Virida, Verdy, Verdey, Verde, Verdi, Verdie

Verenase (Swedish) One who is flourishing
Verenese, Verennase, Vyrenase, Vyrennase, Vyrenese, Verenace, Vyrenace

Veronica (Latin) Displaying her true image
Veronicah, Veronic, Veronicca, Veronicka, Veronika, Veronicha, Veronique, Veranique, Ronni

Vesna (Slavic) Messenger; in mythology, the goddess of spring
Vesnah, Vezna, Vesnia, Vesnaa

Vespera (Latin) Evening star; born in the evening
Vesperah, Vespira, Vespeera, Vesperia, Vesper

Vevila (Gaelic) Woman with a melodious voice
Vevilah, Veveela, Vevyla, Vevilla, Vevylla, Vevylle, Vevyle, Vevillia

Vibeke (Danish) A small woman
Vibekeh, Vibeek, Vibeeke, Vybeke, Viheke

Vibhuti (Hindi) Of the sacred ash; a symbol
Vibuti, Vibhutie, Vibhutee

*Victoria (Latin) Victorious woman; winner; conqueror
Victoriah, Victorea, Victoreah, Victorya, Victorria, Victoriya, Vyctoria, Victorine, Tory

Vidya (Indian) Having great wisdom
Vidyah

Viet (Vietnamese) A woman from Vietnam
Vyet, Viett, Vyett, Viette, Vyette

Vigilia (Latin) Wakefulness; watchfulness
Vigiliah, Vygilia, Vygylia, Vijilia, Vyjilia

Vignette (French) From the little vine
Vignete, Vignet, Vignetta, Vignett, Vigneta, Vygnette, Vygnete, Vygnet

Vilina (Hindi) One who is dedicated
Vilinah, Vileena, Vileana, Vylina, Vyleena, Vyleana, Vylyna, Vilinia

Villette (French) From the small village
Vilette, Villete, Vilete, Vilet, Vilett, Villet, Villett, Vylet

Vimala (Indian) Feminine form of Vamal; clean and pure
Vimalah, Vimalia, Vimalla

Vincentia (Latin) Feminine form of Vincent; conquerer; triumphant
Vincentiah, Vincenta, Vincensia, Vincenzia, Vyncentia, Vyncyntia, Vyncenzia, Vycenzya

Violet (French) Resembling the purplish-blue flower
Violett, Violette, Violete, Vyolet, Vyolett, Vyolette, Vyolete, Violeta

Virginia (Latin) One who is chaste; virginal; from the state of Virginia
Virginiah, Virginnia, Virgenya, Virgenia, Virgeenia, Virgeena, Virgena, Ginny

Virtue (Latin) Having moral excellence, chastity, and goodness
Virtu, Vyrtue, Vyrtu, Vertue, Vertu

Viveka (German) Little woman of the strong fortress
Vivekah, Vivecka, Vyveka, Viveca, Vyveca, Vivecca, Vivika, Vivieka

Vivian (Latin) Lively woman
Viv, Vivi, Vivienne, Bibiana

Vixen (American) A flirtatious woman
Vixin, Vixi, Vixie, Vixee, Vixea, Vixeah, Vixy, Vixey

Vlasta (Slavic) A friendly and likeable woman
Vlastah, Vlastia, Vlastea, Vlastiah, Vlasteah

Voleta (Greek) The veiled one
Voletah, Voletta, Volita, Volitta, Volyta, Volytta, Volet, Volett

Volva (Scandinavian) In mythology, a female shaman
Volvah, Volvya, Volvaa, Volvae, Volvai, Volvay, Volvia

Vondila (African) Woman who lost a child
Vondilah, Vondilla, Vondilya, Vondilia, Vondyla, Vondylya

Vonna (French) Form of Yvonne, meaning "young archer"
Vonnah, Vona, Vonah, Vonnia, Vonnya, Vonia, Vonya, Vonny

Vonshae (American) One who is confident
Vonshay, Vonshaye, Vonshai

Vor (Norse) In mythology, an omniscient goddess
Vore, Vorr, Vorre

Vulpine (English) A cunning woman; like a fox
Vulpyne, Vulpina, Vulpyna

Vyomini (Indian) A gift of the divine
Vyominie, Vyominy, Vyominey, Vyominee, Vyomyni, Vyomyny, Viomini, Viomyni

Wafa (Arabic) One who is faithful; devoted
Wafah, Wafaa, Waffa, Wapha, Waffah, Waphah

Wagaye (African) My sense of value; my price
Wagay, Wagai, Wagae

Wainani (Hawaiian) Of the beautiful waters
Wainanie, Wainany, Wainaney, Wainanee, Wainanea, Wainaneah

Wajihah (Arabic) One who is distinguished; eminent
Wajiha, Wajeeha, Wajyha, Wajeehah, Wajyhah, Wajieha, Wajiehah, Wajeiha

Wakanda (Native American) One who possesses magical powers
Wakandah, Wakenda, Wakinda, Wakynda

Wakeishah (American) Filled with happiness
Wakeisha, Wakieshah, Wakiesha, Wakesha, Wakeshah, Wakeesha, Wakeeshah, Wakysha

Walda (German) One who has fame and power
Waldah, Wallda, Walida, Waldine, Waldina, Waldyne, Waldyna, Welda

Walker (English) Walker of the forests
Wallker, Walkher

Walta (African) One who acts as a shield
Waltah

Wanetta (English) A pale-skinned woman
Wanettah, Wanette, Wannette, Wannetta, Wonetta, Wonette, Wonitta, Wonitte

Wangari (African)
Resembling the leopard
*Wangarie, Wangarri,
Wangary, Wangarey,
Wangaria, Wangaree*

Wanyika (African) Of the
bush
*Wanyikka, Wanyicka,
Wanyicca, Wanyica*

Waqi (Arabic) Falling;
swooping
Waqqi

Warma (American) A car-
ing woman
*Warm, Warme, Warmia,
Warmiah, Warmea, Warmeah*

Warna (German) One who
defends her loved ones
Warnah

Washi (Japanese)
Resembling an eagle
*Washie, Washy, Washey,
Washee, Washea, Washeah*

Waynette (English) One
who makes wagons
*Waynett, Waynet, Waynete,
Wayneta, Waynetta*

Wednesday (American)
Born on a Wednesday
*Wensday, Winsday,
Windnesday, Wednesdae,
Wensdae, Winsdae,
Windnesdae, Wednesdai*

Welcome (English) A welcome guest
Welcom, Welcomme

Wendy (Welsh) Form of
Gwendolyn, meaning "one
who is fair; of the white
ring"
*Wendi, Wendie, Wendee,
Wendey, Wenda, Wendia,
Wendea, Wendya*

Wesley (English) From the
western meadow
*Wesly, Weslie, Wesli, Weslee,
Weslia, Wesleigh, Weslea,
Weslei*

Whisper (English) One
who is soft-spoken
Whysper, Wisper, Wysper

Whitley (English) From
the white meadow
*Whitly, Whitlie, Whitli,
Whitlee, Whitleigh,
Whitlea, Whitlia, Whitlya*

Whitney (English) From
the white island
*Whitny, Whitnie, Whitni,
Whitnee, Whittney,
Whitneigh, Whytny,
Whytney*

Wicapi Wakan (Native
American) A holy star

Wijida (Arabic) An excited
seeker
*Wijidah, Weejida,
Weejidah, Wijeeda,
Wijeedah, Wijyda, Wijydah,
Wijieda*

Wileen (Teutonic) A firm
defender
*Wiline, Wilean, Wileane,
Wilyn, Wileene, Wilene,
Wyleen, Wyline*

Wilhelmina (German)
Feminine form of
Wilhelm; determined pro-
tector
*Wilhelminah, Wylhelmina,
Wylhelmyna, Willemina,
Wilhelmine, Wilhemina,
Wilhemine, Helma, Ilma*

Winetta (American) One
who is peaceful
*Wineta, Wynetta, Wyneta,
Winet, Winett, Winette,
Wynet, Wynett*

Wing (Chinese) Woman of
glory
Winge, Wyng

Winnielle (African) A vic-
torious woman
*Winniell, Winniele,
Winniel, Winniella,
Winniela*

Winola (German) Gracious
and charming friend
*Winolah, Wynola, Winolla,
Wynolla, Wynolah,
Winollah, Wynollah*

Winta (African) One who
is desired
*Wintah, Whinta, Wynta,
Whynta, Whintah,
Wyntah, Whyntah*

Wisconsin (French)
Gathering of waters; from
the state of Wisconsin
*Wisconsyn, Wisconsen,
Wisconson, Wysconsin,
Wysconsen, Wysconson*

Woody (American) A
woman of the forest
*Woodey, Woodi, Woodie,
Woodee, Woodea, Woodeah,
Woods*

Wren (English) Resembling
a small songbird
*Wrenn, Wrene, Wrena,
Wrenie, Wrenee, Wreney,
Wrenny, Wrenna*

Wynda (Scottish) From the
narrow passage
Wyndah, Winda, Windah

Xalvadora (Spanish) A
savior
*Xalvadorah, Xalbadora,
Xalbadorah, Xalvadoria,
Xalbadoria*

Xanadu (African) From the exotic paradise

Xantara (American) Protector of the Earth
Xantarah, Xanterra, Xantera, Xantarra, Xantrrah, Xanterah, Xanterrah

Xaquelina (Galician) Form of Jacqueline, meaning "the supplanter"
Xaqueline, Xaqueleena, Xaquelyna, Xaquelayna, Xaqueleana

Xerena (Latin) Form of Serena, meaning "having a peaceful disposition"
Xerenah, Xerene, Xeren, Xereena, Xeryna, Xereene, Xerenna

Xhosa (African) Leader of a nation
Xosa, Xhose, Xhosia, Xhosah, Xosah

Xiang (Chinese) Having a nice fragrance
Xyang, Xeang, Xhiang, Xhyang, Xheang

Xiao Hong (Chinese) Of the morning rainbow

Xin Qian (Chinese) Happy and beautiful woman

Xinavane (African) A mother; to propagate
Xinavana, Xinavania, Xinavain, Xinavaine, Xinavaen, Xinavaene

Xirena (Greek) Form of Sirena, meaning "enchantress"
Xirenah, Xireena, Xirina, Xirene, Xyrena, Xyreena, Xyrina, Xyryna

Xi-Wang (Chinese) One with hope

Xochiquetzal (Aztec) Resembling a flowery feather; in mythology, the goddess of love, flowers, and the earth

Xola (African) Stay in peace
Xolah, Xolia, Xolla, Xollah

Xue (Chinese) Woman of snow

Xyza (Gothic) Of the sea
Xyzah

Y

Yachne (Hebrew) One who is gracious and hospitable
Yachnee, Yachney, Yachnie, Yachni, Yachnea, Yachneah

Yadra (Spanish) Form of Madre, meaning "mother"
Yadre, Yadrah

Yaffa (Hebrew) A beautiful
woman
Yaffah, Yaffit, Yafit, Yafeal

Yakini (African) An honest
woman
*Yakinie, Yakiney, Yakiny,
Yackini, Yackinie, Yackiney,
Yackiny, Yakinee*

Yalena (Greek) Form of
Helen, meaning "the shin-
ing light"
*Yalenah, Yalina, Yaleena,
Yalyna, Yalana, Yaleana,
Yalane, Yaleene*

Yama (Japanese) From the
mountain
Yamma, Yamah, Yammah

Yamin (Hebrew) Right
hand
*Yamine, Yamyn, Yamyne,
Yameen, Yameene, Yamein,
Yameine, Yamien*

Yana (Hebrew) He answers
*Yanna, Yaan, Yanah,
Yannah*

Yanessa (American) Form
of Vanessa, meaning
"resembling a butterfly"
*Yanessah, Yanesa, Yannesa,
Yannessa, Yanassa, Yanasa,
Yanessia, Yanysa*

Yanka (Slavic) God is good
Yancka, Yancca, Yankka

Yara (Brazilian) In mythology, the goddess of the
river; a mermaid
Yarah, Yarrah, Yarra

Yareli (American) The Lord
is my light
*Yarelie, Yareley, Yarelee,
Yarely, Yaresly, Yarelea,
Yareleah*

Yaser (Arabic) One who is
wealthy and prosperous
Yasera, Yaseria

Yashira (Japanese) Blessed
with God's grace
*Yashirah, Yasheera,
Yashyra, Yashara, Yashiera,
Yashierah, Yasheira,
Yasheirah*

Yashona (Hindi) A
wealthy woman
*Yashonah, Yashawna,
Yashauna, Yaseana,
Yashawnah, Yashaunah,
Yaseanah*

Yasmine (Persian)
Resembling the jasmine
flower
*Yasmin, Yasmene, Yasmeen,
Yasmeene, Yasmen,
Yasemin, Yasemeen,
Yasmyn*

Yatima (African) An
orphan
*Yatimah, Yateema, Yatyma,
Yateemah, Yatymah,
Yatiema, Yatiemah,
Yateima*

Yedidah (Hebrew) A beloved friend
Yedida, Yedyda, Yedydah, Yedeeda, Yedeedah

Yeira (Hebrew) One who is illuminated
Yeirah, Yaira, Yeyra, Yairah, Yeyrah

Yenge (African) A hardworking woman
Yenga, Yengeh, Yengah

Yeshi (African) For a thousand
Yeshie, Yeshey, Yeshy, Yeshee, Yeshea, Yesheah

Yessica (Hebrew) Form of Jessica, meaning "the Lord sees all"
Yesica, Yessika, Yesika, Yesicka, Yessicka, Yesyka, Yesiko

Yetta (English) Form of Henrietta, meaning "ruler of the house"
Yettah, Yeta, Yette, Yitta, Yettie, Yetty

Yi Min (Chinese) An intelligent woman

Yi Ze (Chinese) Happy and shiny as a pearl

Yihana (African) One deserving congratulations
Yihanah, Yhana, Yihanna, Yihannah, Yhanah, Yhanna, Yhannah

Yinah (Spanish) A victorious woman
Yina, Yinna, Yinnah

Yitta (Hebrew) One who emanates light
Yittah, Yita, Yitah

Ynes (French) Form of Agnes, meaning "pure; chaste"
Ynez, Ynesita

Yogi (Hindi) One who practices yoga
Yogini, Yoginie, Yogie, Yogy, Yogey, Yogee, Yogea, Yogeah

Yohance (African) A gift from God
Yohanse

Yoki (Native American) Of the rain
Yokie, Yokee, Yoky, Yokey, Yokea, Yokeah

Yolanda (Greek) Resembling the violet flower
Yola, Yolana, Yolandah, Colanda

Yomaris (Spanish) I am the sun
Yomariss, Yomarise, Yomarris

Yon (Korean) Resembling a lotus blossom

Yoruba (African) Woman from Nigeria
Yorubah, Yorubba, Yorubbah

Yoshi (Japanese) One who
is respectful and good
*Yoshie, Yoshy, Yoshey,
Yoshee, Yoshiyo, Yoshiko,
Yoshino, Yoshea*

Ysabel (Spanish) Form of
Isabel, meaning "my God is
bountiful; God's promise"
*Ysabelle, Ysabela, Ysabele,
Ysabell, Ysabella, Ysbel,
Ysibel, Ysibela*

Ysbail (Welsh) A spoiled girl
*Ysbale, Ysbayle, Ysbaile,
Ysbayl, Ysbael, Ysbaele*

Yue (Chinese) Of the
moonlight

Yuette (American) A capa-
ble woman
*Yuett, Yuete, Yuet, Yueta,
Yuetta*

Yulan (Spanish) A splendid woman
Yulann

Yuna (African) A gorgeous
woman
Yunah, Yunna, Yunnah

Yuta (Hebrew / Japanese)
One who is awarded
praise / one who is superior
Yutah, Yoota, Yootah

Yvonne (French) Young
archer
Yvone, Vonne, Vonna

Zabrina (American) Form
of Sabrina, meaning "a
legendary princess"
*Zabreena, Zabrinah,
Zabrinna, Zabryna,
Zabryne, Zabrynya,
Zabreana, Zabreane*

Zachah (Hebrew) Feminine
form of Zachary; God is
remembered
*Zacha, Zachie, Zachi,
Zachee, Zachea, Zacheah*

Zafara (Hebrew) One who
sings
*Zaphara, Zafarra,
Zapharra, Zafarah,
Zafarrah, Zapharah,
Zapharrah*

Zagir (Armenian)
Resembling a flower
*Zagiri, Zagirie, Zagiree,
Zagirea, Zagireah, Zagiry,
Zagirey, Zagira*

Zahiya (Arabic) A brilliant
woman; radiant
*Zahiyah, Zehiya, Zehiyah,
Zeheeya, Zaheeya, Zeheeyah,
Zaheeyah, Zaheiya*

Zahra (Arabic / Swahili)
White-skinned / flowerlike
*Zahrah, Zahraa, Zahre,
Zahreh, Zahara, Zaharra,
Zahera, Zahira*

Zainab (Arabic) A fragrant flowering plant
Zaynab, Zaenab

Zainabu (Swahili) One who is known for her beauty
Zaynabu, Zaenabu

Zalina (French) Form of Selene, meaning "of the moon"; in mythology Selene was the Greek goddess of the moon
Zalinah, Zaleana, Zaleena, Zalena, Zalyna, Zaleen, Zaleene, Zalene

Zama (Latin) One from the town of Zama
Zamah, Zamma, Zammah

Zambda (Hebrew) One who meditates
Zambdah

Zamella (Zulu) One who strives to succeed
Zamellah, Zamy, Zamie, Zami, Zamey, Zamee, Zamea, Zameah

Zamilla (Greek) Having the strength of the sea
Zamillah, Zamila, Zamilah, Zamylla, Zamyllah, Zamyla, Zamylah

Zamora (Spanish) From the city of Zamora
Zamorah, Zamorrah, Zamorra

Zana (Romanian / Hebrew) In mythology, the three graces / shortened form of Susanna, meaning "lily"
Zanna, Zanah, Zannah

Zane (Scandinavian) One who is bold
Zain, Zaine, Zayn, Zayne, Zaen, Zaene

Zanta (Swahili) A beautiful young woman
Zantah

Zarahlinda (Hebrew) Of the beautiful dawn
Zaralinda, Zaralynda, Zarahlindah, Zaralyndah, Zarahlynda, Zarahlyndah, Zaralenda, Zarahlenda

Zarifa (Arabic) One who is successful; moves with grace
Zarifah, Zaryfa, Zaryfah, Zareefa, Zareefah, Zariefa, Zariefah, Zareifa

Zarna (Hindi) Resembling a spring of water
Zarnah, Zarnia, Zarniah

Zarqa (Arabic) Having bluish-green eyes; from the city of Zarqa
Zarqaa

Zaylee (English) A heavenly woman
Zayleigh, Zayli, Zaylie, Zaylea, Zayleah, Zayley, Zayly, Zalee

Zaypana (Tibetan) A beautiful woman
Zaypanah, Zaypo, Zaypanna, Zaypannah

Zaza (Hebrew / Arabic) Belonging to all / one who is flowery
Zazah, Zazu, Zazza, Zazzah, Zazzu

Zdenka (Slovene) Feminine form of Zdenek, meaning "from Sidon"
Zdena, Zdenuska, Zdenicka, Zdenika, Zdenyka, Zdeninka, Zdenynka

Zebba (Persian) A known beauty
Zebbah, Zebara, Zebarah, Zebarra, Zebarrah

Zelia (Greek / Spanish) Having great zeal / of the sunshine
Zeliah, Zelya, Zelie, Zele, Zelina, Zelinia

Zenaida (Greek) White-winged dove; in mythology, a daughter of Zeus
Zenaidah, Zenayda, Zenaide, Zenayde, Zinaida, Zenina, Zenna, Zenaydah

Zenechka (Russian) Form of Eugenia, meaning "a well-born woman"

Zenobia (Greek) Child of Zeus
Sinobia

Zephyr (Greek) Of the west wind
Zephyra, Zephira, Zephria, Zephra, Zephyer, Zefiryn, Zefiryna, Zefyrin

Zera (Hebrew) A sower of seeds
Zerah, Zeria, Zeriah, Zera'im, Zerra, Zerrah

Zeraldina (Polish) One who rules with the spear
Zeraldinah, Zeraldeena, Zeraldeenah, Zeraldiena, Zeraldienah, Zeraldeina, Zeraldeinah, Zeraldyna

Zerdali (Turkish) Resembling the wild apricot
Zerdalie, Zerdaly, Zerdaley, Zerdalya, Zerdalia, Zerdalee, Zerdalea, Zerdalea

Zesta (American) One with energy and gusto
Zestah, Zestie, Zestee, Zesti, Zesty, Zestey, Zestea, Zesteah

Zetta (Portuguese) Resembling the rose
Zettah

Zhen (Chinese) One who is precious and chaste
Zen, Zhena, Zenn, Zhenni

Zhi (Chinese) A woman of high moral character

Zhong (Chinese) An honorable woman

Zi (Chinese) A flourishing young woman

Zia (Arabic) One who emanates light; splendor
Ziah, Zea, Zeah, Zya, Zyah

Zilias (Hebrew) A shady woman; a shadow
Zilyas, Zylias, Zylyas

Zillah (Hebrew) The shadowed one
Zilla, Zila, Zyla, Zylla, Zilah, Zylah, Zyllah

Zilpah (Hebrew) One who is frail but dignified; in the Bible, a concubine of Jacob
Zilpa, Zylpa, Zilpha, Zylpha, Zylpah, Zilphah, Zylphah

Zimbab (African) Woman from Zimbabwe
Zymbab, Zimbob, Zymbob

Zinat (Arabic) A decoration; graceful beauty
Zeenat, Zynat, Zienat, Zeinat, Zeanat

Zinchita (Incan) One who is dearly loved
Zinchitah, Zinchyta, Zinchytah, Zincheeta, Zincheetah, Zinchieta, Zinchietah, Zincheita

Zintkala Kinyan (Native American) Resembling a flying bird
Zintkalah Kinyan, Zintkalla Kinyan, Zintkallah Kinyan, Zyntkala Kinyan, Zyntkalah Kinyan, Zyntkallah Kinyan, Zyntkalla Kinyan

Zintkala Lowansa (Native American) Resembling a songbird
Zintkalah Lowansa, Zintkalla Lowansa, Zintkallah Lowansa, Zyntkala Lowansa, Zyntkalah Lowansa, Zyntkallah Lowansa, Zyntkalla Lowansa

Ziona (Hebrew) One who symbolizes goodness
Zionah, Zyona, Zyonah

Zipporah (Hebrew) A beauty; little bird; in the Bible, the wife of Moses
Zippora, Ziporah, Zipora, Zypora, Zyppora, Ziproh, Zipporia

Zira (African) The pathway
Zirah, Zirra, Zirrah, Zyra, Zyrah, Zyrra, Zyrrah

Zisel (Hebrew) One who is sweet
Zissel, Zisal, Zysel, Zysal, Zyssel, Zissal, Zyssal

Zita (Latin / Spanish)
Patron of housewives and
servants / little rose
*Zitah, Zeeta, Zyta, Zeetah,
Zytah, Zieta, Zietah, Zeita*

Ziwa (Swahili) Woman of
the lake
Ziwah, Zywa, Zywah

Zizi (Hungarian)
Dedicated to God
*Zeezee, Zyzy, Ziezie,
Zeazea, Zeyzey*

Zoa (Greek) One who is
full of life; vibrant

★ᵀZoe (Greek) A life-giving
woman; alive
*Zoee, Zowey, Zowie, Zowe,
Zoelie, Zoeline, Zoelle, Zoey*

Zofia (Slavic) Form of
Sophia, meaning "wis-
dom"
*Zofiah, Zophia, Zophiah,
Zophya, Zofie, Zofee, Zofey,
Zofi*

Zora (Slavic) Born at
dawn; aurora
*Zorah, Zorna, Zorra,
Zorya, Zorane, Zory,
Zorrah, Zorey*

Zoria (Basque) One who is
lucky
Zoriah

Zoriona (Basque) One
who is happy

Zubeda (Swahili) The best
one
Zubedah

Zudora (Arabic) A laborer;
hardworking woman
*Zudorah, Zudorra,
Zudorrah*

Zula (African) One who is
brilliant; from the town of
Zula
*Zul, Zulay, Zulae, Zulai,
Zulah, Zulla, Zullah*

Zuni (Native American)
One who is creative
*Zunie, Zuny, Zuney, Zunee,
Zunea, Zuneah*

Zurafa (Arabic) A lovely
woman
*Zurafah, Zirafa, Zirafah,
Ziraf, Zurufa, Zurufah,
Zuruf, Zuraffa*

Zuri (Swahili / French) A
beauty / lovely and white
*Zurie, Zurey, Zuria,
Zuriaa, Zury, Zuree, Zurya,
Zurisha*

Zuwena (African) One
who is pleasant and good
*Zuwenah, Zwena, Zwenah,
Zuwenna, Zuwennah,
Zuwyna, Zuwynah*

Zuyana (Sioux) One who
has a brave heart
*Zuyanah, Zuyanna,
Zuyannah*

Zuzena (Basque) One who
is correct
Zuzenah, Zuzenna,
Zuzennah

Zwi (Scandinavian)
Resembling a gazelle
Zui, Zwie, Zwee, Zwey,
Zwy, Zwea, Zweal